GNER

GNER

The Route of the Flying Scotsman

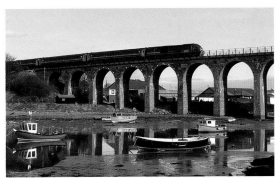

John Balmforth

Ian Allan
PUBLISHING

First Published 2008

ISBN 978 0 7110 3318 4

© John Balmforth 2008

Published by Ian Allan Publishing

an imprint of Ian Allan Publishing Ltd,
Hersham, Surrey KT12 4RG
Printed in England by Ian Allan Printing Ltd,
Hersham, Surrey KT12 4RG

Code: 0812/B2

Visit the Ian Allan Publishing website at
www.ianallanpublishing.com

The Railway Children Charity
Registered charity No 1058991

The Railway Children Charity helps runaway and
abandoned children who live in and around the
world's railway stations. Working through partner
organisations, the charity offers shelter, healthcare,
education, training, protection and, above all,
friendship.

   The work of the Railway Children would not be
possible without the generosity of its supporters.
There are many ways you can help the charity
help the millions of street children around the
world. Thanks to loyal supporters, The Railway
Children now helps around 7,000 children every
year, and helps counsel or refer on about another
12,000.

   All of the royalties due to the author from the
sale of this book are being donated to The Railway
Children Charity.

   You can read more about the charity on its web
site at http://www.railwaychildren.org.uk and,
should you wish to support the charity, donations
can be sent to:

The Railway Children
1 The Commons
Sandbach
Cheshire
CW11 1EG
United Kingdom

PAGE 3 CLOCKWISE FROM TOP LEFT:
DVT No 82228 rests under the ornate roof of
King's Cross station after arriving with a busy
service from Leeds.
Allan Stokes
'Regional Eurostar' sets Nos 373310 and
373309, on hire to GNER but wearing their
home 'Eurostar' livery, are seen nearing
journey's end on the ECML.
Rich Mackin/railwayscene.co.uk
A GNER electric train passes a fairground
at Peterborough.
railphotolibrary.com
Power car No 43039 *The Royal Dragoon
Guards* heads its train across Rossie Viaduct,
just south of Montrose, in March 2004.
railphotolibrary.com

FACING PAGE: A perfect side profile of
HST power car No 43108 *Old Course
St Andrews*, seen as it passes Sedgefield
en route to King's Cross in November 2003.
railphotolibrary.com

Contents

Foreword

by Jonathan Metcalfe
GNER Chief Executive, 2006-2007

I was delighted when I heard that a book was to be published about GNER.

It was a special company that enjoyed a special place in many people's hearts, not least mine.

The name GNER deserves to live long in the railway lexicon, as a byword for good service. It led the post-privatisation silent cultural revolution, placing the passengers' interests firmly at the centre of its business.

Based on a strong unifying vision and binding values, staff attitudes and behaviours were transformed and liberated, and passenger satisfaction rose.

Where GNER led, others subsequently followed.

Under Christopher Garnett's inspiring leadership, eye for detail and passion for service, a remarkable family spirit and 'can do' attitude prevailed. It created a cultural bond and resilience that guided us through good times and bad.

GNER was also the only operator that, in its distinctive brand image, doffed its corporate cap to the past, deliberately harnessing the 'Route of the Flying Scotsman' heritage, but at the same time projecting itself in a modern forward-looking way.

Remarkably, in just 11 years it became a household name that commanded impressive levels of loyalty. It attracted almost 50% more passengers on 36% more trains. It created the most reliable long-distance train fleet in Britain and won more than 60 awards.

However, the journey was rarely smooth but never dull. At times, as we battled through regular periods of franchise uncertainty and two awful tragedies, it felt like the worst kind of roller-coaster ride.

GNER was its own fiercest critic and the first to recognise areas for improvement. While proud of its achievements, it always recognised that it was a journey of continuous improvement. It was a great shame that the journey was sadly cut short, due to factors beyond the company's direct control.

But what is done is done. Of one thing I am sure: GNER's legacy will live on in all those who rightly expect and demand a high-quality railway in Britain – one that puts the passenger first and combines the best of private-sector flair with a strong sense of public duty.

I hope that readers of this book will treat it as a celebration of GNER, rather than a corporate obituary.

Having worked for GNER since its inception, I was privileged to become its Chief Executive in the last chapter of its journey, as the business was stabilised and after the collapse of the franchise. Throughout all my time at the company I could not have hoped to have worked with such a fantastic and impressive group of people. Their efforts continue to this day, albeit under a new name and new owner. I wish them well.

Jonathan Metcalfe
February 2008

Preface

by Christopher Garnett
GNER Chief Executive, 1996-2006

By railway standards, GNER had a relatively short life, yet it enjoyed amazing loyalty from its passengers and, importantly, its staff. Our pre-eminent position for providing customer service was keenly supported by our parent company Sea Containers and its president Jim Sherwood. Jim shared in our belief that success depended on our ability to give our passengers consistently excellent service.

Rail travel in the United Kingdom is relatively expensive, and everyone in the industry has a responsibility to serve passengers to the very best of their ability. GNER's staff rose to that challenge time after time – and the passengers responded so well to their efforts that, at the end of their journey, many people went away satisfied.

Through the terrible dark days of Hatfield and Great Heck, the most amazing camaraderie of everyone in the company kept us all going.

We would never claim to have always got it right – mechanical breakdowns were an issue in the early years – but we always aimed to improve, and whenever we fell short of our own high standards, we were ready to say so.

We showed that our people wanted to give good service, and that they could draw satisfaction from doing a job to the best of their ability. Yet for this to come about, managers had a great responsibility to treat people properly. You cannot run a train company from your office, as you are reliant on everyone in the organisation to deliver. All our managers could do was to set the culture, and to lead by example.

And the GNER journey was never dull. There were wonderful events, such as the day in October 2003 when Her Majesty Queen Elizabeth II came to King's Cross to unveil our rebuilt 'Mallard' train. Many of our staff shared in that memorable occasion.

I look back over my 10 years with GNER with great happiness and pride in what we achieved. I wish our people well for the future and thank them, and our passengers, for their amazing support over the years. I also hope that the standards we set on the East Coast are built on, and not seen as a one-off. The passengers and staff deserve it.

Christopher Garnett
February 2008

CHAPTER ONE

The privatisation of Britain's railways: a brief outline

When the Conservative Party under John Major's leadership won the General Election in 1992, it did so with a mandate for Britain's railways to pass into private ownership, although it did not specify in what form that should be. Many, including, it is thought, the British Railways Board, favoured using the model that had previously been used in privatising most government utilities, which would have required the railways to be sold as a single going concern. However, in the end privatisation saw the rail infrastructure separated from the actual operation of both passenger and freight services, with a new company, Railtrack, formed to take over ownership and maintenance of the infrastructure, and many other companies, both passenger and freight, to operate the trains.

At the same time the rail network was divided into 25 new franchises, created to provide rail passenger services; the winners of the franchises became known as Train Operating Companies (TOCs). To oversee the franchising programme the Office of Passenger Rail Franchising (OPRAF) was set up, being given special responsibility for letting the new franchises. For the changes to be politically acceptable, it also had to agree a core investment programme with Railtrack, although the East Coast Main Line (ECML) had recently been the beneficiary of a major infrastructure upgrade with the provision of new electrification, re-signalling in the north and some increases in line speeds.

The winners of the 25 passenger franchises had to enter into track access agreements with Railtrack, which in turn would allow them to use the infrastructure. When Britain's railways were privatised the old InterCity sector had been operating profitably, but the new access charges would virtually double the operating costs pertaining in British Rail (BR) days. The theory was that the additional income would go towards bringing the infrastructure back into good order, as most routes, with the notable exception of the East Coast, had not

seen real investment for many years. The TOCs would also need to pay leasing charges to the rolling stock companies (ROSCOs) for the use of the trains, ownership of which had also passed into private hands. All of this required the payment of government subsidies to most TOCs through OPRAF. Ironically, the total required to compensate the TOCs for the higher access charges was £1.6 billion in 1994/95, an increase of some 58% on the previous year, which was BR's last. With staffing and station costs still to be added, and the TOCs' only real income being from the fare-box, it was obvious that government support would be required by some franchises well into their franchise period, although ultimately the intention was that most operators would be paying a premium before their franchise ended.

Unlike the TOCs, Railtrack did not have to be successful in bidding for a franchise since it was effectively a licensed custodian owning its assets in perpetuity, provided it did not seriously breach its licence conditions. As we shall see later in this book, some of the causes of its relatively early demise also had serious consequences for GNER.

ABOVE: A GNER Class 91 electric locomotive supplies the power as it provides the 'push' part of the 'push-pull' service seen departing from Edinburgh Waverley on its way to London. *John Balmforth*

LEFT: A diesel 'under the wires' as power car No 43118 *City of Kingston upon Hull* heads a GNER service along the East Coast Main Line. *Matthew Clarke*

TOP: An HST set in GNER livery races past Spittal, south of Berwick-upon-Tweed, in 1998. *railphotolibrary.com*

CHAPTER TWO

The East Coast Main Line:
a brief description

The use of 'East Coast Main Line' as the route description dates back to pre-British Rail days and is a little misleading, because a passenger travelling from London will not glimpse the sea until the train is well north of Newcastle approaching the border between England and Scotland. However, the United Kingdom has two main-line railway routes operating between London and Scotland; one runs up the western side of the country and the other up the eastern side, hence the names West Coast Main Line (WCML) and East Coast Main Line.

The East Coast Main Line – providing the principal rail link between London and Edinburgh – was developed piecemeal by a number of railway companies mainly in the 1840s and 1850s. The earliest sections of the current route arose out of the railway empire of George Hudson, the so-called 'Railway King' of the 1840s, when there was great competition between the promoters of both the East and West Coast routes to be the first to complete their services into Edinburgh, though until completion of the Great Northern Railway between King's Cross and York in 1852, East Coast trains used Euston as their London terminus. From the 1860s the principal day train linking the two capitals, departing at 10.00am, was to become generally known as the 'Flying Scotchman', later the 'Flying Scotsman', though it was not officially named until the 1920s.

The consortium of companies operating the route until 1922 (the Great Northern Railway and North Eastern Railway between York and Berwick-on-Tweed, and the North British Railway beyond) were in constant competition with the West Coast, on both journey time and provision of improved facilities for passengers. Similarly, while there is no longer head-to-head West Coast competition, air and road competition drive the development of services over the two routes through to the present day. This push for faster trains and reduced journey times culminated in two major events in British railway history.

The first of these was the 'Railway Race' to Aberdeen in 1888 between the East and West Coast consortiums, but this was overtaken by the events of the summer of 1895 when the races appeared again, though this time with the East Coast companies being able to take advantage of the newly completed bridges over the firths of Forth and Tay. Acute competition was to erupt again in the 1930s, this time with the 'grouped' companies of the London & North Eastern Railway and the London Midland & Scottish Railway. The outcome was greatly accelerated services over the East Coast route, from London to Leeds, Newcastle and Glasgow, with the famous engineer Sir Nigel Gresley designing the exceptional streamlined 'A4' class of locomotive, one of which, No 4468 *Mallard*, was to achieve the world's fastest speed by a steam locomotive when it reached 126mph descending Stoke Bank in Lincolnshire on a test run in 1938. It was an incredible feat and the record still stands to this day. *Mallard* can still be seen in the National Railway Museum at York, together with numerous other top-link locomotives that worked express trains on the East Coast route from the 1870s onwards, including the famous *Flying Scotsman* of 1923, which had made the first 100mph run along the route.

Equally famous – arguably the most famous of all diesel locomotives – and able to consistently maintain 100mph, were the 3,300hp Class 55 'Deltics'. A fleet of 22 was put to work on the route between 1962 and 1988, some surviving into preservation today.

The principal services along the East Coast Main Line connect London with Peterborough, Doncaster, Hull, Leeds, York, Newcastle, Edinburgh, Glasgow, Dundee, Aberdeen, Stirling, Perth and Inverness, but it should not be forgotten that a number of other important destinations are also served.

The case for electrification of the route was supported by British Rail's need to consider the future of its High Speed Train (HST) diesel

ABOVE: Ex-LNER streamlined 'A4' class 'Pacific' No 60022 *Mallard* awaits departure from King's Cross in 1958, some 20 years after setting the still unbeaten speed record for a steam locomotive. *railphotolibrary.com*

ABOVE RIGHT: In this view from the driver's cab, engineers working on the Forth Bridge stand aside to allow No 43110 and its train to pass en route to Aberdeen. *John Balmforth*

RIGHT: A DVT leading an InterCity 225 train in British Rail's InterCity livery speeds south along the ECML, powered from the rear by a Class 91 locomotive. *railphotolibrary.com*

sets, which it used to operate the punishing East Coast timetable. With high mileages being run daily, maintaining the trains was becoming ever more expensive and it was known that electric trains were cheaper to run – one electric locomotive replacing the two diesels used in an HST set, and with many fewer complex moving parts. BR also had a wish to replace the non-air-conditioned carriages so often used on East Coast services. However, the Government had set a target of a 7% return on capital investment for the upgrade, and this would prove challenging. Indeed, it was first thought that this would restrict improvements to simply replacing the diesel power cars with electric locomotives.

Much debate took place within the senior management of BR, both at boardroom level and also with Chris Green, who was then in charge of ScotRail. There was great concern that electrification would mean the loss of through running beyond Edinburgh, which passengers had enjoyed for years. Consideration was even given to using pairs of redundant HST power cars marshalled back-to-back to haul the trains. Eventually the problem was not found to be as insurmountable as at first thought, because the saving in time by using Class 91 haulage between the English and Scottish capitals far outweighed the delay

that would be caused by a potential locomotive change, or change of train, at Edinburgh.

Ultimately new Class 91 electric locomotives with Mk 4 carriages and Driving Van Trailers (DVTs) would be used in a 'push-pull' formation, but there would still be a need for the HSTs to remain – particularly north of Edinburgh, where the route remained non-electrified. The number of electric trains ordered required the retention of a smaller fleet of HSTs, thus allowing the continuation of the same level of through services to Hull, Inverness and Aberdeen.

The upgrade works carried out in the late 1980s and completed by July 1991 saw Mk 4 coaches and DVTs hauled by Class 91 electric locomotives regularly attaining speeds of 125mph, although not along the route's entire length – the dream of 140mph running for service trains is unlikely to be achieved in the foreseeable future. Like many commentators I consider this an opportunity lost, since, after all, the diesel HST sets had been running at 125mph over the route since the 1980s. However, the high cost of the required signalling upgrade and the large numbers of level crossings along the route were significant factors in the Government reaching that decision.

Just like its West Coast rival Virgin Trains,

GNER had trains capable of attaining 140mph – hence the name 'IC225' (225kmh) given to the electric services – but sadly the infrastructure will need considerable further enhancement, as was the case on the WCML, and will almost certainly prove to be too costly. Nevertheless the electrification project, described at the time of the upgrade as 'Britain's longest construction site', did bring major improvements in capacity and was certainly value for money, being completed on time and within budget. The magnitude of the project is borne out when it is considered that 157 bridges had to be raised or rebuilt, nine station layouts altered and modern electronic signal control installed. Electricity supply was taken from the National Grid at 16 different locations, with BR's three electric control offices at Hornsey, Doncaster and Cathcart in Glasgow managing the supply. Furthermore, the upgrade did not cause widespread disruption to passengers, unlike earlier upgrades elsewhere in the 1950s and 1960s. The Project Director at the time, Don Heath, explained that the project had not only been completed on time but also on budget. Indeed, electric trains were able to run between London King's Cross and Leeds a full 12 months earlier than had been originally planned. The cost of the upgrade, including trains, was good value at

around £1 billion – substantially less than the £8 billion plus trains for the later West Coast Main Line upgrade, though it should not be forgotten that the West Coast route was in a very run-down condition.

Under the watchful eyes of the business managers, the late Simon Fraser and his team of Stuart Baker (BR East Coast South Route Manager), David Watters (BR East Coast Route Manager Newcastle-Scotland) and Resources Manager Peter Strachan, renewals were not simply undertaken like for like. Instead improvements were always looked for in planning infrastructure renewals. A good example of this was the new signalling on the York-Tyneside section, which was commissioned in 1991 at the same time as the overhead wiring.

Dr Prideaux, who spearheaded the beginning of the revival of InterCity for British Rail, was followed by Chris Green, who continued the good work when he became head of InterCity. Green told me that he had a philosophy for a vertically integrated InterCity business that would focus on one total route modernisation every decade. The plan was for 1990-2000 to cover the West Coast route, 2000-2010 the Great Western/CrossCountry network, and 2010-2020 the Midland Main Line, Anglia and Gatwick routes, before returning again to the

ABOVE: One of GNER's 'Mallard' trains, headed by a Class 82 DVT, passes engineering work at Little Bytham on its way to King's Cross.
Gordon Valentine

RIGHT: The southern approach to Montrose is seen from the driver's cab on 4 December 2007. New colour light signals are already in place awaiting commissioning, after which they will replace the nostalgic semaphore signals.
John Balmforth

East Coast to restart the cycle. The cost of such a major programme of investment would have been high but would certainly have had considerable merit.

It is not unreasonable to conclude that the East Coast Main Line was historically better managed than its rival West Coast route, being kept in far better condition with the exception of the overhead wire, which suffered a lack of robustness, and BR handed over the route in reasonably good condition to Railtrack for GNER to use for franchising in 1996.

CHAPTER THREE

The East Coast rail franchise is won

The Bermuda-based shipping company Sea Containers, which had owned the Venice-Simplon Orient Express (VSOE) since the 1980s, had in fact made previously unsuccessful attempts to win both the Great Western and South West Trains franchises. In an in-depth interview with Christopher Garnett, he revealed that after the failure of the bid to win South West Trains it was Sea Containers President Jim Sherwood, a man whom GNER would always be able to rely on for invaluable support and advice, who felt that a bid should be made for the East Coast rail franchise. It was also Sherwood who had arranged for the purchase of the elderly Orient Express coaches, overseeing their restoration that led to the re-launching of the brand. His attitude was never to do anything unless it was done right.

After the bid was submitted to the Office of Passenger Rail Franchising (OPRAF), Garnett and Sherwood both had gut feelings that things were not going as well as had been hoped with the bid, and that they might be slipping behind Stagecoach. Then, out of the blue, all bidders received a letter from OPRAF, which now wanted the bids to include some works to the north of King's Cross related to the Channel Tunnel route into St Pancras. This recognised that bidders might wish to revise bids to include any associated costs for the extra work. Christopher Garnett recalled that Sea Containers had been very cautious in its bid and was now actually able to reduce the bid by around £10 million. This was very significant because ultimately Sea Containers, through its subsidiary 'The Great Northern Railway Company Ltd', was successful by a narrow margin, believed to be around £5 million, over Stagecoach. The winning bidder then purchased the shares of InterCity East Coast Ltd, the company that had previously operated the East Coast rail services in BR days.

It is not generally realised that, pre-privatisation, a group of British Rail employees had been giving consideration to getting involved in a management buyout scheme,

ABOVE: The unusual sight of a GNER Class 91 running 'slab end' first gives an impression of speed as the camera gets close to it at a level crossing.
railphotolibrary.com

and had been looking at a number of potential franchises. That group had come up with, and registered, a possible operational name for the East Coast Main Line franchise; 'The Great North Eastern Railway Company'. Ultimately the group did not fulfil its dreams, with all except one choosing to remain in employment with British Rail. The remaining group member, Ian Yeowart, continued to pursue his plans and, ironically, eventually succeeded when he became head of the Open Access Operator Grand Central Railway Company Ltd, which features significantly later in the GNER story. Sensibly Yeowart had retained the rights to the name 'The Great North Eastern Railway

Company', ultimately selling it to 'The Great Northern Railway Company Ltd' for a fee believed to be in the region of £10,000. This enabled the company to switch to its new name, GNER Holdings Ltd, and ultimately to use the initial letters only for its operational trading name – GNER.

The newly won franchise included commitments to:

• Maintain the train mileage operated in the 1995/96 timetable for two years with a view to increasing it thereafter.

BELOW: GNER's headquarters was based in the old LNER building, itself the subject of a book, in Station Road, York.
John Balmforth

LEFT: DVT No 82231 waits for the road at Edinburgh Waverley in August 2007, ready to begin the long journey south to London.
John Balmforth

TOP: A Class 91 hauling a rake of MK 4 coaches and a DVT crosses the Royal Border Bridge. The locomotive carries the temporary white GNER brand lettering, and the coaching stock still has blue doors *GNER*

ABOVE: An artist's impression of Vignelli's proposed livery for GNER rolling stock. *GNER*

- Refurbish all existing rolling stock.
- Provide a buffet and trolley service on all services, with onboard restaurants on many weekday trains. (Subsequently the number of restaurant cars increased from 66 to 90 on every weekday.)
- Improve access and security at stations where GNER was the station facility operator (SFO).
- Improve business travel facilities.
- Increase car parking spaces at stations.
- Establish road coach links from Bradford to Wakefield Westgate and Lincoln to Newark.

(It has to be said that this commitment did not go down well with a number of rail industry supporters who felt, with some justification, that a TOC had no business furthering the interests of road competitors – especially at Newark, where a rail-based link already existed.)

Additionally, very high performance targets were set, with 90% for punctuality and a huge 99% for reliability. GNER's confidence in achieving the targets was highlighted by its passenger charter commitment:

- On GNER trains delayed by one hour or more passengers would receive complimentary refreshments and compensation totalling 50% of the fare paid in the form of Rail Travel Vouchers (RTVs); these could be exchanged towards the cost of tickets for rail travel on any of the UK's main-line services.
- On GNER trains delayed by two hours or more the compensation was increased to 100% of the fare paid, again in the form of RTVs.
- On GNER trains delayed by three hours or more the refund was given in the form of cash.

The Great North Eastern Railway Company was a wholly owned subsidiary of Sea Containers Ltd, falling within that company's Ferries, Ports

and Trains division, and operated services over some 935 route miles between London and the North East of Scotland, with its headquarters in York. The longest journey was the 568 miles from London King's Cross to Inverness, closely followed by the 520-mile trip from King's Cross to Aberdeen.

The original GNER franchise commenced on 28 April 1996, when the company won the right to operate the East Coast Main Line rail services for a period of seven years. The winning bid included the provision for payment of a subsidy by OPRAF; the latter was later disbanded, its duties taken over by the newly formed Strategic Rail Authority (SRA), which initially operated in shadow form (sSRA) throughout the franchise period. When it bid for the franchise, GNER had anticipated the healthy increase in passenger numbers that would occur and planned to move from a subsidy totalling £67 million in 1996/97 to a profit within seven years of taking up the franchise.

The Sea Containers Senior Vice President (passenger transport), David Benson, was appointed as Chairman, with Christopher Garnett joining to take up the post of Chief Executive. They were the only 'outsiders' to join the company, the rest of the management team already being in post with British Rail. Garnett

had previously been appointed by Sherwood in 1986 to run the cross-Channel section of the former state-owned Sealink Ferries after its purchase by Sea Containers following privatisation in 1984. He therefore had valuable experience of running a former state-owned company and told me that the East Coast Main Line had run well under British Rail, so he did not see the need for wholesale changes, choosing instead to make use of the excellent in-house knowledge held by the former management team. This also included one or two recent

appointees such as Jonathan Metcalfe, who had joined the business as HR Director only months previously, in order to participate in the wider railway privatisation process.

The requirement for subsidy was removed in January 2002 when the company signed a franchise extension to 30 April 2005, at the same time agreeing to invest some £100 million in extra carriages, smarter stations, train refurbishment and improved passenger compensation. In March 2005 GNER successfully overcame bids from Danish State Railways (DSB) and English Welsh & Scottish Railway (EWS); First London and Scottish & North Eastern Railway; and Inter-City railways (the latter being an initial consortium of Deutsche Bahn, which later withdrew from the bidding after deciding it did not like the financial risk of the UK rail franchise process, and Stagecoach Group/Virgin Group). By so doing it won the right to continue to operate the East Coast rail franchise until 2015, commencing a couple of months later on 1 May 2005.

On taking up the original franchise GNER found itself operating over a recently refurbished route with relatively new electric locomotives hauling Mk 4 coaches with Driving Van Trailers (DVTs), but also using High Speed Train (HST) sets, which were

already approaching 20 years old. Unfortunately there is a view that the new infrastructure owner, Railtrack, did not continue to lavish as much care on the route as had been the case prior to privatisation, seemingly allowing it to degrade below a sustainable level with problems in track quality and other maintenance, which, arguably, would lead to the Hatfield accident some four years after the line passed into private ownership. This view gains support when taking into account a report commissioned by Railtrack, which highlighted money savings by reducing maintenance and renewals. It is thought that the first Railtrack East Coast Route Director in post refused to make the reductions and subsequently left his post. Christopher Garnett highlighted the example of weeds growing on the trackbed as being totally unacceptable, and a situation that he described as 'being of a third world standard', adding that 'passengers paying high fares were entitled to a good travel experience and certainly the undergrowth blooming from the infrastructure on the approach to London tarnished this.'

The GNER business plan included a target to achieve 18% growth over the life of its new franchise, but such was its immediate success that 21% was achieved inside the first three years of operations, and under much tighter control than had been the case in British Rail days. Wanting to build on BR's achievements, GNER decided that it would use a quality-driven approach with a good balance of old and new but, above all, very visible staff both on board the trains and at stations. Despite this, Garnett revealed that the company started cautiously, and there were no repainted trains or new uniforms visible on the first day of operation, and neither were there any new services. He felt he needed to know what would work before endorsing things with the company logo, so at first GNER still used BR-uniformed and liveried staff and trains, rather than have a branded train.

Virgin Trains went down the opposite route and operated a branded train on day one of its franchises; Garnett admits that when he saw the hype in the media celebrating Virgin's arrival in the rail business, he wondered if he had got it wrong: 'Should we have gone for immediate rebranding?' He told me that subsequently his worries disappeared because it was soon realised that rebranding brings with it very high public expectations, which a Train Operating Company could not hope to achieve from day one. Indeed, this was an issue from which Virgin Trains itself suffered, later admitting that, with hindsight, doing so had been a mistake. It is an interesting comparison to note that, when National Express succeeded GNER as the operator of the East Coast Rail Franchise in

Craigentinny

mtu 43300

2007, it chose to introduce a branded train on the first day of its operation, the difference being that it was taking over a rail franchise that already had a high degree of customer confidence.

New livery and uniforms

Considerable time and effort was subsequently put into designing the livery and uniforms. Jim Sherwood was able to engage the highly acclaimed New York designer Vignelli, who had previously done some work with the Orient Express, and it was his idea to use the dark blue livery with red stripe along the carriage sides. By now the inherited fleet of HSTs and Mk 4 coaches was due for repainting. Jim Sherwood visited Rosyth in Scotland, where the vehicles were to be repainted with two to three coats of paint to ensure a lasting finish. He gave an instruction that the trains should be repainted using a high gloss paint. The engineers were sceptical, saying it couldn't be done and that anyway trains do not get painted in a gloss finish. Garnett recalls that an angry Sherwood retorted, 'Don't tell me what I can't have – I have painted the Orient Express Pullmans.' Ultimately a compromise of sorts was reached and the paint used gave an 85% gloss finish, but in sticking to its guns GNER became the first UK Train Operating Company to have its trains repainted to that standard.

Sherwood was equally adamant that he wanted the trains to carry the company crest, and, after studying Andrew Dow's book on railway crests, actually came up with his own design, which was approved and issued by the Court of the Lord Lyon in Edinburgh. He understood the need for the branding to reflect the high-quality service the company intended to provide, but even so the issue of the crest on trains became problematic. Metal crests were extremely expensive and, due to the high costs, GNER switched to using vinyls instead. In fact, only nine locomotives, all HST power cars, were fitted with cast nameplates, and approximately 200 coaches, some of which were Mk 4s, had cast metal crests. Each of the company's carriages carried the legend 'Route of the Flying Scotsman' in white lettering above the crest, located just below the red waist-rail band, creating an air of permanence, historic pedigree and nostalgia.

The letters 'GNER' in gold lettering were added to the body sides of each of the company's locomotives, but unfortunately in the early applications the dark blue paintwork showed through,

so for a short period in 1999 the colour of the lettering was changed to white until a more durable version of gold could be obtained.

Request for franchise extension and Open Access Operator rights

Towards the end of 1997 GNER wrote to the then Deputy Prime Minister, John Prescott, who was also the Government Minister responsible for transport, requesting an extension to its franchise in order to facilitate the purchase of new trains. This request was non-productive, although the possibility of a 20-year franchise would come under consideration some years later during Sir Alistair Morton's reign at the head of the then shadow Strategic Rail Authority. The company followed this up with a meeting at the Office of the Rail Regulator, asking for rights to operate as an Open Access Operator alongside its main franchise. This request was also refused, something that GNER and Garnett would find very annoying in years to come when two other operators, Hull Trains and Grand Central Railway, were granted Open Access rights along the East Coast route.

CHAPTER FOUR

Rolling stock

Despite these setbacks, Garnett revealed in another in-depth interview that he knew they had to do something about capacity or the company would start to suffer from chronic overcrowding. He said, 'It was impossible to simply lease more trains because none were available, although one option would have been a new train build.' At an earlier press conference journalists had picked up on a casual remark by Sherwood that the company was considering buying two 'Pendolinos', and it is true that they were looking hard at the possibility, in fact spending some £2 million on the project, and a train with traction distributed along its length would certainly have been better for capacity than the existing practice of locomotive-hauled trains with DVTs, which resulted in two wasted vehicles in every train because they could not carry passengers in them.

Subsequently Jim Sherwood, Christopher Garnett and David Benson, and the then GNER Operations Director Mike Tham, visited the Fiat Ferroviaria factory in Italy to take a look at the Italian tilting 'Pendolino' train. Sherwood made it quite clear to the others that he did not like the small window apertures of the 'Pendolino', which certainly restricted some passengers' views from the train, but at the same time it was the only suitable off-the-shelf long-distance electric train available. However, without an extension to the franchise it would be difficult to finance the trains and ultimately the idea was not followed up. Instead Sea Containers purchased some old Mk 3 sleeper stock with the intention of converting it for use on GNER services, although this never happened due to a number of issues, including the high cost of conversion and rolling stock changes within the Virgin Trains fleets, which eventually saw some former Virgin HST sets become available to GNER. This also provided an opportunity to strengthen the fleet by including an extra carriage on each train in the existing HST fleet. In the meantime, as we shall see, GNER was also able to hire some of the spare regional 'Eurostar' trains for service on the ECML.

Unfortunately the sleeper stock suffered badly at the hands of vandals and was written off; a sad indictment of some members of today's society.

In hindsight Garnett revealed that he was glad that the 'Pendolino' plan had failed because he felt the Mk 4 coaches were better for the East Coast Main Line route, but admits that the 'Pendolino' is the right choice for the West Coast because of the more curved nature of that route. Proud of his plans to refurbish his entire fleet to 'Mallard' standards (described later in the book), his sense of humour was evident when he made a tongue-in-cheek remark describing Virgin's new 'Voyager' fleet as 'cheap

RIGHT: High speed on the East Coast Main Line: a King's Cross-Glasgow Central service races past Fenwick, north of Doncaster, in March 2004.
railphotolibrary.com

BELOW: A GNER HST set makes its way over the Forth Bridge at South Queensferry on a dull day in late August 2007.
John Balmforth

TOP RIGHT: A GNER Class 91 and Mk 4 train set crosses Newcastle's King Edward Bridge over the River Tyne in November 2003. *railphotolibrary.com*

and nasty for long-distance travel', calling them 'Spinster Specials' because 'they had 19 litres throbbing away beneath their feet'. The comment caused a few ripples at Virgin, but Garnett recalls that the Bombardier sales team were pleased with the publicity, which inferred that the 'Voyager' design was cheap to buy.

Good reliability and performance was paramount to GNER and the TOC could not allow trains to stand out of service for lengthy periods awaiting attention when faults arose. The Class 91 fleet, which was being used intensively, is a specific example because there were no spare wheels in stock. This was a practice inherited from British Rail days and one that had to be remedied quickly. In BR ownership it was easy for a locomotive to be borrowed from another depot to cover for a shortage, but GNER would have either to hire one, which had financial implications, or cancel services. It was not long before the owning Rolling Stock Company (ROSCO) had spare wheels available.

ABOVE: The unusual sight of a pair of Class 91s double-heading a GNER service is caught at Darlington South Junction. All is not quite as it seems, however, as the leading loco is assisting its failed sister. *Rich Mackin/ railwayscene.co.uk*

At the privatisation of BR's East Coast trains, the rolling stock had been transferred to the ownership of ROSCOs from whom GNER had to hire them:

EVERSHOLT: This ROSCO provided electric traction and, Garnett told me, was difficult to deal with (lack of spare wheels for the Class 91 locomotives being just one of a number of issues). Later, it was taken over by HSBC and subsequently things improved dramatically. The new owner came in with a mission to improve the Class 91 fleet, which by now had a high failure rate in service. The maintenance programme improved them so much that drivers eventually came to prefer them to the HST sets. Today it is rare for a Class 91 to fail in service.

ANGEL TRAINS: This ROSCO provided the High Speed Train sets and is a wholly owned subsidiary of the Royal Bank of Scotland Group.

The Class 89 AC electric:
a unique locomotive

Locomotive No 89001 was designed by Brush Traction to a British Rail specification and was built at British Rail Engineering Ltd (BREL) Crewe in 1986 as a potential replacement for the Class 86 AC electric locomotives that were nearing the end of their planned life (though most are still at work more than 20 years later). It was the only one of its type built, had a top speed of 125mph, and featured electric traction control, speed selection, a Co-Co wheel arrangement and a continuous rating of 4,500kW (6,000hp). Ultimately the lighter Bo-Bo-configured Class 90s and 91s were the preferred choice of BR's InterCity sector, but No 89001's uniqueness justifies a detailed description in this book.

Named *Avocet* at Sandy station on 16 September 1989 by the then Prime Minister, Margaret Thatcher, it was fitted with appropriate cast nameplates. After the locomotive suffered an unacceptable number of in-service failures it soon found itself stored out of use at Bounds Green depot and was officially withdrawn in July 1992. Fortunately this unique locomotive escaped the cutter's torch when it was rescued by a group of staff at Brush Traction, finding itself moved to the Midland Railway Centre, Swanwick, in 1994.

When Sea Containers won the right to operate the East Coast franchise, it reviewed several options for its motive power requirements, which needed to be increased in order to cope with planned capacity expansion. As part of this review Christopher Garnett told me that GNER purchased No 89001 for £25,000, spending around a further £100,000 in bringing it back up to standard for main-line use, the plan being to use it on King's Cross to Leeds and Bradford services. The overhaul, which took place at the Loughborough works of Brush Traction, was made easier because the locomotive was already fitted with Time Division Multiplex (TDM) circuitry, enabling it to be used in a 'push-pull' capacity in conjunction with a Driving Van Trailer at the opposite end of the train, thus saving the lengthy 'run-rounds' incurred by locomotive-hauled trains.

No 89001 received the new Vignelli-inspired GNER corporate livery in 1998 soon after joining the fleet, but reappeared from the works without the *Avocet* nameplates. It was able to operate at 125mph over parts of the East Coast Main Line but was not tested to its full capability over the route to Leeds and Bradford since the line speed there was 110mph. Driver knowledge of the locomotive was also a major factor in the machine being used mainly on the

Yorkshire services, but even so it was a regular sight on the ECML hauling crack GNER expresses between 1996 and 2000. This was only interrupted by a period from 1999 to the summer of 2000, which it spent at Doncaster Works after bogie and traction motor failure. The end of its service on the main line came later in 2000 when it suffered a further traction motor failure. It was subsequently stored at Doncaster Works.

In the early part of 2002 No 89001 was dragged to the GNER depot at Bounds Green for use as a static train power supply unit, though later in the year it was returned to Doncaster for further storage. With GNER having no further main-line use for it, the locomotive was transferred in December 2004 into the care of the AC Locomotive Group and can be seen by visitors at Barrow Hill Roundhouse near Chesterfield. Following a successful funding appeal the preservation group was able to purchase No 89001 in November 2006, and by June 2007 it had been returned to its original InterCity livery, although it is unlikely that it will ever appear again hauling trains under its own power on the main line.

Class 90 AC electric locomotives: a brief introduction

The Class 90 electric locomotives were originally intended to operate along the West Coast Main Line route alongside the Class 87s, and in fact were planned to be designated Class 87/2. The first of a fleet of 40 was delivered to the Railway Technical Centre at Derby in the late autumn of 1987. Capable of use both on

ABOVE: The unique Class 89 AC electric locomotive No 89001 was once used on crack GNER expresses but is now owned in preservation by the AC Locomotive Group. It can still be seen today by visitors to the Barrow Hill Roundhouse, near Chesterfield.
Rich Mackin/railwayscene.co.uk

LEFT: A view inside the driver's cab of No 89001.
John Balmforth

locomotive-hauled trains and in conjunction with a DVT in 'push-pull' mode, these machines had bogies configured to Bo-Bo format and were rated at 5,000hp with a maximum permitted speed of 110mph.

Rising passenger numbers required GNER to have more trains. Availability was difficult but early in the franchise the company managed to hire a number of Class 90 electric locomotives from the English Welsh & Scottish Railway on a daily basis for use on the King's Cross to Leeds services, to compensate for lack of serviceable Class 91s. Almost immediately the company repainted one of them into GNER livery and Garnett remembers that rather ironically it spent much of its time, still wearing GNER colours, hauling freight trains up and down the West Coast Main Line. The hired locomotives did not let GNER down, but subsequent reliability improvements and a Class 91 refurbishment programme eventually resulted in GNER being able to discontinue the use of Class 90 locomotives in its fleet.

Class 91 AC electric locomotives: a brief introduction

When the fixed-formation concept of the Advanced Passenger Train (APT) was abandoned by British Rail, the need for a powerful electric locomotive with high speed (140mph) and also tilt capability to haul more conventional rolling stock became ever more paramount. Hence the Class 91 AC electric locomotive was born.

The first ten were designed and built by BREL at Crewe Works in February 1988, being introduced into passenger service in the autumn of the same year, although this was

before the Mk 4 coaches and DVTs were delivered. To overcome this, a number of HST power cars were converted to act as surrogate DVTs, with Mk 3 carriages being used. The locomotives operate from a 25kV 50Hz AC overhead line electricity supply and are fitted with GEC G426AZ body-mounted traction motors with cardan shaft drives. Weighing 84 tonnes, they have a power rating of 6,090hp (4,540kW) and are fitted with rheostatic brakes. At the time of manufacture they were hailed as the most powerful locomotive ever to work in the UK.

The Class 91 Bo-Bo electric locomotive formed the backbone of GNER's locomotive fleet hauling Mk 4 carriages with Driving Van Trailers at the opposite end of the train, usually at the southern end; this removed the need for time-consuming 'run-rounds' at terminating destinations. The entire fleet of 31 vehicles was leased to GNER for its East Coast Main Line services when it won the franchise in 1996, and this effectively meant that they would not be used on the freight or overnight parcels work that the locomotive's designers had also intended for it. They were all repainted into GNER's blue livery and received names (a full list is reproduced at Appendix B) featuring places along the route or famous people.

The class was intended to operate at 140mph (225kmh), hence the trains they hauled becoming known as 'IC225'. The present-day 125mph maximum line speed prevents the class being used to its full potential, though it is little known today that, during testing, speed restrictions were relaxed between Peterborough and Grantham and the test locomotive set a new UK speed record for rail by reaching 154mph, fittingly at Stoke

Bank where steam locomotive *Mallard* had set the all-time speed record for a steam locomotive in 1938. Indeed, that section of line still has the 'flashing green' signals installed to give a greater braking distance for 140mph running. All of the class are based at Bounds Green depot, though the early test trains tended to be found at Edinburgh's Craigentinny depot and Millerhill Yard.

The Class 91 locomotive has a sloping streamlined look at one end while the other is upright and known as the 'slab end'. However, the locomotive is equipped with a cab at both ends, allowing it to be driven from either, although the streamlined cab is usually found at the northern end of a fixed formation of 'Mallard' Mk 4 coaches plus DVT. If the locomotives are operated 'slab end' first the maximum line speed is reduced to 110mph. They were not often used in that mode in GNER service except for occasional

operational needs, such as a fault in the cab at the streamlined end or TDM.

They are capable of conversion for tilt operation but the full technology has never been put to use, mainly due to the failure of the Government and Network Rail to upgrade the route to a line speed where it would be

ABOVE: A line-up of four Class 91 GNER locomotives as they await their next turns of duty at King's Cross. *Rich Mackin/ railwayscene.co.uk*

ABOVE: The side profile of Class 91 No 91107 *Newark on Trent* is seen to good effect as it nears Newark on a King's Cross-Leeds working in April 2004.

railphotolibrary.com

LEFT: The western end of Edinburgh Waverley station sees the arrival of a Glasgow Central – King's Cross service powered from the rear by a Class 91 locomotive.

railphotolibrary.com

beneficial. Nevertheless, and despite their high level of technical capability, GNER found that the locomotives were troublesome, often failing in service and giving poor results performance-wise. To remedy this the company invested in an extensive upgrade and refurbishment of the class between 2001 and 2003 (further reviewed later in this book). Classified as a Heavy General Repair (HGR), this proved highly effective, and by 2007 GNER had one of the best-performing long-distance fleets in the UK, some arguing that it was in fact the best.

Class 373/3 'Regional Eurostar': 'The White Rose'

The Class 373/3 'Regional Eurostar' trains, so called because they were intended to operate through services to the continent from the major regional UK cities north of London, were built as part of the 78 half-set (7-10 cars) 'Eurostar' fleet. They were designed to operate through the Channel Tunnel as 14-car sets with two power cars (all of their sister units consisted of 18 cars with two power cars for the London, Paris and Brussels services), connecting the North of England via London with direct services to Paris, Lille and Brussels. It was a purpose-built fleet based on the French TGV design and variously owned by the French

national rail operator Société Nationale des Chemins de Fer Français (SNCF), Belgium's national rail company Société Nationale des Chemins de Fer Belges (SNCB) and Eurostar UK, with the half-sets coupled in the centre and provided with a driving motor car at each end. Built to very high technical standards, the trains have proved to be very successful, albeit heavy and expensive to operate. They boast a superb ride quality at high speed, resulting from the use of articulated trailers on two-axle bogies. Each half-set mirrors its neighbour, containing First Class accommodation and restaurant facilities.

Manufactured by a combination of GEC Alstom, Brush, ANF, De Dietrich, BN and ACEC, the fleet first appeared in 1992 and had the capability of drawing power from three

TOP: The only Class 90 locomotive ever to recieve GNER colours is seen in a 'later life' heading a private charter train through York.
Matthew Clarke

ABOVE: 'Regional Eurostar' set No 373304 shows how well the GNER livery suits the train's profile, as it speeds along the ECML near Peterborough on a non-stop service to York.
railphotolibrary.com

different sources: 25kV 50Hz AC overhead line, 3kV DC overhead line, or 750-volt DC third rail. The electrical equipment used three-phase GEC/Brush asynchronous traction motors producing a power rating of 16,350hp (12,200kW) and a maximum speed of 186mph (300kmph). All sets were fitted with both friction and rheostatic brakes.

Five 'Regional Eurostar' sets were hired by GNER and saw service with the company between 2000 and 2005, three of the sets receiving vinyls in the GNER Vignelli livery, though the remaining two ran in GNER service wearing their home 'Eurostar' livery but without any branding.

GNER Mk 3 coaches: a brief description

Introduced in 1976 and designated by British Rail as Mk 3, these coaches were originally designed for use as part of the High Speed Train sets, although they were perfectly at home on locomotive-hauled services. The final batch was built in 1988, but some multiple unit carriages based upon the Mk 3 design continued to be built well into the 1990s. The design has certainly stood the test of time, and since 1977 the Royal Train has included nine specially adapted Mk 3 carriages.

The Mk 3 body shell is 75 feet (22.86 metres) in length, of full monocoque construction and has gained a well-deserved reputation for its exceptional strength and crashworthiness. The vehicles are also fitted with air suspension between the bodies and bogies, resulting in a particularly smooth ride. The bogies themselves, classified as BT10, were designed specifically for the Mk 3 and have coil spring primary suspension with hydraulic dampers, enabling a maximum speed of 125mph (200kmh). Electrical and air-conditioning systems are mounted in modules housed behind the aerodynamic skirts between the bogies (on earlier carriage designs these components were located above and below the passenger cabin area), with the actual fittings integrated into the ceiling panels for the first time.

Like their predecessors, the Mk 3 coaches are equipped with pneumatically-operated automatic gangway doors triggered by pressure pads located under the floor, and a guard-operated central door-locking system for the manually operated slam doors (following a number of incidents across the national network of passengers falling out of the doors of moving trains, the guard-operated central locking system was fitted to the whole fleet in the early 1990s).

All of the Mk 3s in service with GNER

were used in HST formations and, unlike the locomotive-hauled variants, did not require fitting with alternators, since the power required to operate the heating, lighting and air-conditioning systems was drawn directly from the train's power cars. The TOC had plans to refurbish the Mk 3s to the same 'Mallard' standard as their Mk 4 sisters; that programme commenced in January 2007 and is described later in this book.

Most of the Mk 3s used across the rail network in HST sets were of eight-car Class 253 formation, but the Class 254 HSTs in service with GNER were increased to nine cars in line with its franchise commitment.

GNER Mk 4 coaches: a brief description

British Rail's final design of passenger coach, designated as Mk 4, was specifically designed for use in the InterCity 225 sets operating along the East Coast Main Line. Built between 1989 and 1991 at the Washwood Heath, Birmingham, works of GEC Alstom, the fleet totalled 302 vehicles, all to be used in dedicated formations with a Class 91 locomotive and Driving Van Trailer.

The design was based heavily upon the abandoned Advanced Passenger Train concept, this being most obvious externally by the profiled sides, which would have allowed retrofitting of a tilting mechanism if the trains were to operate at their 140mph design speed. Sadly the opportunity to do so was never taken up and the trains have run in service at a reduced speed of 125mph. The vehicles incorporated many improvements over the Mk 3 design including the provision of push-button-controlled plug-type doors to replace the manual slam doors previously used. Doors and vestibules were wider to allow disabled access and vestibules were given carpets and better lighting, together with flip-down seats. They were the first BR vehicles not to use the iconic 'Rail Alphabet' typeface in any of their interior signage and operating notices.

British Rail introduced the Mk 4 coaches, and they were subsequently refurbished to a very high ('Mallard') standard by GNER between 2003 and 2005, as detailed later in this book. However, despite their popularity with passengers, railway engineers had to tackle a number of issues, including:

- The weight of each vehicle was some 30% heavier than a Mk 3 carriage.
- The suspension and tuning, which was initially wrong.
- The rigidity of the bogies, especially on the Class 91s that were used to haul them.
- They were expensive to operate, so their

ABOVE LEFT: The scene at King's Cross on 1 November 2007 as GNER trains formed of Mk 4 coaches left and Mk 3 carriages right prepare for departures on services to Leeds and Aberdeen. *John Balmforth*

ABOVE RIGHT: Two rakes of GNER coaches seen at Newcastle Central on 8 October 2005. On the left are Mk 4 'IC225' vehicles, and right the earlier Mk 3 'IC125' coaches. *Chris McKenna*

LEFT: A GNER Class 91 electric locomotive and a Class 43 power car rest at the King's Cross platforms as they prepare for their next duties on services to the north on 3 July 2006. *Rich Mackin/railwayscene.co.uk*

longevity in service was questionable.
- They suffered serious failures in their air-conditioning systems.

It should also be acknowledged that, as with the Mk 3 carriages, the Mk 4s have gained widespread praise for their exceptional crashworthiness, as was proved in the accidents at Hatfield and Great Heck. Safety experts agreed that the integral construction of the coaches was a major factor in restricting the number of lives lost.

The Mk 4 coaches, even in British Rail days, experienced problems with their air-conditioning and, due to the lack of suitable alternative vehicles, GNER was often forced to run trains in service with the air-conditioning out of order. This led to the famous occasion when, on a very warm day, with inoperative air-conditioning, Garnett made the never-to-be-forgotten announcement to passengers that 'GNER would always give them a warm welcome'. Despite his joke, it was a serious problem and one that irked him immensely; after all, there were days when temperatures reached 30-plus degrees and even higher in the drivers' cabs. He recalls one passenger approaching him and asking why GNER hadn't resolved the problem. The customer added that he understood to a degree why British Rail had failed to do so under government control, but GNER was a private company and, with the backing of its parent company, should surely be able to get things working properly. Garnett agreed and turned to GNER's Manager Fleet & Engineering, Tony Brown, for the solution.

Brown told me that the problem lay in the actual air-conditioning system, which had originally been designed by Metro Cammell. It used a heat pump but did not include a separate refrigeration pump, and a number of its components, while fine for use in a static environment, were not ideally suited for use in transit. The fan motors were powered by DC current but designed to run under their own battery power should the overhead line electric power supply fail. Brown felt that this was not really required as other batteries were available on board and extras only increased the vehicle's weight. The air flows to the system's ducting also frequently became blocked by insulation that became dislodged due to poor workmanship during installation. This in turn caused the air-conditioning units to become so hot that on occasions the solder in them melted. When the units overheated, their electrical control system would automatically shut down the air-conditioning and, because the control was located below the carriage and behind the aerodynamic skirts, it could not be re-set during service. Instead it required the train to visit a depot, and even though it would then re-enter service with the air-conditioning working it wasn't long before the system deficiencies took a hand and shut it down again. Not only did this result in carriages becoming uncomfortably hot to ride in, but a further design fault was causing the air inlets to become choked with dust from the coaches' brake pads whenever the friction brakes were applied, resulting in a burning smell entering the carriages. The problems were not insurmountable, however, and by correctly refitting the insulation, together with new valves and other equipment modifications, the matter was resolved, with passengers no longer having to suffer journeys in unpleasant temperatures.

BELOW: A DVT at the rear of a northbound GNER express having just crossed the only remaining flat crossing on a UK main line, near Newark.
railphotolibrary.com

Class 82 Driving Van Trailers:
a brief description

A Driving Van Trailer (DVT) is a purpose-built vehicle that allows the driver to drive a train from the opposite end to its locomotive, thus avoiding the need for locomotives to run-round trains at their destination or a terminus station. British DVTs resemble Class 90 and 91 locomotives externally, and when the train is operating in 'push' mode it does not give the impression that it is actually travelling 'backwards'.

Built by British Rail in 1988, GNER had a fleet of 32 DVTs in service in dedicated formations with a rake of Mk 4 coaches and a Class 91 electric locomotive. Although capable of a top speed of 140mph (225kmph) – to achieve which they would need to be retro-fitted with a tilt mechanism – they have, like the Class 91 locomotives and Mk 4 coaches, been restricted to the maximum 125mph line speed of the East Coast route. DVTs use a Time Division Multiplexer to send control signals along specially screened cables that run along the length of the train. The control signals are encoded and multiplexed onto the cables by the TDM equipment on the DVT. At the locomotive end the signals are de-multiplexed, again by the TDM equipment, and used to control the locomotive. The exception is the air braking system, which is always operated from whichever cab the driver is driving from.

In the event of a TDM failure, and an inability to reconfigure the equipment, the train can still continue to operate, but if the DVT is the leading vehicle it will be necessary to uncouple the locomotive and attach it to the front of the DVT.

Class 43 HST power cars

The Class 43 power cars are used to power the InterCity 125 High Speed Trains, which consist of a rake of Mk 3 coaches with a power car at each end – in effect a fast diesel multiple unit. The prototype power car was designated Class 41 and developed at the Railway Technical Centre, Derby, but built at BREL, Crewe. Two prototype power cars were built in 1972 and, after successful trials, authority was given to develop the present-day versions, with 197 eventually being built. As with the prototypes, the production versions were constructed by BREL at Crewe between 1976 and 1982, and have a maximum permitted speed of 125mph, although the class is officially deemed to be the fastest diesel locomotive in the world, having attained 148mph on 1 November 1987 when

TOP: The side profile of a Class 82 Driving Van Trailer can be clearly appreciated as it speeds past the photographer near Newark while working a Leeds-King's Cross train in April 2004. *railphotolibrary.com*

ABOVE: Two Driving Van Trailers stand side-by-side at the rear of their trains under the ornate station roof at King's Cross while awaiting their next turn of duty. *GNER*

the fixed formations were abandoned by BR, allowing the power cars to be easily removed for maintenance purposes.

Many of the early London-Leeds services were stopping trains, while those to York and beyond were usually fast express services.

descending Stoke Bank while testing a new type of bogie. It is claimed that the record has been broken on two occasions: in Russia in 1992 (168mph) and in Spain in 2002 (159mph), although neither have been officially recognised. Another HST, carrying passengers, reached 144mph north of York on 27 September 1985 during a special press run to celebrate the launch of the 'Tees-Tyne Pullman' service.

The vehicles have been powered by a number of engines: Paxman 12RP200L Valenta, Paxman 12VP185 and MTU 16V4000. Weighing in at 35 tonnes, they have a power rating of 2,250bhp (1,680kW). Fitted with air brakes, the units have a Bo-Bo wheel arrangement and diesel-electric transmission.

During 1987 eight Class 43s were converted for use as DVTs and fitted with buffers and TDM equipment, allowing them to be used in 'push-pull' mode with a Class 91 on the East Coast Main Line. Subsequently returned to their normal duties, the power cars so converted can be easily identified today because they still retain their buffers.

When operated with rakes of eight coaches they are known as Class 253, but the versions used by GNER containing an additional carriage are known as Class 254 sets. Originally intended for use as permanently coupled units,

The trains used on the fast York services tended to be HSTs because they operated most effectively once they had reached high speed, making them ideal for use on non-stop journeys. Their overall performance levels dropped when used on stopping services, but, as more sets were introduced to help cater for growth, by 2007 they were found operating on a greater number of routes. Additionally they were employed on services to Skipton because, although the route was electrified, it was not to a high enough power rating to enable regular Class 91 operation.

FAR LEFT: A rare photograph of a GNER HST using bay platform No 2 at York station. *GNER*

LEFT: The driver's cab controls of HST power car No 43110 *Stirlingshire*, photographed at Edinburgh Waverley on 4 December 2007. *John Balmforth*

LEFT: A GNER Inverness-King's Cross service passes through Princes Street Gardens, Edinburgh, in February 2003 on the approach to the city's Waverley station.
railphotolibrary.com

ABOVE: An Aberdeen-King's Cross express passes Fenwick in March 2004.
railphotolibrary.com

RIGHT: A Class 43 power car, at King's Cross on 1 November 2007, prepares for the 520-mile journey to Aberdeen.
John Balmforth

CHAPTER FIVE

Maintenance and depots

Fleet maintenance was a top priority for GNER and behind the scenes a 550-strong engineering team looked after the maintenance of the fleet, usually carried out at one of four depots. The depots located at Bounds Green (Alexandra Palace) and Craigentinny (Edinburgh) were operated by GNER, but other operators' depots at Neville Hill (Leeds) and Heaton (Newcastle), supported by two mobile teams, also carried out maintenance. GNER also had a contract with ScotRail to provide maintenance for the HST sets used on the Inverness-King's Cross route as well as a service point at Aberdeen. Alstom's Glasgow depot at Polmadie also had a role in preparing Mk 4 sets for service on a nightly basis.

Heavy maintenance of the Class 91 locomotives was contracted out to Bombardier Transportation at Doncaster. Special arrangements were made for maintenance of the unique Class 89 locomotive to be carried out by a dedicated team of staff from Brush, which could be provided at any of the depots or the Brush works in Loughborough. The Class 373/3 'Regional Eurostars' always returned to the Eurostar depot at North Pole (London) for maintenance procedures to be carried out. Quite simply, the importance of work carried out at the depots cannot be underestimated, so let us take a look behind the scenes at one of them.

Behind the scenes:
Bounds Green depot (Depot Code BN)

Bounds Green depot was built in the 1970s to service HSTs and in reality resulted in the early 1980s closure of Finsbury Park depot and the locomotive fuelling point at King's Cross. The depot was electrified later in the decade as part of the ECML upgrade.

The judges at the National Rail Awards in 2005 voted the staff at Bounds Green 'Best London Operational Team', after which

GNER's Business Process Manager (Depots), Tim Sayer, told *Rail* that he felt the award reflected the way in which staff worked together as a team and management encourage ideas from the bottom for self-improvement. He cited the Class 91 exam routine, which had evolved over the years to become more efficiently managed, offering economies and reducing costs. He said that the team pioneered continual improvement within GNER and was ahead of the rest of the company in that respect. He said, 'The employees come up with ideas for improvement. It helps to have a good team focus – it's good for generating ideas. The overnight cleaning teams have subdivided their work to create a better flow to eliminate unproductive practices. There is a strong sense of ownership, which makes staff feel proud. It is very rare that we do not deliver a train for the booked service.'

Bounds Green depot is located in Bridge Road, not far from Alexandra Palace and just a 5-minute walk from Alexandra Palace station. GNER's 31-strong fleet of Class 91 electric locomotives was based there, alongside 30 rakes

ABOVE: Engineer Brian Guilfoyle carries out an overhaul on a Class 91 locomotive's Voith gearbox at Bombardier, Crewe. *GNER*

CENTRE RIGHT: Engineers carrying out a wheel-set overhaul at Crewe Works. *GNER*

RIGHT: Bounds Green depot is seen from Bridge Road near Alexandra Palace station. The East Coast Main Line can just be glimpsed curving away to the extreme left of the picture. *John Balmforth*

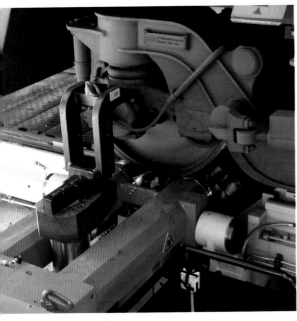

ABOVE: GNER's electric shunting locomotive, purchased to shunt vehicles requiring attention onto the wheel lathe at Bounds Green depot.
John Balmforth

ABOVE LEFT: The newly installed wheel lathe is re-turning the steel tyres on a Mk 4 carriage at Bounds Green.
John Balmforth

LEFT: A Mk 4 carriage shows off its shiny re-turned tyre after a session on the wheel lathe.
John Balmforth

of Mk 4 coaches. While the HST fleet was generally looked after at Craigentinny, Neville Hill and Heaton, Bounds Green staff were qualified to undertake limited work on them. Similarly the other depots had staff who are qualified to carry out limited repairs on the electric fleet and Mk 4 coaches.

Maintenance procedures

Most major rail depots in the UK provide a 24-hour service, and in Bounds Green's case that is provided 363 days of the year. As might be expected, at night, when rail services are reduced, the depot becomes a real hive of activity. Up to nine trains return for servicing every night, though this can increase to as many as 13 at weekends. Even so, it may come as a surprise to some that one of the non-GNER depots (Heaton) actually saw the most GNER

RIGHT: Class 08 diesel shunter No 08892 poses at Wabtec, Doncaster, in GNER livery.
Rich Mackin/ railwayscene.co.uk

trains each night, but this was the direct result of the large number of GNER services that ended their day at Newcastle.

Nevertheless all major servicing of the Class 91 fleet is carried out at Bounds Green. This includes the 'A' examination required every 10 days, as well as the much more in-depth 'B' exam, which has to be carried out every 30

days. In between the 'B' examinations Class 91s undergo the 'Z' exam, which requires a thorough check of the locomotive's traction motor brushes. The depot is also capable of carrying out Level 4 and 5 maintenance, much of which previously had to go to specialist works such as Bombardier and Wabtec. Level 5 maintenance is required every 750,000 miles; locomotives take around two years to reach this mileage.

GNER's train diagrams were designed to allow for two Mk 4 sets to be spare at Bounds Green every day for between four and five hours. The depot staff used this time to carry out basic maintenance on the carriages; on occasions repairs took longer than expected, so then the set would be swapped with a spare set, thus avoiding the need to cancel a service.

Typical train examination timetables at Bounds Green are:

Mark 4 coaches

Minor exams	'S' exam – daily
	'A' exam – 15,000 miles
	'Z' exam – 45,000 miles
Major exams	'B' exam – 90,000 miles
	'C' exam – 270,000 miles
	'D' exam – 540,000 miles
	'OH' exam *(Level 5)* – 1,000,000 miles

The exam sequence is B, B, C, B, B, D, B, B, C, B, B, OH

Class 91 locomotives

Minor exams	'S' exam – daily
	'A' exam – 15,000 miles
	'Z' exam – 30,000 miles
	'B' exam – 65,000 miles
Major exams	'XM01' – 120,000 miles
	'XM02' – 240,000 miles
	'XM03' – 360,000 miles
	'XM04' – 480,000 miles
	'XM05' – 600,000 miles
	'XM06' *(Level 5)* – 720,000 miles

ABOVE: This 'old lady' was a stalwart at Bounds Green. No 08853, still wearing BR blue, lasted in service with National Express until 6 February 2008. She is seen at Bounds Green awaiting collection by road transport at the end of her last day's service.
John Balmforth

RIGHT: The driver's cab controls of Class 08 diesel shunter No 08853.
John Balmforth

The engineering team was required to provide 26 of the electric train sets every weekday in order to meet the demands of the ECML timetable. In addition, the depot's staff tried to keep a 'hot spare' that would always be available for immediate use in the event of train failures. Of the remaining sets one would be undergoing Level 4 planned maintenance and another, at either Craigentinny or Bounds Green, for tyre turning on the wheel lathes. The depot also provided a daily spare Class 91 locomotive stationed at King's Cross, which was used to keep delays minimal should a rostered locomotive fail close to departure time.

In order for carriages to be up to acceptable service standards they were given a basic clean whenever they arrived on depot, but in any case every 30 days they underwent a heavy clean of the interiors, with a 60-day cycle seeing specialist cleaning of all carpets and seat fabrics. Cleaning could be, and often was, carried out while carriages were being serviced.

Bounds Green is equipped with jacks capable of lifting the heavy 84-tonne Class 91s, and a new wheel lathe was installed in 2007 at a cost of £500,000, which included the provision of an electric shunter used to position the carriages. The new lathe at Bounds Green is capable of turning tyres on each axle in approximately one hour. Vehicles needed to visit the wheel lathe every 250,000 miles for tyre turning. At the fourth, 1-million-mile, visit the wheels were replaced.

The depot has a six-road shed with holding roads, but not all roads are electrified, thus one of its two Class 08 diesel shunters is required to assist with stock movement. To access the shed, trains coming from King's Cross need to take the down Hertford line round the back of Alexandra Palace, head over the flyover and reverse at Bowes Park. Trains leaving the depot for King's Cross have an easier task, using the direct connection off shed to the up Hertford line and through Finsbury Park for the 3.75-mile trip to the terminus.

Trains arriving at Bounds Green after their day's work visit the carriage wash at Ferme Park, which, although located on the other side of the ECML, is officially part of Bounds Green depot. After passing through the carriage wash, the train's toilet tanks are emptied before it is shunted to the shed via Bowes Park. HSTs also have refuelling facilities at Ferme Park.

Staffing levels

GNER had 220 staff based at Bounds Green, made up of 65 cleaners, 45 stores, administration and training staff, and 110 maintenance personnel working four shift patterns to give 24-hour cover. Although not part of the depot staff, Bounds Green also saw many drivers who, although being rostered at King's Cross, started and finished their shifts at Bounds Green, taking trains off shed to start their day's work and doing the same in reverse in the evening. The depot was also home to a team from Bombardier who carried out warranty work on the 'Mallard' sets, and likewise there was a small team from Alstom to work on the Class 91s.

ABOVE: A GNER DVT stands on No 9 road at Bounds Green ready to return to service in May 2005. *GNER*

RIGHT: Assisting the author with research for this book, Allan Stokes is seen in the driver's seat of DVT No 82224 at Bounds Green depot in February 2008. *John Balmforth*

ABOVE AND LEFT: Ironically, GNER, and its successor, held a contract to maintain the hired heritage blue/grey-liveried train used on Hull Trains' weekend services. This train was required following damage to a Class 222 set after it fell off the supporting jacks at Bombardier's works during maintenance. Seen at Bounds Green depot, the train is headed by Class 86 No 86101 *Sir William A. Stanier FRS*, the driver's cab of which is seen at left. *Both: John Balmforth*

CHAPTER SIX

Customer service

It took in excess of 12 months before GNER was able to launch its new branding, but in the spring of 1997 the major switchover took place. A proud Garnett asked staff what they thought of it and was genuinely surprised at what could be interpreted as a negative response. All too often it was simply 'it's different'. Strangely enough, though, the passengers he quizzed did like it. After a short time the positive reaction of passengers began to have a good effect on staff, who began to reveal that they now liked it. This time, when Garnett asked why, he got the response 'because the passengers like it'. A classic case of happy customers equals happy staff. Within a further three months the new uniforms and liveries had become a regular sight, being highly visible to the rapidly increasing numbers of passengers, and by 2002 the number of staff employed had risen to 2,833, an increase of more than 12%.

While GNER had ensured that a lot of engineering improvements took place on its train fleet, Garnett felt that the company was just as progressive in its attitude to customer service. He argued that the main driver behind customer service for GNER was to take on the airlines, so it became imperative that passengers be given a good experience. At the end of the day Garnett felt that they succeeded in winning the battle against the short-haul airlines, but not those operating from Scotland or Newcastle to London. He felt that GNER should have been able to obtain at least 50% of the market, and remains very disappointed that this was never achieved.

GNER's progress resulted from the use of a two-pronged approach. The first was directly concerned with investment in trains, maintenance, stations and service improvements, while the second concentrated on its people, with flexibility and career opportunity seen as important. Recruitment was done on the basis of 'attitude and train up'. If candidates showed good attitude and a willingness to learn, GNER was prepared to invest in them, and during the first three years of the franchise many training workshops were held for all levels of staff. By the end of the franchise in 2007 the company had developed some of the best training facilities in the industry. The Harvard Business School philosophy interestingly refers to 'The Service Profit Chain', which it defines as:

Committed staff ⟶
satisfied passengers ⟶
commercial success

GNER's Head of Communications, Alan Hyde, told me that the company discovered a few years later that it had been using that philosophy without realising it, and the Service

LEFT: Former Chef of the Year Colin Patty prepares dinner on GNER's 1100 King's Cross-Edinburgh service on 3 December 2007.
John Balmforth

Profit Chain was used to post-rationalise what GNER had done instinctively. The philosophy created a very loyal staff, terrific customer support and strong revenue growth for much of the time.

Dirty trains

Early on in the franchise Garnett noticed that the exterior of trains was often dirty in service and told depot engineers, 'For a start, passengers want to be able to see out of the windows.' He was given what he considered to be an unacceptable excuse that water freezes in cold weather and the carriage wash machines could not operate at low temperatures. Garnett knew that there must be an answer and it was provided by the staff at Bounds Green. They knew that hot air blown into an industrial standard washer would resolve the problem, but that would require investment that they simply didn't have authority to implement. The authority was immediately forthcoming from Garnett. Passengers and staff alike, none more so than Garnett himself, were delighted with the results. Headquarters staff were also encouraged to help clean trains' exteriors and windows as trains came through a station to show how serious GNER was.

ABOVE: GNER Customer Service staff member Fiona Mullen assists with directions at Newcastle Central station.
GNER

Bacon sandwiches

Christopher Garnett's love of bacon sandwiches is well known within the UK railway industry, and he was amazed when he found that they were not available on his trains. At the end of the British Rail era there had been a practice whereby catering staff could purchase their own ingredients to make them, but this practice had been stopped because it was difficult to manage stock control. Instead the offer had become, in Garnett's words, 'those awful microwaved burgers'. It was, he felt, a good example of not putting passengers first, and the company

donated the last burger to the National Railway Museum in York, where it can still be seen by visitors today.

The issues of clean train exteriors and availability of bacon sandwiches were by themselves only small ones, but were noticeable. Rectifying them showed customers that improvements were being made. GNER Customer Service Director Mike McKechnie held the responsibility for service development, and for around half of the GNER workforce. Among the improvements he wanted to introduce was a better standard of food on the trains. He held a view that a train is not an aeroplane, so 'let's do what they cannot do and avoid using microwaves'. A big internal debate followed concerning the First Class onboard offer. GNER already provided complimentary tea and coffee to First Class ticket holders, but only had a small onboard staff with which to provide the service. The decision was taken to increase staffing with the consequent ability to improve the First Class offer. Christopher Garnett describes this as a 'speculate to accumulate situation'. He feels it is often wrongly assumed that British Rail was inefficient, and as many savings in staff on the ground had already been implemented by BR, it was not possible for GNER to further reduce staffing or divert them from elsewhere to improve the First Class service. The increased staffing levels and consequently improved service produced an immediate increase in revenue.

By the time the Mk 4 coaching stock 'Mallard' refurbishment programme was completed in 2005 (covered later in this book),

ABOVE: Former Prime Minister Tony Blair takes a break from his paperwork to enjoy a complimentary festive mince-pie served to First Class passengers. *GNER*

RIGHT: First Class passengers enjoy breakfast in a refurbished Mk 4 'Mallard' coach. *GNER*

GNER found itself achieving £15 million worth of meal and snack sales every year. In addition to being a train operator it had effectively become a major catering business requiring expertise and staffing numbers to plan and provide the service. The original congested café/bar area was redesigned and improved with the provision of an enlarged standing area and curved counter, resulting in a quicker and smoother service for passengers. The complimentary First Class at-seat service of tea and coffee was extended to include biscuits and fruit and nuts, while a full restaurant service provided breakfast, lunch and dinner on more than 90 services each weekday.

In 1998 Jonathan Metcalfe, later to become Chief Executive, found himself in charge of the customer-facing side of GNER. During that time he was responsible for overseeing the introduction of 130 Customer Service Managers on board trains. Metcalfe did not pretend that the move was universally accepted within the company, particularly by its Train Guards, who saw it as a partial erosion of their traditional role of being in charge of the train. But he is adamant that with the passage of time onboard customer service improved dramatically, fully justifying the multi-million-pound annual cost to the

ABOVE: Passengers are served breakfast on a northbound GNER service to Newcastle on 6 March 2006. *GNER*

LEFT: In December 2007 Mk 4 'Mallard' at-seat service is provided to passengers travelling First Class. *John Balmforth*

company. Metcalfe said, 'It sent a clear message throughout the organisation that Customer Service is at the heart of our vision – either accept it or get out of the business.'

Lorraine Flower also joined the company early on as Sales & Marketing Director. She had been recruited from British Airways and was given the mission to establish GNER's early years vision and values (reproduced in the Postscript to this book), service standards, etc. with the aim of providing an ultimate travel experience. She found that a cultural change was needed from British Rail's days in order to put customers at the heart of operations, though despite this shortcoming it cannot be denied that BR was actually quite good at running trains. The changes included better dialogue with trade unions, and GNER is proud that it never lost a single day's service due to industrial action.

Part of the customer service improvements saw the provision of more accurate information to passengers, particularly during any delays, through the use of hand-held computers for on-train crews, a new station management centre at London King's Cross, staffed customer information points at stations, and a new Integrated Control Centre in York. Ticket purchase was made easier by the installation of self-service fast ticket machines and a Ticket on Departure facility.

CHAPTER SEVEN

Staff training

GNER had developed one of the best training schemes in the industry, investing substantial sums in supporting its staff, spending about the same on training as it did on marketing the business.

GNER recognised the need for high-quality training for its drivers. King's Cross-based Driver Training Manager Paul Lartey told me that it took around 16 months from commencing training before a driver was able to take out a train on his or her own. The company invested £1.5 million in four Driver Training Simulators located at King's Cross, Leeds, Newcastle and Edinburgh. Designed by the French company Corys TESS, the facilities allowed instructors to input just about every situation drivers could find themselves facing, whereas previously on-the-job training could have resulted in a driver completing his training without ever coming across an 'out of the normal' incident. The facility also included special train control software with a touch screen that recreated the ability to operate every control or switch on the train, including external items such as air pipe cocks.

Alan Hyde revealed that many GNER drivers were recruited from outside the rail industry, a trend becoming more and more prevalent at many Train Operating Companies; they included a former police superintendent and a bank manager.

The company also invested heavily in a state-of-the-art training centre at York station. Located in the former signal cabin on platform 8 and named 'The Studio', it provided several classroom and conference room facilities contained over three floors. Classes were usually of ten students or less, and training courses for all grades of staff could be provided. The self-contained unit was busy on most days and saw an extremely high pass rate among those attending.

In addition GNER provided training courses for its management staff via both the University of York and the Open University, successful completion of which earned students certificates or diplomas in Management Studies. It was therefore, perhaps, no surprise when the TOC was successful in gaining the coveted 'Investor in People' award, an achievement of which it was rightly proud. Further evidence resulting from the investment in staff, stations and rolling stock are plain to see, exemplified by the high number of rail industry awards for quality won by the company (included in Appendix E), together with its exceptional performance results over most of its stewardship. The company frequently topped national customer surveys among long-distance operators, with punctuality regularly topping the 90% mark for trains arriving at their destination on time. Indeed, figures supplied by Alan Hyde showed the average cause of delay to its services that were attributable to GNER was as low as 17%.

ABOVE: The 'Investor in People' award plaque won by GNER reflected the company's investment in its staff. *John Balmforth*

RIGHT: The Class 91 Driver Training Simulator at King's Cross. *John Balmforth*

CHAPTER EIGHT

Fares, car parking and stations

Fares

If the media and press are to believed, potential customers could be forgiven for thinking that they need to take out a mortgage to buy a rail ticket, but it really isn't true and some terrific value fares can be obtained, especially if journeys can be planned in advance. Indeed, advance purchase tickets have an important role to play in attracting passengers to travel at off-peak times when trains are more lightly loaded. Intense competition from other TOCs, the private car and airlines all played a part in attracting new customers to GNER, the £20 Standard Class return fare from Newcastle to London being an excellent example.

Despite the availability of these cheaper fares, there has been an increase in the numbers of passengers attempting to travel without purchasing a ticket (not a new phenomenon as BR was victim to ticketless travel too). Mike McKechnie believed that GNER took a firm but fair approach to making sure passengers paid their way, at the same time promising to come down hard on determined fare-evaders. The TOC felt that the punitive penalty fares system devised in the final days of InterCity was counterproductive in the longer term. McKechnie said in an interview for a rail magazine special in the first years of the franchise, 'I took the view two years ago that the whole idea was anti-customer, heavy-handed and bureaucratic. We caused an awful lot of problems for genuine customers who did not understand our fare regimes. For this reason, against a good deal of criticism from within British Rail, I tried to urge our Senior Conductors to be far more liberal and give them discretion to waive rules when they saw fit. We scored a lot of goodwill out of that approach, but it took a long time to get Senior Conductors to think that way. However, society has moved on in those last two years and there seems a willingness to exploit looseness and liberalism. We must respond accordingly.' GNER therefore tried to recapture some of the discipline that

revenue protection gave it. The company put in spot checks and teams of people to check trains in an ad-hoc way, but did it in a supportive way. McKechnie said, 'We will be reasonable, but we will identify individuals who consistently flout the rules, and take action. However, I must stress that we don't want a penalty fares system.'

On the subject of fares, Jonathan Metcalfe, who succeeded Christopher Garnett as Chief Executive in 2006, told me that in his opinion rail fares already compared favourably with air travel, and that GNER was able to boast that 10% of its fares were cheaper at the end of the franchise than they were in British Rail days. He said that GNER would never have subscribed to the £1 Megatrain-type fare, preferring to offer the more traditional range of tickets through all sorts of media, be they internet, telesales, at the station or through travel agents. These fares varied from the £8.45 from York to London in 2007 right up to the off-peak walk-up or full-priced premium fares. Alan Hyde explained that while walk-up fares were still very popular, there was a rapid increase in online ticket sales following the opening of GNER's own web retail site at Newcastle, and within two years of taking on the franchise GNER was regularly achieving in excess of 30,000 online ticket sales every week, generating a weekly turnover of £1 million. Hyde admitted that busy trains were getting busier and that there was a premium to be paid to travel in the peak, but that conversely the cheaper range of tickets had also seen a reduction in price. He added that around 10% of GNER passengers actually travelled on cheaper tickets in real terms than the pre-privatisation British Rail fare, and certainly in 2005 some 900,000 passengers had taken advantage of:

- First Class off-peak travel starting at £59 from London to Glasgow, Edinburgh, Newcastle, York and Leeds.

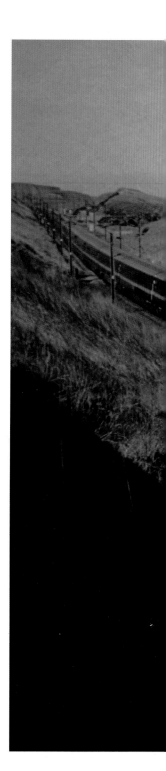

ABOVE: A GNER service heads north in 1998, where the East Coast Main Line skirts the North Sea near Berwick-upon-Tweed. *railphotolibrary.com*

• Standard Class off-peak travel return fares beginning at £19 from London to Leeds or York £20, to Newcastle and £25 to Edinburgh.

Hyde went on to point out that 30-40% of the company's income came from travel agent and corporate ticket sales, and that more than 2,000 extra car park spaces had been provided since 1996. Nevertheless Christopher Garnett did admit that some of GNER's retail prices were high, but thought that this was justified by the provision of the additional parking spaces, which had worked out at roughly £10,000 per space. Like most Train Operating Companies GNER did not offer refunds of parking charges against fares, but it did introduce car park season tickets for regular customers, which Garnett said continued to offer considerable discounts. He also pointed out that the gap between full-price Standard Class fares and season tickets had widened, making the season ticket more attractive. When the franchise began, passengers making an average of 3.5 journeys per week benefited from having a season ticket, but by 2007 the number of weekly journeys to make the season ticket better value had dropped to 2.5. This, coupled with London house prices, had resulted in longer-distance commuter travel from places like Grantham and Newark – it also created an onus on GNER to provide more early-morning trains to get people to work in London.

RIGHT: Two GNER expresses formed of Class 91 locomotives, Mk 4 coaches and Driving Van Trailers pass at Newcastle on 19 February 2003. *railphotolibrary.com*

BELOW: An artist's impression of the proposed GNER Parkway station close to the M18 motorway near Doncaster. *GNER*

Car parking

GNER always recognised the need to increase car parking spaces at stations, with Metcalfe saying, 'Frankly, we can't get enough of them.' The policy had been to buy up or lease any land that became available near stations, but the company was also supportive of the idea of a high-speed north-to-south line or, if that was not financially viable, an improvement to the current infrastructure to allow faster journey times between London and Scotland. Metcalfe told me that he felt 3½ hours was necessary to take on the air market more successfully. Such far-sighted thinking is without doubt the way forward and hopefully future franchises will again allow incumbents

to consider developing innovative ideas as part of a franchise.

GNER had also looked long and hard at providing 'Parkway' stations as part of its 20-year bid. Serious consideration was given to providing 'park and ride' stations at Musselburgh near Edinburgh, a site close to the point where the M18 motorway crosses the ECML near Doncaster, and at Hadley Wood on the southern section of the route. Ultimately, however, the TOC elected to fund improvements and expansion to its car parks at Grantham, Newark Northgate, Wakefield Westgate and Darlington. Even so, growth was such that the extra spaces were soon filled.

Stations

GNER recognised that stations are the gateway to local communities as well as the railway itself, and delivered a £28 million programme of investment, providing new lounges for both Standard and First Class passengers, as well as cycle storage facilities and improved access for customers with mobility difficulties. Indeed, the new First Class Lounges were some of the best in the industry when they were introduced, with those at King's Cross, Leeds, Newcastle and Edinburgh being equipped with a meeting room, fax machine, modem and internet facilities as well as complimentary refreshments and newspapers.

The programme included improving passenger information systems and screens, some being located in nearby shopping centres and bus stations, new subways, modernised Travel Centres, additional cycle stands, better signage and refurbished toilet facilities.

At York a £600,000 extension was added to the station footbridge providing quicker direct access to the National Railway Museum and areas to the west of the station. Improved passenger security was provided by the installation of closed circuit television (CCTV) in stations, lounges and car parks. The city's Victorian-age station, which handles the services of several different rail companies, is a positive delight and stands alongside a multi-million-pound development of an adjacent triangle of empty railway land, which is one of Europe's largest inner-city regeneration projects.

BELOW: A busy, bustling scene on York's platform 3 as a GNER service for London King's Cross takes on passengers. *GNER*

ABOVE: GNER's First Class Lounge at Edinburgh's Waverley station. The décor and theme were similar in all of the TOC's First Class Lounges. *John Balmforth*

RIGHT: GNER train dispatcher Jonathan Healy indicates to the train's guard that he has completed platform duties and the train is ready to depart from York. *GNER*

ABOVE: 'The Highland Chieftain' departs from Aviemore station on a cloudy day in June 2005 as it traverses the Scottish Highlands.
railphotolibrary.com

RIGHT: A GNER Edinburgh-King's Cross train awaits departure time at Darlington in November 2003.
railphotolibrary.com

Newcastle was one of GNER's busiest stations and is arguably better now than when it was built in 1849, benefiting from a large Travel Centre, shops, food outlets and easy access to each of its nine platforms. All 12 GNER managed stations benefited from the programme of investment that was recognised in the number of awards won by the company (see Appendix E), impressing judges regularly in the National Rail Awards competitions; three –

Doncaster (2001), York (2006) and Newcastle (2007) – won the ultimate accolade of being named Station of the Year.

Although King's Cross was not a GNER-operated station, it did of course see all but one of GNER's services starting and ending there, and the company was happy to invest in major improvements. The station frontage (only ever intended to be temporary, but now more than 40 years old) is due to be replaced as part of a

local regeneration scheme and includes a reconstruction of the London Underground interchange. Christopher Garnett told me that he hated the impersonal glass screens that existed in the station's Travel Centre, which separated staff from customers, and wanted them removed to provide a more modern open-plan atmosphere, but he fully understood that some staff had concerns over their safety. Garnett said he had been able to point out that Barclays Bank, which had a branch opposite the station, had recently made similar changes. Ironically, a few months later the bank was the victim of a hold-up, but despite this the GNER staff and their customers liked the new arrangements and were happy to keep them.

ABOVE: A DVT-headed rake of Mk 4 coaches powered by a Class 91 locomotive arrives at King's Cross after the long journey from Edinburgh. Waiting to depart at the adjacent platform is an HST with a service to Aberdeen. *railphotolibrary.com*

LEFT: A newly arrived HST set unloads its passengers at platform 8 at King's Cross, while close by, a DVT and its Mk 4 coaches are readied for a northbound departure behind a Class 91 locomotive. *John Balmforth*

LEFT: Passengers disembark from a GNER express service newly arrived at King's Cross from the north in May 2005. *railphotolibrary.com*

ABOVE LEFT: An aerial shot of King's Cross station, where 70% of GNER's services started or finished. The view dates from 1992 before the Channel Tunnel work and the upgrade of neighbouring St Pancras to take international Eurostar services. *railphotolibrary.com*

CHAPTER NINE

Accidents:

Sandy, Hatfield and Great Heck

The company was unfortunate to find three of its trains being involved in major accidents in just over 2½ years, and although GNER was not at causal fault in any of them, the effect on passenger and staff morale, as well as the financial implications, were serious and far-reaching. Two of the incidents resulted in the tragic loss of 14 lives and had a profound and lasting effect on Christopher Garnett and his staff.

Sandy,
Bedfordshire

On 17 June 1998 a GNER InterCity 225 express service headed by a Class 91 locomotive formed the well-loaded 6 o'clock service out of King's Cross, and while travelling at a speed in excess of 100mph derailed at Sandy in Bedfordshire, not far from Hatfield, after suffering a broken wheel. The cause was quickly

found to be a fracture leading from one of the fixing points that are drilled into the wheel for counterbalance weights to be attached and ensure smooth running. The accident came just weeks after a similar wheel failure had caused a major train accident in Germany involving a high-speed inter-city express train.

Christopher Garnett was among the team of GNER staff who met passengers when they finally reached York station very late at night after considerable delay. A telephone call from Operations Director Mike Tham alerted Garnett to the fact that there might be a wider implication for the company, and indeed the rail industry as a whole. Could it be that a design fault was the cause? If so, could he afford to allow the trains to continue in service without the fleet being inspected thoroughly? By 0300 he still did not know whether this was an isolated equipment failure or if other vehicles might be carrying the same problem. No senior manager would knowingly put people's lives at risk, so Garnett took the decision to pull all similar vehicles from the next day's service for initial examination and limit the speed to 80mph until full ultrasonic testing was completed. Other train operators did the same, and nationally some 2,000 vehicles were checked using ultrasonic techniques. The timetabled service was devastated but the decision was totally justifiable.

Following accidents elsewhere on the national network, the media was rightly critical at what appeared to be a lack of anyone senior from within the industry taking immediate charge at the accident scenes. Recognising this criticism, the GNER board took the decision that, if ever the company was unfortunate enough for one of its trains to be involved in another major accident, it would be essential for senior people to immediately attend the scene. In addition, Sea Containers would make available its own emergency incident room – a quite excellent and superbly equipped facility. GNER employed the services of a specialist

company, Black Mountain, to provide emergency training scenarios. Again, looking back, Garnett was able to recall just how useful the role-plays had been and how they reinforced the decision by the board that someone senior needed to attend major incidents as quickly as possible.

Hatfield,
Hertfordshire

If the Sandy derailment had been bad enough, the Hatfield accident on 17 October 2000 is indelibly planted in Garnett's mind. He told me, 'I will never forget the tragedy and trauma that resulted for all involved.' The train was GNER's 1210 service from King's Cross to Leeds, carrying more than 200 passengers. Even though GNER was again blameless, the tragic loss of four passengers' lives, all of whom had been in the buffet car in the 115mph accident, was felt by everyone at the company, and it had a devastating effect on revenue as passengers lost confidence in rail, preferring instead to travel by air or by road. The blanket nationwide Temporary Speed Restrictions (TSRs) imposed by Railtrack while it carried out checks of similar locations elsewhere on the network did not help either, and the journey time from London to Scotland shot up to more than 12 hours, longer than it had been at the end of the 19th century. In an interview for *the Guardian* in July 2001, Garnett described the restrictions as 'draconian', saying, 'That company caused the Hatfield accident and I don't think it understands to this day the cumulative damage it has caused the industry. Dealing with Railtrack is like watching somebody performing the dance of the seven veils. You think you've seen everything when they reveal more.' This was a widely held view within the rail industry and it was some months before all of the TSRs were lifted and the national rail timetable could return to normal.

While it is understandable that serious infrastructure damage will cause major service disruption, it is also true that any rail accident that results in serious damage to rolling stock also has the potential to do the same. The size of an operator's fleet incorporates the need for trains to be out of service for maintenance, planned or otherwise, but when rolling stock is written off following an accident a shortage of serviceable stock can follow. In the case of the accidents at both Hatfield and the later Great Heck collision, such damage was indeed serious. The GNER fleet did, however, include a spare train set, which was brought into service while further vehicles were hired to cover its use until permanent replacements for the damaged vehicles could be obtained.

GNER Operations Director Richard McClean told me that there was a period when Railtrack seemed to try to pin the blame on the Train Operating Companies; a lot of discussion was taking place with the infrastructure custodian, which argued that the TOCs would not let Railtrack take possession to carry out repairs, as well as claiming that new trains were wearing the track out quicker than the older ones. The second point may well be a factor, but McClean reminded me that Railtrack had, in fact, had routes under absolute block possession for several weekends prior to Hatfield when a junction was replaced south of that station. He said, 'The simple fact is that the system didn't deliver output.'

On the day of the accident GNER's executive team had been due to meet at the Devonshire Arms near Skipton to finalise the 20-year franchise bid. Garnett remembered being in conversation with Jonathan Metcalfe about installing Wi-Fi on GNER services. He had been travelling through a poor radio signal area and been unable to receive radio signals to his pager, but upon arrival at the hotel he was informed by a colleague that a pager message had been received advising that a GNER train had been involved in an accident but that no further information was available. Immediately the meeting was cancelled and the entire group headed back south. At first the news filtering through was that no serious injuries had occurred, but gradually the grim news was received that loss of life was involved. At York Christopher Garnett, accompanied by Nick Pollard, Railtrack Zone Director, immediately accepted the offer to use the Jarvis helicopter to get to the site as quickly as possible, while Jonathan Metcalfe remained at York to co-ordinate operations from there. Garnett says, 'It was a journey that seemed to take for ever, all the while turning over possible causes in my mind, particularly wondering if another broken wheel might be involved.' The sight of a train lying spread across the tracks is one that he says will never leave him – tears were filling his eyes even as he recounted the facts to me some years afterwards. He even wondered if he would be arrested on his arrival and, once again, would he need to pull the rest of the fleet from service?

There was an absolute need to gain access to the scene to enable rational decisions to be made about pulling the fleet from service, but access was barred by the police. It transpired initially that the Metropolitan Police Anti-Terrorist Branch had taken control of the accident site in case the cause had been a terrorist attack. A passing policeman eventually mentioned that it looked as if a broken rail had been the cause, but there was still nothing official. Journalists had now appeared and Garnett, supported at the scene by Jim Sherwood and Railtrack's Nick Pollard, were in demand, fronting for the industry, followed up by a television interview with Jeremy Paxman, all the time still not knowing the cause. He told me, 'I felt so sad, especially when visiting the injured in hospital. What could I tell them? Sympathy and apologies seemed so insufficient.'

On the morning after the crash came the calls for Gerald Corbett, head of Railtrack, to resign. Some asked Garnett if he thought Corbett should go. Garnett did not think either resignation or the question was appropriate at that time. A further visit to the scene by Garnett followed, this being the first time he had been allowed trackside, and Railtrack officials were able to confirm that a broken rail was indeed the cause; one of them reported that he had never seen a rail shatter into so many pieces. Accident investigators later revealed that it had crumbled into more than 300 pieces. Damage marks on the train's wheels had proved beyond doubt that the rail was broken before they had passed over the rail break.

Away from the scene the GNER boss formed the opinion 'that Railtrack did not seem to know what was going on', and it took several meetings between Railtrack and the TOCs even to get an emergency timetable in place, and moreover one in time for the busy Christmas period. Meanwhile business continued to be haemorrhaged to the airlines, which could transport passengers to Scotland in around 2 hours, not the 12 now offered by the railway. Garnett said that he 'found Railtrack arrogant'. He had been used to having constructive relationships with suppliers in his pre-rail days, but in previous meetings with Railtrack, even on matters as simple as getting undergrowth removed, things had proved difficult. However, Garnett does accept that GNER was very demanding of both Railtrack and its successor, Network Rail. Jonathan Metcalfe told me that he was sure it was not intended, but the debate between Railtrack and the ORR over funding and regulation became very public, and was

very distracting at the top at a time when it was essential for the industry to concentrate on its day-to-day job.

Passengers know that if their drinks don't spill then the track is generally in reasonable condition – what Garnett describes as the 'coffee cup run'. Everyone also knows that the infrastructure custodian needs to run special trains to carry out ultrasonic testing of the rails to identify imperfections that the 'coffee cup run' does not show up. However, it is also important that any defects shown up are acted upon, and subsequently Garnett was very angry when the failings within Railtrack and its maintenance and renewals policy were found to be such immense factors in the Hatfield crash. When he found that Railtrack's maintenance contractor, Balfour Beatty, had reported a fault with the rail several months earlier, requiring renewal of the rail, and nothing had been done to replace the damaged section, Garnett's annoyance was again apparent. Lives had been lost and he now realised that there was no need for the crash to have happened. His feelings were compounded and replicated by the public at large when it transpired that no one would be prosecuted over the accident. Referring to the later accident at Great Heck near Selby, Garnett told me, 'Great Heck made me weep but Hatfield still makes me very angry – it was terrible.' He revealed to me that he found the attendance at funerals and memorial services extremely debilitating, but felt that he had to attend personally and would not delegate the task to someone else. Such was his grief that he felt he understood what friends and relatives of the deceased were going through. A trackside memorial to remember those whose lives were lost has now been placed near the site of the crash.

A huge lesson learned from Hatfield was that the infrastructure custodian found it could not, in practice, pass on its safety responsibilities to maintenance contractors. At that time maintenance was used to maintain line speeds, etc. but if renewals were required then a separate contractor was used with specific Railtrack authorisation and funding. In other words, a contractor doing day-to-day maintenance was never expected to undertake renewals work. The Government had supported Railtrack's contracting-out of infrastructure maintenance as part of the rail privatisation, but Hatfield had proved that this was a bridge too far and Network Rail took the brave, and expensive, step of bringing maintenance back 'in-house', recognising that infrastructure maintenance was such a core safety activity that it could no longer be delegated out of the mainstream business. Nevertheless, it must not be overlooked that Railtrack had plenty of time to rectify the processes, but for whatever reasons failed to do so.

Great Heck,
near Selby

Great Heck saw the third major accident in less than three years involving a GNER express, but although Hatfield could and should have been avoided this time there was nothing the railway could have done to prevent it. Effectively, the railway and the 10 people who lost their lives were the victims of a road accident that spilled over onto the railway, and Garnett says, 'I vividly remember 28 February 2001 – Ash Wednesday.'

The fast GNER express travelling from Newcastle to King's Cross, ironically hauled by locomotive No 91023, which had also been involved in the accident at Hatfield, was passing under the M62 motorway when it was in collision with a Land Rover that had crashed off the motorway and onto the railway track below the bridge, after its driver fell asleep at the wheel. The train was being driven correctly and its driver could do nothing to avoid the collision with the road vehicle. Fate then took a hand and the derailed train was struck by a loaded coal train travelling from Immingham to Ferrybridge, which was approaching in the opposite direction. The freight train was actually running

early and also being correctly driven. Fate also had a second hand in the accident because a Temporary Speed Restriction on the route had only recently, though correctly, been removed; had it still been in place neither train would have been present.

This time GNER's Chief Executive was leaving home when he received a pager message that a GNER train had again derailed. Without delay he telephoned the GNER Control and was told they did not know how serious it was. Garnett set out for King's Cross post haste but it soon became obvious just how serious things were; 10 people had died and 82 were seriously injured. Heading for the accident site, he managed to reach Doncaster by train, and from there was taken to the scene of the accident. Once again he was presented with an image that will never leave him: 'The appalling sight of a train's carriages lying on their side in a field.' He told me that 'it still haunts me to this day and I just thought, not again – what have we done to deserve this?' Once again the emotions of the man came through as he recounted the facts.

Garnett felt adamant that the situation was not helped by the appearance on television of all sorts of experts providing uninformed speculation as to the cause. When it quickly became clear that a road accident was to blame, he couldn't resist asking a Highways Agency official 'if they would be putting blanket speed restrictions on all similar motorway bridges'. When asked why, he retorted, 'Because that's what would have happened on the railway if it had been our fault.' Obviously Garnett was not suggesting that speed restrictions should be imposed all over the country's motorways, but merely highlighting the unfair way in which he and many others felt the railways were treated following accidents.

Jonathan Metcalfe also has vivid recollections of the accident. He was on duty and had made a routine telephone call to Control intending to enquire whether an

ABOVE: The appalling damage inflicted on the GNER express train involved in the accident at Great Heck, near Selby, is clearly seen in this photograph taken during recovery of the wrecked train.
Nigel Harris

engineering possession had been completed on time. During the conversation the controller asked him to hold the line while he took an urgent call. Metcalfe could hear every word the controller said on the other line and explained that it was a terrible feeling as he heard the controller repeating the caller's words detailing what had happened. He still does not like talking about it to this day, but says that he learned how organisations can show strength in times of crisis. GNER's top two executives met at Doncaster and Garnett went to the accident scene while Metcalfe remained at Doncaster dealing with the press and media before returning to York to co-ordinate matters from there. He remembers the low morale of staff in the immediate aftermath, but, despite this, staff at all levels again volunteered to help in any way they could, be it hospital visiting, comforting relatives, or sorting out accommodation and refreshments.
The assistance they gave, without being asked, was, he says, unbelievable.

Christopher Garnett recalls all sorts of stories of survival, and once again commenced a round of hospital visiting, not because he had to, but because he wanted to. Some 18 months after the crash he was being head-hunted for a job and his interviewer told him, 'I bet you don't remember me.' The interviewer turned out to be one of the accident victims whom he had visited in hospital after the crash. The Chief Executive was not the only representation from GNER at the bedsides of the injured or giving comfort to friends and relatives of the deceased and injured. In fact, many staff at all levels, be they train crews, station staff or even secretarial personnel, volunteered their services, despite the sense of grief many of them were feeling. Garnett revealed his pride in the professionalism shown by the GNER staff. He told me, 'They did their jobs and very much more, thus ensuring GNER's mission statement [see the Postscript] was carried out,' and revealed how he found their reaction very humbling, especially after staff had lost respected working colleagues. Again Garnett's compassionate nature shines through when he highlights the traumatic effect on people, staff or public, as being very real. Some experienced staff have not been able to travel by train since. Counselling was provided, but every time a rail accident happens the full trauma is bought back to the

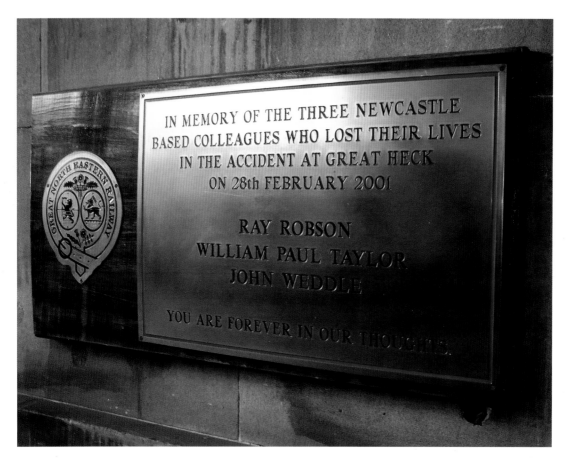

IN MEMORY OF THE THREE NEWCASTLE
BASED COLLEAGUES WHO LOST THEIR LIVES
IN THE ACCIDENT AT GREAT HECK
ON 28th FEBRUARY 2001

RAY ROBSON
WILLIAM PAUL TAYLOR
JOHN WEDDLE

YOU ARE FOREVER IN OUR THOUGHTS

ABOVE: A memorial plaque remembering the Newcastle-based GNER staff whose lives were lost in the accident at Great Heck is located at Newcastle depot.
Tim Hedley-Jones

victims, and some of them are really strong people. Garnett fears that they will never be able fully to put the experience behind them. Indeed, such was his style of management that he considered all the GNER staff to have been his friends, feeling the loss of valued working colleagues as much as everyone else.

Subsequently GNER ensured that all of its train windows were replaced by laminated glass windows to help prevent passengers being thrown out of them in an accident. On this occasion the police did not treat the accident site as a potential crime scene, allowing recovery equipment to be deployed quickly, and ensuring that the line was back in use without undue delay. The financial consequences arising from the accident at Great Heck did not have the same disastrous effect as Hatfield, mainly, Garnett feels, because of the speed with which the railway was repaired, and because passengers realised that what had happened was beyond the railway's control and was something of a freak accident.

The driver of the Land Rover, who allegedly had fallen asleep at the wheel, was charged with and found guilty of Causing Death by Dangerous Driving. He was sentenced to five years imprisonment by Mr Justice Mackay.

In the aftermath of the accident at Great Heck a memorial garden was built near the site, and a plaque placed at Newcastle where the three GNER train crew members who lost their

lives had been based. A moving memorial service was held at Selby Abbey on Thursday 28 February 2002 in honour of the 10 people who lost their lives in the accident.

The 14 people (10 passengers and four railway staff) whose lives ended so tragically are named below:

Hatfield
Robert James Alcom, 37
Steve Arthur, 46
Leslie Gray, 43
Peter Monkhouse, 50

Great Heck
Professor Steve Baldwin, 39
Stephen Dunn, 39 *(Freightliner driver)*
Alan Ensor, 44
Barry Needham, 40
Raymond Robson, 43 *(GNER Customer Service Operations Leader)*
Robert Shakespeare, 43
Paul Taylor, 42 *(GNER Chef)*
Christopher Terry, 30
Clive Vigden, 39
John Weddle, 47 *(GNER driver)*

The Class 66 Freightliner locomotive involved in the accident at Great Heck, No 66521, was returned to service after repair and named *Driver Steve Dunn (George)*, its body side receiving a memorial plaque.

CHAPTER TEN

Class 373 'Regional Eurostars': 'The White Rose'

GNER had earlier investigated ways of obtaining additional trains. With the 'Pendolino' plan scuppered, and the operator seeing increased overcrowding on many services, the company turned its attention, nearly four years into its franchise, to the possibility of hiring some of the 14-vehicle Class 373/3 'Regional Eurostar' sets that were standing unused on sidings. Although it is undeniably a fine train, the 'Eurostar' uses large amounts of power and this would have caused difficulties, particularly south of Hitchin where the supply just could not cope. There would also be a requirement for the wire tension to be especially high for double-pantograph operation at 125mph running. This was easily achieved, but because of the steep contact wire gradients around level crossings and the lack of wire tension on some sections of the ECML, it meant that these 186mph-capable trains had to

be restricted initially to 110mph, later eased to 125mph south of Grantham. Higher speeds would have resulted in excessive stresses being placed upon the overhead line equipment (OLE) by the pantograph tensioning. Fortunately the 'Eurostar' is a train that has a high degree of redundancy built in, and it was found to be possible to operate it with some features switched off. Doing this did not in any way detract from the train's performance, and the switched-out facilities would not have been required by GNER anyway. In the event of any other equipment failure in service, that too would need to be locked out of use, and when the trains returned to North Pole depot at the end of a shift the engineers faced stiff challenges to have them back in working order by the next morning.

All trains operating on the UK rail network require a safety case, and the 'Eurostar' sets

RIGHT: Christopher Garnett is pictured alongside unit No 373306 as he launches the GNER 'White Rose' service to Leeds using hired 'Regional Eurostar' stock in 2002. *GNER*

ABOVE: The GNER livery suited these train sets, as displayed to good effect on No 373304 travelling at high speed on the East Coast Main Line. *railphotolibrary.com*

RIGHT: A GNER-liveried Class 373/3 'Regional Eurostar' set hurtles past Little Bytham on the East Coast Main Line. *Gordon Valentine*

were no different. GNER's services ran across three different Railtrack/Network Rail zones, and even though 'Eurostars' had been running satisfactorily in the South of England for some years, separate safety case applications had to be made to each of the regions independently. Outcomes could be, and often were, variable and the operator found some routeing difficulties that had to be resolved before the

sets could enter GNER service. However, 20 April 2000 saw the trains undergoing test running to York, and by May they had received authority to operate in service, and south of Grantham had permission to travel at 125mph. Later signalling and power supply modifications made it possible for them to be put to work on the lucrative services to Leeds. The company understandably took the opportunity to do so, benefiting from the additional revenue the trains earned, but it was a move that did not go down well with some passengers who had become used to travelling in the superior comfort they provided on services to York; some user groups conducted a campaign to keep them running to York.

For certain the 'Eurostars' were a huge hit with passengers, who instantly took to their smooth ride and classy interiors. The services on which they were used were named 'The White Rose', firstly operating from King's Cross to York, but subsequently King's Cross to Leeds, and by 2002 the company was operating an additional 11 services daily between London and Leeds, an increase of some 44% in the number of GNER trains operating on the route since 1996. All the 'Eurostars' were originally intended to run on scheduled non-stop services because of the time taken for the train doors to be opened and closed, though in practice they did operate on stopping services, made possible by being fitted with 'selective door control'.

It was also found necessary to make some alterations to the trains in order to comply with the GNER policy of making full breakfasts available, and once again the company found itself up against a 'can't be done' attitude, with its own engineers having to insist on a 'can do and will do' approach. The difficulty arose from the fact that 'Eurostar' trains have to satisfy Channel Tunnel fire regulations, which meant that standard cooking equipment could not be used on them. Not even water can be brought to the boil, and Eurostar insisted that the sets be kept in a condition whereby, should they need to recall them at short notice, they could virtually go straight back into international service. GNER's engineers overcame this by the introduction of removable modular kitchen equipment, which enabled tea, coffee and other refreshments to be provided on board.

LEFT: 'Eurostar' No 373303 is seen at Calais Frethun wearing GNER livery on French soil. *GNER*

ABOVE: This close-up of No 373303 shows the stylish front nose of these trains. Note the lack of side windows in the driver's cab. *GNER*

BELOW: No 373302, new paintwork gleaming, awaits its next turn of duty. The aerodynamic front end was essential for the 186mph speed required of these trains through France and Belgium. *GNER*

The five 'Eurostar' sets, three of which had received full GNER corporate livery, were withdrawn from GNER service in 2005 and replaced by HST sets, not because the operator was dissatisfied with them, but because the lease period had ended and alternatives were available at lower cost. Today the sets can be found on hire from the UK Government operating services for the French operator SNCF, though they are still fondly remembered by GNER's customers on the southern half of the ECML.

CHAPTER ELEVEN

Train refurbishment

Class 91: refurbishment and upgrade

Recognising that its train fleet was becoming tired from the intensive service it was required to provide (Tony Brown went as far as describing the Class 91 fleet he had inherited as 'a dog'), GNER and HSBC Rail agreed on a programme of Heavy General Repair (HGR) for the fleet commencing in July 2000. The HGR programme required a major investment of some £30 million, but it was money well spent as performance improved impressively over a four-year period, seeing the initial 3,000 miles between casualty rate climb to 70,000, thus providing GNER with the UK's most reliable long-distance train fleet. Like the Mk 4 carriages, the Class 91 locomotives suffered from air-conditioning problems. Some of the insulation had been provided by the use of a varnish on pipework, but this had flaked and was getting sucked into the flow ducts. Brown revealed that an engineering-led approach, with a lot of help provided by former GEC head of research Dr Mike Reece, eventually solved the problems.

The air flow management system inside the locomotive was located in the engine room, where temperatures were found to reach 60 degrees, and due to poor management of the air flow it would frequently shut the engine down. On top of this, the same air flow system also controlled the air-conditioning in the driver's cab, and the problems frequently resulted in unpleasantly high temperatures for drivers to work in. The upgrade included new air flow management but required holes to be cut into the locomotive's bodywork to allow in extra air. Brown told me that a lot of effort went into resolving the problem and engine room interiors were 'positively pressurised', which had the effect of keeping the inside clean and preventing the air flow system from blocking up. In addition, the HGR programme included:

- pantograph development
- choke replacement
- parking brake and compressor development
- replacement of the gearboxes
- re-engineering of the bogies
- modification of the transmission
- redesign of the cab

Overall Brown felt the upgrade was very good for the locomotives, providing a reliable machine for many years to come. However, as we shall see, he did not feel the same about the refurbishment carried out on the Mk 4 carriages.

After the Class 91 fleet was upgraded the fleet numbers on the cab sides were increased by 100, but No 91023 was the exception. The locomotive had been involved in the accidents at both Hatfield and Great Heck, so it was renumbered 91132, thus helping to ease some drivers' superstitions.

RIGHT: A Class 91 shows off its 'slab end' and pantograph area to the photographer outside Bounds Green depot on 6 February 2008. Taken after the change of franchisee, the photograph shows both the white vinyl stripe applied to carry the National Express branding, and the two additional air intake holes cut into the bodysides to resolve air management flow problems.
John Balmforth

LEFT: The driver's cab controls of Class 91 No 91106 *East Lothian*. *John Balmforth*

ABOVE: Class 91 No 91119 *County of Tyne & Wear* waits to depart from York, heading a service to Edinburgh in December 2007. *Matthew Clarke*

GNER Mk 4 coach refurbishment: the 'Mallards'

To improve the quality of the existing fleet GNER put its 302 Mk 4 coaches through a total redesign and rebuild of their interiors in an upgrade dubbed 'Project Mallard', the name being adopted from the 1938 East Coast record-breaking 'A4' steam locomotive No 4468. The total cost of the refurbishment would top the £30 million rebuild of the Class 91 locomotives, but was intended to increase their working lives through to 2025. The trains had covered more than one billion train miles and had carried more than 100 million passengers in service. The work required the complete stripping out of everything inside the body shell, which allowed access to the structure should it require any work.

The refurbishment work was contracted out to Bombardier Transportation and was undertaken at that company's Wakefield works in West Yorkshire. The refurbishment, carried out on two sets at a time under the watchful eye of GNER Head of Design Neal Stone, on secondment from British Airways, commenced in early 2003 and was completed by 2005. Stone told *Modern Railways* in May 2003 that his starting point was 'How can we make best use of this long metal tube piece of real estate?' His prime objective was to create a more comfortable, reliable, and improved service for customers, and a better working environment for onboard staff. Starting with a blank sheet of paper, he was able to create a 'big picture' group consisting of passengers, engineers, maintenance staff, train crew, chefs, cleaners and marketing people off whom to trade ideas before finalising the design.

The biggest feature in the upgrade was the redesign and reconfiguration of the catering vehicles. The existing layout of the food preparation and bar area restricted the catering offer that GNER could provide. Since this was an area GNER considered to be important, the opportunity was taken to pay particular attention to this feature. Pre-privatisation the catering concept used a 'cook-chill' airline-style tray service. Experience had shown that this type of catering fell well short of the wishes of GNER's customers. The catering service cars

ABOVE: HM Queen Elizabeth II accepts a bouquet from a young lady after she unveiled the final upgraded rake of Mk 4 'Mallards' at King's Cross on 9 October 2003. *GNER*

RIGHT: An external view of an upgraded Mk 4 'Mallard' Restaurant Car, in service at Edinburgh Waverley. *John Balmforth*

became the classic dividing point between First and Standard Classes, with the internal plan being turned round and given a completely revised layout, consisting of four distinct sections. The new layout saw the kitchen positions at the London end of the carriage next to the First Class seating areas. Chefs were given their own dedicated workstation.

The original Mk 4 takeaway service was designed on the assumption that passengers in the Standard Class carriages would prefer an at-seat trolley service, but practice showed that many liked to have the opportunity to stretch their legs during the journey and walk to the buffet bar. A static buffet bar was able to carry a much wider variety of goods than the trolley service, but queuing in cramped conditions was a perennial source of complaint. The previous Mk 4 bar/counter was much too short and passengers could not see what items were offered for sale until they arrived at the front of the queue. The 'Mallard' upgrade resolved this by introducing a curved counter together with an enlarged area for passengers waiting to be served. Equipment included improved glass-fronted refrigerated display cabinets, a bean-to-cup coffee machine, an improved work surface and a separate hand wash basin for staff. The unused area of the coach was fitted with Standard Class seating. The upgrade also saw the

First Class accommodation increased to three carriages, having previously been two and a half (except a few Pullman sets used on peak services to Leeds and Newcastle, which had three and a half), providing an additional 27 First Class seats, but resulting in the loss of 45 in Standard Class.

The first completed rake of what became known as 'Mallards', top-and-tailed by Nos 91129 *Queen Elizabeth II* and 82219 *Duke of*

TOP: The upgraded Mk 4 'Mallard' Standard Class coach interior. *John Balmforth*

ABOVE: The interior of a Mk 4 Standard Class coach prior to the 'Mallard' upgrade. *GNER*

Edinburgh, was unveiled by Her Majesty Queen Elizabeth II at King's Cross on 9 October 2003. The monarch had also launched the fleet of Mk 4 coaches when they first entered service with British Rail, the two events being a truly unique honour bestowed upon the fleet. The final 'Mallard' rake was greeted by the former Transport Secretary, Alistair Darling, at the same location in a ribbon-cutting ceremony on 9 November 2005. A proud Christopher Garnett said, 'This major project has been delivered on

time and on budget, without any disruption to passengers' journeys or our normal timetable. The result is a fantastic fleet of stylish new trains that give passengers a much better travel experience. What better way to travel than on a superb train, as you enjoy the most scenic rail route in the country, relax, surf the net, or dine in comfort?' During an interview while researching this book he told me that in some ways he was glad that the 20-year franchise hadn't materialised as it would certainly have

required the use of 'Pendolinos'. He feels that the Mk 4 carriages refurbished to 'Mallard' standard not only have better window spacing but are also more comfortable. Nevertheless he is tinged with disappointment that the long-term franchise didn't come about because it would have resulted in some major investment in infrastructure, rolling stock and services.

The First Class coaches received better soundproofing, high-backed biscuit and blue-coloured reclining seats with flip-up arm rests –

toilet in each coach was adequate, though a universal toilet (suitable for passengers with impaired mobility) was located in coaches E and H. A more logical layout of the hand basin, soap, water supply and hand dryer was installed, with the water supply being gravity fed and a drain hole in the floor to dispose of cleaning liquid. Finally, doors were fitted with new handles and locks.

While the upgrades were generally welcomed, GNER fleet engineer Tony Brown

described as akin to armchairs – veneered tables, overhead halogen spot lighting and sound-absorbing carpet. The overall effect was described as 'an oasis of calm'. Wi-Fi, which allows wireless internet access, was fitted to some carriages during the refurbishment, but had been retrofitted to all 'Mallards' by 2006. GNER was the first UK train operator to offer the system for use on the move, allowing passengers to read and send emails, check the news and sport, or even shop online. The list is not exhaustive. To take advantage of the facility passengers required a laptop computer that was Wi-Fi enabled, with a wireless network card installed. Passengers travelling First Class had free use of the system and it was also available to passengers in Standard Class for a charge of £2.95 for 30 minutes, rising to £9.95 for 3 hours.

In Standard Class the improvement in quality was also most noticeable. High-back padded seating and the same level of sound-proofing as in First Class was provided, with all vestibule doors being suitable for wheelchair access. The redesigned layout allowed leg room to be increased by 2 inches, thus allowing for 6-foot-tall people to work comfortably at their seat on their laptop computers. The final improvements saw the toilets being completely rebuilt. Research had shown that one standard design of

told me that he was disappointed that some aspects of the refurbishment had needed to be revisited following problems with the lifting armrests in Standard Class, and the seat-reclining mechanisms in First Class. Nevertheless, they were not insurmountable and the carriages have continued to be popular with passengers.

High Speed Trains (Class 43) and Mk 3 coach refurbishment

Following on from the completion of the upgrades to the Class 91 locomotives and Mk 4 carriage train sets, GNER turned its attention to its fleet of HSTs, some of which had been in service on the route since 1977, nearly three decades. The power cars had already undergone overhauls, and reliability had doubled in the four years to the turn of the millennium; now all of the company's 25 HST power cars were to be fitted with new high-performance engines designed to give more reliable and environmentally friendly travel for the next 10 years. The sets' existing Paxman Valenta engines were to be replaced with the new German MTU 16V000R41 diesel engines, installed by Brush Traction at its Loughborough works. GNER had high expectations of the new engines, which were of proven technology in

TOP: Class 91 No 91129 *Queen Elizabeth II* heads its train across the Royal Border Bridge on a northbound service to Edinburgh. *GNER*

ABOVE LEFT: The 'Mallard' refurbishment programme saw major changes to the Café/Bar area with a new curved counter, extra queuing space and additional Standard Class seating in the coaches. *John Balmforth*

Europe and had performed almost faultlessly in the HSTs working on the Great Western Main Line between Paddington and Penzance for nearly 12 months. The new engines included the latest control systems and a new cooling system, as well as quieter running and reduced emissions, plus the benefit of consuming 15% less fuel. On trains delivering around 3 miles per gallon, the fuel saving was an important additional factor. The trains were also fitted with a new wheel slip detection system, enhanced braking capability and improved crashworthiness as part of the redesigned driver's cab.

The High Speed Train fleet used by GNER was leased from Angel Trains and was due to be refurbished at Wolverton. Normally it is the practice of the owning Rolling Stock Company to pay for this, but GNER wanted a better interior ambience and again turned to Vignelli for his help. His design included changes to carriage lighting and shade, making it appear a major alteration. Some train engineers opposed the design, as did many of the staff at Wolverton, and Garnett recalls some fairly big arguments. However, Sherwood and Garnett knew it was achievable and again stuck to their guns, insisting that Vignelli's design be

RIGHT: A delightful night-time scene on Edinburgh Waverley's platform 19 as GNER staff prepare to give the guard of a southbound HST the ready to depart signal. The distinctive cloud of exhaust smoke hovers above the leading power car in February 2003.
railphotolibrary.com

LEFT: HST power car No 43320 *National Galleries of Scotland* undergoes an engine change at the Brush works on 30 November 2006; it is being fitted with a new MTU engine. *GNER*

MIDDLE RIGHT: A GNER HST set headed by power car No 43039 *The Royal Dragoon Guards* takes a well-earned rest at Inverness after arriving with GNER's longest-distance service, 568 miles, from London. *railphotolibrary.com*

BOTTOM RIGHT: A GNER HST awaits departure time at Aberdeen's platform 5 for the 520-mile run to King's Cross in March 2004. *railphotolibrary.com*

National Galleries of Scotland

implemented, even though Garnett remembers 'some frightful rows' taking place with the trains' owners. To achieve its goal GNER agreed to make a payment to Angel Trains covering part of the cost, and eventually the trains underwent refurbishment in accordance with GNER's wishes. When upgraded and returned to service, many passengers were convinced that they were actually riding in brand new trains, not 20-year-old ones that had merely undergone refurbishment. It has to be said that the designs have stood the test of time and, apart from the introduction of red doors, the only real change of any note came in 1999, when the company logo on the sides of the locomotives was temporarily changed to white lettering following a problem with the gold paint previously used, which had deteriorated and allowed the blue paintwork of the bodysides to show through. This was an issue that also affected the electric fleet.

The HST sets contained 99 carriages of the older Mk 3-type coaching stock, but in 2006 GNER commenced a £27 million refurbishment programme, aimed at bringing them up to a similar standard to that of the 30 rebuilt electric 'Mallard' trains. The work was planned to provide new seating, new tables, new lighting, refurbished vestibules and additional luggage racks. As the upgraded trains

re-entered service passengers found themselves travelling in more contemporary surroundings, including brighter and more spacious interiors, and on softer contoured seats with improved lumbar support and fold-up armrests for easier access. The upgrade also included improvements to toilets with the provision of new vanity units. While East Coast Main Line passengers had already benefited from the Mk 4 'Mallard' refurbishment, the upgraded HST sets now provided a completely new travel experience for passengers travelling to locations such as Inverness, Aberdeen, Harrogate, Skipton and Hull. The contract for the work was awarded to Wabtec Rail, to be carried out at its Doncaster works, and by November 2007 four sets had been completed and handed over to GNER. Under the contract the HST sets were scheduled to benefit from work aimed at improving reliability and to undergo a complete exterior repaint. The contract required the refurbishment work to be completed early in 2009; following the change of franchise owner in December 2007, the new incumbent, National Express, completed the project.

GNER's then Development Director, Richard McClean, later to become Operations Director, was impressed with the planned upgrade. He said, 'This is the most comprehensive package of improvements ever fitted to this type of

train. The new engines will deliver 21st-century standards of performance, replacing the pioneering but now tired 1970s technology. The former InterCity 125 trains have given a fantastic service over the past 30 years and, in their new condition, will set a very high standard for the next decade. In the longer term, the current fleet will be replaced by a totally new High Speed Train, as part of a national procurement exercise being led by government.'

Equally impressed with the refurbishment programme was Haydn Abbott, Managing Director of Angel Trains, who said, 'Re-powering and upgrading our HST fleet is just another example of the innovation and investment that Angel Trains has brought to Britain's railways. The new engines, together with the interior refurbishment, will ensure that the existing HST fleet can continue to operate reliably and cost-effectively until their successor is introduced.'

Under a separate programme of investment the HST sets were also fitted with a unique onboard wireless internet (Wi-Fi) system, which allowed passengers to surf the internet as well as send and receive emails while on the move; this had previously only been available to passengers travelling in the refurbished electric train fleet and in some lounges.

RIGHT: One of GNER's High Speed Train sets is caught on camera as it speeds through Chester-le-Street in November 2003.
railphotolibrary.com

BELOW: A GNER High Speed Train headed by power car No 43096 *Stirling Castle* traverses one of the single-track sections through the Scottish Highlands on its way to Inverness.
railphotolibrary.com

CHAPTER TWELVE

Franchise renewal

The original franchise granted in 1996 was for a seven-year period and, as we have seen, GNER had unsuccessfully attempted to have it extended to facilitate the purchase of new trains. However, as the time for re-letting the East Coast rail franchise approached the specification issued by the shadow Strategic Rail Authority to potential bidders was for a 20-year period. This was viewed by some as an about-turn when considering the refusal of GNER's earlier request to both Government and the Office of Rail Regulation. It should be remembered, however, that by now Stephen Byers had taken over governmental responsibility for transport, succeeding John Prescott. GNER and a combined Virgin/Stagecoach bid were the front runners resulting in innovative bids, including tilting trains, new-build high-speed sections over part of the route, parkway stations and freight loops. Useful though all of these would have been, none of them would have resolved the big issue of how to get more trains into King's Cross station.

At the end of the day the sSRA closed the bidding, possibly becoming worried about the escalating costs of upgrading the West Coast Main Line, preferring instead to re-let the franchise at a later date but, in the meantime, extending GNER's franchise for a further two years. As Garnett jokingly pointed out, 'I wanted 20 years but effectively the sSRA knocked off the nought and gave me two.' It was a shame, because the GNER bid had also included plans not only to replace the stand-by rolling stock, but also to strengthen the overhead line wiring.

An interview with the *Guardian*'s Transport Editor, Keith Harper, in July 2001 revealed the depth of disappointment felt within GNER. The article says that Garnett bit his lip as he told the newspaper that he was astonished at what seemed to be a 48-hour turn-round by the Government. He said, 'On Monday we were being told that the 20-year franchise was ours and that the Strategic Rail Authority had recommended us to Mr Byers [the new Transport Secretary]. Somewhere between then and Wednesday the Government dropped a nought out of the equation. It makes you think: what on earth has happened?' The feeling was that the Treasury had become frightened about the arithmetic surrounding Railtrack's £2.6 billion upgrading of the line, promised for completion by 2010. Garnet said, 'Ministers see the problems and the escalating costs and they wonder who will pay, but it does not help companies who are planning to invest millions of pounds in new rolling stock and provide better services by getting rid of overcrowding.'

When the East Coast Main Line franchise eventually came up for re-letting it was for a period of almost 10 years, commencing on 1 May 2005 and ending on 31 March 2015, although to run for the full period the new franchisee would have to meet performance targets from 2012. In order to retain the franchise GNER had to prove itself as the preferred bidder in competition with DSB/EWS, First London, and a consortium of Stagecoach and Virgin Group. The successful bid was led by Tim Hedley-Jones, GNER Market Development Manager,

RIGHT: A photograph that suggests that young boys still have ambitions of becoming train drivers! *GNER*

LEFT: One of GNER's onboard advertising posters, which suggests that small girls also have ambitions to drive trains! *GNER*

and Richard McClean, GNER Development Director. It would require GNER to pay a premium of some £1.3 billion over the life of the franchise, which was considered by many to be excessively high, but Garnett and the bid team were confident that the prevailing economic climate coupled with growth in passenger numbers made it sustainable. Indeed, the Department for Transport must have agreed since it had a duty to ensure that winning bids were sustainable before awarding a franchise. Any feeling that the bid was not too high is supported by the fact that the successful National Express bid in 2007 promises a higher premium over a shorter period, albeit with additional capacity planned.

After months of talks GNER was announced as the preferred bidder for the new franchise due to commence on 1 May 2005. However, even then things were not straightforward because Sea Containers had hoped to obtain protection from the Government against Open Access Operator Grand Central, which had entered an application to operate services along part of the East Coast route early in 2005. In a *Sunday Times* article dated 6 August 2006, GNER's Planning and Development Manager, Adrian Caltieri, is quoted as saying, 'The Strategic Rail Authority had immediately offered protection when the question of Grand Central was raised.' However, at a meeting in March 2005, at which Christopher Garnett was due to sign the agreement on behalf of GNER, the SRA announced that the promised protection had been withdrawn. It is now known that the SRA gave GNER an ultimatum – sign within 2 hours or we put the franchise out for re-tendering. Both issues put the TOC in a difficult situation, arising as they did at the 11th hour. Indeed, it should be remembered that the original InterCity East Coast (ICEC) Invitation to Tender, issued in October 2004, told bidders to assume no change to the pattern of other passenger operators on the ECML, although it did warn bidders to note 'the Rail Regulator's recent approval of a supplemental track access

agreement granting Hull Trains additional rights including a fifth service in each direction each weekday'. GNER's bid had been made in line with the assumption that no other changes to passenger operations would be made and Garnett now had to make a difficult decision – sign or miss out on the franchise. Faced with the risk of losing the franchise Garnett signed, and GNER now had the rights to operate the East Coast franchise for a further ten years.

The *Sunday Times* article also carried a quote from an unnamed GNER spokesman who said, 'Obviously, at the time being faced with such an ultimatum at the eleventh hour was a surprise, given the value that had previously been offered, and the threat that the franchise would have to be re-tendered if we did not sign there and then put us in an impossible position. What is worse is that the verbal assurances that the SRA gave us at the time, that Open Access would not adversely affect GNER, have now been shown in the High Court to have been of no use whatsoever.'

The newly won franchise required GNER to pay premiums totalling almost £1.3 billion over the ten-year franchise. The DfT's own figures show the agreed premium profile as:

Year	£million
2005/06	49.7
2006/07	31.4
2007/08	68.2
2008/09	90.0
2009/10	122.3
2010/11	145.8
2011/12	165.8
2012/13	183.5
2013/14	201.8
2014/15	219.3
Total	**£1,278 million**

The May 2005 bid included:
- A £42 million rebuild of GNER's diesel High Speed Trains, which operated on the route including the non-electrified parts to Hull,

Harrogate, Aberdeen and Inverness. The interiors would gain the style of the Mk 4 'Mallards' and all power cars would get new engines.
- GNER's innovative onboard wireless internet service on all trains by May 2007.
- A 90% punctuality target by 2010, achieved by a new Integrated Control Centre in York, upgrade of overhead electric supply lines and an extra rescue locomotive.
- A £25 million station modernisation programme, including more car parking and cycle spaces, automatic ticket barriers, lifts, information points, improved facilities and access, the aim being to provide quality, consistency and accessibility.
- More passenger security, better information on stations and in shopping centres, new bus-rail links, through ticketing, self-service machines at stations, and more on-line ticket sales.
- The 'Electric Horseshoe Project', designed by GNER's own Adrian Caltieri to provide 14 extra electrified route miles between Neville Hill, Leeds, and Hambleton, allowing 15 extra trains daily with trains able to continue beyond Leeds and loop back onto the East Coast Main Line, reducing time-consuming run-rounds and congestion at Leeds station.
- Half-hourly services between London and Leeds.

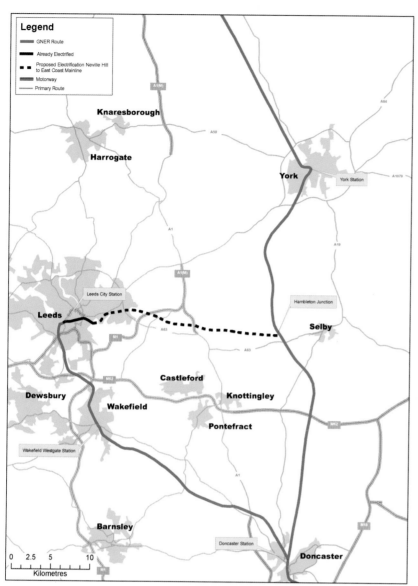

Legend

- GNER Route
- Already Electrified
- Proposed Electrification Neville Hill to East Coast Mainline
- Motorway
- Primary Route

LEFT: A map showing the proposed 'Electric Horseshoe Project', which Christopher Garnett wished had been a definite commitment in the May 2005 franchise bid. *GNER*

BELOW: GNER installed self-service Fast Ticket machines at its major stations, as seen here at Newcastle, which can issue tickets to the most popular destinations. The facility literally removes the need for passengers to queue at ticket sales windows and enables customers to collect tickets purchased online. *GNER*

Christopher Garnett told me that his big regret was that the bid did not include a firm contractual commitment to the 'Electric Horseshoe Project'. With hindsight he wished it had and is sad that the plan may well be lost to the railway for ever. In addition to reducing run-round times or time taken by crews changing ends, the project would also have provided GNER with the potential of tapping into the 'park-and-ride' market north of Leeds in the nearby 'golden triangle' more or less bounded by Ripon, Boroughbridge and the A1. This is an area in which households have the highest average disposable income outside London and which has excellent road links, but from which rail travel is presently unattractive.

LEFT: The modern easily accessible ticket sales point on the concourse at Newcastle Central station. *GNER*

CHAPTER THIRTEEN

Financial disaster:

the franchise becomes unsustainable

Not long after GNER had won the rights to operate the franchise for a further ten years the company was hit by a series of disasters, many of which it rightly insists were out of its direct control. Despite this, many were quick to point their fingers at what they had described as an over-the-top bid. However, both Christopher Garnett and his eventual successor Jonathan Metcalfe told me that with the hindsight of knowing that the other bids were so much lower, the GNER bid might have been higher than was needed, but that it included everything that GNER wanted to do; they were adamant that it had been sustainable at the time it was made. The bid had been based upon the continuing high growth the company had seen during the first franchise, and the Gross Domestic Product (GDP) projections it used were lower than the Treasury's assumptions of GDP growth. It also included the franchise requirement to increase the number of services between King's Cross and Leeds; the stations between Leeds and London were by now accounting for approximately 70% of passengers carried by GNER. The TOC was, after all, proven to be a good franchisee and had met all the requirements of its earlier franchise and extension. It had built a good reputation with both passengers and

government and was generally well respected within the rail industry.

Change at the top

Around the time of the Hatfield tragedy Sea Containers had been involved in bidding for other businesses as they became available, looking to expand its business empire. These included an unsuccessful 2002 attempt to buy GB Rail, the offer made as part of a consortium consisting of Management Consortium Bid (MCB), itself the parent company of Freightliner, and GNER, as well as unsuccessful attempts to win the Great Western and South West Trains franchises (both which were ultimately bid for three times). Christopher Garnett, in addition to his role as GNER Chief Executive, was also chairman of the Association of Train Operating Companies (ATOC). Both were extremely time-consuming. Realising that he needed to reduce his workload, Garnett asked Jonathan Metcalfe to take over responsibility for the day-to-day running of GNER, promoting him from Customer Operations Director to Chief Operating Officer in April 2001. Metcalfe told me, 'I felt this was a very magnanimous decision by Christopher because GNER really was his baby, but he just couldn't fit everything in.'

LEFT: Class 91 No 91129 *Queen Elizabeth II* departs Darlington's platforms on a snowy 3 February 2003.
Rich Mackin/ railwayscene.co.uk

LEFT: Northbound and southbound GNER HST services pass at Newcastle. No 43111 *Scone Palace* is seen on the left with a service for Aberdeen. *Rich Mackin/ railwayscene.co.uk*

A driver's-eye view from the cab of HST power car No 43110 *Stirlingshire* heading a GNER service to Aberdeen in December 2007 as it runs on to the famous Forth Bridge. *John Balmforth*

Metcalfe had top-level experience, having joined British Rail in January 1996 and being involved in the original management buyout bid led by Brian Burdsall, which finished third behind Sea Containers and Stagecoach. Remaining with GNER, he spent the next two years leading organisational changes, particularly front-line and cultural changes to the Customer Services-based organisation.

In August 2006 Christopher Garnett made the decision to step down completely from his role at GNER, and Bob Mackenzie, Sea Containers' new President, appointed Metcalfe as GNER's Chief Executive. At the same time Mackenzie took over as Executive Chairman of the Train Operating Company. There was considerable speculation that Garnett was carrying the can for the GNER bid being too high. However, Metcalfe is adamant that this was not the case, pointing out that the bid had been put together by the company as a whole and with the blessing of Sea Containers. He said, 'Everyone was involved in it. There was a bid team responsible for putting it together. It wasn't Christopher's bid but it was a GNER and a Sea Containers bid.' The new Chief Executive told me that 'he had worked for Garnett for ten years and they had an excellent relationship, but he could be a nightmare to work for because his attention to detail was relentless, right down to worrying about teaspoons. I remember him phoning me from King's Cross and telling me that he was standing on the platform at King's Cross at 1355 and the train for the 1400 service was not yet in. He wanted to know where it was and when I suggested he should be concentrating on future strategic issues he retorted, "If we haven't got a train we haven't got a strategy."'

What the bid team could not have anticipated was the July 2005 terrorist campaign, resulting in lower revenue than predicted, which together with unexpectedly high increases in the cost of fuel and electricity meant that the company needed support from a parent that simply could not give it. The fact that the company had been refused protection from Open Access Operators exacerbated a feeling that the Government seemingly wanted rid of Sea Containers. Garnett himself said that 'the London bombings knocked hell out of the business and made forward projections in revenue extremely difficult'. He added that it was only the second occasion on which GNER had needed the help of its parent company, Sea Containers, and it was unfortunate that this was not available. The previous time had been in the aftermath of the Hatfield accident when Jonathan Metcalfe revealed that the company had found itself losing up to £3 million per week, and said that legal issues had delayed the payment of compensation to GNER, giving it little choice other than to stop paying track access charges to Railtrack. Metcalfe told me that 'without taking that course of action GNER would not have survived'.

Garnett told me, 'If our parent company had been able to bankroll GNER, things would have worked out OK, but sadly it was unable to do so, having filed for Chapter 11 protection in the United States, which in reality meant that the company was bankrupt.' Garnett also revealed that an unsuccessful attempt was made to sell GNER, but, in his own words, 'Who would want to help a sick company with a really sick parent?'

This was also a view held by Jonathan Metcalfe, who calculated that the loss of passenger revenue following the bombings had cost the company £10 million in lost revenue. He felt that unexpected increases in fuel and electricity charges cost the company a further £10 million. He said that 'GNER's business was running operationally well but financially the company was very sick. A cash-rich parent could have kept things going, but with that help not forthcoming it was clear that we could not keep going.' He added that, 'Contrary to many reports GNER did not threaten to hand in the keys to the franchise or ask to renegotiate the premiums, as we knew that was not tenable.' Indeed, Sea Containers, under the leadership of Bob Mackenzie, proved themselves to be exceptionally responsible and committed owners of the franchise right up till the very end in December 2007, with ironically more investment being facilitated across the business in the previous 18 months than ever before!

Uneven playing-field

Another issue in which both men were in agreement was the matter of Open Access Operator rights being granted to two other operators, Hull Trains and Grand Central Railway, to operate along the East Coast Main Line. Both made it clear that they are not against Open Access rights being granted in principle – after all, GNER had once attempted to become such an operator itself – but they simply wanted a level playing-field. Metcalfe told me that 'the Department for Transport was adamant that there would not be another operator on the route', and consequently there was no need for protection to be built into the GNER franchise. He went on to say that 'the whole thing was a muddled mess with, on the one hand, the DfT saying there should be no competition to the GNER East Coast Main Line franchise from Open Access Operators, while another arm of government, the Office of Rail Regulation, ruled that there could be. If it had been transparent it wouldn't have been an issue – we just wanted a level playing-field.'

Christopher Garnett's view was that the effect on GNER was certainly an issue, in particular the ORCATS raid by Grand Central when it announced its intention to stop at York, which was estimated to be at a potential cost of £10 million in lost revenue to GNER. He feels that the risk of Open Access applications needs to be identified and made clear to bidders. Garnett said that franchisees have costs that Open Access Operators don't, and when the GNER franchise, specified by a government department, the DfT, contained a requirement

BELOW: The driver's view from the cab of a GNER HST set as it approaches the entrance to Scotrail's Haymarket depot, just after leaving Haymarket station on a northbound service. On the right of the picture can be seen the home of Scottish Rugby Union, Murrayfield stadium. *John Balmforth*

to increase the service to Leeds it did not seem right for another arm of government, this time ORR, to make a ruling that seemed to prevent those services being provided. Garnett said that 'when taking into account the fact that the route would have been taken up to capacity by the additional Leeds paths, GNER did not see any need for protection to be built into the franchise.' It became a major issue when Network Rail announced that there were no paths available for the extra GNER services to Leeds, but that it was granting paths along the East Coast Main Line for Grand Central's proposed services. GNER had always considered that the infrastructure custodian had a duty to provide the Leeds paths in accordance with the terms of its franchise agreement with the Department for Transport. The whole issue was taken before the High Court, where Mr Justice Sullivan ruled that the granting of Open Access Operator rights to Grand Central was not illegal.

At this point it is worth exploring the GNER argument that competition from Open Access Operators was unfair. In *Rail* magazine (issue 534, published in March 2006) Richard Bowker, the former SRA Chairman and now, ironically, head of National Express, which succeeded GNER as operator of the East Coast rail franchise, wrote under the sub-heading 'Let's compile the evidence':

'First, GNER. It's recently signed a franchise agreement based on a service specification set by the SRA and adopted by DfT Rail. In pricing its bid GNER would have had regard to known risks, one of which had been bobbing around

the annual timetable conferences for several years, namely Ian Yeowart's wish to be allowed to start up his own train service, this time on the East Coast.

More fool them, you might say, if GNER chose to presume Ian Yeowart's ambitions would continue to be thwarted, but nonetheless GNER agreed to return to the taxpayer a very large amount of money for the privilege of running ICEC and that, as is well known, depends primarily on revenue growth. Why? Because the costs of a franchise are largely fixed through labour, track access and rolling stock charges. If you want to change the net income line, it is revenue – and more precisely management of yield – that is your major weapon. The GNER franchise is due to return very large sums that significantly reduce the cost of the railway to the public sector, a material factor when arguing the industry's corner with HM Treasury.

Second, Grand Central (and Hull Trains) will be operating on a different basis from GNER. Open Access Operators pay only the variable component of their track access charges whereas GNER pays both fixed and variable. The fixed bit represents GNER's share of the cost of providing the ECML in the first place, whereas the variable bit represents the marginal costs of running X number of trains on it.

The battle for who got that extra path was fought on variable track access terms only – that is, both GNER and Grand Central would have paid only variable charges for their extra paths, which misleadingly enables the Office of Rail Regulation to suppose that it is dealing with a level playing-field; at the margin maybe it is, but Grand Central, having won the argument, will itself in practice be directly competing with GNER on an unequal basis.

It may offer a choice to consumers but its product is priced on the basis of variable track access only whereas GNER's is based on variable and fixed, not to mention a contribution on top back to the exchequer. A very different proposition.'

Ultimately the matter of extra paths was resolved when Network Rail did an about-turn and mysteriously managed to find the extra capacity required for GNER's additional services to Leeds, as well as those required by Grand Central. However, on the issue of the ORCATS raid on its revenue GNER could do nothing further, having to accept the predicted drop in revenue.

A Transport Select Committee report released in 2006 was welcomed by GNER, especially as it largely backed the TOC's own experience. The report questioned the fairness of Open Access when the franchisee takes all the risk, and suggests that this risk be shared with the Government. It also notes that safeguards to protect franchisees do not offer much protection if problems hit companies in the first year or two. The committee recommended that specifications for premium-paying franchisees, as opposed to those receiving subsidy, should be a little looser to allow room for innovation.

In an editorial page in *Rail* magazine (issue 542), Managing Editor Nigel Harris wrote, 'You have to concede, the GNER story oozes not only drama, but also more twists, turns and heated emotions in its plot than the best of Agatha Christie and D. H. Lawrence combined. You really couldn't make it up.' He is right: we have seen a prolonged refranchising campaign, a bitterly fought war with the Office of the Rail Regulator, courtroom drama, previously unavailable ECML paths mysteriously appearing from the ether, and the financial meltdown of the TOC's parent company, Sea Containers.

There have been other issues, too, arising from the GNER experience. Under the headline 'Rail franchise process to be changed after east coast battle', the Independent newspaper's transport correspondent, Barrie Clement, wrote that ministers had ordered a key change in awarding franchises, which should not be signed-off until track access is established. Even ORR conceded on reflection that the bidding process should have taken place after the decision on access. The *Rail* editorial continued with a quote from ORR Chairman Chris Bolt, who said, '…there would be a more sensible way of doing things in the future.'

BELOW: The view from the driver's cab of power car No 43110 *Stirlingshire* as it prepares to shunt into Aberdeen's carriage wash and refuelling lines. In the distance the two white 'cat's eyes' of the position signal are illuminated, indicating to the driver that the signalman has already set the route. *John Balmforth*

Access rights would not be 'set in stone' but '...new franchises should know how much competition there would be in the foreseeable future'. While government ministers were clearly furious at the ORR decision, there is a strong feeling that the finger of blame should be pointed at the DfT's rail franchising team.

The new 10-year franchise depended upon an 8.5% growth in revenue, but this only ever reached 3% in the first 12 months, and was quite simply not viable if the business was to operate profitably; most of today's franchises operate on around 4% profit margins. Jonathan Metcalfe revealed that GNER approached the Department for Transport to advise it that 'it was not financially viable to operate the existing franchise in the longer term but that it still wanted to continue operating the services'. The TOC advised the DfT that, if it wished to go down the path of refranchising the business, it would understand, but said it would be happy to continue to run the franchise on a management contract basis with the Department for Transport underpinning it in the meantime. In fact, Mike Mitchell, head of the DfT, agreed to this proposal and, at the same time, allowed planned investment in stations and other areas such as rolling stock to go ahead. In addition, GNER had also proceeded with its plan to introduce a half-hourly timetabled service between King's Cross and Leeds, commencing in May 2007. Within two months the move was proved to be fully justified as an extra 60,000 passengers had been attracted to the Leeds services, an increase of 8% on the equivalent period in the previous year.

Nevertheless there continued to be problems with the East Coast Main Line infrastructure, particularly the robustness of the overhead lines, which, when coupled with GNER's own stability issues, saw the previously high performance standards slipping. GNER Operations Director Richard McClean revealed his disappointment when he told me, 'Since taking over the franchise in 1996 the company had been unable to make the impact it wanted concerning the condition of the route, and there has been no real improvement with very little in the bank account of ideas for improvement.' While this was certainly true of both Railtrack and Network Rail, McClean also held the view that by 2007 GNER itself was not performing to its accustomed standards in any aspect of the business. This viewpoint was ably supported by the performance levels for the May/June 2006 reporting period, which showed that it had dropped to an unacceptable level (an all-time low for the company), with only 81.6% of trains arriving at their destinations within 10 minutes of their booked arrival time. McClean

continued: 'The last 18 months have been very difficult for all of us and it showed through in the end product and the opportunity for a new start with a new owner is right. It is so difficult working in a company nearing bankruptcy, with a parent that is already bankrupt.'

It is impossible to argue with McClean's comments, but during my interview with Jonathan Metcalfe he revealed that GNER was able to keep the front line going, albeit with a slight drop in the accustomed standards, on behalf of the Department for Transport, and redundancies were kept to a minimum, occurring mainly at director and management level. He told me that 'there was no point in stripping services, as passengers would have just walked away from the business'. He continued, 'I am extremely proud of the professional way our staff conducted the business through what were undoubtedly worrying times for them.' Christopher Garnett was equally proud of the way his former staff reacted during the period of uncertainty over future ownership of the franchise. Garnett says that 'one of the downsides of the rail franchising system is that periodically staff have to be picked up on taking over a franchise only for them to have to be passed on to someone else if the franchise is lost. It makes investment in people difficult to justify – is this a good way to treat people?' In addition Garnett felt that GNER employed so many competent people who, while protected by the Transfer of Undertakings (Protection of Employment) Regulations 2006 (TUPE) for transfer to the new franchise holder, must have felt some uncertainty about their future careers.

Even so, some rail commentators felt that the company should have taken greater account of the potential risk in not achieving the passenger growth required, which could have been as badly hit by a financial recession as it was by the London bombings. They may have a point, but GNER also has a very strong point when it states that it should not have stood alone shouldering all of the blame. Metcalfe told me that 'franchises are publicly specified but privately delivered, and since winning bids are a public-private partnership, and GNER's figures were given the SRA's seal of approval at the time, the company is not happy to be left shouldering the full responsibility for getting the projections wrong. I really don't think one side or the other can really take all the responsibility or accountability, or stand back from it and say it's not our problem. We have to take responsibility for our problems, but I think the DfT have got a responsibility as well.' After he left the company Garnett said that GNER's survival was now in the hands of the Government. Asked if he agreed in an interview for *Rail Professional* magazine, Metcalfe said that

he would qualify it slightly, feeling that it was really down to GNER, Sea Containers and the Department for Transport. Garnett also considers that bids for franchises are now being forced up too high, a viewpoint that attracts much agreement from the rail media and many commentators. Metcalfe said, 'I think the pendulum has swung too far. The original franchises were not specified clearly enough and, in some cases, I think the margins were rather high. What's happened now is that the franchises are probably too tightly specified in some cases and the margins have become far too tight. In the fullness of time the balance might be restored.'

On the other hand, Richard McClean told me that his own feelings were that the Office of the Rail Regulator would like a good portion of inter-city routes to be Open Access operations, with subsidy-supported regional franchises covering the remaining routes. He explained that there would be big debates about route utilisation strategy and who gets what on the inter-city routes, with the consequences lying at the door of the Department for Transport. The outcome will affect the Train Operating Companies but funding will inevitably come from the taxpayer in the form of reduced premiums. He said, 'If a route is commercially profitable the ORR seems to feel it should be

Open Access – franchises only being required for routes requiring subsidy.'

Jonathan Metcalfe revealed that he had found 2007 to be a very challenging year but, despite the loss of the franchise, the business was now back on a sound financial footing following the signing of a management contract with the DfT in December 2006. This was in large part due to the very strong support Metcalfe and his team received from Bob Mackenzie at Sea Containers, who played a major part in helping navigate GNER through the difficult last 18 months and back into a much healthier financial state. This also ultimately enabled the DfT to be able to successfully re-franchise the business as reflected by the high levels of premiums offered to the Government in the bids ultimately received, including National Express's £1.4 billion winning bid. The Department for Transport also indicated that GNER could be involved in the bidding when the franchise was re-let since it was still held in high esteem by government at parliamentary and DfT levels. The suggestion was that, while it would probably be unacceptable for GNER to bid in its own right, it would be acceptable for a bid to be made jointly with another bidder. Internally GNER was giving serious thought about which bidder to partner with, but Metcalfe says, 'This possibility was scuppered by the ridiculously

ABOVE: A driver's-eye view of an approaching GNER HST, heading south. Although GNER was still operating the East Coast franchise the passing train already has the white vinyl stripes covering the red of the GNER to allow speedy rebranding at the end of the franchise.
John Balmforth

short time set by the deadline for prequalification of bidders, allowing only three to four weeks.' He went on to say that this made it extremely difficult to get into partnership with bidders. Having said that, GNER did enter negotiations with a number of companies, and one partnership (not named here for reasons of confidentiality) was very close to being finalised, but almost at the last minute decided that it was not in a position to do so.

Despite its own parlous financial state, any bid involving GNER had to have Sea Containers' approval, and a great deal of discussion took place between the company and its parent, eventually concluding that a joint bid with Stagecoach/Virgin Group should be progressed. GNER's agreed holding in the bid was set at 10%, and the new consortium worked hard, with the final bid costing several million pounds. Ultimately the bid came third behind Arriva Trains and National Express Group (NEG). Even so, it is thought that the gap between the bids was quite close, somewhere between £100 million and £200 million, which, in railway terms, is not very wide, especially in a franchise worth considerably more than £1 billion, and when taking into account the full cost of rebranding the business.

The franchise period will run from 9 December 2007 to March 2015, with the last 17 months being dependent upon franchise targets being attained. Interestingly, when taking into account that the premium payable by the winner was £1.4 billion, the winning bid submitted by National Express Group, which will operate services under the title 'National Express East Coast', and had higher premium payments, as well as being for a shorter time span than the failed GNER franchise, it was perhaps not surprising that a few eyebrows were raised. Responding to the question 'Was the NEG bid too high?', Metcalfe said he didn't necessarily think so, adding that he saw a lot of good things in the winning bid that would further improve the railway, although, ultimately, a lot would depend on the economy and no further franchise shocks. Metcalfe does feel, however, that the longer-distance franchises do need to be for longer periods, perhaps a minimum of 15 years, but he is still convinced that the privatisation of the railways was the right thing to do, although he comments that the franchising structure is complicated and especially costly for the unsuccessful bidders. Nevertheless, Jonathan Metcalfe feels that the time was right for a change of franchisee, given the particular circumstances preceding the franchise changeover. He said, 'I'm sad, but it seems a natural break point for GNER, which has ended on a high, and I wish Richard Bowker and his team at National Express every success. He is taking over a good railway with an exceptional staff.'

I also asked Christopher Garnett if he felt that the National Express bid was too high, but he also did not think so. He told me, 'I wish the new franchise owner every success, and that after GNER's experience National Express will have been well aware of any threat that could come from Open Access applications, and will have factored this into their bid.' He too concluded that he could see no reason why users of the East Coast Main Line should not continue to enjoy a high-quality service under the new franchise owner.

Postscript

When GNER commenced operation of the East Coast Main Line rail franchise, one of the first things it did was publish a mission statement, which is reproduced here:

Our Service Vision

The essence of our customer promise: Creating the ultimate travel experience for you.

Our Core Values

Who are we?   People
Customer Focus
Safe
Progressive
Pride in our work

Our Mission Statement

What do we plan to achieve and how? Through our people, GNER will create a golden era of rail travel. We will do this together by setting the highest standards of service, convenience and quality in the UK. We will be the ultimate travel experience for every customer.

Our Customer Promise

Whatever your journey length, GNER will ensure that the time you spend with us is of high quality, however you choose to use it because:
- We have a high staff-to-passenger ratio because we believe that this is the best way to ensure your needs are attended to.
- Our extensive training programmes are designed so that our staff can help you get the most out of our retail outlets, stations and onboard facilities.
- We continuously monitor customer satisfaction through a number of measures with the aim of continuous improvement.
- We take care of you from city centre to city centre.
- From our car parks, through our lounges to our onboard facilities, we are continually striving to ensure safety, cleanliness, convenience and comfort.
- Our award-winning onboard catering brings you the best of British ingredients, with ready-to-go options and cuisine freshly prepared by our onboard chef in our restaurant cars.
- Our fares are competitive, so this quality time is great value.

What We Do Best

What does this mean for the customer? Traditional, personal service delivered in a contemporary way. Respectful of customer needs and reflective of the romantic past of rail. The best of both worlds.

What Makes Us Different?

A service ethic that commits us to delivering 'quality time' to you the customer, however you want it.

Did GNER achieve its aims? I think that, in terms of the service and standards it provided to passengers, it undoubtedly did. Without doubt passengers received a very high level of service and performance from a Train Operating Company that became much loved, led from the top by a highly respected management team who were backed up by a loyal and dedicated workforce, but even so it was not loved in all circles around the rail industry.

Jonathan Metcalfe told me that GNER may sometimes have had an appearance of arrogance, but that is not what was intended. He says, 'We just wanted to run the franchise our way, to our beliefs in values, etc. with all stakeholders. We believe this is a public railway delivered by private firms and we have been unashamed in our view of taking on stakeholder values. We always tried to take on views of those who use the railways. We haven't always toed the line and at times this has caused ripples but it was done for the right reasons – we had a responsibility to be a good custodian and look after the railway. If we didn't speak up for the railway then who would?'

He has a point, and surely no one should dispute that GNER, so often held up as the benchmark-setting train operator in terms of service quality and outlook, has earned itself the right to a place alongside the other famous names that have featured in the history of the East Coast Main Line. It really was 'a true thoroughbred'.

ABOVE: The author seen enjoying the comforts of a Mk 4 'Mallard' First Class carriage, courtesy of GNER, while carrying out research for this book. *John Balmforth collection*

Appendix A
The GNER Fleet (2007)

GNER was one of a small number of franchises that continued to operate only trains that were designed and built (or, in a limited number of cases, specified) by British Rail, some of them dating back to the 1970s. The exception to this was, of course, the use of five Class 373 'Eurostar' electric multiple units (EMUs) on 'The White Rose' service, though none of the five ever appeared in daily service at the same time. Below is a list of all the types of locomotives and carriages used by GNER, though not necessarily at the same time:

Locomotives/power cars/DVTs

Class	Type	Maximum speed (mph)	Number used	Years built	Withdrawn
08	Diesel shunter	20	4	1953-1962	-
43	(HST)Diesel	125	27 (power cars)	1976-1982	-
47	Diesel ('Thunderbird')	100	4	1963-1968	1999
67	Diesel ('Thunderbird')	125	4	1999-2000	-
82	DVT	125	32	1988	-
89	Electric loco	110	1	1986	2001
90	Electric loco	110	1	1987-1990	2003
91	Electric loco	140 (restricted to 125 max in UK)	31	1990	-
373/1 ('Regional Eurostar')EMU		186 (restricted to 125 max in UK)	5	1993	2005

Carriages

Class	Maximum speed (mph)	Number used	Years built	Withdrawn
Mk 3	125	99	1976-1988	-
(HST formation; four refurbished to 'Mallard' standard by November 2007)				
Mk 4	140 (restricted to 125 in the UK)	302	1989-1991	-
(All refurbished to 'Mallard' standard)				

ABOVE: A northbound GNER express crosses one of the numerous level crossings on the ECML in about 2000. Note that the coaches still have blue-painted doors.
Gordon Valentine

ABOVE: Looking like a scene from a Christmas card, a Class 91 locomotive and its train are seen rushing through a snowstorm on the ECML in 2004.
railphotolibrary.com

LEFT: The driver's cab controls of Driving Van Trailer No 82224.
John Balmforth

 **RIGHT:** A GNER HST set speeds along the ECML carrying a 'Discover other worlds' advertisement for 'Tutankhamun and the Golden Age of the Pharaohs'. *GNER*

Appendix B
Locomotive numbers and names

GNER fleet and vehicle names carried in service usually, though not exclusively, referred to places or famous people associated with the East Coast Main Line route

Class 89 AC electric locomotive
89001 *Avocet* (BR nameplate not carried in GNER service)

Class 91 AC electric locomotives
(number before upgrading in brackets)
91101 (91001) *City of London*
91102 (91002) *Durham Cathedral*
91103 (91003) *County of Lincolnshire*
91104 (91004) *Grantham*
91105 (91005) *County of Durham*
91106 (91006) *East Lothian*
91107 (91007) *Newark on Trent*
91108 (91008) *City of Leeds*
91109 (91009) *The Samaritans*
91110 (91010) *David Livingstone*
91111 (91011) *Terence Cuneo*
91112 (91012) *County of Cambridgeshire*
91113 (91013) *County of North Yorkshire*
91114 (91014) *St Mungo Cathedral*
91115 (91015) *Holyrood*
91116 (91016) *Strathclyde*
91117 (91017) *Cancer Research UK*
  (previously *City of Leeds*)
91118 (91018) *Bradford Film Festival*
91119 (91019) *County of Tyne & Wear*
91120 (91020) *Royal Armouries*
91121 (91021) *Archbishop Thomas Cranmer*
91122 (91022) *Tam the Gun* (previously
  Double Trigger)
91123 – this number was never allocated
91124 (91024) *Reverend W. Awdry*
91125 (91025) *Berwick upon Tweed*
91126 (91026) *York Minster*
91127 (91027) *Edinburgh Castle*
91128 (91028) *Peterborough Cathedral*
91129 (91029) *Queen Elizabeth II*
91130 (91030) *City of Newcastle*
91131 (91031) *County of Northumberland*
91132 (91023) *City of Durham*

Class 82 Driving Van Trailers (DVT)
82200 (involved in Hatfield accident,
  17 October 2000)
82201
82202
82203
82204
82205
82206
82207
82208
82209
82210
82211
82212
82213
82214
82215
82216
82217 *Off to the Races*
82218
82219 *Duke of Edinburgh*
82220
82221 (written off in Great Heck crash,
  28 February 2001. Presently in store
  at Doncaster)
82222
82223
82224
82225
82226
82227
82228
82229
82230
82231

Class 43 High Speed Train power cars
43006 *Kingdom of Fife*
43008 *City of Aberdeen*
43038 *City of Dundee*
43039 *The Royal Dragoon Guards*
43051
43053
43056
43057
43077
43090 *MTU Fascination of Power*
43095 *Perth*
43096 *Stirling Castle*
43099
43102 *Diocese of Newcastle*
43105 *City of Inverness*
43106 *Fountains Abbey*
43107 *Tayside*
43108 *Old Course St Andrews*
43109 *Leeds International Festival*
43110 *Stirlingshire*
43111 *Scone Palace*
43112 *Doncaster*
43113 *The Highlands*
43115 *Aberdeenshire*
43116 *The Black Dyke Band*
43117 *Bonnie Prince Charlie*
43118 *City of Kingston upon Hull*
43119 *Harrogate Spa*
43167 *Deltic 1955-2005*
43300 *Craigentinny*
43314 *East Riding of Yorkshire*
43320 *National Galleries of Scotland*

LEFT: Seen at King's Cross, the similarity in front-end styling is clearly shown in this photograph of a Class 82 DVT and an HST, many years its junior, in the background. *John Balmforth*

Appendix C
GNER-managed (SFO) stations

Berwick-upon-Tweed
Darlington
Doncaster
Dunbar
Durham
Grantham
Newark Northgate
Newcastle
Peterborough
Retford
Wakefield Westgate
York

The stations at Doncaster, Newcastle and York all won the national Station of the Year award during GNER's custodianship.

In addition GNER also made calls at approximately 50 other stations managed by Network Rail and other Train Operating Companies, including London King's Cross, Leeds, Edinburgh Waverley, Glasgow Central, Dundee, Inverness and Aberdeen.

GNER catering: total items sold per year

Item	1997/98	2006/07
Full meals (breakfasts, lunches and dinners)	250,000	275,000
Hot drinks	1,500,000	3,000,000
Soft drinks	1,500,000	n/a
Bottles of wine	100,000	n/a
Spirits (measures)	250,000	n/a
Cans of beer	900,000	n/a
Sandwiches	1,000,000	n/a
Hot snacks	800,000	n/a
Cakes/pastries	800,000	n/a
Crisps/peanuts	1,100,000	n/a
Confectionary	300,000	n/a

GNER customers' profile

Reason for travel	%
On company business	25
Leisure customers	60
Commuter travellers	5
Other customers	10

RIGHT: HST power car No 43300 *Craigentinny* pauses at York on 8 December 2006 as it makes the inaugural run by a GNER HST fitted with the new MTU engine. *GNER*

Appendix D
Some facts about GNER

Headquarters Station Road, York
GNER is a wholly owned subsidiary of Sea Containers, Bermuda.
Presidents Jim Sherwood (1996-2006); Bob McKenzie (2006-2007)
Chairman David Benson (1996-2004)
Chief Executives Christopher Garnett (May 1996-August 2006); Jonathan Metcalfe (August 2006-December 2007)
Number of staff Initially 2,800; 3,100 in 2007
Total route miles Initially 920; 935 in 2007
Number of stations directly managed (SFO) 12
Franchise start date 28 April 1996

Franchise end date 9 December 2007; franchise ownership transferred to National Express Group at 0200; NEG operates the route as 'National Express East Coast'
Passenger journeys (2006/2007) 17.6 million
Passenger miles (2006/2007) 2.67 million
Train miles (2006/2007) 11.7 million
Number of services per day 123
Longest journeys Kings Cross to Inverness (568 miles); King's Cross to Aberdeen (520 miles)
Most popular long-distance journey – King's Cross to Leeds
HST power cars owned (not leased) – 5
Complimentary onboard magazine *Livewire*

Appendix E
GNER: a brief chronology

1996
GNER starts seven-year franchise

1997
GNER launches rail industry's first customer loyalty programme
Launch of re-liveried GNER trains and new staff uniforms
New telesales facility opens in Newcastle

1998
New car park opens at Newark Northgate station
New website goes live
Broken wheel causes derailment at Sandy, Bedfordshire
Daily Skipton-Keighley-London return service reintroduced after absence of 22 years
New Lounges and Travel Centres provided across route

1999
Last GNER microwaved burger consigned to history at NRM
New Travel Centres and Lounges open at King's Cross, Doncaster, Newcastle and Berwick-upon-Tweed
At On Board Services International Awards held in Florida, GNER receives Best Food Service: Diamond Award; Best Tableware: Diamond Award; Best Catering: Diamond Award; Best Uniforms: Emerald Award

2000
Introduction of 'The White Rose' 'Eurostars' between London and York
Introduction of daily Selby-London direct service (withdrawn by BR in 1983)
New 270-space car park opens at Peterborough
133 extra car parking spaces provided at Wakefield Westgate
Broken rail causes derailment at Hatfield, Hertfordshire – four lives lost
New First and Standard Class Lounges open at Darlington station
At Rail Business Awards 2000, GNER wins Rail Business Manager of the Year
At Railway Innovation Awards 2000, GNER wins Customer Service award
At CBI Yorkshire & Humberside Fit for the Future 2000, GNER wins Service Sector Award

2001
Withdrawal of reservation charge for bicycles on trains
£5 fare anywhere on route (post-Hatfield recovery)
On-line ticket booking service launched
Road vehicle crashes onto line at Great Heck,

Selby, derailing GNER train and causing collision with freight train – ten lives lost

Partnership agreements with trades unions, applauded by TUC

In SRA National Passenger Survey, GNER wins Best Long-Distance Operator

At Railway Innovation Awards 2001, GNER wins Customer Service Achievement through Teamwork

In National Rail Awards 2000, Doncaster is named Station of the Year, and GNER wins Best Customer Experience, and Best Train Operator (jointly with Great Eastern)

Green Award ISO 14001 Environmental Management Certification awarded to Clayhills Depot, Aberdeen (International Standard for Environmental Compliance)

2002

GNER is first TOC to be granted 'Investor in People' award by UK Government

Eleven extra services on London-Leeds route results in record levels of passengers, 44% more than in 1996

'The White Rose' 'Eurostars' switch to London-Leeds on completion of Leeds 1st upgrade

New First Class off-peak fares launched

Original franchise extended by two years

Fast ticket machines become available at all GNER-managed stations

At National Rail Awards 2001, Dunbar is named Best Small Station of the Year

Onboard Service Magazine awards GNER Outstanding Overall Service: Diamond Award

York station awarded Integration of Bike and Rail Travel Award in Best Station category ('Cyclemark' – Strategic Rail Authority)

2003

New national Control Centre opens

Completion of Class 91 improvement programme

Overhaul of HST power cars commences

220 new car parking spaces at Newark Northgate

100 extra car parking spaces provided at Grantham

IC225 fleet reaches 1 billion miles and 1 million passengers

HM Queen Elizabeth II launches first rebuilt Mk 4 'Mallard' train

Extra Standard Class coach added to all HST sets

GNER becomes first TOC to launch Wi-Fi on the move

230-space car park opens at Grantham

GNER wins RoSPA Gold Award for promoting safety-first culture on trains, and at stations and depots

At Railway Innovation Awards 2002, GNER wins Train Operator of the Year (FOREST)

At CBI Yorkshire & Humberside Fit for the Future 2002, GNER wins Service Sector Award

2004

Customer Information Points installed at all GNER-managed stations

Hand-held computers introduced with real-time running information for on-train crews

New footbridge opens at York in time for NRM's 'Railfest'

Increased cycle spaces at GNER stations (extra 954 spaces in total)

New Travel Centres open at Peterborough and Doncaster

One millionth 'Mallard' passenger carried

Connections Award for cyclists at York (Strategic Rail Authority)

Best Customer Service (Bike & Trail Awards)

At National Railway Heritage Awards 2004, GNER wins Principal Station

Christopher Garnett awarded Honorary Degree from Northumbria University

2005

GNER wins new 10-year franchise from May, ending 5½ years of uncertainty

Transport Secretary Alistair Darling witnesses arrival at King's Cross of final rebuilt Mk 4 'Mallard' train

Class 393 'Regional Eurostar' 'The White Rose' sets recalled for further service with Eurostar

Trade Magazine PR Week: GNER wins Best Campaign of the Year Award

Associated Publishing Agencies: GNER wins APA Online Publishing Solution of the Year Award for Livewire

At National Rail Awards 2004, Darlington is named Best Large Station of the Year, and Bounds Green depot is named London Operational Team of the Year

Chartered Institute of Public Relations: GNER wins Excellence Award – 'Back or bid'

2006

Ten years of GNER

Halfway mark reached in Wi-Fi roll-out

New phase of station improvements commences

Contracts signed for new HST engines

Christopher Garnett steps down as Chief Executive; Jonathan Metcalfe appointed

Jim Sherwood steps down as President; Bob McKenzie appointed

Financial issues threaten franchise

Sea Containers requests Chapter 11 protection in American courts

Refurbishment of HST sets to 'Mallard' standard begins

At National Rail Awards 2005, York is named national Station of the Year

At National Rail Heritage Awards, York station wins Heritage Award for work to improve facilities for passengers

At British Travel Awards, London, GNER wins Britain's Best Rail Operator

Charter Mark – National Standard for Excellence in Customer Service – awarded by UK Government

At York Festival of Food & Drink, David Buchanan (Newcastle depot) wins Chef of the Year

At Cost Sector Catering Awards, London, GNER wins GOEAT Award for on-board catering

Green Award ISO 14001 Environmental Management Certification awarded to Craigentinny depot, Edinburgh (International Standard for Environmental Compliance)

At HSBC Rail Business Awards, Rail Industry's Top Leader is awarded to Christopher Garnett

2007

In Station of the Year Awards, Newcastle is named national Station of the Year

Fourth HST set 'Mallard' refurbishment completed

In European Call Centre of the Year Awards, GNER's call centre is Highly Commended in Best Improved category

Chartered Institute of Public Relations: GNER wins Outstanding In-house Public Relations Team award

RoSPA Gold Award

European Cyclists Federation: GNER awarded Best in Europe for Cyclists

At HSBC Rail Business Awards, GNER wins Wireless Internet Award for roll-out to all of its trains

Franchise ends (9 December)

LEFT: Shortly after the franchise changed hands, a rake of Mk 4 'Mallards' is seen alongside a rake of 'barrier' coaches (owned by HSBC Rail and still carrying GNER's famous blue and red livery) at Bounds Green depot on 6 February 2008.
Allan Stokes

Bibliography

Balmforth, John *Virgin Trains: A Decade of Progress* (Hersham: Ian Allan Publishing Ltd, 2007)

Boocock, Colin *East Coast Electrification* (A *Modern Railways* Special) (London: Ian Allan Publishing Ltd, 1991)

Bowker, Richard *Grand Central: Not such a grand decision* (*Rail*, No 534, March 2006, p30) (Peterborough: EMAP Active)

Comment (Ed) 'Revealed: how GNER was bounced into accepting IC East Coast' (Rail Manager online, No 57, 7 August 2007; www.KT-365.com)

Dunn, Pip 'Bound to impress' (*Rail*, No 524, October 2005, pp38-41) (Peterborough: EMAP Active)

Flowers, Andy 'Farewell Great North Eastern Railway' (*The Railway Magazine*, January 2008, pp28-31 (London: IPC Media Ltd)

Great North Eastern Railway 'Building on Success' (York: *Rail*, 1998)

Harper, Keith 'Starting all over again' (the *Guardian*, 21 July 2001, Finance section, p3)

Harris, Nigel (Ed) *Rail* magazine, No 542, July 2006 (Peterborough: EMAP Active)

Johnston, Howard (Ed) *The Comprehensive Guide to Britain's Railways* (7th Ed) (Peterborough: EMAP Active Ltd, 2004)

The Comprehensive Guide to Britain's Railways (8th Ed) (Peterborough: EMAP Active Ltd, 2005)

The Comprehensive Guide to Britain's Railways (10th Ed) (Peterborough: EMAP Active Ltd, 2007)

GNER: 10 YEARS GOING FURTHER 'A Beacon of Excellence' (Peterborough: *Rail*, 2006)

Johnston, Howard and Harris, Ken *Jane's Train Recognition Guide* (London: Collins, 2005)

O'Connell, Dominic 'Rail firm given two hours to sign £1bn deal' (the *Sunday Times*, 6 August 2006, Business section, p3)

Semmens, Peter *Speed on the East Coast Main Line: A century and a half of accelerated services* (Wellingborough: PSL, 1990)

Simmons, Jack and Biddle, Gordon *The Oxford Companion to British Railway History* (Oxford: Oxford University Press, 1997)

Sylvester, Katie 'The Rail Professional Interview' (*Rail Professional* magazine, December 2006, pp18-20) (Cambridge: Rail Professional Ltd)

Acknowledgements

I should like to thank the following for their help in the preparation of this book: Helen Atkinson, GNER Communications Executive; Stuart Baker; Andy Balmforth; Shirley Balmforth; Mark Botlazzi, GNER Bounds Green depot; Peter Brown, GNER Communications Team; Tony Brown, GNER Manager Fleet & Engineering; Alun J. Caddy; Christopher Garnett, Chief Executive, GNER 1996-2006; John Gelson, GNER Media Relations Manager; GNER; Chris Green; Tim Hedley-Jones, GNER Manager Strategic Planning; Janet Huck, GNER Legal Director; Alan Hyde, GNER Head of Communications; Mick Ingledew, GNER Driver Team Manager, Newcastle; Paul Lartey, GNER Driver Team Manager, King's Cross; Richard McClean, GNER Operations Director; Rich Makin (www.railwayscene.co.uk); Jonathan Metcalfe, Chief Executive, GNER 2006-2007; Andrew John Page; Michael Pead (www.michaelpead.co.uk); railphotolibrary.com; Peter W. Robinson; Allan Stokes; and Will Whitehorn.

RIGHT: A Class 82 Driving Van Trailer is silhouetted at sunset as it rests after a hard day's work on the East Coast Main Line.
railphotolibrary.com

THE DOULTON LAMBETH WARES

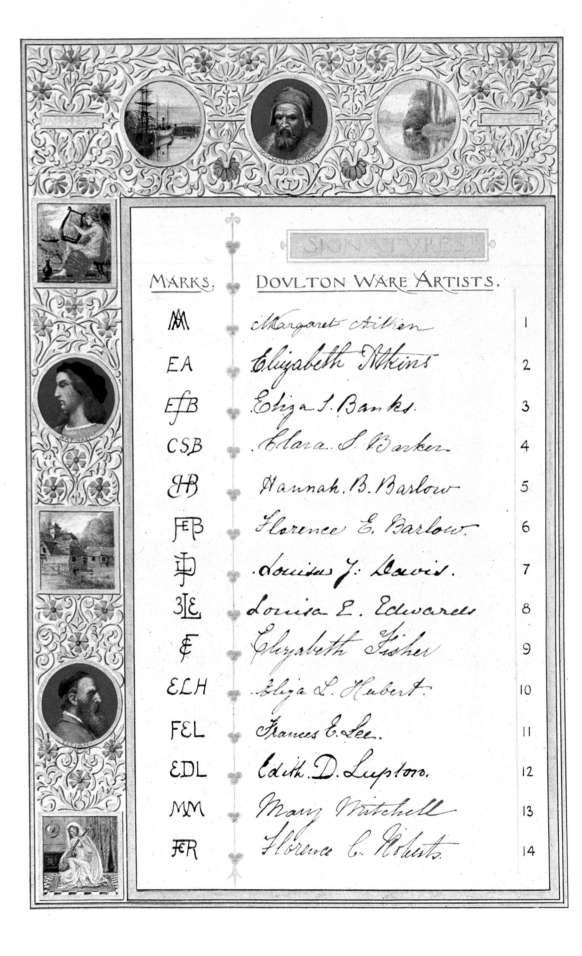

SIGNATURES

MARKS.   DOULTON WARE ARTISTS.

Mark	Artist	No.
AA	Margaret Aitken	1
EA	Elizabeth Atkins	2
EJB	Eliza S. Banks.	3
CSB	Clara S. Barker	4
HBB	Hannah. B. Barlow	5
FEB	Florence E. Barlow.	6
LJD	Louisa J. Davis.	7
LE	Louisa E. Edwards	8
EF	Elizabeth Fisher	9
ELH	Eliza L. Hubert.	10
FEL	Frances E. Lee.	11
EDL	Edith. D. Lupton.	12
MM	Mary Mitchell	13
FCR	Florence C. Roberts.	14

DESMOND EYLES

The Doulton Lambeth Wares

HUTCHINSON OF LONDON

Hutchinson & Co (Publishers) Ltd
3 Fitzroy Square, London W1

London Melbourne Sydney Auckland
Wellington Johannesburg and agencies
throughout the world

First published 1975
© Desmond Eyles 1975

Set in Monotype Bembo
Designed and produced by Hutchinson Benham Ltd

Printed in Great Britain by Flarepath Printers Ltd
St Albans, Herts and bound by Wm Brendon & Son Ltd
Tiptree, Essex

ISBN 0 09 124240 1

Contents

Acknowledgements

The photographs in this book are reproduced by kind permission of the following. Colour plates are indicated by Roman numerals.

Julian Barnard, Esq.: LXXII

Blackpool Gazette and Herald: 154

Michael Collins, Esq.: XV, XIX, XX, XXXV, XXXVI, LV

Davidson & Kay, Aberdeen: 109

Richard Dennis, Esq.: XXIV–XXVI, LII, LIV, LVIII, LX, LXII–LXIV, LXVII, LXVIII, LXXIII, LXXIV, 12, 19, 20, 22–24, 30–32, 34, 36, 37, 42–44, 46, 47, 56–59, 62–65, 69, 70, 73–76, 82, 85, 86, 88, 90–93, 95, 101, 102, 115, 120, 121, 123, 139, 143, 145, 150

Doulton & Co. Limited: I–IX, XI, XII, XIV, XVII, XVIII, XXI–XXIII, XXVII–XXXIV, XXXVII, XXXVIII–L, LXV, LXVI, LXIX, LXX, LXXV–LXXVII, 1–11, 13, 17, 18, 21, 26–29, 33, 35, 38, 41, 48–55, 60, 66–68, 71, 72, 77–79, 83, 84, 87, 89, 96–99, 103–108, 110–112, 114, 116–119, 122, 124–138, 140–142, 144, 146–149, 151, 152, 156, 157, 160–167

A. Gee, Esq.: 39, 40

Directors of Library and Amenity Services, Borough of Lambeth: frontispiece

J. McLennan, Esq.: 155

National Westminster Bank Limited: LXXI

Smithsonian Institution, Washington, D.C.: 14, 15

Sydney (N.S.W.) Museum of Applied Arts and Sciences: 16, 25, 45, 72, 81, 94, 100, 113, 159

Michael S. M. Thomson, Esq.: X, XIII, XVI, LI, LIII, LVI, LVII, LIX, LXI

Victoria & Albert Museum (Crown Copyright): 61, 71, 153, 158

Foreword

DURING the past ten years or so there has been a great resurgence of interest in the salt-glazed stoneware and other art ceramics produced at the Doulton Pottery in Lambeth, on the London Thames-side, in the nineteenth and early twentieth centuries. These, it is being realized more and more, offer a fascinating and still relatively accessible field for forming a collection of pottery of unusual artistic, technical and historical interest.

The revival is reflected in the increasingly frequent appearance of these wares in Christie's, Sotheby's and other salerooms; in the many references to them in newspaper and magazine articles, television and radio programmes and collectors' reference books; and in the ever-growing number of enquiries received by the Doulton Company and myself concerning specific pieces, artists' monograms, factory marks and the like.

The magnificent exhibition of nearly 700 items of Doulton Stoneware and Terracotta presented by Richard Dennis in London in 1971 was another important stimulus to the interest now being shown by collectors in these products. I am greatly indebted to Mr. Dennis for allowing me to reproduce illustrations not only of some of the pieces shown in that exhibition but also of others which he has since acquired and hopes to show to the public in the near future.

In my now out-of-print history of the Doulton Potteries (*Royal Doulton 1815–1965*, Hutchinson, London, 1965) I gave a general survey of the rise and expansion of this enterprise over a period of a century and a half. Only a relatively small section of the text and illustrations dealt, however, with the Lambeth art wares; the greater part was necessarily devoted to the family, social and economic background of this now world-famous concern, and to the many industrial and technical ceramics for which it is just as well-known as for the art pottery.

The Doulton Lambeth Wares, on the other hand, has been written specifically for *the collector*, in response to many requests for further information about these ceramics and the designers and artists who created them. It incorporates relevant material from the earlier book but contains also much new material, many illustrations never before published, and a greatly enlarged list of artists and assistants with their monograms and other identifying marks. Short biographical details are given about some of the most important artists and the alphabetical glossary contains a great deal of new information of the kind constantly being asked for by collectors. The chapter on Commemorative Wares has the most extensive list of these so far published.

There are, it must be admitted, still some regrettable gaps in our knowledge of the Doulton Lambeth Wares. Many internal factory and studio records which would have been invaluable to the ceramic historian have unfortunately been lost for ever as the results of ignorance of their value, fire, flood, war damage and other mishaps to which the Lambeth Pottery seems to have been singularly fated. Much of the information in this book has had to be built up gradually, over many years, from various other sources, such as contemporary accounts in art magazines and other journals, advertisements, exhibition and trade catalogues, and diaries and letters fortunately preserved by the descendants of former artists and others associated with the Lambeth Pottery. The examination of marks and monograms on many hundreds of examples of the Doulton Wares has made it possible to add to the knowledge of the periods of activity of certain artists.

I have been fortunate in acquiring several unique handwritten and beautifully illustrated volumes, entitled *Studio Notes*, which were produced in the 1880s and 1890s for private circulation among the Lambeth artists. Although evidently only part of a series, they have brought to light useful new information. I have been greatly helped too by data previously collected by the late Mr. J. H. Mott and the late Mr. W. Fairhall, both of whom were intimately associated with the Lambeth Art Department for many years. My grateful thanks are due also to all those collectors, dealers and museum officials who have given me information concerning pieces in their possession or have allowed me to examine these.

Several people have kindly supplied photographs or have allowed photographs to be taken of examples of the Doulton Wares; these sources are acknowledged on page vi. I wish to thank also Miss Frances Lovering, Miss Olive Manders and Mr. John Tustin who have helped me in preparing the work for press, and Mr. Stuart Shrimpton who took nearly all the colour photographs, to the preparation of which he has devoted much time and patience.

If any readers can augment in any way the information given in the following pages, I would greatly appreciate it if they would send me details with a view to these being included in a subsequent edition, if such be required.

A list of commemorative wares is given in chronological order in Chapter VI. Artists and assistant artists are listed in alphabetical order in Appendix I. A detailed alphabetical glossary is given in Appendix III. An index has thus been rendered superfluous.

Over 420 different examples of the various Lambeth Art Wares are illustrated. These are indexed in Appendix I under the relevant artists' or assistants' names. They represent of course but a minute fraction of the vast variety produced. Further illustrations will be found in the following publications:

A.B.C. of English Salt-Glaze Stoneware, J. F. Blacker.
19th Century English Ceramic Art, J. F. Blacker.
George Tinworth, Edmund Gosse.
Doulton Stoneware Pottery 1815–1925, Richard Dennis.
Royal Doulton 1815–1965, Desmond Eyles.

The
Doulton Lambeth
Wares

I

Doulton Wares and the Collector

THERE are several good reasons, apart from the now general revival of interest in nineteenth-century English arts and crafts, why the Doulton Lambeth Wares are proving particularly alluring to discerning collectors.

One is the extraordinarily extensive range of materials, processes and decorative treatments they evince. Another is the fact that, in addition to over 9,000 designs which were reproduced in varying quantities, there are probably still in existence, dispersed over many parts of the world, hundreds of thousands of individual artist-signed pieces to which that often-abused word *unique* may unhesitatingly be applied.

It is known, to give but one example, that Hannah Barlow and her brother Arthur designed in the four years between 1871 and 1874 some 9,000 different pots. Unfortunately, Arthur died at an early age in 1879 but Hannah continued to work with scarcely diminished energy until 1913, producing from 20 to 30 new pieces a week. Sometimes, when she was in particularly creative mood, she would even decorate 20 pieces in a day. Their sister, Florence – known particularly for her bird studies in *pâte-sur-pâte* painting as Hannah is for her spontaneous life-like etchings of animals – was almost equally creative over a period of 36 years. It will be seen, therefore, that the scope for Barlow enthusiasts alone is immense.

George Tinworth was another prolific artist. He first became known for his terracotta panels and other sculptures, usually inspired by the Bible, but he also produced during his 47 years at the Lambeth Pottery thousands of vases and other pots in an unmistakably individual vein, as well as the greatly sought after comical studies of mice, frogs and other creatures.

The creations of Eliza Simmance, Esther Lewis, Edith Lupton, Mark Marshall, Frank Butler and other artists who spent many years in the Lambeth Studios also offer wide scope for collectors. Some, on the other hand, may find it more challenging to look out for examples of pots by artists such as Eliza Banks, Edith and Martha Rogers and Mary Capes, whose periods of artistic activity at Lambeth were relatively short.

A further attraction of the salt-glaze stonewares in particular – and these formed the greater part of the Lambeth Art Pottery's production – is that because of the unusual strength of this tough vitrified material, with its closely integrated hard-wearing glaze, the vast majority of pots have survived in perfect condition. Even those which may have become coated with the dust and grime of decades need only be washed with soap and water, or a mild detergent, to be restored to the same glistening freshness they had on the day they first emerged from the kilns. Compared with more fragile delft-wares, soft-paste porcelains and fine earthenwares, they have the great advantage that it is seldom necessary to consider buying chipped, cracked or otherwise damaged specimens.

'The Lambeth Thrower', *terracotta study by John Broad*

The fact that the Lambeth Pottery ceased to make stoneware in 1956 – production having already been on a very limited scale ever since 1914 – has made the collecting of even the later wares by Vera Huggins, Agnete Hoy, Simeon, Rowe, Pope, Harradine and other artists well worth-while. They will certainly be sought after more and more as the years go by, and some of them have already found their way into important museum collections in Great Britain, Canada, the United States, Australia and other countries.

The Doulton Lambeth Wares as a whole embraced such an extensive range of materials and types of decoration that they offer the opportunity to specialize in one or more particular *genres*, as for example: the 'Impasto', 'Carrara', 'Silicon', 'Chiné', 'Marqueterie', 'Lambeth Faïence' and 'Crown Lambeth' wares, all of which are described later in this volume. These wares have distinctive factory marks or backstamps; many bear also artists' and assistants' monograms, initials or other means of identification.

Another approach which has its appeal for some collectors is to concentrate on certain types of product, such as tobacco jars (of which I have so far noted some 260 different shapes, designs and sizes), jugs, tea-pots, paper-weights, menu-holders, spirit flagons, decanters, wall plaques, tiles, lamps, relief-figured 'hunting' or 'Toby' wares, clock-cases, commemorative wares, figures and animal models. In all these groups the Doulton Lambeth Wares are well represented. The range of Doulton commemorative items is particularly large and few if any other potteries in the world can compete with it in interest, variety and number.

It is becoming more and more difficult, especially for those of moderate means, to build up a collection of good specimens of Bow, Chelsea, Bristol, Plymouth, delftware and other earlier productions of the English potter. In contrast, numerous Doulton items of great historical, technical and general interest may still be acquired at prices from under £5 to £25 or so. Although outstanding pieces by Tinworth and the Barlows have recently been fetching higher sums than these in leading London sales-rooms and antique shops, the patient average collector can still come across exciting and reasonably-priced 'finds' elsewhere – particularly in small second-hand shops and open markets somewhat 'off the beaten track', not only in country towns and villages but even in parts of London and other cities not generally frequented by American and Japanese tourists, for whom the Doulton Wares have recently become a great draw. Private house auctions, concerning which the notice of sale merely says 'items of china and pottery' are often worth investigating.

Generally speaking, the collector who derives the most satisfaction from his or her hobby is not concerned primarily if at all with questions of financial gain. The excitements of the search; the thrill of an unexpected 'find' in some unlikely place; the comparing of notes with other collectors; the correction of some widely-held but erroneous assumption – these are among the most rewarding 'highlights' of collecting for the ardent and persevering seeker.

None the less, even though profitable investment may not be the main consideration, most of us have to exercise prudence and common-sense in what we spend on our hobby. It is, moreover, a natural and human trait to feel a certain satisfaction in 'picking up for a song' – or, at any rate, for a surprisingly reasonable sum – a choice example of the work of a certain artist in whom one has a particular interest. This, as I know from letters I receive, is still by no means an uncommon experience for the Doulton Lambeth Ware collector though it must naturally become an ever rarer one as time goes on. He or she can also have the satisfaction of knowing that, should it become necessary to dispose of part or all of a collection some years hence, there is every indication that it will have appreciated considerably in value.

Yet another noteworthy feature of the Doulton salt-glaze stoneware and other Lambeth ceramics is that, as far as I am aware, fakes and forgeries are non-existent.

3

Doulton Ware Vase. by Frank A. Butler.

One occasionally comes across *unmarked* pieces which are obviously of Doulton origin but for some reason, perhaps because of an oversight or because they were not considered up to standard, they were not stamped; on the other hand, any similar piece which is clearly printed or impressed with a Doulton trade-mark or back-stamp may almost certainly be accepted as genuine.

II

The First Fifty Years of Doulton

THE year 1815, when Napoleon Bonaparte's fate was finally decided at Waterloo, is a famous date in British history.

Compared with the issues then at stake, the fact that a young 22-year-old man, called John Doulton, had just ventured his entire savings of £100 in a one-third partnership in an obscure backyard pot-house in Vauxhall Walk, Lambeth, was seemingly of little moment. From that humble beginning, none the less, was to evolve the now world-famous Royal Doulton Group.

Links with Early Traditions

The Vauxhall Walk pot-house was but one of some twenty similar small enterprises to be found in the late eighteenth and early nineteenth centuries on or near the London Thames-side, which had long been associated with the craft and 'misterie' of pottery-making.

In 1570 Jasper Andries and Jacob Janson, tin-glaze maiolica potters from Antwerp, petitioned Queen Elizabeth I, for permission to settle in London 'by the Waterside' and there 'to exercise the same Science in this Realme'. Janson, who later anglicized his name to Johnson, was one of the early makers in England of that type of earthenware now known to collectors as Lambeth delftware. Like Italian maiolica and early French faïence, this ware was coated with a lead glaze containing tin oxide which gave it an attractive white finish, superficially resembling porcelain although, underneath the glaze, the 'body' – to use the potter's term – was actually dark and porous.

During the seventeenth and eighteenth centuries, several tin-glaze earthenware or 'gallyware' potteries were established in Southwark, Lambeth, Vauxhall and other riverside parishes. One of the largest of these, established in 1751 on the site of an earlier pottery, lay between the Thames and Lambeth High Street, then known as Back Lane; it later became part of the Doulton Pottery.

5

The development of cream-glazed earthenware in Staffordshire by Whieldon, Wedgwood and other potters, in the second half of the eighteenth century, led to the more fragile delft gradually going out of use for tablewares. The making of delft tiles, wine bottles, apothecaries' pots and drug jars was continued by some Lambeth and Vauxhall potters into the early nineteenth century. But, by that time, most of the pottery made in the district was salt-glaze stoneware.

This dense and highly vitrified ceramic material owes its name partly to its strength and durability and partly to the fact that it is glazed by inserting salt (sodium chloride) in the kiln—either through holes in the crown or through the fire-holes or both – when the temperature reaches a white heat of some 1,250° centigrade. Upon volatilization, the chlorine constituent of the salt is expelled in fumes while the sodium unites with alumina and silica in the clay to form a thin but exceedingly durable and corrosion-proof transparent glaze, intimately integrated with the vitrified body. One of the great advantages, and part of the unique attraction, of the thin salt-glaze is that it in no way masks or obscures the most delicate or intricate modelling, carving, *pâte-sur-pâte* painting or other decoration. Normally all decoration is completed before the ware is fired and salt-glazed, and there is only one firing as compared with the two, three or even more required in the production of china and porcelain.

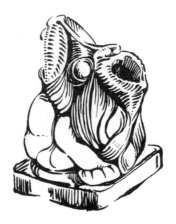

Grotesque paper-weight, by M. V. Marshall

During the reign of Elizabeth I there were increased imports of stoneware bottles and wine flagons made in the Rhineland and commonly known as 'Cologne Ware'. Compared with the porous and relatively fragile English pottery then available, the impervious German pots had the advantages of strength, durability and cleanliness. The Queen was petitioned by one William Simpson who wished to import 'drinking Stone Pottes' in opposition to a foreigner named Garnet Tynes, living in Aachen. Simpson promised to try to set up a manufactory, 'wherebie manie a hundred poore Men may be sett a Work', but it is not known whether or not his request was granted.

In 1626, Charles I granted a patent to Thomas Rous (or Ruis) and Abraham Cullyn (or Cullin) for 'the sole making of the Stone Pottes, Stone Jugges and Stone Bottells', and in 1635 three Westminster brewers obtained a similar concession. Stoneware potteries are known to have existed near the Bear Garden in Southwark and at Gravel Lane, Bankside, in the second half of the seventeenth century; manufacture at Lambeth probably began much about the same time. Evidence given in a lawsuit brought by John Dwight in 1693 against certain other potters, for infringing his patent, suggests that stoneware was being made in Lambeth 25 years before that date. While the sites for the Headquarters of the London Fire Service, Doulton House and other modern buildings on the Albert Embankment were being excavated, specimens of both delft-ware and stoneware, including 'wasters' (rejects) were found at similar levels, implying that over a long period the two manufactures had been pursued side by side.

A famous name in the history of early English stoneware is that of the John Dwight referred to above. He has been called 'the father of English pottery'. In his first patent of 1671 he mentioned, among other achievements to which he laid claim, that of the 'Mysterie and Invention of making the Stone Ware vulgarly called Cologne Ware'. Although his assertion that this material had 'not hitherto been wrought or made' in England was incorrect, there is no doubt that his researches effected great improvements in ceramics. He established a works at Fulham, near the riverside, where he brought the art of pottery-making to a height previously unattained in England. Among his successes were some finely finished white and red stonewares, a great variety of relief-figured brown salt-glaze stoneware jugs and other pots, and a number of ceramic sculptures (some possibly modelled by Grinling Gibbons) of an exceptionally high order. He was one of the first English potters to try to make translucent porcelain.

John Doulton

John Doulton, who was born at Fulham – then a small Thames-side village – on 17th November 1793, served his apprenticeship from 1805 to 1812 at the pottery founded by Dwight. It was then owned by a descendant of Dwight, on the female side, named White. While there, Doulton was considered one of the most skilled throwers in London and he and the owner's son, Charles White, sometimes had a wager as to who could make the most pint pots in a day. (A thrower shapes pots by hand from a lump of clay which he centres on a revolving wheel – a fascinating and, to the uninitiated, almost magical art, the origins of which go back to the early civilizations.)

By 1800, the staple products of the Fulham Pottery were blacking, beer and ink bottles, spirit jars, chemical vessels, and other essentially utilitarian wares. Artistic endeavours were confined more or less to relief-figured 'hunting' jugs and mugs, sometimes (because of the toper motifs) called 'Toby' ware, of a traditional type made in Fulham and Lambeth for generations. Unlike the anthropomorphic Staffordshire Tobies, modelled as seated or standing figures, the London types were in conventional jug or mug shape but decorated with quaint applied reliefs (made separately in small plaster moulds) of topers with foaming tankards, horsemen and hounds, stags, foxes, hares, cottages, windmills and trees.

In 1812, when John Doulton came out of his apprenticeship, he found employment at a small pot-house in Vauxhall Walk, Lambeth, of which, three years later, he became part proprietor. It was one of three or four in the same street and almost faced one of the entrances to the once famous Vauxhall Gardens immortalized in Thackeray's *Vanity Fair*. Although by 1812 this somewhat notorious pleasure haunt (where Pepys 'walked, and ate, and drank, and sang' after the restoration of Charles II) was already greatly shorn of the glory and gaiety which had earlier made it a fashionable resort, it was still high in local favour as a place of popular amusement.

The story of how John Doulton came to be involved in the Vauxhall Walk pot-house is somewhat unusual. This tiny establishment had previously belonged to a potter named Jones. In 1812 it was being carried on by his widow, Martha, with the help of a foreman, John Watts; her intention was to hand it over eventually to her son, Edward, who was then learning the craft.

Unfortunately, young Edward became involved in some trouble with the law and, to avoid arrest, absconded to South America, leaving his mother and Watts with only one thrower and an apprentice to cope with the work. It happened that Watts was acquainted with John Doulton who had just then come out of his apprenticeship at Fulham and was seeking work. An interview and a demonstration showed that he was not only a superb thrower but also had a good overall knowledge of pottery processes. And so he was engaged. It is tempting to speculate about the subsequent history of the small pot-house and the future careers of John Doulton and his son, Henry, had young Jones not run away!

Jones, Watts & Doulton

Doulton worked assiduously, always willing, if need be, to take on any task in an emergency, from preparing the clay to setting, firing and drawing the kiln, apart from his own specific job as a thrower. In this way he amplified the experience already gained at Fulham, laying the foundations of his future successful career as a master potter. He saved hard too, unlike many of his fellows in Lambeth who were inclined to spend much of their wages at 'The Jolly Potter' and other local ale-houses.

8

Early in June 1815, Martha Jones, not having heard from her son for three years, took both Watts and Doulton into partnership and the firm became Jones, Watts and Doulton.

It was an exciting, challenging and often anxious time for a young man at the beginning of his career. A short-lived post-war boom was followed by an economic crisis. Wages were cut, exports fell, and a catastrophic drop in prices ruined many small farmers and businesses. Competition from the other London stoneware potters was intense. Some days Doulton worked at his wheel from six in the morning until late in the evening; other days he would spend the morning calling on customers to take orders and collect payments, returning in the afternoon to help make the ware.

For the first year or so, the men continued the long-established practice of breaking the roughly-shaped balls of Dorsetshire clay ('ball clay' as it is still called) with hammers and mallets and then, after mixing it with water, treading it out into slabs with their bare feet; this was practically all the preparation needed for the ordinary wares then being made. Later on, the partners rented a piece of land adjoining the pot-house, where a grinding and mixing mill was installed, worked, it is recorded, 'with exemplary patience' by a blind but sturdy horse. A second kiln was built about 1818 to cope with increasing orders.

Watts, besides helping to fire and repair the kilns, tested the ware before despatch, supervised the packing, and kept the accounts. He was not a practical potter, having originally been a carpenter, but he was an astute and fairly well-educated man. His part in later developments, though presumably important (he remained a partner until 1853) is obscure, being completely over-shadowed by the achievements of John Doulton, and still more so by those of John's second son, Henry.

Early Products

Among the early products of the Vauxhall Walk pot-house, apart from the ordinary bottles and jugs, which formed the bulk of the output, were some fish-shaped spirit flasks and others in the form of pistols and powder horns, also dog and bird whistles, money-boxes and small replicas of constables' truncheons. Things of this kind were also made by Stephen Green and other London potters, as were small ink-wells somewhat crudely representing the Duke of Wellington, David Garrick, a Beadle and other characters, and spirit bottles in the shape of a tipsy sailor dancing or sitting on a barrel. Most of these were unmarked and are difficult to ascribe to a particular pottery; any with the name Doulton & Watts impressed were probably made after 1826.

The only other early Doulton products with any artistic pretensions at all were relief-figured hunting jugs and mugs of the traditional type already mentioned. This kind of ware had been popular in the so-called 'mug-house' clubs of the eighteenth century, patronized by hunting and other sporting types. Hot punch was served in the larger jugs, which were often mounted with silver or pewter rims. They remained popular for generations and they, as well as similarly relief-decorated bowls, tobacco jars, tea and coffee-pots, were made almost continuously (except during the two World Wars) up to the time the Lambeth Pottery closed in 1956. They were in fact the only ornamented wares made in really large quantities, running eventually into hundreds of thousands, particularly the jugs of which there were several sizes, ranging from tiny miniatures up to 3 pints capacity (or more for special orders). Collectors should be particularly careful when buying these relief-figured hunting jugs and similar items, as absurd prices are sometimes asked for them. Those with a Doulton & Watts mark are rare and those with a Doulton Lambeth mark, without the word 'England', are becoming more difficult to find. Later types, especially those with the Lion and Crown or Lion without the Crown trade marks still abound and fancy prices should not be paid for them.

An account book for 1818–19, one of the very few early records to have survived, gives details of other salt-glaze stoneware products then being made. They included pipkins (small pots with handles), druggists' phials, gallipots (ointment pots), pitchers, gorges (large jugs), candlesticks, butter pots, tobacco jars, soap dishes, quicksilver bottles, tumblers, cups, goblets, cider jars, tamarind pots, rushlight holders, jars and barrel-shaped containers for spirits, cordials and ales. The main production, however, was of bottles for beer, spruce beer (then popular as a preventive against scurvy), blacking and oil bottles, and jars for anchovy and other pastes. These were probably all unmarked.

Doulton & Watts

In 1820, Mrs. Jones decided to withdraw from the partnership and the business was carried on by John Watts and John Doulton until the former retired in 1853. At first it was known locally as Watts & Doulton but soon became Doulton & Watts—doubtless reflecting the fact that Doulton, the practical potter, though much the younger man, had become the predominant partner.

An interesting production of 1820 was a salt-glaze figure flask, somewhat crudely representing Queen Caroline, the wife of George IV. She holds a scroll on which is inscribed 'My Hope is in my People'. The King tried unsuccessfully to get Parliament to pass a Bill to dissolve the marriage and deprive her of the right to the title of Queen. The Radicals, whom John Doulton at that time supported, took the side of the Queen. It is not known how many of these flasks were made but they are now exceedingly rare. An almost identical figure flask, but without the scroll, is also known. A peculiar thing about some figure flasks, such as those depicting the young Queen Victoria, the

Duke of York, Prince Albert and other personages, is that similar designs were made by Doulton & Watts, Stephen Green, Northen and other Lambeth potters. It would seem that they either employed a common modeller or did not object to others copying a good selling line. There is evidence too that the Lambeth potters sometimes co-operated in executing orders for certain lines.

Business had increased sufficiently by 1826 to warrant moving to Lambeth High Street, where the old-established pottery which Doulton & Watts took over included what was said to be the largest garden in Lambeth, apart from that of Lambeth Palace, the London residence of the Archbishop of Canterbury. The move took a year or more to complete and work at Vauxhall Walk continued meanwhile. In the High Street property, it seemed, would be ample room for any further expansion likely to be needed; in fact, the next fifty years were to see a long series of new developments until the Doulton Works, at the height of their activity, extended from opposite the entrance gates to Lambeth Palace half-way to Vauxhall Bridge.

It was probably about the time of the move to Lambeth High Street, when the firm was becoming better known, that it was decided to mark the wares with the name *DOULTON & WATTS*, with or without the words *LAMBETH POTTERY*. Among the products of the 1820s were some well-modelled figure jugs and mugs in the likenesses of Nelson, Wellington and Napoleon, a distinct advance on anything of the kind previously attempted.

Between 1829 and 1830 two new kilns were built, one of them designed for firing unglazed chimney-pots, ridge-tiles, garden vases and other red and buff terracotta wares. Three years later these had to be superseded by still larger kilns, and between 1837 and 1840 seven properties in and around the Doulton & Watts pottery were bought to provide space for further developments, including the supply of vessels of various kinds to the rapidly growing chemical industries.

In 1832, the year of the passing of the First Reform Act, spirit flasks and larger containers, now generally known as 'Reform Flasks' and 'Reform Bottles' were made by Doulton & Watts to commemorate this historical measure which did away with some of the worst abuses connected with the election of Members of Parliament. The necks of these pots depicted the heads and shoulders of William IV and the Lords Grey, Brougham and Russell who were associated with the Bill. Most of the flasks and bottles bore slogans such as 'The Second Magna Charta', 'The People's Rights', 'Reform Cordial' and 'The True Spirit of Reform'. A somewhat similar and rarer flask, produced about 1829 or 1830, portrayed Daniel O'Connell, the great Irish Catholic patriot. Although many thousands of these various flasks were made, Sir Henry Doulton recorded that, even by 1890, they had become very rare, and today they seldom come on the market at all. Perhaps being used largely by gin drinkers, and having political implications, they were more liable to damage than other Doulton Wares!

Henry Doulton Enters the Firm

Henry, John Doulton's second son, was born in 1820. Although given the opportunity, when the time came to choose a career, to study for the Church or the Law, he told his father that he wished, above all else, to become, like him, a practical potter. And so, in 1835, at the age of 15, he joined the firm as an informal apprentice to the craft. 'In those early days of my factory life,' he recalled on his 70th birthday, 'I had anything but an easy time of it. I had to kick my own foot wheel, for there were neither string nor steam wheels at that time.' He had to be up at six in the morning to ring the bell which called the men together; then he took his place among them, learning with extraordinary aptitude the fundamentals of pottery-making, as it was then practised, from the preparation of the clay body to the final stages of firing and salt-glazing. After about two years he was able to make large 20-gallon chemical receivers on the potter's wheel, and in this and similar ways he acquired that practical and intimate knowledge which was one of the secrets of his later phenomenal success.

'Mouse on Bun', by George Tinworth

An early outcome of his inventiveness was the application of steam to drive the potter's wheel – in this the Lambeth Pottery being ten years in advance of any other. In 1841 he celebrated his coming-of-age by making a 300-gallon 'Ali Baba-type' transport jar for chemicals; this his father proudly exhibited outside the entrance to the pottery, with a notice reading: 'The largest stoneware vessel in the world'. It still stood there in 1875 when it was described by a visitor to the factory as being 'big enough to hold five or six of the forty thieves!'

In 1840 a large new kiln was built for firing terracotta sculpture. A Coat of Arms for a school in Kennington Lane was one of the first important orders; a little later on, a much more ambitious piece of work was undertaken – a large figure of Sir John Crosby for the front of Crosby Hall, Bishopsgate. In this venture into an entirely new field, which called for designing abilities of an entirely different order from what was required for the industrial products, Henry Doulton was influenced and greatly helped by an acquaintanceship he had formed with a well-known Kennington sculptor, Samuel Nixon, who carried out a number of special commissions for the firm, including a fine bust of John Doulton.

The manufacture of terracotta, especially for architectural use, gradually became an important part of the Doulton activities, reviving an art for which Lambeth had been famous during the eighteenth century when the Coade Manufactory at King's Arms Stairs, Narrow Wall, near Westminster Bridge, had produced 'artificial stone' of a high quality which was used by the Adams Brothers, Nash, Repton, Wyatt and other architects in the construction of several famous London residential streets and squares, as well as for important buildings in other parts of the country.

Apart from developing this interest in ceramic sculpture and architectural terracotta, and an unsuccessful attempt to revive the manufacture of delftware, Henry Doulton, during the first thirty years of his career at Lambeth, concentrated his energies almost entirely on industrial ceramics. The only items of interest to collectors of which we find any mention in the 1840s and 1850s are some 'Tam o' Shanter' mugs and jugs; other jugs with moulded reliefs depicting boar and stag hunts or Silenus and satyrs (the latter being presumably what Henry Doulton once described as the Bacchanalian jugs). There were also some mugs and figure flasks to commemorate the accession of Queen Victoria; flasks inscribed 'Triumph of the Pen' featuring Punch and Dog Toby; and 'Caudle flasks', inspired by Douglas Jerrold's *Mrs. Caudle's Curtain Lectures* in *Punch*, with moulded relief figures of Mr. and Mrs. Caudle and Mrs. Prettyman. The 'Caudle flasks' were often stamped with the names and addresses of tavern-keepers; although made in fair quantities over a period of several years, they are becoming more and more difficult to obtain nowadays.

At the Great (Crystal Palace) Exhibition held in Hyde Park in 1851, except for some terracotta garden vases and Tudor-style chimney pots, a large terracotta figure of Father Time with his Scythe, and a few jugs of the kind already mentioned, the Doulton exhibits were all of an industrial nature. They gained two First Class Medals – the forerunners of almost 400 exhibition honours to come during the next hundred years.

The Driving Force

By the time he was 30, Henry Doulton had become the driving force in the business and the most far-seeing member of his family in furthering its interests. He had a lively and questing mind and an intensely creative imagination. He had a great gift of concentrating on the immediate task in hand, leaving aside all other ideas until time would show whether or not it would be feasible and appropriate to put them into practice. He foresaw new industrial and social uses for ceramics which he proceeded to develop one by one. A striking observation of his was this: 'There are three steps in the Law of Nature that it is well to remember. If there is stagnation, decay soon follows and finally dissolution. Such a calamity can only be avoided by introducing new methods and manufactures as the old become obsolete.' 'You must,' he also said, 'be ready to put yourself out of business in order to stay in business.' The story of Henry Doulton's life is a fascinating one; here we are concerned only with those aspects relating to the development of the art wares. Readers who would like to know more about him are recommended to obtain the biography *Sir Henry Doulton*, by Edmund Gosse (Hutchinson, London, 1970).

Adaptation to changing circumstances; anticipation of coming trends and requirements; and, above all, the introduction of entirely new uses for pottery – these were three of the factors which contributed to Doulton's growing success and eventual rise to fame by the 1860s.

The many developments connected with the supply of acid-resisting stoneware to the expanding chemical and allied industries; the production of insulators for the new telegraph, telephone and electricity supply companies; the establishment at Lambeth in 1846 of the first factory in the world for the manufacture of salt-glaze vitrified stoneware pipes and conduits; the pioneering work in bathroom and sanitary equipment – these and many other achievements in the industrial ceramic field do not come within the scope of this book. They are mentioned, however, because in one respect they had a considerable bearing on our story, for they led to the financial success which later enabled Henry Doulton to become an enthusiastic and generous patron of the arts and to sustain the heavy expenditure involved in sponsoring and successfully establishing the revival of decorated salt-glaze stoneware in the 1870s.

By 1860, according to a contemporary report on the pottery industry, there were in Lambeth some 70 kilns each turning out on an average £50 worth of ware, compared with only 16 kilns in 1840 producing under £20 a kiln. The increase was largely due to the expansion of the Doulton Pottery.

14

It was said of Henry Doulton (Sir Henry as he then was) after his death in 1897 that 'he made a fortune out of drainpipes but spent it on art.' This was an exaggeration, for despite the large sums he certainly spent on the Lambeth Art Wares (the development of which will be described in the next two chapters) he still died an extremely wealthy man. It is true, however, that these wares became his altogether special love and that he could and did indulge his enthusiasm for them without having to worry unduly whether or not they were profitable. According to a writer in *The Graphic* on 11th December 1897, 'Sir Henry Doulton used to say that although he delighted in his art-work it had never paid its expenses. . . . Doulton Ware is one of the few sacrificial tributes of Commerce to Art.' Tinworth's studio alone is said to have involved losses up to £1,000 a year; it is doubtful if the works of the Barlows, Butler and the rest ever really paid their way, so far as book-keeping entries were concerned. As against this it must be remembered that the value of the prestige they brought to Doulton and to his industrial wares was incalculable.

On the retirement of John Watts in 1853 the style of the firm became Doulton & Co. The 'Doulton & Watts' trademark was continued for several years and is, therefore, not at all a reliable guide to dating salt-glaze items made before 1866. Fortunately this need not worry collectors unduly, for almost all the wares produced before that date were undecorated industrial and domestic wares.

John Doulton died in 1873 at the age of nearly 80. He had seen the small business he had helped found 58 years earlier grow into a large and thriving concern, with the promise of still greater things ahead. He also saw the first beginnings of what came to be known specifically as *the Doulton Wares* – that is to say, the salt-glaze art stoneware which, under the guidance and encouragement of his son, Henry, was to bring the name Doulton world-wide renown in an entirely different field of ceramic activity from those in which he himself had laboured for so many years.

'*Going to the Derby*', humoresque by George Tinworth

III

The Doulton Wares

AT the International Exhibition in London in 1862 one item on the Doulton Stand might have struck one as incongruous, for it was in complete contrast to the filters, pipes and other exhibits. It was a large salt-cellar, obviously an imitation or copy of *grès de Flandres*, as Rhenish stoneware was then generally called. It has been decorated with applied reliefs and an incised design into which cobalt blue had been rubbed as a colouring medium; during firing, however, most of the colour had fled.

Unsatisfactory as it was, this modest piece could be said to have been the first of the Doulton Wares, in the sense which that designation later acquired.

The manufacture of decorated salt-glaze stoneware had been a flourishing industry in Siegburg, Raeren, Hoehr, Grenzhausen and other parts of the Rhineland between the sixteenth and early eighteenth centuries. Large quantities of butter pots, pitchers, jugs, bottles and flagons, including the well-known 'Bellarmines,' were exported to England, France, Switzerland, the Netherlands and Scandinavia. In the mid-nineteenth century attempts were made in Germany to revive and extend the tradition, but the results were largely disappointing.

The revival in Lambeth of the art of salt-glaze art stoneware was in a style which, except for some early pieces, was almost completely original – owing little to either the *grès de Flandres* or to the Staffordshire salt-glaze of the eighteenth century. The genesis of the Doulton Wares was intimately connected with the rise of the Lambeth School of Art. This branch of the Central School of Design at Marlborough House had been founded in 1854 in a small schoolroom in Princes Road, Lambeth, by Canon Robert Gregory who later became Dean of St. Paul's. Canon Gregory, who had been associated with Lambeth since the time he was a junior curate at the Parish Church, felt the acute need for some centre of artistic and cultural activity and influence in his drab industrial parish. With the help of an enthusiastic and brilliant young art master, John Sparkes, who took charge of the school two years later, the Lambeth School of Art, despite early setbacks, gradually developed into what the *Art Journal* of July 1875 was to describe as 'one of the most successful in the kingdom'.

16

It seemed to Sparkes that, because of the long association of Lambeth with the attractively painted blue and white and polychrome delftwares, his school should try to do something to encourage the pursuit of beauty as well as utility in what had once again become a prosperous pottery-making centre, though of a completely different product. With this in mind, he approached Henry Doulton with the suggestion that school and pottery should co-operate to see what could be done to further this aim. The outcome of his first discussion with Doulton was a bitter disappointment to him. Doulton made it crystal-clear that his sole interest in ceramics at that time was the technical perfection of his industrial wares and that, recalling his abortive attempt many years earlier to revive Lambeth Delftware, he was not to be side-tracked into any dubious 'artistic' ventures.

In 1860, none the less, Henry Doulton did agree to make a small edition of presentation jugs, now among the rarest of Doulton commemorative pottery, to mark the laying of the foundation stone for a new building in Vauxhall Gardens to house the by then greatly enlarged and flourishing art school. This ceremony was the first public act of the young Prince of Wales, later to become King Edward VII. Doulton & Watts had in the past already made Nelson jugs, Reform Flasks and other commemorative items so that, in acceding to Sparkes' request, Henry Doulton felt he was not really departing from his previous stand.

His reluctance to co-operate more freely with Sparkes was not because of any lack of appreciation of the arts. On the contrary, despite the preoccupations of a constantly expanding business, he always found time for cultural pursuits, especially in the realms of poetry, music and oratory. He visited many of the famous art centres of Europe, encouraged young painters and sculptors by giving them commissions for their work, and took a leading part in South London in establishing and fostering literary, debating and musical societies. He had a sincere and thoroughly well-grounded admiration for the great English poets, Shakespeare, Milton and, above all, Wordsworth whom he could quote from memory at great length. He revered the memory of Wedgwood and Palissy among the European potters but had seemingly no desire whatever to try to emulate them. His ambitions, in so far as pottery-making was concerned, were focused on quite other – to him equally important even if more prosaic – ends.

It happened that an old friend and business associate, Edward Cresy, had become very interested in the early 1860s in *grès de Flandres*, of which he built up a small collection. Cresy was an architect and one of the founders of the Metropolitan Board of Works. He had had much to do with Henry Doulton in popularizing the use of stoneware pipes for sewerage and drainage; they belonged to the same clubs and visited one another's homes. It was Cresy who persuaded Doulton to allow one of his potters to attempt to make a reproduction of a sixteenth-century Rhenish salt-cellar and it was this that was shown in the 1862 Exhibition. Doulton thought it dull and unattractive; the blue colour, as he had predicted, had almost vanished in the firing. The salt-cellar seemed to him unworthy to take a place among the technically superior utilitarian wares on the Doulton Stand but to please his friend, he agreed to its being included.

Among the thousands of visitors to the exhibition was John Sparkes and, of them all, he was probably the only one to appreciate the possible importance of this 'poor thing', as Doulton had called it. The sight of it gave him renewed hope that his dream of the art school and the pottery working together and helping each other might yet be fulfilled. When he called on Doulton again in the early part of 1863 he was received much more cordially and Doulton even accepted an invitation to become one of the committee of management of the now thriving school. A year later the association was further strengthened by a commission which Doulton gave the school for a series of over life-size heads, modelled in terracotta and fired in the Doulton kilns, for the façade of an extension to the pottery. Designed by Sparkes and executed by one of his most promising pupils, Percival Ball, these portrayed Wedgwood, Böttger, Palissy and other famous potters, the head of each potter alternating with a female head, symbolizing the country in which he had worked. (Ball later gained high distinctions at the Royal Academy and became a well-known sculptor in Florence.)

George Tinworth

Another of Sparkes' young students, George Tinworth, had assisted Ball with the terracotta heads and had possibly modelled one or two of them himself. Tinworth was born in 1843, in Walworth, of humble parents, his father being a wheelwright in a small way of business. In any spare moments he could snatch from working at his father's trade, which he began to learn while still a boy, he tried surreptitiously to develop a spontaneous and untutored gift for carving little figures in wood and stone. These efforts were frowned upon by the father who, if he had had too much alcohol, was liable to destroy what he called 'such graven images' and to upbraid George for wasting his time. Mrs Tinworth, on the other hand, quietly encouraged the youth and to her he owed his phenomenal knowledge of the Bible which became an inexhaustible source of the romance, history, imagery and poetry for which his developing artistic nature craved.

When he was about 19, Tinworth heard of the Lambeth School of Art and was accepted there by Sparkes on the strength of a carved head which he brought along. His progress as a modeller and sculptor was rapid and successful especially considering the complete severance of his humdrum daily work from his evening studies. At the end of 1864 he was admitted to the Schools of the Royal Academy and two years later exhibited at the Academy a little group, based obviously on his own observations in

Walworth, entitled 'Peace and Wrath in Low Life'. This proved to be the first of many examples of Tinworth's work to be shown at the Academy exhibitions.

Sparkes was greatly concerned about Tinworth's future. His heart ached, he once said, to see one of his most talented students having to devote the greater part of his time to earning a living by making cart-wheels and repairing cabs and wheel barrows. It gave him real joy when, towards the end of 1866, he was able to persuade Tinworth to give up his uncongenial work altogether and to accept a somewhat nebulous opening as a pottery modeller which Henry Doulton had been induced to offer him.

Doulton at first hardly knew what use to make of Tinworth's gifts. Some of the potters looked rather askance at the newcomer who seemed to them an exceedingly odd combination of artist and puritan, eschewing alcohol, tobacco and the very mildest of expletives, and devoting his dinner-break to reading the Bible. He was assigned at first by the foreman a smoky corner of the factory near a kiln, and was given a square board on top of a barrel for a table and a smaller board on top of a terracotta chimney-pot for a seat. Had it not been for Sparkes' sustaining encouragement he would not have stayed long at the Lambeth Pottery.

Tinworth began his career with Doulton by modelling some outer cases, of rather Gothic design, for charcoal water filters. Then, at Sparkes' suggestion, Henry Doulton allowed him to model several large terracotta medallions, based on the designs of Greek and Sicilian coins and gems in the British Museum. One of these, showing Hercules wearing a lion's head as a hood, attracted the attention of John Ruskin, who later did much to encourage Tinworth and to bring his work to the notice of the art world. These medallions were reproduced from moulds in small quantities over a long period of years. Seven of them, depicting Arethusa, Hercules, Alexander the Great, Proserpina, Medusa and two unnamed females, were still being illustrated in a 1901 catalogue.

Now came another great step forward. Encouraged by Sparkes and Cresy, and with Henry Doulton's blessing, Tinworth began to design some well-shaped stoneware jugs, tankards and vases, using an off-white clay which had been originally prepared for making chemical vessels. He himself was not adept in throwing but fortunately there was a potter in the factory, who had been trained under Henry Doulton himself, who could interpret exactly his sketches and verbal indications. When they were firm enough to handle, Tinworth then decorated the pots, some with raised bosses and beaded runners (for which he always had a great partiality), others with incised concentric lines filled in with blue or brown colour or with the tops dipped in blue glaze. The brown withstood the high-temperature salt-glaze firing well but the blue gave trouble for a long time and often disappeared altogether.

Tinworth seldom did any preliminary sketches of his decorative schemes but worked directly on to the clay, incising the design rapidly with a piece of pointed box-wood.

Scroll and leaf decorations and free-trailing seaweed-like forms are characteristic of his work in this *genre* and often almost run riot over the piece. He frequently used relief bosses to pull the design together; these bosses and the little relief dots and florettes often found on his vases were later applied by assistants from small face-moulds and dotting-moulds.

Sparkes enthused over these first developments, as did Cresy, and between them they managed to inflame Doulton with some of their own excitement. And so it came about that at the Paris Exhibition of 1867 some 30 pots of the kind described above appeared amid the industrial ceramics on the Doulton stand. Most of these had been designed and decorated by Tinworth but a few were by W. Christian Symons, another talented student at the Lambeth School of Art. Some of Symons' incised designs were copied from drawings by Flaxman; a large unmarked mug in the Doulton Museum may be an example. So far as is known, Symons was not engaged at the Lambeth Pottery but, later on, did occasional freelance work for Doulton. A 'dry impasto' panel (see page 44) by him, which he designed for St. Luke's Church, Norwood, was shown in a reduced copy on the Doulton stand at the Chicago Exhibition of 1893.

The general effect of these first 'Doulton Wares' (as they came to be described) gave some promise of a new development in English art ceramics and they were generously commented on by some of the French art critics.

The International Exhibition of 1871

The modest success of the small display of decorated stoneware in Paris was for Henry Doulton the spur to greater efforts for the International Exhibition to be held at South Kensington in 1871. Immediately the programme was published, he held a meeting at the pottery and announced that with the help of Sparkes, who had promised to interest some of his students, he would try to build up a small art department. Tinworth, whom Doulton ever afterwards singled out as the one mainly responsible for the successful development of the ware in the early days, set to work on another series of vases and jugs, and Miss Hannah B. Barlow and her brother, Arthur, two other Lambeth Art School students, were commissioned to do some others. They both began to work permanently for Doulton later in 1871.

During seven months of intense activity and many disappointments two or three hundred pots were made and of these about 70 were eventually selected by Sparkes as being good enough to exhibit. Most of the pieces were decorated with incised designs in the style which Mr. Drury Fortnum, a well-known china collector and connoisseur, christened as 'Doulton *Sgraffito*'. The artist cut into the clay with a sharp tool which threw up a fine burr on either side to retain the colour – generally brown, black or blue

– afterwards inserted. Strictly speaking, the term '*sgraffito*' or '*sgraffiato*' applies to a decoration incised or scratched through a coating of white or coloured slip, revealing the contrasting colour of the underlying clay. Some of the Doulton Wares were indeed later decorated in this way but in most of the early examples the incisions were made directly into the uncoated clay. ('Slip' is the name given by potters to a semi-liquid clay mixture of a cream-like consistency, used for making, coating or decorating pottery.)

The Doulton exhibits were at first relegated to an inconspicuous position, in a badly lit corner of the porcelain and pottery section, but fortunately Mr. Soden Smith, a member of the Exhibition Committee, noticed them and, realizing that here was something out of the ordinary, had them moved to a central showcase alongside the work of Wedgwood, Minton, Spode and other famous potteries. From that moment the future of the Doulton Wares was assured.

The *Art Journal* of January 1872 commented interestingly on the Doulton exhibits in an article, from which the following are some extracts:

'The specimens exhibited in the pottery gallery were selected from a small number made specially to illustrate the application of ornament of simple character to ordinary stoneware. It was not then intended to carry this class of manufacture further, but the result of the idea was such that no active firm could, for many reasons, afford to overlook. These examples were received with so much satisfaction, and commented on so favourably by persons of known taste and learning in such matters that the firm, consulting their own interests and reputation, determined to continue the manufacture of these products, in so far as they should find favour with the public . . .

'The objects produced by Messrs. Doulton include many beautiful forms that have descended to us from antiquity . . . We are never weary of contemplating them and return to them with increasing admiration after considering the abuses of proportion and vulgarity of ornament induced by desire of novelty . . .

'The designs are various and are tastefully adapted to the style of the vessel or object; for instance, on the occasion of our visit to these works, the artist was working on a small vase of Pompeian shape, around which were drawn laurel leaves reaching to the neck of the vase; this was held in the left hand while the draughtsman operated on the surface by marking the outline with a stile, following the lines of a pencil sketch; thus, this process, although conducted with the utmost precision, is comparatively rapid . . . To the ornament thus engraved in outline, especially to the leafage, colour is applied with an ordinary water-colour brush, and so burnt in.'

Sir George Birdwood, K.C.I.E., who was actively concerned with British participation in almost every important international exhibition between 1871 and 1893, recalled in 1885:

'I was one of the first . . . to be attracted to the tall glass case in the art gallery in which (these) wares were shown and was charmed by the beauty of the forms they presented which, having just returned from Bombay, I perceived was due to their having been all thrown on the wheel, as in India . . . I at once purchased half the contents of the case and I have ever since been extremely proud to know that I was one of the first – if not the very first – to buy a portion of the first batch of "Doulton Ware" offered to the British public for sale.'

Within a few days all but six of the Doulton pots had been sold, several to foreign museums and well-known connoisseurs such as Professor Sir Arthur Church. The new salt-glaze wares, 'with their sober, quiet, harmonious and deep colours, so full of quality,' as one collector described them, were quite different from any produced previously either in Staffordshire or Germany. No attempt was made to imitate the dainty, fragile graces of china and porcelain. The stoneware pots were uncompromisingly robust and virile, expressing the personality of the makers and designers, and redolent of the earthly elements that gave them substance. In shape and texture they not only pleased the eye but demanded to be handled and fondled instead of being merely gazed at from afar.

The Doulton Wares impressed both critics and public and even attracted the attention of Queen Victoria who ordered some to be sent to Windsor. The Queen, accompanied by Princess Beatrice and Prince Leopold of the Belgians, watched one of the Doulton throwers shape a vase and a jug on the wheel. Throughout the remainder of her long reign, she continued to show great interest in the achievements of the Doulton designers and artists; her example was followed by the Prince of Wales, by several foreign rulers, and by members of the nobility and aristocracy. In introducing the Doulton Wares to a cultured and discerning public, the leading china dealers of the period, Howell and James of Regent Street, played an invaluable part. About 1875 they had built, and extensively advertised, a special gallery to display them to the best advantage.

Apart from the salt-glaze wares, a large fountain, an eagle figure and what became known as the 'Amazon Vase', all modelled in terracotta by George Tinworth, attracted much attention. The theme of the vase, encircled with bold relief figures of female warriors and other combatants, with projecting handles in the form of horses, is said to have been inspired by a sarcophagus found near Ephesus.

The Growth of the Doulton Wares

From these small beginnings there developed in an astonishingly short time a veritable renaissance of salt-glaze stoneware in England which was remarkable for three special reasons. The Doulton Wares created their own tradition, a very different one from that of the white salt-glaze stoneware school of eighteenth-century Staffordshire; they opened up an entirely new field of activity for women of some culture and artistic ability; and they were the precursor of a movement to foster the production of hand-made and hand-decorated pottery which spread all over the civilized world. Mr. Hugh Wakefield of the Victoria & Albert Museum in his book *Victorian Pottery* (Herbert Jenkins, 1962), commented on the last-mentioned aspect of the Doulton revival in these words: 'In many respects this ware can be said to mark the beginning in this country of the long process which was to lead to the development of modern studio pottery.' Léon Solon, the brilliant Minton artist and ceramic historian pointed out that 'little had been done to turn stoneware's merits into an artistic channel since the days of Dwight, until Henry Doulton created the new style by which the Lambeth ware has become known and admired by amateurs of ceramic art all the world over'.

Behind the scenes, despite the public success in 1871, there had been many frustrations and disappointments. The empirical knowledge of ceramic bodies and glazes built up over the years since 1815, in the production of various industrial ceramics, fell far short of what was required for the new Doulton Wares. Had it not been for the steadfast encouragement of Sparkes and Cresy and for a fortunate friendship recently formed with a distinguished scientist, Professor Sir Arthur Church, who probably knew more about the chemistry and physics of ceramics than any other man in England at that time, Henry Doulton might have been tempted to abandon the whole project. Kiln losses were often disastrous; sulphur and other products of combustion could play havoc with the colours; the blues often turned black in the firing and the browns and yellows muddy; sometimes the whole of a week's artistic endeavours by Tinworth and Arthur and Hannah Barlow came from the kilns stunted, cracked or discoloured, or marred beyond redemption by grit which had dropped from the roof or the walls of the kiln.

The decorated salt-glaze stoneware – unlike delftware, fine earthenware, bone china and porcelain – was not protected from the direct effect of the flames by being placed in fireproof saggers or boxes. On the contrary, the volatilized fumes circulated freely around them in the large 30-ft. diameter ovens. Moreover, because the decorated wares were fired in the same kilns as the industrial ceramics, which took several days to fire, the colours were sometimes scorched beyond recognition or else the salt vapours failed to reach them adequately. These problems were gradually overcome by modifying the design of the kilns, by disposing the decorated wares on slabs in the centre of the kiln where there was the least risk of damage from grit and scorch, and by evolving new bodies and glazes which would stand up to the severe conditions. Right up to 1956, however, when manufacture at Lambeth ceased, fireproof saggers were never used for the salt-glaze Doulton Wares; in fact some totally unexpected but delightful effects were very often achieved just because they were exposed to the action of the swirling heat and vapours. Because of slight over-firing, for instance, a blue pigment might become slightly burnt at the edges, thereby fading gradually into green or brown. The

23

absence of a mechanical, dead uniformity of colour, just because of the 'open firing' is one of the attractive features of the salt-glaze wares.

The wares shown at the 1872 International Exhibition at South Kensington scarcely fulfilled the promise of the previous year. During the interval between that exhibition and the one in Vienna in 1873 innumerable experiments were carried out, Henry Doulton unstintingly provided fresh funds for development, and a small laboratory was established with the help of Church. As a result, the exhibits at Vienna showed great strides in design, colour and techniques. Several of them were bought by Professor Archer, the then President of the Royal Scottish Society of Arts and Director of the Museum of Science and Art in Edinburgh, who in the following year wrote of the Doulton Wares in the *Art Journal*:

'The workers who produced the old German, Flemish and English stonewares were all possessed with an artistic feeling of the most genuine kind, which was modified and guided by the nature of the material; this they studied closely and never played tricks with it by trying to make it do more than it was capable of being made to do well; and it is particularly pleasing to see that the new school for this branch of the Ceramic Art in the works of Doulton & Watts is actuated by the same sentiment and feeling, and is guided by a higher artistic taste than ever before prevailed amongst English workers in this material.'

Archer made the significant and prophetic comment that, except for pairs of vases, each piece was unique, 'having in perspective the time when such wares may be sought for and gathered into collections and museums'. (It is interesting to note that he refers to Doulton & Watts, although the firm had become Doulton & Company almost 20 years before this.)

A striking feature of some of the pots exhibited at Vienna was their rich glistening cobalt-blue colouring, enhanced by the thin salt-glaze integrated coating. After many failures, the Lambeth Pottery had at last found a satisfactory method of preparing this capricious pigment and wedding it to a compatible stoneware 'body' in such a way that it would endure the ordeal by fire. This particular colour (usually distinguishable from the Sèvres, Coalport and other cobalt-blues on porcelain and bone china) became particularly associated with the Lambeth stoneware in the popular mind and was widely known as 'Doulton Blue'.

In Germany, under the auspices of the Museum for Art and Industries in Berlin, an attempt had also been made to revive interest in salt-glaze stoneware. The art had largely degenerated during the wars of the seventeenth century in Germany and many potters had emigrated. A collection was made of fine examples of Rhenish pots of earlier centuries in the hope of inspiring contemporary potters by letting them see and even borrow beautiful pieces that their predecessors had produced in this medium. Unfortunately, as John Sparkes told the Society of Arts in April 1874, 'the laudable experiment failed . . . The modern worker moulded the old pots in plaster of Paris,

Painting Doulton Ware (from 'The Queen', Oct. 1, 1887)

pressed clay into the mould, and thus made in some sense copies of the pieces, but that was all. The (German) potters of today showed no real perception of the principles which had guided the old work. It was the same with all the loan articles; but the astonishing thing is that these poor copies sold well'. Many in fact were sold by unscrupulous dealers as genuine old examples and were accepted as such not only by unsuspecting tourists but also by some museum authorities who might have been expected to know better.

Owing mainly to a different method of firing, whereby the volume of air reaching the inside of the kiln was reduced at a certain stage, the German stoneware was generally grey or bluish-grey in colour, whereas the Lambeth ware had a warmer brown or yellowish-brown hue – unless a special iron-free clay was used or the ordinary Dorset body was coated with a white or coloured slip before being decorated and fired. One important feature of the Lambeth stoneware as compared with the German was the much richer blue it could take once the early problems had been overcome.

Professor Sir Arthur Church, F.R.S., to whom reference has already been made, met Henry Doulton for the first time about 1868 and soon became a frequent caller at the Lambeth Pottery. His expert knowledge helped considerably in the development of the Doulton Wares. He encouraged Doulton and Sparkes in their efforts and even allowed an eighteenth-century Staffordshire white salt-glaze plate from his own collection to be refired in a Lambeth kiln to show that the blue colouring *could*, under suitable conditions, stand up to the same high-fire (1,250° C.) as that used for chemical ware and drainpipes.

Church, Doulton and Sparkes had many discussions on how to obtain a more extensive range of colours in a single firing. 'The gamut of colours,' Church recorded, 'was slowly augmented by taking hints from the *flambé* porcelains of China, and by adding oxide of tin, purple of Cassius and, I think, oxide of chromium to the palette of the stoneware potter. There was no servile copying here. Henry Doulton had no wish to suggest it and no occasion to permit it.'

Under Church's guidance, Doulton studied the problems of chemical reactions taking place during the process of salt-glazing and of the influence of sulphur and iron on the results. Church also initiated him into the study of thin sections of porcelain stoneware, delft and other fired bodies with the aid of the best microscope then available. From then onwards he was pleased to note that Henry Doulton 'was not content with outer appearances but wanted to penetrate beneath the surface of things'.

Great encouragement in these critical early days was also given to Doulton by Mr. George Wallis, Keeper of the South Kensington Museum, by Mr. Trenham Reeks, Curator of the Museum of Practical Geology which was then in Jermyn Street, London, and by unknown writers in *The Times*, *Observer*, *Daily News*, *Examiner*, *Spectator*, *Athenaeum* and other journals who realized the potential significance of the novel liaison between pottery and art school which was developing at Lambeth.

Further Expansion of the Art Studios

Wilton P. Rix, the first art director at the Lambeth Pottery, played a predominant role, from 1870 onwards, in the evolution of the Doulton Wares, for it was he who followed up Church's suggestions and, after hundreds of experiments, perfected the coloured pigments, glazes and slips which would withstand the severe firing conditions required to produce vitrified stoneware. He also developed some finer-textured and lighter-coloured bodies as well as a range of self-coloured bodies, which he termed 'silicon' (see page 45). In Church's opinion, Rix by 1880 had already far surpassed earlier German and English stoneware potters in the range of tints which he had perfected.

The first three designers in Rix's embryonic 'Art Department' were Tinworth and

Hannah Barlow and her brother, Arthur. (Further details of these and other artists yet to be mentioned will be found in Appendix I.) In 1872 they were joined by another student from the Lambeth School of Art, a deaf and practically dumb young man named Frank Butler. At first they had no studios of their own but worked in a corner of the general showroom behind a folding screen. Customers who came to buy the few specimens that were available for sale to the public in those early days – the majority had to be reserved for exhibitions and dealers – 'persistently intruded on the privacy of the artists by craning their necks over the screen'.

Tinworth was assisted for a short period by Edward and Walter Martin whom he had met at the Lambeth School of Art. Another Martin brother, Robert Wallace, became a life-long friend of Tinworth and, before he and his brothers set up their own pottery, is said to have designed some vases, terracotta garden ware and stoneware water filter cases for Doulton. Many years ago I was shown a Doulton-stamped vase which also bore what appeared to be Robert's initials; I have never since seen another.

Towards the end of 1873, Henry Doulton, who was becoming ever more enthralled by his new interest, invited Sparkes – who of course was only too willing to comply – to send a fresh batch of students to the pottery. The new group included Florence E. Barlow (sister of Hannah and Arthur), Eliza S. Banks, Louisa J. Davies, Eliza Simmance and H. Bone Nightingale. Some of these had already been doing occasional freelance designs for Doulton; they continued their art school studies in the evenings. It is possible that some other students, whose names are not now known to us, also did some freelance designing. This could account for a number of so far unidentified initials on early Doulton Wares. The question of accommodation for the artists and their assistants was temporarily solved in the following way, according to Sir Edmund Gosse:

'It was of no use to disperse them about, in holes and corners; they must have a definite home of their own. It happened that some twenty years earlier, the Doultons, in extending their property, had put up a block of workmen's dwellings with a view to helping their men to a better sort of habitation. In time, however, the project failed. The tenants had been found undesirable, and had been allowed to disperse, but these houses with their numerous little rooms had never been conveniently subjected to the general purposes of the works. They were practically unused, with their clusters of small, useless rooms, like a rabbit-warren. It immediately suggested itself to Henry Doulton that this was the place for his hive of decorators. Accordingly, these houses were put in perfect repair, made into comfortable little sets of studios and all prepared for the installation . . . Henry Doulton did not attempt to direct (the artists). With the most enthusiastic gaiety and curiosity, he would hasten from one to the other, to see what each was contriving to do, and his praise was unstinted in its welcome of each successful experiment.'

It was not long before Henry Doulton was writing to a friend: 'If all turns out as I fully expect, I shall build an art pottery on some ground I have on the Southern Embankment.'

Sparkes became Director of Art Studies at South Kensington in 1875 but he continued to supervise at the Lambeth School of Art and to co-operate as ardently as ever with Doulton and Rix.

During the next two decades, the number of designers, artists and assistants at the Lambeth Pottery grew into hundreds and their work was shown at one great exhibition after another, gaining a host of *Grands Prix*, gold and silver medals and other awards. The expansion may be gathered from the following figures: *1873*: 7 artists; *1874*: 30; *1875*: 44; *1878*: 113; *1880*: 171; *1881*: 231; *1885*: 250; *1886*: 290; *1890*: 345. Of the 250 at work in 1885, Sparkes stated that all but ten had been students at the Lambeth Art School.

In 1876, because of the growth of the Doulton Wares and the demand also for terracotta and faïence for architectural purposes, it became imperative to provide additional studios, workshops, kilns and showrooms. Two large buildings were erected on the Albert Embankment and a smaller one (which still survives today) on the corner of Lambeth High Street and Broad Street (now Black Prince Road). Built in a 'freely-treated modern Gothic style' of blue and red brick, enriched with terracotta mouldings, columns and foliation, interspersed with coloured stoneware panels and bosses, and hand-painted faïence tiles and tile panels, they were indisputably *sui generis* and attracted great attention. Everything except the red bricks had been made in the Lambeth Pottery or Doulton's blue brick factory in the Midlands. A German architectural journal described the buildings as being 'more like Italian Renaissance palaces than factories'. The 233-feet high campanile-like chimney of red brick blossoming into terracotta was a well-known London landmark for over 70 years. Its design, partly inspired by the tower of the Palazzo Vecchio in Florence, is said to have been suggested to Henry Doulton by John Ruskin, who took a great interest in all the developments at the Lambeth Pottery.

In 1877 an interest was acquired in the fine earthenware factory of Pinder, Bourne & Co. in Burslem, the 'mother-town' of the Staffordshire Potteries. Five years later this became Doulton & Company, Burslem, and in 1884 a new wing was added for the manufacture of bone china. Before the end of the century the Doulton Burslem products had become as famous as those of Lambeth and today they represent an important part of the Royal Doulton Group's total turnover.

Exhibition Successes

By the time of the Philadelphia Exhibition in 1876, at which Doulton received five First-Class Awards, immense progress had been made. Nearly 1,500 pieces of Doulton Ware were shown there, compared with some 70 in London in 1871. Gladstone, then leader of the Liberal Opposition in Parliament, and Spurgeon, the famous Baptist preacher, were among the 2,000 invited visitors who came to the new showrooms at Lambeth to view the vast collection before it was shipped to America. At times the queue stretched half-way from the showrooms to Vauxhall and it was estimated that in all some 10,000 people saw the display. Shortly afterwards Henry Doulton wrote to a friend:

'We kept the exhibition open for two days for Ruskin. He came at last, and expressed himself warmly as to the merit of the work. He declared that Tinworth is "an indubitable genius". Of course he was critical but he explained that this was because he was so immensely interested. *One thing that this exhibition has taught me is that in art-criticism there are many mansions, for equally good judges and authorities had very different opinions as to which were the most excellent specimens.* Happily, all seemed to agree that the work was good.'

In a speech which he made a few days later, when he received the Freedom of the Worshipful Company of Turners, Gladstone commented on what he had seen.

'These works,' he said, 'were delightful for the eye to behold. They were also highly satisfactory upon the distinct ground that the price of production seemed to be so moderate, but thirdly and most of all, they were delightful to me because they were true products of the soil. There was a high faculty of art, as it seemed to me, developed in the production of these wares, and that faculty of art had grown up in Lambeth.'

Gladstone mentioned one piece in particular by Frank Butler that had greatly impressed him.

'It was,' he said, 'a beautiful piece of work produced by a youth who from his birth was both deaf and dumb. What a cutting off of resources! What a stinting of the means of training and improvement! And then consider, notwithstanding this, how through an inborn resolution in the centre of his being, it was in the power of this lad to make himself a producer of works that could command admiration on the score of beauty.'

A writer in *The Times*, in a passage which fairly reflects the impact of the Doulton Wares on contemporary critics, commented as follows:

'Taken as a whole the collection affords a marvellous evidence of the growth of artistic taste and of technical skill in this country; and its vigour, vitality and originality are not only highly pleasing and encouraging in themselves but also in the contrast which they offer to the somewhat namby-pamby prettinesses, cast out of moulds by the gross and painted in strict adherence to a copy, which form the bulk of what is generally known as ornamental porcelain . . . Mr. Doulton is obviously engaged in a labour of love . . . Everything which is made in this department at Lambeth is unique . . . Everything is the direct result of the mind and the hand of the workman or of the artist.'

Several impressive works in terracotta by George Tinworth were also shown at Philadelphia, including a font and a large pulpit. Two other terracotta exhibits which attracted great attention were a reproduction, nearly 11-feet high, of the statue of 'Diana and the Stag' in the Louvre, and a colossal terracotta group symbolizing America – an exact reproduction of one of the marble groups in the Albert Memorial in Kensington Gardens, designed by the well-known Victorian sculptor, John Bell. Bell persuaded Henry Doulton to allow Tinworth to co-operate with him in the reproduction of this

'The Lute Player', by S. Nicholson Babb

group. 'Nobody before,' he said, 'has ever dared to produce terracotta on a really heroic scale.' It proved to be, as Bell predicted, 'one of the most remarkable feats any English potter has ever accomplished'. The colossal group was fired without a flaw or crack; each figure was moulded separately and the number of joins was considerably less than in the marble original.

The Doulton display as a whole aroused fantastic interest in the United States and marked the dawn of a close and rewarding relationship between Doulton and the

North American market which has continued to grow to this day. The *New York Times* wrote:

'The collection of Doulton pottery, about which the critics are wild, is indeed rarely beautiful . . . Doulton has produced out of the simplest elements a creation which may be considered the Etruscan vase of the nineteenth century. Weighed in unprejudiced and unbiased scales, the vases of Doulton will, in fact, be found to be much more valuable to the world than all the pottery that ever came from the cities of the Rasena.'

This is but one of many comments which could be quoted to evidence the extraordinary stir which the Doulton Wares made in Great Britain and overseas in the last quarter of the nineteenth century. Such praise, had it been accorded to a long-established, enterprise, would have been very satisfying; what is really remarkable is that Doulton with the help of the Lambeth School of Art, had been able to accomplish all this *within just over a single decade.*

The award of the *Grand Prix* at the Paris Exhibition of 1878, and the bestowal on Henry Doulton, by the President of France, of the personal dignity of Chevalier of the Legion of Honour, were further proofs that the Doulton Wares, which may be said to have begun in that obscure corner of the Lambeth Pottery where George Tinworth had been somewhat diffidently installed twelve years previously, had more than justified John Sparkes' hopes for a revival of English ceramic design which, generally speaking, had been at such a low ebb at the time of the Great Exhibition of 1851.

The first examples of *pâte-sur-pâte* painting on Doulton stoneware were shown at the Paris exhibition; experiments in this technique had already been going on for a year or two. It is a particularly delicate form of ceramic decoration in which several coats of semi-liquid pigmented clay (slip) are applied by a brush or pencil to build up a slightly raised design. Sparkes in 1880 described it as 'by far the most important introduction up to that time'. Among its first exponents were Eliza Banks, Florence E. Barlow and Eliza Simmance.

Pâte-sur-pâte painting on translucent bone china was introduced into England by the famous French ceramic artist, Marc Solon, who came from Sèvres in 1870 to the Minton factory in Stoke-on-Trent. It is a subtle form of relief decoration, applied by delicate brush-work, which builds up a series of different thicknesses of one coloured body upon another. The effect is entirely different from that of relief decoration applied from moulds as, for instance, in the Jasper and Silicon wares. To adapt this intricate process to stoneware fired only once at the high temperature of 1,250° Centigrade was an exceedingly difficult undertaking and success came only after a long series of experiments by Rix.

Sparkes described the process in the following way:

'To paint with the earthy pigment requires great decision of hand and accuracy; and as each

31

touch with the brush delivers the exact amount needed . . . it requires much practice and unerring certainty in planting the material on the ware firmly and in the right place.

'The peculiarity of the method has produced a certain conventionality in the decoration, and a crisp-leaved sort of parsley-fern pattern seems to be the one mostly adopted. Small patterns also are arranged somewhat as an Italian ornament, but with peculiar and fine details, and often with broader, larger treatment. Both are the product of different artists' tastes, and may serve to show how much is gained by allowing the individuality of the designer to have full swing.

'There are eighteen colours and tints which can now be used in these ways – giving a possibility of form and colour.

'The difficulties here overcome were great and numerous, but a very accurate adjustment of flux and pigment has been worked out, so that the opaque portions partly burn away and become semi-transparent, showing the ground through. One great trouble was to obtain adhesion between the body and the colour; this, however, is now successfully overcome. This (technique) is absolutely new in the (stoneware) potter's art, and is a true example of the *pâte-sur-pâte* principle, inasmuch as it is not enamel but body that is the basis of the decorating material.'

The method, as Sparkes indicated, led at first to a certain conventionality and sameness in treatment but Florence E. Barlow and other artists soon mastered it to such an extent that they were able to use it in a wide variety of other ways besides those mentioned by him.

Individual Artistic Expression

A sign of the recognition officially accorded to the comparatively new Doulton Wares occurred in September 1878. After many vicissitudes, the Egyptian obelisk from Heliopolis, popularly known as 'Cleopatra's Needle' (though it predates that 'Serpent of Old Nile' by some 1,500 years) was re-erected by the Office of Works by the Thames-side. Doulton stoneware cylinders were chosen to contain and preserve for posterity a variety of records inserted in the pedestal, and several specimens of decorated Doulton Ware were also included as examples of contemporary British ceramic art.

With the growing fame of the art-ware, Henry Doulton devoted more and more time to this now for him supremely fascinating branch of his ceramic interests. 'If a thing is worth doing at all, it is worth doing well' was one of his favourite sayings. There was also the spur of the appeal to his vanity, from which he was by no means immune, and which Church hinted at once when he said: 'It was a source of satisfaction to H. D. that some at least of his ware would be visible and admired (in future times) though most of it would of necessity be buried in the earth or hidden in the dingy recesses of chemical works and laboratories.'

From the outset of the stoneware revival Henry Doulton had insisted that each creative artist should be given the utmost scope for individual expression, unhampered by any dictation from himself, Rix or anyone else at the Lambeth Pottery. He deplored and abhorred with his whole sensitive nature any tendency – politically, educationally, socially or otherwise – 'to deal with people in masses, to make them all go in one direction'. 'Those who have imagination, let them cultivate it,' he advised, 'for imagination is a valuable gift. Others may not have imagination but they can develop patience, industry and fineness of touch.' Another pregnant remark of his which illustrates the attitude he adopted towards the creative designers and artists at Lambeth was this: '*To distinguish between eccentricity and genius may be difficult but it is surely better to bear with singularity than to crush originality.*'

It is largely because of this liberal and self-excluding spirit on the part of Henry Doulton that we have today such an incalculable number of unique examples of the wares which he sponsored. The very freedom accorded to the Lambeth artists not surprisingly led in some instances to over-exuberance, over-decoration, and ornament merely for ornament's sake. This applies particularly to some of the earlier pots which were over-influenced by Rhenish stoneware and which, as one critic wrote, 'show an astonishing taste, with elongated and distorted forms, decked out with bizarre excrescences and overloaded with decoration, carved and modelled'. But the remarkable thing about the Doulton revival is that despite the general tendencies of the period in which it took place, so many fine pots were produced which can still win our admiration and appreciation today. And even those which we may consider over-decorated for our taste have their own interest as examples of a mastery of a whole gamut of decorating techniques which is probably without parallel in the field of ceramics.

Each specimen of individually-designed and decorated Doulton Ware bore the monogram, initials or signature of the artist, and often also the initials or other identifying marks of the assistants responsible for subsidiary aspects of the decoration or infilling with colour.

By the 1880s the art of throwing was already in danger of becoming extinct in Staffordshire. The great majority of the Lambeth Wares, however, were thrown on the wheel, the shapes taking form and life in the hands of the potter, thereby attaining a quality – difficult to put into words but readily apparent to the connoisseur – which differentiates them from stereotyped products made in moulds. Even after it was decided in the 1880s to meet popular demand by introducing a range of vases and other pots to be reproduced in some quantity (seldom exceeding 2,000), these were invariably designed by the leading artists and with certain exceptions (such as hand-moulded or slip-cast figures and animal models or non-circular pots) each one was individually hand-thrown and hand-finished. This gave even the 'repetitive' or 'series' wares a distinctive quality compared with the general run of popular mass-produced pottery.

Some of the Lambeth designers, such as Hannah Barlow and George Tinworth, had themselves done some throwing on the wheel and all of them knew both the possibilities and the limitations of this age-old method of shaping. But the usual procedure was for the artist to design on paper, or to mould as miniature clay prototypes, the shapes he or she required; these were then produced by a thrower who had had long years of practice in the craft. The same shape, of course, could be used for a whole range of different decorations appropriate to its contours. Already by 1882 over 1,600 different shapes had been produced and many times that number of different decorations. There was the closest collaboration between artist-designer and thrower and, indeed, some of the more creatively-gifted throwers, such as Thomas Ellis, William Askew, John Coggins and Harry Peacock, sometimes submitted to the artists, and had accepted by them, suggestions for new shapes or modifications of old ones. The standard of throwing at the Doulton Potteries in both Lambeth and Burslem was unsurpassed by any other in the country and Doulton throwers and turners constantly won the highest awards, usually for their own original designs, in competitions organized by the Society of Arts, the Worshipful Company of Turners and other bodies. At the Turners exhibition of 1886, for instance, Doulton craftsmen-potters secured fourteen out of the eighteen awards made.

The majority of the thrown pots, after they had partly dried to the state which the potter calls 'green hard', were then shaved or turned in a lathe to give them the precise dimensions required. This turning process also gave them the fine smooth surface necessary for many of the decorative processes. Not all were turned, however; some were left in the somewhat roughly-textured surface condition in which they came from the wheel; there are delightful examples signed by Butler, Marshall, Simeon, Pope, Harradine and other artists which form a quite distinct type of Lambeth stoneware.

Methods of Decoration

Sparkes described the eight main methods of decoration in vogue in 1880 as follows:

'(1) By scratching in the pattern while the pot is still wet, soon after removal from the wheel. The line is scratched with a point which leaves a burr raised up on each side. This is useful and serves to limit the flow of any colour that is applied, either within the pattern or to the ground that surrounds it.

'(2) At a later period, when the vessel has left the wheel twenty-four hours, the clay is too hard for this treatment. In this condition a burr is not raised up but breaks off and leaves a broken blurred edge. When in this state the ware is scratched with an implement which scoops out a line and delivers the clay that is removed cleanly away from the cut. *It makes a clear, incised depression with no burr;* it too has its own beauty and subserves a use. Colour applied to the pattern, or to the ground, flows into it, fills it up, and is darkened by its deeper thickness at the place where a line crosses it.

34

'(3) Carving away a moulding or collar left on the ware by the thrower or turner is a fruitful source of excellent light-and-shade effects. This system is not only applicable to mouldings but also to flatter members, as for instance, where a row of leaves is first turned in a mass and then carved in detail.

'(4) Another method is by whitening the body. But the material used for this purpose is of too short a texture to allow of ornamentation by the first method of scratching the wet clay with a point; it is, however, tough enough to be decorated with patterns taken out with the incised line. In this body we observe a difference from the ordinary brown ware body. It has less affinity for the soda in the process of glazing with salt. It does not shine with the full glaze, as the brown ware does; it has what is called a "smear" by potters. On the other hand, it takes the blue colour much more kindly . . .

'(5) Another system becomes imperative when a vessel of ordinary dark brown clay is dipped into a slip or coating of white colour. It is obvious that a cut made on such a vessel would expose the brown colour of the body made visible by the removal of the white covering. This method offers many varieties of treatment, with or without the addition of colour to the cut surface.

'(6) Now, in addition to these various methods there is still another which was extensively used by the old Rhenish potters. It is by the application of dots, discs, flowers, borders etc., by a process of sealing on a form of clay – usually of a different colour from the ground – from a mould . . .

'(7) Similar in principle is the method of cutting in patterns from a mould. Such lines of sharp environment serve to set bounds to the little rivulets of flowing colours, when fused and fluid by the intense heat of the kiln; they seem to limit the flow which, if not thus checked, would run down the surface of the vessel.

'(8) Again, it is quite possible to stamp on a disc or series of dots with such a material that it will burn away with the fierce heat, and leave a small circular inlay of beautiful crystallized brown-grey substance, flush with the surface of the ware. This opens up a new field of decoration not yet developed.'

Two or more of the above techniques could, of course, be combined. The use of coloured slips, in addition to the white mentioned under heading (5) was also introduced. Another method just being developed in 1880 was the use of self-coloured bodies, such as for the Silicon Wares (see page 45). *Pâte-sur-pâte* painting has already been described on page 31. Then again there was the method, particularly well exemplified by Butler and Marshall, which Sparkes described as follows:

'Another very beautiful source of decoration is due to the manipulation of the clay, while still plastic in its recently thrown form. Saucers, dishes and plates, with their edges, may be completely turned over as to their margins; others have their rims only partially turned, so as to form a shell-like cavity and handle; others are completely fluted and frilled at their edges.

'This principle is a very beautiful one, and one that lends itself to the taste of the designer in a variety of ways, for not only can the edges of the ware be thus treated but also the vessel itself . . . This goes to the extent of shaping the object afresh; for example, out of a circular bowl, as thrown on the wheel, a square one or a polygonal one or an elliptical one – or a shape combining all these forms – may be produced. On these shapes again, we may have depressed grooves in rings, or in upright series, or in spiral windings, and these crossed by others, giving a most pleasant variety of surface and of light and shade. No two can possibly be alike, and all are the immediate product of the artist's mind.

'A beautiful method of decorating some of these squeezed or hand-moulded pots is by inlaying a ribbon of pierced work over the depression, so that the appearance is given of a perforated band of ornament in front of a rich background of shadow. There are many instances of this perforation in Eastern porcelain and in our own English manufactures, but none in stoneware, so far as I know. The effect is always interesting and rich, and has a certain mystery of light and shadow but the difficulties in applying it to stoneware were very great, and even now the absolute certainty of success is not so assured as to lead us to hope it will be a very general method of decoration.'

Examples of this technique are comparatively rare and are much sought after by collectors. The designs and models for some of these perforated bands of ornament were made by Arthur Barlow during the last months of his life, after he was too ill to handle heavy pots or to leave his room at home (see page 90).

The above descriptions give some idea of the variety of decorating techniques which had been evolved at the Lambeth Pottery in the space of ten or twelve years, starting from the simplest beginnings. But even these do not exhaust the methods which had been evolved by one or other artist. Here are some others, as described by Sparkes:

'In a certain relationship with the application of perforated discs is a similar use of *solid* discs on which may be modelled any appropriate pattern – such as a head or an ornament. This may be a simple relief or it may be an *appliqué* in coloured clays. It might be called "medallion ware", as up to now the idea of using it for the reception of models after antique heads has been the prevalent one.

'The system of moulding a modelled piece of ware, which is the commonly used one in all potteries with which I am acquainted, is discouraged at Lambeth as much as possible, as tending to mere mechanical reproduction, and as leading to a lifeless kind of repetition. In the case, however, of some kinds of bottles of octagonal shape, not possible to press by hand, it is used, but in this case the ornament is added by hand or carved on the moulded form by hand. (Another method) is where the designer models on the piece that the thrower makes . . . it is hardly necessary to do more than dwell for a moment on the demand this treatment makes for originality, and we may say distinctly that no two cases can be designed on the same lines . . . It is a stimulus to individuality and comes as a change from the etching or cutting-in of a pattern in which some ladies, notably Miss Hannah Barlow, excel. She occasionally feels that she can best express her intentions by a modelled figure in low relief (on a pot) and she is, of course, quite free to do this or adopt any other method she chooses.'

It has been thought worth while to give these descriptions in John Sparkes' own words rather than to paraphrase them. With their slightly Victorian colouring, they take us right back into that exciting period where one new development came fast on the heels of another. Here in Lambeth in the 1870s and early 1880s, a host of techniques – several of them entirely new to stoneware – were evolved and quickly put into successful practice. It was only possible because profitability was not the primary aim as it had to be in other potteries whose financial success depended on bulk production of more or less stereotyped designs. There had to be bulk production at the Lambeth Pottery also, if it was to pay its way, but it was of drainpipes, conduits, insulators, crucibles, chemical storage jars and the like. The profit on them made the venture of the Doulton Wares possible.

'The Yawn', by M. V. Marshall

After the decorating stage, the wares had to undergo the ordeal by fire. Sparkes has left us a picturesque description of this also:

'The skill of the thrower, the handiness of the turner, the gifts of the artist, the knowledge and science of the colourist, are all in vain if the intelligence which keeps guard over the kilns, where all these works of beauty are tried in the fire, is unequal to the task of urging the heat to the proper pitch of intensity, of staying his hand when this has been attained, of knowing by instinct, as it appears to me, when the critical instant has arrived when the ware will take the salt. The gift of thus piercing the secrets of the fiery furnace, whence emerge either things of beauty that live forever, or amorphous masses of "wasters", belongs eminently to William Speer. He spares himself no sacrifice of comfort or health to give up from the kilns the objects of loveliness that have been entrusted to his care to pass through the most critical period of their existence in the white heat of the furnace'.

This William Speer's father had worked for John Doulton as burner and his descendants continued to supervise the firing of the Doulton Wares right up to 1956 when the Lambeth Pottery closed for ever.

Changing Styles

Each artist had his or her own distinctive style but some such as Eliza Simmance, Butler, Marshall, Broad and Rowe had a wider range than others and were more open to experiment and new artistic trends.

The following are some very broad characteristics of the salt-glaze stoneware produced during the periods 1867–1875, 1876–1890 and 1891–1914. It must be remembered, however, that earlier techniques were often carried over into later periods and techniques which later became general were sometimes anticipated by individual artists. (Some productions, of course, such as the hunting jugs and other relief-figured wares, the 'black leather' and 'copper' wares, and the 'natural foliage' ware do not fall into any of the following categories.)

1867–1875: cream-coloured, light buff, brown and greyish-blue bodies. Simple bands and runners; scratched, incised and carved decoration; raised or modelled ornament; dotted and beaded outlines. Much use of bosses and rosettes to hold designs together. Quiet colour schemes using mostly simple browns, blues and occasional greens. The rich cobalt blue which became popularly known as 'Doulton blue' was evolved in 1873.

1876–1890: a wider range of light, dark and self-coloured bodies; richer colourings including pink, yellow and purple and a much wider and subtler range of blues, greens and red-browns. Greater variety of decorative treatments with use of modelling, carving, perforating and raised line techniques, also dotted, stippled and otherwise textured backgrounds; *pâte-sur-pâte* painting, etching, gesso and gilding. From 1884 a white body was widely used, as well as lighter coloured slip backgrounds and brighter coloured glazes and pigments.

1891–1914: a period, generally speaking, of more formal and restrained designs with indications of New Art influence at the turn of the century. An increasing use of mixed colours giving marbled and mottled effects. A new technique of freely-drawn brush-line painting with flat pigments introduced in 1897, less use being made of incised lines to contain the colours. Ivory, white, green and blue colour schemes popular, also designs with Moresque and Celtic types of scrolling. From 1900 onwards extensive use, especially on the series wares, of tube-tool decoration to contain coloured pigments (a process similar to iced decoration on cakes). After about 1909 a limited production of metallic lustred and *flambé* stonewares.

IV

Other Lambeth Wares

As soon as the decorated stoneware had been successfully established, Henry Doulton was ready to consider suggestions from Sparkes, Rix and Church for the launching of other art ceramics. Although it means departing from the chronological order which our story has hitherto more or less followed, it will be more convenient to describe the most important of these other Lambeth Wares in a separate chapter. In the broadest sense of the word they can, of course, all be described as 'Doulton Wares' but the tendency is to reserve that term for the decorated salt-glaze stoneware.

LAMBETH FAÏENCE

About 1872 the first experiments were made in an attempt to revive some of the features of painted maiolica in producing a type of earthenware to which the name 'Lambeth Faïence' was given. In one sense this was a misnomer for – unlike tin-glazed maiolica and early French faïence – the Lambeth product was decorated on a biscuit (i.e., once fired) body, prior to glazing and further firing or firings, whereas they had been painted on an opaque unfired lead glaze containing tin oxide which gave the ware a superficial whiteness. The terms *'faïence fine'* and *'faïence anglaise'* were, however, in use in France to describe fine under-glaze decorated earthenwares of the type produced in Staffordshire by Wedgwood, Spode, Minton and other makers, so that Sparkes' choice of the description 'Lambeth Faïence' was not altogether unjustifiable, although criticized by some writers on ceramics.

Sparkes envisaged in this new Lambeth ware, which was launched in 1873, yet another field of activity for his ever-growing band of art school students. For the Lambeth Faïence the unglazed biscuited shapes required by the artists were at first obtained from Pinder, Bourne & Company of Nile Street, Burslem, and then, after this firm had been taken over in 1877, from Doulton & Company, Burslem. This explains why, on some examples of Lambeth Faïence, a Pinder Bourne or Doulton Burslem mark is found in addition to the Lambeth one.

40

By about 1879, if not earlier, Rix had evolved a suitable earthenware body from a mixture consisting mainly of plastic Dorsetshire clay, Cornish china clay (kaolin), ground Cornish stone and ground flints. Generally speaking, the colour of the fired Lambeth body was softer and warmer in tone than that of the Staffordshire. Tiles, however, were still bought in, unglazed, from Minton and Maw and Co. and it would seem that even after an earthenware body was being made at Lambeth, some biscuited shapes, especially for large items such as wall plaques, were at times obtained from Burslem.

On the biscuit ware the designs were painted with vitrifiable colours. This called for sure and unhesitating brush-work because of the porous nature of the biscuit ware. The colours themselves were compounded mainly from metallic oxides and in applying them an oil medium was generally used. Several of the colours underwent very great changes in the firing so that the artist needed considerable experience and imagination to visualize the final result of his or her painting. After this came a second firing, known as the 'hardening-on' firing in order to fix the colours.

The decorated piece was then glazed by dipping it into the fluid mixture of which the glaze was composed, and this was followed by a third firing in a muffle kiln which, as the name suggests, protected the ware against the direct action of the fire. Constant care had to be exercised to ensure that the colours and glaze would expand and contract compatibly to avoid the development of fine hair-like cracks ('crazing') and other defects. A lead glaze with a rich brownish-yellow hue was used up to 1900; after this, a leadless glaze, noticeably colder and whiter took its place.

Lambeth Faïence decorated with over-glaze enamel colours – the range of which was wider than that of the underglaze pigments – or with gold required yet another firing (or even two more firings) in special 'enamel ovens', which were fired at a lower temperature than the usual kilns. Until ovens of this type were installed at Lambeth, about the turn of the century, such items were sent for firing to a Mr. Battam of Johnson's Court, Fleet Street, or to the glassworks then in Soho Square.

The Lambeth Faïence range included vases, plaques, pilgrim bottles, tazzas, tiles, tile panels and others items, the majority painted underglaze with realistic or slightly conventionalized flowers and foliage, landscapes, portraits, geometrical and other conventional ornamentation. Other forms of decoration included modelling, *cloisonné* and gilding treatments.

In training the artists and assistants who were to specialize in Lambeth Faïence, Sparkes began with a study of the principles which had guided the earthenware potters of Persia, Turkey, Japan, China and Italy. These influences are reflected in some of the wares; many, however, are free from any obvious traces of foreign inspiration, owing their appeal, as a writer in the *Academy* of January 1879 put it, 'to no imitation or adaptation of previous work'. What Sparkes was aiming at, he expressed as follows:

'The perfect surface of porcelain, its semi-vitreous fracture and imperviousness, and its white colour, gave it at once the place it so properly holds in universal esteem for household uses. The ordinary white earthenware of Staffordshire and other potteries is an imitation of porcelain, and is so good for common everyday use, and so cheap, that it must be long before it meets with a rival in the markets of the world. But the perfection of the material did not lead to any very high-class decoration; china painting in Europe almost entirely went wrong, inasmuch as artists were attracted by the perfect surface to paint miniatures on it, and on no china that I am acquainted with has an attempt been made to rival the large and decorative treatments that the material received in China, Japan and Persia.

'The small and exquisitely-finished productions of the European porcelain factories were eminently unsuitable for the decoration of the walls of our rooms. Hence the demand for a better, larger, more comprehensive treatment of *plaques* and panels, which should be of harmonious colour, not too elaborated, simply and more artistically treated than could be expected from workshops or potteries where trade limitations of ideas prevailed. Again, there was a demand for colour, which the glaring white ground of earthenware bodies (much used for tiles) did not satisfy. Hence the introduction of our present faïence bodies and their popularity; the colour of natural clay, not whitened, forms an agreeable base of operations for the painter; the range of colours is sufficiently extensive to do anything with, and, by the union of underglaze colours with enamel or over-glaze treatment, any colours whatever can be used.'

The Lambeth Faïence was well received by the public. The *Court Journal* of May 1876 reported, moreover, that 'these productions have been considered worthy of special inspection by Her Majesty'. Queen Victoria drew the attention of the Empress of Germany to the Lambeth Faïence and both purchased specimens.

At the Philadelphia Exhibition in 1876 numerous examples of the new Lambeth product were shown. A large tile panel painted by Catherine Sparkes, John Sparkes' wife, aroused immense interest. Consisting of 252 tiles, six inches square, it depicted the Pilgrim Fathers standing in strong relief against an evening sky, bidding farewell to their friends and relatives in England. 'Her large and effective drawing and fine sense of colour,' wrote John Forbes-Robertson, 'make every piece of Lambeth faïence which comes from her hand an art-object worthy the cabinet of the most fastidious connoisseur.' An important specialized market was later developed for faïence tiles and panels for the interior decoration of churches, theatres, restaurants, cafés, banks, hospitals, stores and large mansions. They were also used extensively for fireplaces.

A writer in *Design and Work* in July 1876 expressed the view that the Lambeth Faïence, generally speaking, held a balance 'between the irregularity of the Japanese types of ornament and the too mechanical and exact symmetry which distinguished a good deal of modern work of this kind, especially the French'.

At the Paris Exhibition of 1878, in addition to numerous vases and plaques, some beautifully painted tile panels by Walter Gandy were shown, depicting scenes from Shakespeare's *Tempest*, also some paintings of birds on tiles, specially done for Doulton by a distinguished French artist, Georges Léonce. Castellani, the famous jeweller, said of these exhibits: 'Doulton is on the true path. When I think what English pottery in general was in 1851, I am astonished at his show.'

An artist named John Bennett, who had been trained in ceramic painting in Staffordshire, helped Sparkes and Rix to launch the new faïence department at the Lambeth Pottery. Unfortunately his fellow-artists found him 'imperious and touchy' and he did not remain many years. Henry Doulton, while acknowledging his help, said of him: 'You can buy even gold too dear.' Bennett later went to America where Tiffanys of New York sold some of his pots.

Lambeth Faïence Vase, by J. H. McLennan

Generally speaking the harmony of colour of Lambeth Faïence was in advance of the painting, except in the work of the leading artists, such as Esther Lewis, Mary Capes, Florence Lewis, John Eyre, Linnie Watt, John McLennan and James Cruickshank. The work of some less gifted artists did not attain the artistic level of the stonewares, lacking also their vitality, originality and historical interest; the drawing on some is even rather wooden.

Florence Lewis painted what is believed to have been the largest faïence vase ever made at the Lambeth Pottery. It was over six feet in height and two and a half feet in diameter; it was exhibited at the Chicago Exhibition of 1893.

The output of Lambeth Faïence gradually dwindled after about 1910 and was discontinued during the early part of World War I. It was not revived except for occasional special orders for tiles and tile panels.

43

IMPASTO WARE

A new and original Doulton development of the late 1870s was the 'Impasto Ware'. This had a similar type of body to the Lambeth Faïence but the method of decoration was very different. The first specimens were drawn from the kiln on the morning of a visit to the Lambeth Pottery by Princess Alexandra, wife of the then Prince of Wales, on 22nd February 1879. Impasto Ware is rarer than either Lambeth Faïence or salt-glaze Doulton Ware and, at its best, perhaps represents one of the most artistic and unusual products of the Lambeth Pottery.

It was described by Sparkes, who in co-operation with Rix originated it, as follows:

'The ware that is, on the whole, most capable of receiving artistic impressions is that which is called *impasto* ware. It is so named from the special treatment it receives at the hands of the artist who decorates it. *The colour is applied to the raw clay.* It is further so thickened by the vehicle by which it is incorporated that *it models the form as well as paints it.* The small amount of relief that is thus given to the ornament, coloured as it is, adds to the apparent reality of the thing depicted, and is no doubt an additional power in the hands of the artist; it is also a snare, inasmuch as the treatment involves a knowledge of modelling – to some extent at least. And, without some acquaintance with practice of light and shade, it is quite possible to produce a design devoid of effect – too evenly distributed all over the piece. But with taste and judicious use of the raised parts, this new material may add very considerably to the pottery painter's means of producing good work.

'The command over the texture as well as the tint of the background is also a point to be noted, as the application of paint, which has a considerable opacity of substance, gives a quality that is never reached by half transparent films.

'The whole system is, to a certain extent, analogous to painting with opaque colour in oil, while the average pottery underglaze painting is very like water-colour painting, where the reflection from the ground passes through the coloured tints and films of pigment that cover it. *Impasto* painting, therefore, has all the advantages that opaque *tempera* or oil painting possesses, inasmuch as it reflects light from its surface. The opportunity this raised or *impasto* work gives for *a second colouring, with underglaze colours*, is to be remarked as rendering the work of art capable of taking a refinement of finish in detail on the surface prepared for it in relief.'

The Impasto colours, incorporated in fairly thick slip, included rich red browns, soft light yellows, greyish greens and beautiful graduations of blue. By the judicious use of two harmonious pigments of different fusibility unusual effects were obtained. The ware was fired with scarcely any gloss.

Impasto Ware was made mostly between 1879 and 1906 but production continued on a very limited scale until 1914.

VITREOUS FRESCO

Vitreous Fresco was virtually an adaptation of the Impasto Ware technique, on a terracotta type of body, for use in the form of slabs and tiles for mural decoration. It was unglazed but embodied a fine range of strong-toned colours permanently fired into the body and produced an overall effect not unlike fresco painting on plaster – hence its name. Among early examples of Vitreous Fresco were some panels by John Eyre shown at the Indian and Colonial Exhibition in South Kensington in 1886; these depicted an Indian potter, a British blacksmith, an Australian farmer and a gold-miner. At the Paris Exhibition of 1900 were displayed some very impressive panels, designed by Arthur Pearce and executed by J. McLennan, depicting scenes from Malory's *Quest of the Holy Grail*.

Vitreous Fresco was made between about 1885 and 1914.

SILICON WARE

Silicon Ware was made from a smooth, intensely hard, high-fired stoneware body, somewhat like dry jasper ware in appearance but different in composition and fired at a higher temperature and, accordingly, stronger. One variety was not subjected to the salt-glaze of the Doulton Ware kilns and had no gloss at all; another was fired with the Doulton Ware but because of the composition of the body, which contained little or no flint, it took on at most a barely perceptible, dull eggshell gloss known to potters as a 'smear'. Sometimes a slight mottled gloss was produced, giving almost an alabaster effect; this was achieved by placing the pots in those parts of a salt-glaze kiln most exposed to the fire.

The basic silicon ware body, if used in its natural state, was a light terracotta in colour but coloured stains could be infused right *through the whole mass* to develop, during firing, a wide range of self-coloured bodies including bronze, green, brown, black, blue, olive, chocolate and grey in different tones, as well as near-white. These bodies were unabsorbent even though unglazed.

Silicon ware was decorated in a variety of ways – carved, incised, stippled, or perforated ornament; applied relief mouldings; *pâte-sur-pâte* painting; gilding; and combinations of two or more of these methods. On some pieces touches of copper lustre are also found. Two varieties were known as 'Silicon Mosaic' and 'Gilt Silicon Mosaic' because of their overall effect. *Appliqué* florettes and other motifs in different coloured clays were extensively used. Another style of decoration was to raise the edges of the pots by laying on strips of clay while sufficiently soft to ensure firm adhesion; these borders could then be scalloped, indented or modelled upon to produce a variety of effects. Considerable use was also made of the relief application of one coloured clay upon another, a combination of blue and white on a light brown or buff body being particularly popular. Exceptionally great care had to be taken in processing the Silicon Ware because, being unglazed or almost so, it would show up the slightest scratch or defect produced before it was fired.

Lambeth Faïence Vase, by Mary Denley

Silicon Ware was introduced to the public in 1880, after a year or two of intensive research, and production continued on a fair scale until 1914; thereafter it became very spasmodic. A range of flower-pots, fern pots, jugs, tobacco jars and cruet sets, with Egyptian motifs, appeared in the 1920s. Again, between about 1928 and 1932 a series of vases and bulb-bowls with tube-tool decoration was introduced.

'COPPER' AND 'BLACK LEATHER' WARE

Jugs, candlesticks and other items, painted with a copper lustre on a hard silicon stoneware body, were made at Lambeth between about 1887 and 1914. Fired first at 1,250° Centigrade and then, after the lustre had been applied, refired at 850°, 'Copper Ware' proved very popular even though art purists might deplore the fact that rivets, seams, dents and even verdigris were cleverly simulated.

The 'Black Leather Ware', consisting chiefly of jugs, mugs and tankards, was made over a similar period from a dark matt self-coloured silicon stoneware body with an almost black fired finish. Seams and stitching resembling those on Cromwellian 'black-jacks' were imitated and a netted surface was sometimes obtained by pressing real leather into the clay while it was still soft. A combination of simulated leather and copper was also produced, and some of the items bear dates (such as 1623, 1646 and 1658), coats-of-arms and mottoes. The 'Black Leather Ware' was revived between about 1924 and 1926 but the surface was then more glossy and not nearly so effective. Many items were made specially for John Mortlock, china dealers of Oxford Street and bear their name as well as the Doulton mark.

Collectors will also come across other simulated items in silicon stoneware, such as imitation cricket balls and pseudo-iron weights in the form of covered boxes with ring handles.

NATURAL FOLIAGE WARE

Repoussé Ware was the name originally given to a range of salt-glaze stoneware vases, bulb-bowls and flower-pots first produced late in 1883 and announced in the *Gardener's Chronicle* of 26 January, 1884. The description 'Natural Foliage Ware' was later commonly used. Three-handled loving cups, mugs, tankards, pin-trays, cruet sets, teapots and other items were added to the range later in the century.

Real leaves were pressed into the still soft clay and then carefully removed, leaving a faithful impression of even the smallest digitations and veins. The ware was then delicately painted, with the leaves depicted in very realistic autumn tints. It is often singularly attractive with its quiet russet, green and blue colourings.

Natural Foliage Ware was very popular and produced on a fairly large scale up to 1914, then on a much diminished scale until the 1950s (except during World Wars I and II). In a certain sense it could be said that every piece is unique. For some strange reason – possibly the greater risks of damage to bulb-bowls and the like – there do not seem to be nearly as many specimens about as one would expect.

PERSIAN WARE

Between about 1884 and 1912, doubtless influenced by William de Morgan's work, some beautiful tiles and tile panels were produced for wall decoration and fireplace surrounds, in a style based on early Near Eastern designs and colours, notably turquoise blue, green and orange. They were made from a coarse body with a white slip coating on which the painting was done before glazing and firing. (See also page 65.)

MAJOLICA WARE

The so-called 'majolica' glazes, especially green, introduced by the French potter, Léon Arnoux, at Minton's just before the 1851 Great Exhibition, remained popular throughout the Victorian era and even into the Edwardian, for jardinières, outdoor fountains, garden tables and other garden-ware. They bore little or no relationship, except sometimes superficially, to true maiolica.

Doulton's Lambeth Pottery produced, between about 1885 and 1910, a variety of majolica, described as 'modelled glazed faïence', which was mostly moulded in rough clay of great strength and coated with fine cream-coloured slip on which the rather vivid colours showed up with great purity. The modelled ornament was generally in European or Eastern free rococo style. Individual designs were also made to special order.

The ware was either painted with coloured glazes on the still plastic clay or, for repetitive architectural and similar work, was pressed in moulds, biscuit fired, painted and refired. Some very elaborate and brightly coloured so-called 'Indian Style' vases, pedestals and tables were made in Lambeth Majolica.

CHINÉ WARE

The descriptions 'Chiné' and 'Chiné-Gilt' are given to unusual types of decoration, with and without gilding, evolved in the 1880s by John Slater (the then manager of Doulton's Burslem Pottery), and much used, especially on a stoneware body, between 1885 and 1915, and thereafter spasmodically from 1919 up to 1939. The process was patented jointly by Doulton and Slater.

The distinctive feature of these wares is a textured netted background surface obtained by pressing moistened pieces of old point lace, linen and other fabrics into the soft clay soon after the pots had come from the wheel. The superimposed decoration (under-glaze or on-glaze or both) was sometimes very elaborate, involving several assistants, but the method is seen at its most effective in small areas or panels on artist-signed pieces.

Moulded pieces of clay in the form of medallions, lattice-work, scrolls and borders, foliage and flowers, afterwards finished in various colours, were often applied. In some of the popular but more flamboyant series ware the lace-textured effect covered almost the whole surface which was then elaborately finished, after a second firing, with on-glaze enamel colours and gilding.

The process was also applied, but to a lesser extent, to Lambeth Faïence, with which softer effects could be obtained as the enamels sank partly into the glaze. A wider range of colours was available and shaded backgrounds are often found. The process, however, was long, difficult and expensive, involving at least four separate firings, and seems to have been discontinued by 1909.

MARQUETERIE WARE

Probably now the rarest of all the Lambeth Wares, 'Marqueterie' was invented about 1886 and patented the following year in the joint names of Doulton and Rix. The term was borrowed from the method of inlay with woods of different colours used in cabinet-making.

The forms were modelled in delicate and often unusual shapes, a mosaic of patterned geometrical designs or marbled effects being obtained by cutting or compressing thin slices of coloured clay, from previously prepared blocks, in various intersecting and interblending patterns. The difficulty of combining clays of different colours seemed at first insuperable, especially as some of these tended to shrink at different rates, but it was eventually overcome.

Marqueterie Ware was produced in limited quantities up to about 1906, but although it enjoyed a great *succès d'estime* it had then to be discontinued because of the extremely heavy costs of production which could not be covered in the prices the public was prepared to pay. It is now much sought after by collectors for it is a unique *genre* of ceramics. It was particularly admired by Professor Sir Arthur Church from whose account of it in the *Portfolio* for April 1890 are taken the following extracts describing in more detail the complicated processes involved:

'In Staffordshire towards the close of the seventeenth century, and at Fulham somewhere about the same date, a curious kind of pottery known to ceramic collectors as "agate" or "onyx" ware was occasionally made. Its peculiarity consisted in this, that the coloured markings shown on the outside of the pieces were *continued right through their substance, and were not a mere surface decoration* . . .

'After a long interval the making of agate-ware has been revived at Lambeth. It has been more than revived, for results undreamt of by the early potters have been attained by means of improvements in the material, the appliances and the methods employed. Some of the clays are coloured artificially, so securing a great variety of beautiful hues. Complex geometrical or tessellated patterns are a characteristic feature of the new agate or "marqueterie" ware, as it is called. These regular figures are associated, in some of the pieces, with perfectly plain clays, or with regularly striped bands, or with picturesquely variegated patches. The introduction of gilding is also an entirely novel feature, due partly perhaps to a popular demand but capable of legitimate application under certain restrictions. Gold seems to me to look most satisfactory when employed in fine lines and thoroughly conventionalized ornament upon such parts of a piece as are entirely free from any pattern in the coloured clays of the ware . . .

'A mass of plastic clay is cut into leaves or slices of varying thicknesses. A number of such leaves being prepared from plastic clays of various hues, some natural, others artificial, they are superposed in such order that the desired pattern may be produced; then, when a sufficient number have been united, the whole mass is compressed into a solid block or cube of some four or five inches square. This block will present a striped appearance when cut across. Thin sections thus obtained are sometimes employed for the plainer parts of vessels, especially for the borders and for the bands which separate the more complex patterns. The next step consists in building up a definite pattern by superposing very thin leaves, cut from what we may call the primary striped block, upon one another in such a way that the coloured bands of one layer do not exactly coincide with the coloured bands of the next. When a cubical mass has thus been built up its cross section will no longer show stripes or bands, but square or oblong figures of geometrical character, which may be varied infinitely in size, colour, number and arrangement by varying the elements of the primary block and the mode in which the slices cut from this block are superposed.

'In another method of forming the parti-coloured blocks, long rods of any section, of variously coloured plastic clays are laid side by side and above one another in such a manner as to produce, when a cross-section is taken, a pre-arranged pattern. Or such rods may be supported in certain definite positions in a trough, and the interstices between them filled up with clay of any colour in a slip state; the block produced is allowed to consolidate by evaporation and subsequent pressure.

'The patterns producible from the parti-coloured blocks already described may be varied by cutting sections at other angles than a right angle. Another mode of producing new patterns consists in taking a soft mass of plastic clay and running it into any form by means of a template. Upon this a soft mass of clay of different colour may be laid, and so on . . .

'The economy of material and consequent lightness of Marqueterie Ware is remarkable. For instance, a little saucer which measures five inches across weighs very little more than two ounces.'

CARRARA WARE

This variety of Doulton art stoneware was made, on a not very large scale, mainly between about 1887 and 1903. New designs were occasionally produced up to 1914 and there was a limited revival in the 1920s. Some vases with pigment decoration, designed by Willie Rowe for reproduction between 1912 and 1914 are particularly attractive.

Carrara Ware is a dense off-white stoneware containing more Cornish china clay than usual. It has a slightly translucent crystalline matt glaze, giving it an appearance and texture somewhat resembling Italian Carrara marble. It was decorated usually with coloured pigments but lustre effects and gilding were also used. Sometimes the glaze is crackled, whether by accident or design is not certain but the effect in any case is often attractive.

The same name (but spelt as one word: 'Carraraware') was given also to matt-glazed architectural ware and ceramic sculptures in various colours produced extensively between 1885 and 1939. This Doulton material, made in the form of hollow blocks, slabs, tiles and ornamental features was often described in architectural and building circles as 'terracotta' or 'faïence' but it was in fact a high-fired vitrified stoneware.

Among its advantages were its resistance to atmospheric corrosion and the ease with which it could be washed down to restore it to its original freshness.

CROWN LAMBETH WARE

'Crown Lambeth' was made of a finer earthenware than Lambeth Faïence. It was decorated by hand-painting on the biscuit (once-fired) body. After glazing, usually by dipping, the ware was refired and further painting superimposed on the now glazed surface. Then came another firing at the same temperature as before so that the new painting would blend with the glaze. This process might be repeated more than once to achieve certain special effects.

These repeated glazings and firings, while involving great risks, gave Crown Lambeth decorations a richness and transparency and mellow gradation of tone which could not be achieved by the usual overglaze enamel decorations on porcelain and bone china.

The first specimens of Crown Lambeth were shown publicly at the Chicago Exhibition of 1893 but some of these had apparently been produced during the two previous years. Because of the complicated processes involved and heavy kiln losses, production costs were excessively high, and manufacture ceased about 1903. From the accountants' viewpoint it was the worst 'loss-maker' of all the Lambeth Wares and if they had had their way it would have been withdrawn even sooner.

VELLUMA WARE

Specimens of this are rare for it was made only between about 1911 and 1914 when production was halted by the outbreak of war and, so far as can be traced, never resumed. It derived its name from the parchment-like texture of the off-white glaze.

The glazed earthenware shapes were obtained from Doulton's Burslem Pottery and printed at Lambeth with transfers from soft-ground etchings by A. E. Pearce and W. Rowe. The designs, mostly landscape and figure subjects, were lightly tinted with the brush and during the final firing, at about 1,000° Centigrade, the colours sank into the glaze. If it were not for the trademark one would find it difficult to associate most of the examples one comes across with Doulton of Lambeth.

TERRACOTTA

Unglazed buff and brown terracotta garden ware, chimney pots and building components were made at the Lambeth Pottery from the 1820s onwards. Terracotta statuary was introduced in 1840.

The name which will always be indelibly associated with Doulton terracotta sculpture is, of course, that of George Tinworth. His part in the development of the salt-glaze Doulton Wares has already been noted in the previous chapter; a brief account of his subsequent career, particularly his achievements as a modeller and sculptor in terracotta, will be found in Appendix I.

Other designers of terracotta sculptures were Harry Barnard, Arthur Beere, John Broad, Edward Eggleton, Herbert Ellis, William Neatby, Arthur Pearce, F. Pomeroy and Francis Pope. Further information about most of these will also be found in Appendix I.

Carrara Ware Vase, by Esther Lewis

Hundreds of buildings in Britain and overseas are faced with Doulton terracotta and 'Carraraware' (see page 50). The overall designs were the responsibility of the architects concerned but Doulton's designers co-operated in the adaptation of the outside architects' ideas to the ceramic medium and were often entirely responsible for ornamental features, such as figures, figure groups and portrait medallions. Among well-known buildings, in or near London, for which Doulton supplied architectural ceramic facings were Harrods, the Savoy Hotel, extensions to the South Kensington Museum, Manor Lodge, Harrow School, the Birkbeck Bank, Debenhams, Doulton House, W. H. Smith & Sons former premises on the Albert Embankment, the Russell and Imperial Hotels and several other buildings in and around Russell Square. These materials were used also very extensively for theatre, cinema and public house facades.

In addition to terracotta, Carraraware, Vitreous Fresco, and faïence tiles and tile panels, Doulton also developed a polychrome stoneware material for architectural use.

This was employed mainly in mural work from 1897. The stoneware body was coated with a white slip on which, when dry, the colours were painted. In the firing the slip and colours partially fused – the result, in purity of colour and fatness of glaze, being a little similar to Della Robbia work but far more resistant to atmospheric corrosion in large cities and towns.

An early example, still in existence, of the use of polychrome stoneware and other decorative mural ceramics is in the vestibule of Lloyds Bank opposite the Law Courts in London. A later example, unfortunately demolished in 1965 to make way for a far less interesting and less attractive but doubtless commercially more remunerative building, was the Birkbeck Bank (later the Westminster Bank) in Chancery Lane, London, erected 1899–1900 to the designs of a High Victorian architect, Thomas Edward Knightley. In this, Doulton faïence, tile panels, stoneware and terracotta were all used extensively for both the exterior and the interior. Some of the embellishments which escaped damage during the demolition – 'Persian-style' fireplace tiles, winged cherubs' heads, gryphon corbels ridden by naked *putti*, portrait-busts (of Michelangelo, Leonardo da Vinci, Della Robbia, Pugin, Edison, Charles Lamb, Brunel among others) – were bought by dealers and private individuals.

Although outside the field of interest of most collectors, things of this kind do have an appeal for some, and may be acquired from time to time, especially if a watchful eye is kept open for press announcements of new development schemes on the sites of old Victorian and Edwardian buildings. The sad thing is that only too often the expenses involved in taking out inset medallions, sculpture and the like are found to be prohibitive and so most of them seem fated to disappear for ever.

V

Later Developments

BY 1881 the demand for the Doulton Lambeth ceramics of various kinds had become so great that some 60 new artists and assistant artists had to be engaged. The following year a new wing was added to the Art Department to accommodate artists, studios and workrooms. In it were provided fifty separate studios, in many of which three to four assistants and trainees worked under the supervision of a principal designer. Some of the designers had their own private studios; others, like the Barlow sisters, preferred to share a studio with one or two others. The whole set-up was described by Sir George Birdwood as 'one of the noblest *practical* schools of art in any country in Europe'.

'Each artist,' said a contemporary report in the *Queen*, 'is encouraged to perfect her own individual predilections. . . . The encouragement given to the individual artist, the avoidance of any suggestion of a stereotyped character in the work turned out, is exemplified by the number of small rooms where artists of individual distinction carry out their own ideas.'

According to an article in the *Contemporary Review* of February 1884, Henry Doulton used to say to the artists: 'Do what you please, as you please. Follow the bent of your own genius. Send out your creations and I will place them before the world and take its verdict upon them.' It is to this unusual attitude, regardless of the profit motive (and deprecated for that reason by some of his smaller-minded associates) that we owe the surely unparalleled variety and range of original artist-designed wares from a single pottery which are still in existence today. 'Doulton,' said the same article, 'has given the Ceramic Art of England the greatest impulse it has received in the present generation.'

In a letter to Sir Edmund Gosse, written after Sir Henry Doulton's death, Hannah Barlow said: 'Sir Henry was always so encouraging I could not help but enjoy my work . . . In all the many years I have worked at Lambeth, I have never felt that I was working for money. That has been one of the great charms of my work there. Sir Henry's enthusiastic interest in my work always made me feel roused to do better work!'

*   *   *

Each new trainee in the Art Studios was on probation for a month. Then, if she showed promise, she could gradually be promoted to junior assistant, senior assistant and, finally, fully-fledged artist. A small museum of carefully chosen pottery and porcelain from Greece, Rome, Spain, Italy, France, Holland, Germany and other former centres of ceramic art; a well-stocked library of books on art; a music room; recreation rooms; and a dining suite were at the artists' and assistants' disposal. Many of the younger members of the staff spent two hours after work in rest or recreation and then went on to the Lambeth School of Art for evening lessons arranged specially for them.

The art studios and workshops were again extended in 1889 to make room for another group of artists and trainees. Speaking in that year of the continued growth of the Lambeth Wares, Sir Henry Doulton (as he had then become) remarked that he had never found it necessary (as had Minton and others) to import talent from abroad. His designers and artists almost all came from the locality where, with the unfailing help of the Lambeth School of Art, he had found 'a wealth of artistic talent'. 'The nation,' he said, 'only needed to develop a proper system of art education to encourage artists and designers in abundance . . . Every child should learn drawing to secure that concert of hand and eye which is the basis of all art work. But, beyond this, there still remains a rarer and higher gift – that imaginative and creative faculty known as genius, which differs as much from educated mediocrity as does the well-spring from the pool. That *too* is to be had in Lambeth, as the results show.'

In a lecture given at Lambeth in March 1899, William Rix stated that since 1878 he had trained over 1,000 students. 'When you remember,' he said, 'that seven years training is considered necessary before a student can be considered competent, some idea may be gained of the work accomplished.' Not all of these students, the great majority of whom were young women, stayed the course; many left after a time to marry or to take up other work. Moreover, only a small proportion became creative designers and artists; most were engaged in humbler but essential tasks – preparing colours and slips, applying reliefs from moulds, colouring, glazing, repetitive work and the like.

'Repetitive' or 'Series' Ware

Inexpensive plain brown salt-glazed and cream-glazed jugs, tobacco jars, shaving pots, beakers, mugs, carriage warmers, bed warmers, breast warmers, camp kettles, spittoons and many other articles had been produced in large quantities long before the 1870s – many indeed from the very beginning of the firm's activities in 1815. These were entirely different in appearance from what came to be known as the Doulton Wares;

such decoration as they had was of the simplest kind – stamped, rouletted, turned, beaded or printed. Some, such as the brown hunting or Toby wares had applied relief decoration and were top-dipped in a darker brown glaze.

On the other hand, up to about 1881 or 1882, with the exception of pairs of vases and small moulded sculptures, every piece of the new Doulton Ware was individually designed and decorated. Indeed, even in the case of pairs of vases the decoration almost always varied although the shapes were the same. The moulded items too were generally touched up by the original designer after they had been taken from the mould and it is unusual to find two pieces exactly alike.

By the 1880s, however, there had arisen a strident demand from china dealers for well-designed but less expensive items than the artist-signed pots. It was unfair, some of Doulton's friends, both in the trade and outside it, told him, that so many people, because of modest means, should be deprived of the possibility of owning and enjoying Doulton Ware. This pressure was resisted for some time but eventually Doulton agreed to the introduction, under certain strict provisos, of a range of new designs which could be reproduced in quantities varying from a few dozen at first to seldom more than one or two thousand in later years. Such pieces did not bear the designer's monogram but on many of them will be found the initials or symbols of assistants. The 'repetitive' or 'series' wares can generally be distinguished by a printed or impressed number preceded by the letter 'X' (see page 88). Sometimes an impressed factory order number appears as well as, or instead of, the X-number.

These patterns were all designed by senior artists, though executed by assistants, and the standard of potting and finish was equal to that of the individual artist-signed pieces. There was a strict rule in the decorating rooms that the assistants must work always from the designer's *original* example, and not from a copy, so that the standard would be maintained. Each piece had to be approved by a senior artist before being sent out.

It is fortunate from the collector's standpoint that such present-day concepts as 'product rationalization' and 'variety reduction' had no part in the sales organization of the Lambeth Art Pottery. Nor had the advertising technique been evolved of constantly 'pushing' a limited number of designs which it had been decided, on the basis of market research, to 'promote'. The Doulton Wares were seldom advertised. If a particular design had not sold reasonably well within a year or two it was withdrawn without further ado and a new one introduced. The average 'run' was about 1,000 – which today of course would rank as a 'limited edition', justifying a special price! After 1903 the number of new designs launched each year was reduced greatly, and a still more drastic reduction had to be made after 1914, for reasons which will be explained later.

Henry Doulton Honoured

In 1885 Henry Doulton received what he regarded, apart from his knighthood two years later, as the crowning honour of his whole career – the award of the Albert Medal of the Society (now the Royal Society) of Arts. This medal had been instituted in 1863 as a memorial to the Prince Consort and among previous distinguished recipients had been Sir Rowland Hill, Professor Faraday, Sir Henry Bessemer, Professor Louis Pasteur and Lord Kelvin. Doulton was the only potter to have been so honoured.

In a letter to the Society, supporting the proposal to confer the medal on Doulton, Sir George Birdwood wrote:

'(He) has created a school, or rather, several schools of English pottery, the influence of which is being felt in the revival of the ceramic arts in all the countries of the old world, where they had become degraded during the last fifty years . . . The influence of his example in the United States has been quite marvellous.'

In Birdwood's opinion, Doulton's influence had extended also far beyond ceramic circles, and he went on to say:

'All the arts which refine and elevate human life being connected with one another, the improvement of any one of them leads in the end to the improvement of all; and the marked advance in recent years of every branch of higher industrial work in England, which has now placed us at the head of the art manufacturers of the West, may be distinctly traced to the influence of the Lambeth Pottery'.

Henry Doulton was deeply moved by the honour paid him and even more by the fact that the Prince of Wales (later King Edward VII), as President of the Society, had agreed to present the medal, not at Marlborough House, as was the custom, but at Lambeth, in the presence of Doulton's own artists and work people, so that they might share in the distinction. 'For all you have done for art,' said the Prince, 'not only in this country but throughout the world, I do not think there is anyone more deserving of the high compliment we are about to pay you.'

In 1887 Queen Victoria knighted Henry Doulton, who became the first potter to receive such an honour. An American writer in the *China Decorator*, commenting on this remarked 'Sir Henry has done more for the advancement of ceramic art in his country than any potter, not even excepting Josiah Wedgwood.' How fantastic would the suggestion have seemed to Doulton, when John Sparkes set him on the path of art pottery twenty years previously, that such a thing might one day be written about him! Then, much as he personally admired Wedgwood, he saw his own mission as being concerned exclusively with an entirely different branch of ceramics.

The Chicago Exhibition

The Doulton display in Chicago in 1893 was described by Sir Philip Cunliffe-Owen, then director of the Victoria and Albert Museum, South Kensington, as 'Henry Doulton's greatest triumph'. The twin arcaded Doulton pavilions, linked by a central domed hall, all built of terracotta, had been designed by Arthur Pearce. In the hall a magnificent faïence tiled frieze in twelve sections depicted an outline of pottery-making. Below this were seven faïence tile panels, painted by John Eyre, Esther Lewis and Florence Lewis, portraying in beautiful colours incidents in the life of Columbus, and symbolic paintings of other subjects such as 'Agriculture' and 'Commerce'. An eighth panel in 'Dry Impasto' was designed by W. Christian Symons and painted by John McLennan.

Among the hundreds of examples of the various Lambeth ceramics, some of the large 'prestige exhibits' attracted great popular attention, for nothing of their kind had ever before been seen in the United States. These included a tall salt-glaze ewer, 6 ft. high, designed and modelled by Mark Marshall and believed to be the largest ornamental piece ever made in stoneware; large faïence vases designed by Marshall and painted by Florence Lewis and John Eyre; a modelled faïence ewer, 6 ft. 6 ins. high designed and executed by Marshall; and several examples of Crown Lambeth vases, designed and painted by Eyre and now shown in public for the first time. Another outstanding piece was the 'History of England Vase', 4 ft. 4 in. high, a stoneware *tour-de-force* designed and modelled by Tinworth. Around the widest part of the body was a succession of twenty niches containing little groups representing important incidents in English history; around the neck a series of twenty single figures depicting English monarchs.

There were several other exhibits in terracotta by Tinworth and a wealth of choice examples of the work of Hannah and Florence Barlow, Esther and Florence Lewis, Frank Butler and other artists whose names and creations were by 1893 almost as well-known in North America as in Great Britain. The Burslem Pottery too was equally well represented by many magnificent pieces.

Doulton took seven of the highest awards at the exhibition – the largest number granted to any pottery-maker. Nearly all the exhibits shown remained in America, having been bought by museums and private collectors.

Of the hundreds of appreciations in the Press and in letters and telegrams of congratulation, Doulton was most pleased by the words of Sir Henry T. Wood, one of the Royal Commissioners for the Exhibition and a member of the Council of the Society of Arts. He wrote:

'The finest collection of pottery I have ever known to be forwarded by an individual exhibitor to any international exposition. In saying that, I do not except even the magnificent collection sent from Sèvres, the French Government factory. Taken altogether, this collection of Doulton's is the finest ever seen.'

In reading these remarks to his artists and staff, Sir Henry recalled that Sèvres had been in existence for over 150 years, encouraged and subsidized by successive French kings, emperors and governments, whereas the Doulton Ware had barely come of age and had never received a penny of State support.

Another comment which gave Doulton and his friends great pleasure was that of a writer in the *Art Journal*, who described the rise of the Doulton Wares in these words:

'Seldom has it happened *in the experience of a single generation* to see the birth and complete development of an entirely new Art Industry. Yet in the short space of some twenty years, there has been originated and perfected at the Lambeth Potteries, without the aid of previous tradition, a wealth of ceramic method that seems likely to become a conspicuous feature of that Renaissance of English Art which dates from the Victorian era.'

In 1894, the year following the Chicago Exhibition, Sir Henry Doulton was officially appointed 'Potter to His Royal Highness, Edward, Prince of Wales'. By this time the Lambeth Pottery had become a London show-place. Sir Philip Cunliffe-Owen used to tell people: 'Go along to the Doulton Pottery at Lambeth. It's the finest show you'll see in all London.' Among the many visitors were the Prince and Princess of Wales, the Princesses Louise, Victoria and Maud, the Duke of Connaught, Princess Mary of Teck (later Queen Mary), the Empress and Crown Prince and Princess of Prussia, Prince Henry of the Netherlands, the Count and Countess of Flanders, the Empress Eugénie, Gladstone, Dickens, Ruskin, George Eliot, Sir Edmund Gosse, G. F. Watts, M. Gustave Doré, various Archbishops of Canterbury and a host of other ecclesiastical dignitaries who were particularly drawn to the Lambeth Studios by Tinworth's interpretations in terracotta of biblical incidents and texts.

The Twentieth Century

Soon after the turn of the century, the Doulton Lambeth Wares too reached a turning point in their evolution. Several factors combined thereafter to bring about drastic reductions year by year in the volume of production both of the artist-signed pieces and of the series wares until, finally, production ceased altogether in 1956.

Sir Henry Doulton died in 1897, at the age of 77, when, it is probably true to say, the Lambeth Art Wares were at the pinnacle of their fame. The following appreciation of Doulton's contributions to ceramic art, which appeared after his death in the *American Pottery Gazette* is a fair reflection of the general opinion of the time:

'In ceramics especially, most disastrous results have often followed attempts on the part of ill-equipped manufacturers to place upon the market a production that trusts to its novelty alone. The public knows little and cares less about technique, and the manufacturer will explain in vain that such and such difficulties had to be encountered and overcome – that new methods had to be discovered – and that, as a praiseworthy climax, he has succeeded in making a thing the like of which has never been seen before . . .

'It needs patience, enterprise, pluck and artistic discernment to introduce successfully a new ceramic art, and these qualities were never more fully shown than by the late Sir Henry Doulton when – surrounded by only the simplest and most utilitarian of stoneware – he decided to commence the manufacture of an artistic stoneware, and gradually but surely pushed his way to the front by an output of one of the most interesting wares of modern times.'

*   *   *

Already by 1897, trade was becoming more and more difficult. The demand for many of the industrial ceramics as well as for the art wares had fallen away seriously and it was on the former, as we have seen, that the fortunes of the latter, in the long run, depended. Despite the introduction of the series wares in the 1880s the art studios still did not pay their way; in fact they were run at a book loss of some thousands of pounds a year (not taking into account their inestimable prestige value).

Shortly before his death, Sir Henry himself had had to admit that the vast Doulton ceramic empire had grown in complexity far beyond the stage where one man 'could hold the threads in hand'. Henry Lewis Doulton, who succeeded his father as head of the firm, decided to convert the family business into a limited company. This was something that Sir Henry, as an out-and-out individualist, willing to stand or fall on his own merits, had doggedly refused to do, but which he foresaw would probably be inevitable after his death. And so it was that on 1st January, 1899, Doulton & Co. Limited came into being with H. Lewis Doulton as chairman and managing director.

Royal Doulton

For the first few years of the new régime the auguries seemed favourable. In 1901, King Edward VII, in the first year of his reign, conferred an almost unprecedented honour upon the company by presenting its chairman with the Royal Warrant of Appointment and at the same time authorizing it to use the word *ROYAL* to describe its products – a rarely bestowed privilege which is quite distinct from the grant of the Warrant itself. (It is unfortunate and misleading that, in more recent times, a number of concerns have taken unto themselves this description without any official authorization whatever.)

But there were problems looming up. Already back in December 1884, Walter

Gandy (see page 98) had noted in the privately circulated Doulton publication, *Studio Notes*: 'The demand for Doulton Ware has considerably slackened and the brighter key of colour now adopted in glass and in other pottery decoration does not allow the dark colouring of Doulton Ware to hold its own.' To meet this changed state of affairs wrote Gandy: 'Colours must be kept brighter and the general tone lightened through-out. For this purpose, whiter bodies will be used . . . and a new set of lighter colours (half the depth) for backgrounds have been introduced.' He mentions that faïence and Impasto are still being 'freely purchased', that 'good and effective flower painting is sought after more than conventional decoration', and that repetitive wares 'have met with a ready sale and orders continue to come in freely'.

The steps taken in 1884 to combat the threatened danger of a declining market were effective. Demand once again increased steadily during the next ten years and more artists and assistants had to be taken on to meet it. New introductions (described in the previous chapter) – Marqueterie, Carrara, Copper Ware, Black Leather Ware, Crown Lambeth Ware, and the colourful and popular Chiné and Chiné-Gilt Ware – kept the studios and workshops busy up to the turn of the century although they were still being run at a loss. At the Paris Exhibition of 1900 the quality of both the industrial and art ceramics exhibited by Doulton added even further to the company's renown. Doulton, because of earlier successes in Paris, was *hors concours* but the resulting prestige was immense. The *Journal of Decorative Art* described the firm as 'pre-eminent among the English manufacturers of decorated china and pottery'.

A Difficult Period

When Lewis Doulton became chairman, the overall trading situation for Doulton products was vastly different from what it had been in the preceding three or four decades. Since his father's pioneering work in the 1840s in the fields of sanitary, chemical and electrical wares, the firm had gone on from success to success. But, as time passed, Henry Doulton's creation of new uses for ceramics in the industrial sphere and his invigoration of the English tradition in art pottery had not surprisingly pointed the way for others. In addition to the growth of competition, which was only to be expected, there were graver problems to be faced in the twentieth century. The Boer, Russo-Japanese and Balkan wars; international tension caused by growing German militarism; social unrest and strikes at home and abroad; the Irish question – these and other factors brought about a gradual reversal of the expansive and optimistic mood of the Victorians. A large section of British industry entered a long period of depression and recession which brought ruin to many firms and hit particularly adversely the building and contracting industries, upon which the Doulton enterprise relied for the major part of its profits. Competition for the restricted business available was remorse-less and prices for pipes, conduits and sanitary wares sank at times to unremunerative levels.

By 1905 profits had fallen drastically and by 1907 no ordinary dividends could be paid. By 1909 even the preference dividends had to be suspended. This situation continued for several years and just as things were beginning to show signs of improvement came the First World War in 1914 and, with it, renewed difficulties.

It was one thing for a wealthy private individual like Sir Henry Doulton to subsidize the Lambeth art ceramics, but quite another for a limited company faced with the trading problems which prevailed between 1905 and 1920. Lewis Doulton and his fellow directors were forced to recognize that to continue to maintain two large art departments, one in Lambeth and one in Burslem could prove disastrous.

They had to face the fact too that the fine bone china and earthenware tablewares, figurines, vases and other products of the Burslem Pottery showed a profit and were still in good demand whereas once again there was a decline – far more serious than the temporary one in the 1880s – in the demand for the Lambeth Wares. The tendency in the Edwardian era – one which grew in the following reigns – was slowly but surely towards fewer ornaments in the home. The Victorian house, cluttered from attic to basement, and above all in the living rooms, with pictures, ornaments, *objets d'art*, *bric-à-brac* of all kinds, became more and more old-fashioned. It also became more and more impossible to run as the 'servant problem' grew. At the Lambeth Pottery, more-over, there was no compensating production of ever-needed and profitable tablewares to justify the retention of a large staff of designers, artists and assistants when the demand for purely ornamental ceramics continued to fall away. It was decided, therefore, to concentrate the company's interests in decorated ceramics in Burslem but to continue the production of the salt-glaze Doulton Ware at Lambeth on a very reduced scale.

Besides the financial considerations, another factor which influenced this decision was the ever-increasing difficulty in finding in London apprentices for training in throwing, turning, mould-making, glazing, preparation of pigments and all the other processes involved in producing the largely hand-made, hand-crafted Lambeth Wares. This problem became still more acute after the First World War. In Burslem on the other hand, as in the surrounding towns of the North Staffordshire 'Potteries', the greater part of the population was still closely connected with, and indeed largely dependent on, the ceramic industry – unlike London where, except for Doulton and two or three comparatively small concerns such as Stiffs and the Fulham Pottery, the manufacture of pottery had practically ceased and there was already some agitation to prohibit it altogether.

The dwindling production of art ceramics at the Lambeth Pottery is clearly reflected in the numbers of artists and their assistants. In 1897 there had been 370, probably the highest ever. By 1909 the number had fallen to 120, by 1914 to 90, by 1925 to 25. No drastic dismissals were necessary to bring about these reductions. By 1914 most of the leading artists and most of the assistants who had come in the 1870s and 1880s had retired or died; only three or four had been replaced. Most of the other artists and assistants had always been young women and girls, of whom a number left each year to get married or for other reasons; few of these also were replaced. The production of Lambeth Faïence, Crown Lambeth and other non-stoneware ceramics was discontinued in 1914 and not renewed, having become – because of the difficult and expensive firing and other techniques – even more unremunerative than the stoneware. The production of this too was practically suspended during the war years and when it was resumed in 1920 it was with a staff of less than thirty.

The Lambeth Wares after 1900

Although in volume the production of the Doulton Ware and other Lambeth art ceramics diminished steadily after 1905, and rapidly after 1909, the high standards of quality and finish were never slackened.

Tinworth, the Barlow sisters and some other older artists who remained active into the early part of this century continued, generally speaking, their earlier techniques, without any very noticeable changes in styles, except for an occasional flirtation with *Art Nouveau* and then, usually, only in subsidiary details of their designs. Eliza – or, as she now called herself, Elise – Simmance, Frank Butler, John Broad and Francis Pope, on the other hand, showed considerable versatility and adaptation to new trends, producing what many consider to be their most attractive work. Mark Marshall had always been one of the most original and versatile of the earlier generation of Lambeth artists and he continued to demonstrate his unique gifts with undiminished vitality. Among the somewhat younger designers, William Rowe and Harry Simeon were to prove responsible for several interesting innovations, as were the newcomers, Margaret Thompson and Leslie Harradine. Arthur Pearce continued to evince his brilliant flair for design and colour effects both in large-scale architectural, sculptural and exhibition work and in delicate designs for tiles, tile panels and occasionally, vases and other pots. Most of his designs for the latter were executed by other artists and examples of signed pots by him are quite rare.

Joseph Mott, who succeeded Rix as art director at Lambeth in 1897 was responsible for several important introductions, including new matt, semi-matt and crystalline glazes and unusual lustre and flambé effects. He felt strongly that his task was to ensure that, although the Doulton Wares must perforce be drastically reduced in quantity, those that still came from the Lambeth kilns should be worthy of the reputation their predecessors had established. He was a lover of simple functional shapes and although, like Rix, he never infringed upon his designers' freedom, he unquestionably had a strong influence upon them by his example. His knowledge of Oriental ceramics was profound and he was often consulted about them by museum officials. His admiration above all for the T'ang and Sung periods of Chinese ceramics is reflected in many of the designs he executed himself or inspired others to produce. He had considerable technical knowledge and was constantly seeking new developments in bodies, glazes, slips and pigments.

From the turn of the century, under Mott's aegis, freely-drawn brush-work, simple trailed slip decorations and clear pigment colours were used increasingly, with more restrained, but artistically often more effective, use of incised, carved, relief-modelled and *pâte-sur-pâte* decorations. Some very pleasing mottled ground effects were produced by mixing basic colours. Extensive use was made of the technique of dipping the pots in white and coloured slips to cover all or part of the exteriors and thus form a ground for pigment painting.

Slip-cast and moulded shapes were at times used fairly extensively for the series wares but most of the circular shapes continued to be thrown on the wheel, as were nearly all the pots destined for hand-decoration by the leading artists as unique pieces. Throughout the first third of the century, and especially in the 1920s and 1930s a great variety of small slip-cast and moulded items were made such as ash-trays, match-box-holders, match-strikers, trump indicators, ring trays and book-ends, many of them incorporating quaint birds, animals and other figures as part of the design. These were mostly designed by Harradine, Rowe, Simeon and Vera Huggins and were reproduced in quantities seldom exceeding 1,500. The hunting jugs and other relief-decorated wares, the Natural Foliage and Chiné wares remained perennially popular.

Harry Simeon's and Francis Pope's designs for 'leopard skin' or 'orange skin' stoneware pots, introduced about 1910, in a range of new shapes, have a distinct appeal to connoisseurs. The mottled surfaces recall the Rhineland stoneware used by Elizabethan silversmiths as a foil for silver and silver-gilt mounts.

Leslie Harradine, who joined the Lambeth Studios in 1902, proved to be an exceptionally gifted modeller. His stoneware figures of Dickens characters – Pickwick, Sam Weller, Pecksniff, Squeers, Micawber and Sairey Gamp – reproduced both in white and light brown salt-glaze stoneware, and his brown salt-glaze flasks (somewhat in the spirit of the 1832 'Reform flasks', but depicting Asquith, Lloyd George, Haldane, Balfour, Theodore Roosevelt and Dr. Johnson) are now rare collectors' pieces. He and John Broad also modelled in the early 1920s a few figures for reproduction in a hard porcelain body which had been originally evolved during the First World War for making laboratory porcelain. Rowe, Simeon, Broad and Harradine designed several other figures in stoneware, some of which were reproduced both in plain brown and in coloured salt-glaze stoneware.

In the early 1920s a revival took place of the earlier so-called 'Persian Ware' (see page 47). A number of vases, bowls, plaques and tiles were designed in this style, mostly by Rowe but some by Simeon. They were in the technique of the original Near Eastern work by which they were inspired – a coarse once-fired body coated with a white slip or engobe, with a slight bluish tinge, on which the design, often of an intricate nature, was painted, the piece then being glazed and refired. The colours were mainly turquoise blues, emerald greens, orange browns and Venetian red, derived from crude mineral oxides, as were the original Near Eastern colours. A writer in the *Times*, reviewing the Crystal Palace Exhibition of 1921 at which they were first shown, thought they looked so like the early Near Eastern pots that 'they might have come straight from the Victoria and Albert Museum'. Production was on a very limited scale and had ceased entirely by 1936.

In the 1920s, Simeon designed and painted also a series of large hand-painted signed stoneware plaques, usually with decorations of fishes, seaweeds, birds and foliage. These unique pieces are much sought after today. He also modelled for reproduction a series of 'Toby' jugs, ash-pots, tobacco-jars and other shapes, produced in a style quite distinct from, but obviously inspired by, the eighteenth century Staffordshire Tobies. The method of colouring was different from that of their predecessors, being somewhat akin to that used for the coloured Parian wares of the 1880s. The separate sections of the plaster moulds were coated with slip of the required colour and then assembled; the *uncoloured* slip for the body was then poured into the mould, whereupon the two kinds of slip united by adhesion without intermingling.

Collectors' Pieces

Many of the pieces produced in the 1920s and 1930s are among the most attractive ever made in the Lambeth Studios and, although lacking in antiquity, are already much appreciated by discerning collectors. The shapes are generally simple, the decoration uncluttered, and some of the colour effects particularly subtle.

These designs, mostly by Vera Huggins, J. H. Mott, Leslie Harradine, William Rowe and Harry Simeon were the subject of an illustrated article in the *Studio* of April 1929, from which the following is an extract:

'The lure of Stoneware, and, to the initiated, especially that of Salt Glazed Stoneware, is experienced by most who attempt the craft of the potter. The mysterious happenings of firing in the open kilns as distinct from muffle firing, the subtle and harmonious blending of colours, the chances of surprise, all afford an attraction not lightly to be resisted . . .

'The concern of the present article is with the fact that . . . Doultons of Lambeth are still producing decorative, artistic stoneware of highest excellence. Pots, straight from the "thrower's" hands are invested with delicate nuances of amber, apple green, crystalline blue, peach blow in varying surfaces of matt to semi-matt or brilliant glaze. A matt apple-green of great charm has as much viridity of colour as the Chinese *famille verte*, with the additional interest that it is harder and more durable than the eastern enamel. Certain "peach blow" effects are hardly to be distinguished from those of some of the most treasured Chinese specimens and a charming pearl grey matt white is practised in a variety of shadings.

'The trite saying: "There is nothing new" is as well applied to pot shapes as to anything, but in the contours of these Doulton Vessels is a fitness as concerns utility and as concerns the material peculiar to them.'

Vera Huggins came to the Lambeth Pottery in 1923 as a designer. A versatile artist, she produced many original signed pieces which invariably aroused interest and praise when shown at the Royal Academy and at exhibitions in Paris, Johannesburg, Sydney and New York. The delicate colourings, the simple harmonious shapes, and the individual style of decoration which she brought to salt-glaze stoneware gave her productions a quality all their own. A great deal of her work is now in North America, Australia, South Africa and New Zealand. Besides her own signed pieces, she produced a number of designs for reproduction by assistants.

Pottery Sculpture

Another development of the 1920s and 1930s was the reproduction in salt-glazed coloured stoneware of sculptures, bas-reliefs and other decorative features for architectural use. This was referred to in the *Studio* article already quoted above in the following words:

'An interesting development has been the production in these materials of figure work in the round and in low relief; the extreme hardness and durability of the body with its resistance to extremes of temperature make an appeal to those who are in search of colour schemes more capable of wear and tear than enamels and more pronounced than the oft-tried combinations of ivory and bronze, ivory and marble, etc. Conspicuous examples of this treatment of modelled subjects are to be found in the later work of Mr. Gilbert Bayes.'

The great advantages of stoneware in this field were that it yielded sculptors an extended palette of colour – as distinct from the monochrome effects of stone, marble or bronze – and would withstand extremes of climate and atmospheric corrosion far better than softer maiolicas of the Della Robbia type.

Among the well-known sculptors and modellers for whom Doulton reproduced designs in this medium were Richard Garbe, Kruger Gray, Allan Howes, Alex J.

Marshall, George Paulin and James Woodford. The longest association of this kind was with Gilbert Bayes, whose death in 1953 brought to an end nearly thirty years' collaboration. The Lambeth Pottery executed many works by him, one of the largest being the panel 'Pottery through the Ages' over the main entrance to Doulton House erected on the Albert Embankment, London, S.E.1, in 1939.

Occasionally outside artists came to work in the Lambeth Studios. One of these was Reco Capey, industrial designer and Professor of Design at the Royal College of Art. He produced intermittently in 1934 and 1935 a number of unusual pieces which have the Doulton stamp and his signature. They were quite different from anything ever done at Lambeth before but unfortunately did not appeal to most of the retailers – probably because they were in advance of the popular design trends of the period. During occasional visits between 1937 and 1939, Capey produced some further pieces which were fired for him in the Lambeth kilns; these were marketed through his own agent and did not bear a Doulton stamp.

The Maxwell Tiles

Between 1933 and 1936 Mr. Mott co-operated with Donald Maxwell, the well-known topographical artist and painter, in producing a series of hand-painted tiles recording in permanent form the beauties of Kentish architecture and landscape. They became popularly known as the 'modern Domesday Book of Kent'.

Reproduced from original coloured sketches by Maxwell, and fired at a higher temperature than usual for earthenware tiles, they had a beautifully delicate effect; one critic described them as 'coloured aquatints on clay'. The outline print was first transferred from an etched copper plate on to a specially made tile with an oatmeal-coloured glaze; the colours were then filled in by hand by Annie Lyons and Doris Johnson both of whom had been trained in this kind of tile-painting by Mr. Mott and had considerable experience in this field.

The first two tiles, depicting Yalding and Westerham, were presented to H.M. King George V. Queen Mary later bought some for herself and her friends.

Tile-Panels

In 1935 Rowe designed a set of six large picture panels, each 23 ft. 6 in. high, for the decoration of the booking hall of the Singapore Terminal Station. These panels comprised in all 7,500 tiles, individually painted in matt glaze colours – the largest tile contract Doulton ever undertook. Each panel depicted a typical aspect of Malayan products and industries.

Hand-painted tile-panels were also supplied in the 1920s and 1930s for several hospitals and industrial concerns, reviving a branch of Doulton ceramic art which had been much in vogue in the late nineteenth and early twentieth centuries.

The Last Twenty Years

Between 1937 and 1939, Joan Cowper, a young studio potter, worked at the Lambeth Studios, where she produced many unusual pieces. One of the few women throwers in England at that time, she specialized in vases and bowls for flower display and designed each piece individually on the wheel. Her pots were modern and attractive in design without being eccentric. Some, in a coarse stoneware body, were unglazed or only partly glazed, depending for their effect on shape and texture; others were salt-glazed in the traditional Lambeth way. She also produced a number of pots with unusual glaze effects by using different kinds of wood-ash.

During World War II the greater part of what remained of the Lambeth Art Studios had to be turned over to the production of laboratory and technical porcelain, vital for the war effort. It was only with considerable difficulty that a small trickle of decorated salt-glaze stoneware was maintained. Most of this, which was destined solely for export, was designed by Miss Huggins.

Production for the home market was only resumed in 1950 and continued on a very limited scale until the Lambeth Works were finally closed in 1956. During this period the work of Agnete Hoy calls for special mention.

Miss Hoy studied at the famous Copenhagen School of Art and later worked with Natalie Krebs, a well-known Danish stoneware potter, and with Messrs. Bullers in Staffordshire where she created some fine pots in a hard porcelain medium. A studio was put at her disposal at the Lambeth Pottery in 1952, and there between then and 1956 she produced many beautiful individual pieces of stoneware, besides a number of designs for limited reproduction. The individual pieces which she herself decorated are signed in full; the others bear her initials.

She had an immense admiration for the work of the earlier Doulton Ware artists, and she revived many of the traditional Lambeth methods but in an entirely individual way – incised, carved, underglaze, relief-moulded and slip decorations. Apart from her work in the salt-glaze medium she evolved a new type of stoneware decoration with an applied transparent glaze on a fine natural cream coloured body, painted with free brush-work flowers, foliage, birds and other designs. The three-handled loving cup she designed to commemorate the Coronation of Queen Elizabeth II, made in two sizes in limited editions (100 of the larger and 25 of the smaller), is an outstanding example of her work in the traditional salt-glaze *genre*.

With the firing of the last batch of Miss Hoy's designs in 1956 production of the decorated salt-glaze Doulton Wares at Lambeth came to an end. The Lambeth Pottery had for many years been the only one left in Lambeth. Apart from the Fulham Pottery and one or two small studio potteries it was the only one left in London. The many china, delftware and stoneware factories (some famous, some scarcely remembered today) which could at one time have been found in Lambeth, Southwark, Vauxhall, Bow, Chelsea, Cheam, Mortlake, Greenwich and other districts, had long since vanished. London was changing out of all knowledge and it had been apparent ever since the end of the First World War that the site of the Lambeth Pottery, so near Westminster and the centre of government, must soon become totally unsuitable for a vast pottery-works with some thirty large and small coal-fired kilns. Had it not been for the intervention of the Second World War the Lambeth Pottery would in fact have been closed in the early 1940s.

Now that salt-glaze and other Lambeth art wares are all literally 'things of the past', they are naturally of greater interest than ever to collectors. They are still to be found today comparatively easily and at prices that are still reasonable. With the increasing difficulty of procuring eighteenth and nineteenth century earthenware and china, the Doulton Lambeth Wares, as was pointed out in the first chapter of this book, now offer unusual attractions for the collector.

VI

Commemorative Wares

SINCE the early seventeenth century many English potters have felt the urge to produce examples of their craft to commemorate famous (and sometimes infamous) people, important historical and political events, centenaries and other anniversaries.

Apart from some medieval English figure-jugs depicting royalty, one of the earliest commemorative items still in existence is a tin-glazed Lambeth delftware dish dated 1600. Made by an unknown Thames-side predecessor of John Doulton, it is painted with a view of the Tower of London and the patriotic legend: 'The Rose is Red: The Leaves are Greene: God Save Elizabeth: Our Queene.'

This was the forerunner of many Lambeth delftware pieces commemorating not only kings and queens (among them Charles II, James II, William and Mary, Anne and George I) but also notable events such as the Union of England and Scotland in 1707, the American War of Independence, and Vincent Lunardi's famous balloon flight from Moorfields to Ware in Hertfordshire in 1783. After the manufacture of delftware had died out in Lambeth the tradition was maintained by some of the Lambeth stoneware potters – most notably by John and Henry Doulton and their successors.

For those collectors who specialize, or think of specializing, in this intriguing field, Doulton salt-glaze wares offer rewarding opportunities. It is doubtful if any one English potter before or since has produced such a varied range of documentary pieces as Doulton of Lambeth.

The list which follows has been compiled in response to many requests from collectors. Although it notes more than two hundred items, it cannot be claimed to be complete for even since I wrote the first draft of this chapter, five items of which I had no previous knowledge have come to my notice and there are undoubtedly others still unrecorded. (Details are given, for instance, of some pieces issued in connection with the General Election of 1880; there are probably others in existence connected with this and other elections.)

Despite such gaps the following list is, as far as I know, the first of its kind to be published and it will, I hope, be helpful. Anyone who manages to find examples of even a quarter of these items will have a fascinating and unusual collection – and one which may well stimulate a fresh or renewed interest in some of the episodes of English history and social life which they recall.

If any readers can supply details of Doulton stoneware commemorative pieces not included in the list which follows I should be grateful to have these with a view to amplifying the list at some future date.

The dates given are usually those of the events commemorated; the wares themselves may sometimes have been made the following year – especially, of course, if the event in question took place towards the end of the year.

In addition to items of popular interest, reproduced in varying quantities for sale to the general public, many thousands of appropriately inscribed *unique pieces* – loving cups, vases, jugs, bowls, plaques, mugs, etc. – were produced over the years for private presentations; for sports trophies for universities, schools and clubs; and to commemorate births, christenings, confirmations, weddings, wedding anniversaries, retirements, and the like. These it is of course impossible to enumerate but because they are unique – and because they often bear the monograms of the artists who designed and decorated them – they are worth looking out for.

Also not included in the following list are what were referred to in the studios as 'visitors' pieces'. It was the custom at the Lambeth Pottery to invite visitors – especially those regarded as being of some importance – to sign in the soft clay a bowl, vase or other piece which had been thrown on the wheel in their presence. After this had been decorated and fired it would be sent to the person concerned. Between the 1870s and 1956 when the Lambeth Pottery was closed many thousands of visitors received such mementoes – among them British and foreign royalty, members of the nobility and aristocracy, politicians, musicians, artists and writers, scientists, archbishops, bishops and famous Nonconformist divines, sportsmen, actors and others distinguished in various walks of life.

The majority of these visitors' pieces are probably still in the possession of the descendants of those for whom they were originally made but some occasionally appear on the market and the collector who is fortunate enough to come across one signed by Edison, Gladstone, Ruskin, George Eliot or some other notable person will have something of unique interest and value.

*   *   *

1820   Brown salt-glaze figure-flask representing Queen Caroline, the estranged wife of George IV, holding a scroll inscribed 'My Hope is in my People'. (See page 10.)
A similar figure is also found without the scroll.

c. 1821–1830 Napoleon Bonaparte died in St. Helena in exile on 5th May 1821, reviving memories in England of the struggles in which he, Nelson and Wellington had played leading roles. It was probably between then and 1830 (the twenty-fifth anniversary of Nelson's death) that the following items were produced:

Brown salt-glaze figure-mug depicting the head and shoulders of Napoleon; in two sizes c. 3½ in. and c. 6 in. high.

Brown salt-glaze figure-jug depicting Napoleon standing on board ship on his way to exile.

Brown salt-glaze figure-jug depicting Nelson half-length in naval uniform with tricorn hat, wearing a sash and medals, one of which is impressed 'Nile 1798'.

Brown salt-glaze large figure-mug modelled as a bust of Nelson wearing tricorn hat.

Brown salt-glaze large figure-mug modelled in the likeness of the Duke of Wellington.

Brown salt-glaze figure-flask depicting Wellington.

c. 1827 Brown salt-glaze figure-flask depicting the Duke of York, son of George III and one-time heir to the throne; the base inscribed 'Duke of York'.

c. 1829 Brown salt-glaze spirit flask with neck representing Daniel O'Connell the Irish patriot, and inscribed: 'Irish Reform Cordial' and 'Irish Reform and Repeal'.

1832 Large brown salt-glaze spirit bottles c. 14 in. high and similarly designed flasks c. 5–7¼ in. high – made to celebrate the passing of the First Reform Bill, the necks depicting King William IV and Lords Grey, Brougham and Russell; with various inscriptions such as 'The True Spirit of Reform', 'Grey's Reform Cordial' and 'The People's Rights'.

Some of these bottles and flasks are a uniform light-brown in colour but most are top-dipped a darker brown. Some are stamped with the names of the licensed houses for which they were made.

1837 Brown salt-glaze flask with moulded relief figure of the young Queen Victoria holding a sceptre in her hand, her crown resting on a pedestal.

Brown salt-glaze mug with the Royal Arms in relief and applied relief portraits of Queen Victoria and her mother, the Duchess of Kent. (The Duchess was the widow of William IV's brother who, had he lived, would have succeeded William. Her daughter came to the throne in 1837 at the age of 18 and reigned for 64 years.)

Brown salt-glaze jug with relief decorations similar to those on the mug described above.

Brown salt-glaze figure-flask depicting Queen Victoria wearing a crown and holding a scroll; the base inscribed 'Victoria'.

c. 1840 Brown salt-glaze figure of Albert, Prince Consort, who married Queen Victoria in 1840; the base inscribed 'Albert'.

1856 Brown salt-glaze jug with moulded relief figures of soldiers, inscribed: 'Peace Proclaimed'. Issued to celebrate the end of the Crimean War.

1860 Cream-glazed stoneware jug with relief portrait of the Prince of Wales (later King Edward VII) and an inscription commemorating his first public engagement – the opening of the Lambeth School of Art's new premises (see page 17).

1871 Brown salt-glaze jug with portrait medallions of David Livingstone and H. M. Stanley who discovered the missing missionary at Ujiji in 1871.

1877 (?) Coloured Doulton Ware jug decorated with relief portrait medallion of Queen Victoria over the words 'Great Britain'; with shields inscribed India, Australia, New Zealand, Cape Colony, Canada; also inscription: 'Sons be welded each and all into one imperial whole with Britain heart and soul, one life, one flag, one fleet, one throne.'
(It is thought that this jug was issued to commemorate the declaration of Queen Victoria as Empress of India in 1877.)

1879 Brown salt-glaze jug with relief portrait of H. M. Stanley; commemorating the founding of the Congo Free State in that year.
(Henry Doulton was an admirer of Stanley. Other jugs with an association with Stanley were produced in 1871 and 1890.)

1880 Brown salt-glaze jug commemorating the General Election of 1880 after which William Ewart Gladstone again became Prime Minister; relief portrait of Gladstone designed by Harry Barnard; inscribed '26422 votes' and quotation from Gladstone: 'Effort, honest manful humble effort, succeeds by its reflective action upon character better than success'.
Other pieces produced to celebrate the Liberal victory at this election included:
Brown salt-glaze beaker with relief portrait and inscribed 'Herbert J. Gladstone, Returned unopposed Leeds Election 1880'. (Dated 1882).
Similar beaker inscribed 'John Barraine 23674 votes Leeds Election 1880'. (Dated 1882.)
Tyg designed somewhat roughly by Frank Butler (apparently as a specimen) with incised decoration and inscription: 'In commemoration of the General Election of 1880 when for the first time in its history the West Riding of Yorkshire returned six Liberal Representatives to Parliament'; also incised with the White Rose of York, the names of the six Members and that of the High Sheriff (given as Sir George W. Cholmley).

A similar tyg but more carefully decorated and with impressed inscriptions. The name of the High Sheriff is given as Sir Charles W. Strickland, Bart.

1881   Brown salt-glaze jug decorated with primroses and portrait of Lord Beaconsfield (Benjamin Disraeli) by Harry Barnard. Inscribed: 'His favourite flower'.

Similar jug in coloured Doulton Ware.

Another jug with portrait and quotation from Disraeli's maiden speech in the House of Commons on 7th December, 1837: 'I will sit down now but the time will come when you will hear me. I have begun several things many times and I have often succeeded at last.'

The following items – of which further details are not recorded – were also issued to commemorate Lord Beaconsfield's death in 1881:

A Doulton Ware vase

A Lambeth Faïence vase

A Chiné-Gilt tobacco jar

A Silicon tobacco jar

1883   Coloured Doulton Ware two-handled tankard with applied moulded relief figures of soldiers in incised panels. (Issued at the time of the war in the Sudan.)

Coloured Doulton Ware three-handled tankard of similar design.

1885   Brown salt-glaze jug with applied relief portrait of General Gordon by John Broad and several inscriptions: 'By the Help of God I will hold the balance level'; 'I decline to agree that your expedition is for me, 1884'; 'Hero of Heroes'; 'Khartoum'; 'Governor-General of the Sudan 1874'; 'Born Jan. 28, 1833, Betrayed Jan. 26, 1885'.

Not all of these inscriptions appear on all the copies and some have been noted without the dates of birth and betrayal; these may have been issued in 1884   There was great public indignation, supported by Queen Victoria, at the way Gordon, a popular hero, had been treated by Gladstone's government – hence the use of the word 'betrayed'.

There was evidently a continuing demand for this jug, necessitating new editions in 1895 and 1905. The 1895 jugs can be distinguished by the use of the word 'England' in the trade-mark and the 1905 ones by the Royal Doulton lion and crown trade-mark.

(John Broad designed and modelled a large terracotta statue of General Gordon for erection at Gravesend, the General's birthplace.)

1885   Chiné-Gilt small vase with fluted rim; applied white relief portrait of the Prince of Wales (later King Edward VII) on brown oval background; inscribed: 'Albert Medal Society of Arts 1885 for Impulse given to Production of Art Pottery in England'; 'Presented by H.R.H. the Prince of Wales to Henry Doulton, December 21st 1885 at Lambeth Art Pottery'. Also with the Prince of Wales feathers and the inscription 'Honi Soit qui Mal y Pense'.

74

This vase, designed by John Broad, was produced in a small edition for presentation by Henry Doulton to some of his friends.

A large vase, nearly 2-ft. high, with similar inscriptions but elaborately decorated with foliage in high relief and encircled by mythical Welsh dragons; designed and decorated by Mark V. Marshall to commemorate the same event. (Probably a unique piece.)

(See page 57.)

1887 *Queen Victoria's Golden Jubilee*

Among the pieces commemorating this event the following have been noted:

Coloured Doulton Ware 1-pt. and 1-qt. jugs with moulded relief portrait of the Queen and figures symbolizing parts of the Empire, cherubs blowing trumpets, inscriptions 'Honi Soit qui Mal y Pense' and 'Victoria Dei Gratia', and dates 1837–1887.

Similar jug, also in two capacities, but in brown salt-glaze and with applied white reliefs.

Coloured Doulton Ware ½-pt. and 1-pt. mugs with two moulded relief portraits of the young and old Queen, inscribed 'Victoria R.I.' and dates 1837–1887.

Similar mug, also in two capacities, but in brown salt-glaze and with black printed portraits and inscriptions.

Chiné-Gilt vase decorated with applied white relief portraits of the Queen and rose, thistle and shamrock motifs; inscribed: 'The Pillar of a People's Hope: The Centre of a World's Desire: God Save the Queen: 1837 Victoria 1887: Regina et Imperatrix'.

1887   Brown salt-glaze stoneware jug, commemorating the famous Victorian Jockey, Fred Archer; with relief portrait of Archer, the lip of the jug shaped like a jockey's cap. Inscribed verse reading:

> 'Reft from our midst by untimely fate,
> Pledge me his spirit before we sup –
> Pledge me one who, straight as he rode
> For the plate or the cup, through life was straight.
> Ah, Death's pale horse must have felt elate
> As he sped through the shadows with Archer up!'

The jug is stamped with the name of John Mortlock & Co., well-known Victorian china dealers, as well as with the Doulton mark.

1888   Brown salt-glaze three-cornered beaker to commemorate the rebuilding of Islington Chapel, founded in 1788. (Further details not recorded.)

1888   Coloured Doulton Ware three-handled mug to commemorate the Silver Wedding of the Prince and Princess of Wales (later King Edward VII and Queen Alexandra); with portrait busts, coat of arms and inscription in white relief.

1889   Brown salt-glaze jug with applied relief portrait medallion of John Bright, the famous Radical and Quaker statesman and orator who died in 1889.

1890   Brown salt-glaze jug, commemorating the Emin Pasha Relief Expedition 1887–1889; with moulded relief portrait of H. M. Stanley, figures symbolizing Valour and Enterprise, the names of six members of the expedition, and the inscription: 'Out of Darkness into Light'.

1892   Brown salt-glaze jug with moulded relief portrait of Christopher Columbus, a picture of his flag-ship, and the inscription: 'Christopher Columbus sighted America, October 12, 1492'. (Designed by John Broad for the 400th anniversary.)

Brown salt-glaze squat-shaped jug also designed by Broad, with moulded relief portrait of Christopher Columbus, a picture of his flag-ship, inscribed 'Christopher Columbus sailed from Palos Aug. 3, 1492: Sighted America Oct. 12, 1492'. Also inscribed with quotation from Tennyson: 'Thro' the Atlantic Sea which he unchained for all the world to come'.

892   Jug with relief portrait of Alfred Lord Tennyson, Poet Laureate, who died in 1892. (Further details not recorded.)

1893   Coloured Doulton Ware jug, inscribed 'World's Columbian Exposition', with moulded relief of American eagle and portraits of Columbus and Washington between bands of stars. Designed by John Broad to commemorate the Chicago Exhibition of 1893. (See page 58.)

1893   Brown salt-glaze jug with applied white reliefs of Queen Victoria enthroned between two female figures, with various other symbolic figures. Inscribed: 'Imperial Institute of the United Kingdom, Colonies and India', 'Opened by Her Most Gracious Majesty Queen Victoria May 10, 1893'.

1897   *Queen Victoria's Diamond Jubilee*
Coloured Doulton Ware ½-pt. and 1-pt. mugs with relief portraits of the Queen as a girl and in old age, and dates 1837 and 1897.
Similar mugs in two capacities in brown salt-glaze with black printed portraits and dates.
Coloured Doulton Ware 1-pt., 1-qt. and 3-pt. jugs with relief portraits and dates as above, inscribed: 'Dei Gratia Victoria Queen and Empress' and 'She wrought her People lasting Good'; with modelled relief enrichments of roses, shamrocks and thistles. (Produced in two alternative colour schemes, thus making six different items.)
Similar jugs in three capacities in brown salt-glaze with black printed decoration.
Coloured Doulton Ware ½-pt. beaker with relief portraits of the young and old Queen, and inscribed 'Victoria R.I.' (Produced in two alternative colour schemes.)

Similar beaker in plain brown salt-glaze with black-printed decoration.

Brown salt-glaze barrel-shaped jug with black-printed portraits of the young and old Queen and inscribed: 'Dei Gratia Victoria Queen and Empress' and 'She wrought her People lasting Good'.

Brown salt-glaze tall jug printed with two *overlapping* portraits of the Queen in a diamond shape, and inscribed: 'In Commemoration of the 60th Year of Queen Victoria's Reign 1837–1897'.

Large Doulton Ware vase about 2-ft. high, decorated with impressed and incised symbols and applied portraits of the Queen modelled by John Broad; with *pâte-sur-pâte* paintings of birds and animals representing parts of the Empire, designed and executed by Florence E. Barlow.

(George Tinworth and Frank Butler – and perhaps other artists – also produced special pieces to mark the Queen's Diamond Jubilee but details are not recorded.)

Brown salt-glaze mug, of which 700 copies were made for Lees Knowles, M.P., and presented to scholars of St. John's Sunday School, Pendlebury: Royal Arms and date in white relief and inscriptions: 'Fear God, honour the Queen', 'Remember the 60th year of the reign of Queen Victoria' and 'The gift of Lees Knowles, M.P.'

(Designed by W. D. Carol, architect to the Ecclesiastical Commissioners. A specimen was presented to the Queen.)

It is known that other Diamond Jubilee items with relief and printed portraits and various special inscriptions were made for local authorities and other bodies for presentation purposes, but detailed records have not been discovered.

1898   Coloured Doulton Ware jug issued to commemorate the death of Gladstone; moulded relief portrait and inscriptions: 'England's Great Commoner' and 'Effort – honest, manful humble effort – succeeds, by its reflective action upon character, better than success'.

Similar jug in brown salt-glaze with printed portrait and inscriptions.

1900   Brown salt-glaze jug commemorating the Relief of Ladysmith on 28th February 1900; with printed portraits of Captain Scott and Captain Lambton and a figure of a British sailor. Inscribed: 'The Handyman'.

(The two Captains and the Navy played an important part in transporting cannons to Ladysmith for its defence.)

1900   Coloured Doulton Ware jug inscribed: 'In commemoration of the Hoisting of the Flag at Pretoria June 5th 1900'; with the Royal Standard, the Union Jack and portrait of Queen Victoria in relief.

Coloured Doulton Ware three-handled mug similarly decorated.

1901 Light brown salt-glaze figure of Queen Victoria in ceremonial robes seated on throne and holding orb and sceptre; reverse inscribed 'Victoria R.I. 1819–1901'. Modelled and signed by J. Broad.

(Some of these figures have been noted with a brown base, others with blue and green bases. The heights vary slightly, due no doubt to different rates of shrinkage of the clays during firing, but all are under 1-ft.)

1901–2 Light brown salt-glaze figures of British soldiers in Boer War uniforms, modelled and signed by J. Broad. Three different figures have been noted but it is thought Broad modelled four.

1901–2 Terracotta figure of King Edward VII standing bareheaded against a column; base inscribed 'E R I' inside a shield; modelled and signed by J. Broad.

1901–2 Brown salt-glaze jug inscribed 'South Africa', with printed decoration of flags, lion, beaver and kangaroo, and portraits of the three British commanders – Roberts, Kitchener and Baden-Powell.
Brown salt-glaze three-handled mug, similarly decorated.

1902 *Coronation of King Edward VII and Queen Alexandra*
Coloured Doulton Ware two-handled loving cup with portrait bust of Edward VII and Coronation scene in relief; limited edition of 2,000.
Coloured Doulton Ware vase with relief portraits of the King and Queen, inscribed 'In commemoration of the Coronation of Their Majesties King Edward VII and Queen Alexandra, Anno Domini MDCCCCII'.
Coloured Doulton Ware vase with relief portraits of the King and Queen and the ciphers E.R. and A.R.
Coloured Doulton Ware $\frac{1}{2}$-pt. mug, $\frac{1}{2}$-pt. beaker, 1-qt. jug, 1$\frac{1}{2}$-pt. tea-pot, and $\frac{1}{2}$-lb. tobacco jar, with relief portraits of the King and Queen and the ciphers E.R. and A.R.
Coloured Doulton Ware coffee set consisting of pot, jug and mug, with relief portraits of the King and Queen and the ciphers E.R. and A.R.
Brown salt-glaze coffee pot, jug and mug with black-printed portraits and ciphers.
Brown salt-glaze 1-pt. and 1-qt. jugs, $\frac{1}{2}$-pt. beaker and $\frac{1}{2}$-pt. and 1-pt. mugs with black-printed portraits and ciphers.
Coloured Doulton Ware jug with relief portraits of Edward VII, Queen Alexandra, the then Prince of Wales (later George V) and the future Edward VIII.
Brown Silicon busts of the King and Queen modelled by Leslie Harradine.

1902 Brown salt-glaze jug with relief portrait of Austen Chamberlain and inscription: 'What I have said I have said, I withdraw nothing. Birmingham, Jan. 11th 1902'.

1905 *Centenary of the Battle of Trafalgar*

Light brown salt-glaze replica (clearly marked as such) of the large figure-mug modelled as bust of Nelson c. 1835.

Light brown salt-glaze replica (clearly marked as such) of the figure-jug of Nelson made c. 1835.

Brown salt-glaze moulded figure of Nelson standing against a bollard, modelled by John Broad.

Similar figure in green glazed faïence.

Brown salt-glaze ½-pt., 1-pt. and 1-qt. jugs with black print of Nelson and his Captains.

Coloured Doulton Ware relief-figured set of teapot, sugar bowl and cream jug (made in two alternative colourings).

Coloured Doulton Ware relief-figured tobacco jar with portrait of Nelson, coronet, etc. (made in two alternative colourings).

Coloured Doulton Ware relief-figured three-handled mug similarly decorated (made in two alternative colourings).

Coloured Doulton Ware relief-figured tall beer stein with portrait of Nelson, pictures of men-of-war, and inscription 'England expects every man will do his duty'.

Coloured Doulton Ware relief-figured beaker and one-handled and two-handled mugs.

Light brown salt-glaze medallion portrait of Nelson with hole for hanging on wall, designed by J. Broad.

Similar medallion in green faïence.

Brown salt-glaze miniature relief-figured jug, mug and beaker, each c. 1/64th of a pint capacity.

c. 1905–08 Doulton Ware inkwells with hinged tops, one in the shape of a baby wearing a bib and the other (known as 'The Virago') that of a grumpy-looking woman wearing an apron; both inscribed 'Votes for Women'. Designed by L. Harradine.

(The 'Baby' inkwell is also found without the inscription.)

1906 Coloured Doulton Ware jug with moulded relief portrait of Christopher Columbus; made to commemorate the 400th anniversary of his death; designed by John Broad.

1906 Grey terracotta bust of William Pitt (who in 1783, at the age of twenty-four, became Prime Minister). Inscribed 'William Pitt 1759–1806'.

Modelled by John Broad for presentation by the Lambeth artists to Henry Lewis Doulton (only son of Sir Henry Doulton) who lived for many years at Bowling Green House, Roehampton, where Pitt had spent his last years. Mr. Doulton had an interesting collection of Pitt medals and other mementoes.

It is believed that only five additional copies were made for presentation by Mr. Doulton to some of his friends.

Light brown salt-glaze spirit-flask with relief-figured bust of William Pitt, designed by John Broad.

c. 1908–11 Brown salt-glaze figure flasks designed by Leslie Harradine somewhat after the style of the 1832 'Reform flasks' and depicting leading politicians of the early twentieth century – Asquith, Balfour, Haldane, Lloyd George, Austen Chamberlain, John Burns and the American President, Theodore Roosevelt.

Another figure-flask, also designed by Harradine, was produced for the bi-centenary in 1909 of the birth of Dr. Samuel Johnson. (Similar flasks were made for the 'Old Cheshire Cheese' Inn.)

1911   *Coronation of King George V and Queen Mary*

Coloured Doulton Ware three-handled 1-qt. loving cup, with portrait medallions of the King and Queen and various emblems in low relief; inscribed: 'The Coronation of King George V and Queen Mary 1911'.

Coloured Doulton Ware tall 1-qt. jug and squat-shaped ½-pt., 1-pt., 1½-pt. and 1-qt. jugs, with similar decoration.

Coloured Doulton Ware ½-pt. beaker and ½-pt. and ¾-pt. mugs, with similar decoration.

Coloured Doulton Ware ¼-lb. and ½-lb. tobacco jars with similar decoration.

Coloured Doulton Ware 1-pt. and 1½-pt. tea-pots with similar decoration.

Brown salt-glaze ½-pt., 1-pt., 1½-pt. and 1½-qt. squat-shaped jugs with black-printed portrait and inscription.

Brown salt-glaze ½-pt. mug and ½-pt. beaker similarly decorated.

Brown salt-glaze 1-pt. and 1½-pt. tea-pots similarly decorated.

Brown salt-glaze ¼-lb. tobacco jar similarly decorated.

Coloured Doulton Ware 1-qt. jug, decorated with printed portraits and royal arms in heraldic colours with gilding.

Coloured Doulton Ware 1-qt. three-handled loving cup similarly decorated.

Coloured Doulton Ware ½-pt. beaker similarly decorated.

Coloured Doulton Ware ¾-pt. mug similarly decorated.

Coloured Doulton Ware 1½-pt. tea-pot similarly decorated.

Coloured Doulton Ware ½-lb. tobacco jar similarly decorated.

All-blue Doulton Ware jug, mug, teapot, beaker and tobacco jar with moulded relief portraits and inscription.

All-brown Doulton Ware ditto.

Brown salt-glaze 1-qt. three-handled loving cup with black-printed portraits and inscription.

Brown salt-glaze large two-handled loving cup with white applied relief portraits of the King and Queen. (Limited edition of 750.)

Brown Silicon busts of George V and Queen Mary modelled by Leslie Harradine.

1911 *Investiture of the Prince of Wales (later King Edward VIII) at Caernarvon Castle*
Coloured Doulton Ware two-handled 3-pt. loving cup with moulded relief portrait, inscription, arms and emblems.

Coloured Doulton Ware ½-lb. tobacco jar similarly decorated.

Coloured Doulton Ware ¾-pt. mug similarly decorated.

Coloured Doulton Ware 1-qt. jug similarly decorated.

(The above four items were also repeated both in brown salt-glaze with black printed decoration and in cream-glazed stoneware with portrait printed in colour and the arms etc., in heraldic colours with gilding.)

Chiné-Gilt vase with portrait of the Prince of Wales. (Further details not recorded.)

1911 Doulton Ware stamp damper with head of Lloyd George, produced to commemorate the National Insurance Act.

1919 Coloured Doulton Ware jug inscribed 'Peace with Victory', with relief portrait of Field-Marshal Haig and dates 1914 and 1919.

Similar jug with portrait of Marshal Foch.

Similar jug with portrait of Admiral Beatty.

Similar jug with portrait of President Wilson.

(These jugs were also produced in plain brown salt-glaze with black-printed portraits and inscription.)

1935 Brown salt-glaze two-handled large loving cup with portrait busts of George V and Queen Mary in white relief. Produced to commemorate Their Majesties' Silver Wedding.

1936 Brown salt-glaze two-handled large loving cup with white relief portrait of the uncrowned King Edward VIII. Very rare as the intended limited edition of 100 was only partly completed at the time of the Abdication.

1937 Brown salt-glaze two-handled large loving cup with white relief portraits of George VI and Queen Elizabeth; produced in limited edition of 100 to commemorate the Coronation.

A few other pieces were produced but unfortunately records were destroyed during World War II.

1953 *Coronation of Queen Elizabeth II*
Salt-glaze two-handled loving cup in light and dark brown and cream colouring, with carved, incised and modelled decoration; cover surmounted by a crown and

inscribed 'E.R. II 1953'. Designed by Agnete Hoy and produced in a limited edition of 100; 7-in. high overall.

A similarly designed loving cup but only 4¾-in. overall, produced in a limited edition of 25 for presentation to directors and other officials of Doulton & Co. Limited.

Light and dark brown and cream-coloured salt-glaze tankard with incised and carved decoration, applied relief portrait of Queen Elizabeth II, and date 1953. Designed by Agnete Hoy and produced in a limited edition of 500.

Cream-glazed plain stoneware tankard printed in black with crown and 'Elizabeth R. 1953'.

1953   Cream-glazed stoneware tankard produced in 1953 to commemorate the winning of the 1952 County Cricket Championship by the Surrey County XI. Printed with facsimile signatures of the members of the team and inscribed: 'Surrey County XI Cricket Champions 1952 captained by Mr. W. Stuart Surridge'.

Apart from the tankards presented to the members of the team only twelve others were made.

ADDENDA

1887   Bellarmine-type jug commemorating Queen Victoria's Golden Jubilee, inscribed 'Great Albion's Queen for fifty glorious years'.

1892   Brown salt-glaze jug issued to commemorate the death of the Duke of Clarence, Albert Victor, eldest son of the then Prince of Wales (later King Edward VII.) Black print decoration and portrait head of the Duke.

The Plates

I. The Thames-side at Lambeth and Millbank, c. 1793; on the left the kilns of a Lambeth pottery. (From an aquatint by F. Jukes after J. Laporte.)

II. Brown salt-glaze Doulton & Watts jug with moulded relief decoration depicting a boar hunt; top-dipped darker ochre brown; $9\frac{1}{4}$ in. high; c. 1845.

III. Light-brown salt-glaze Doulton & Watts large figure-tankard modelled as bust of Admiral Lord Nelson; $7\frac{1}{2}$ in. high; c. 1821–30.

IV. Light-brown salt-glaze Doulton & Watts 'Reform Bottle'; top-dipped darker ochre brown, inscribed 'The True Spirit of Reform'; 14¼ in. high; 1832.

V. Early example of salt-glaze Doulton Ware; top-dipped ochre brown; 9¼ in. high; 1867.

VI. Salt-glaze Doulton Ware jug; c. 9 in. high; George Tinworth; 1871.

VII. (*opposite*) Salt-glaze Doulton Ware ceremonial 'salt'; 9¾ in. high; George Tinworth; 1874. (Another Tinworth 'salt' is illustrated in Blacker's *A.B.C. of English Salt-Glaze Stoneware*, page 225.)

VIII. Two salt-glaze Doulton Ware humoresques by George Tinworth, 'Hunting' and 'Play Goers'; $4\frac{3}{4}$ in. high; c. 1884–86.

IX. Salt-glaze Doulton Ware jug; $7\frac{1}{4}$ in. high; Arthur B. Barlow; 1874.

X. (*opposite*) Massive salt-glaze Doulton Ware vase; 29 in. high; with incised scenes of lions in their natural environment by Hannah B. Barlow, surrounding applied and incised decoration by Frank A. Butler; 1877.

XI. *Left*: Salt-glaze Doulton Ware beaker; 5½ in. high; monograms of Hannah B. Barlow and Mary A. Thomson; 1875. *Right*: Another beaker 5½ in. high; monogram of Louisa E. Edwards and initials of Rosina Brown; 1879.

XII. Salt-glaze Doulton Ware biscuit barrel; silver lid and handle; c. 6 in. high; Hannah B. Barlow; 1882.

XIII. (*opposite top*) Salt-glaze Doulton Ware jardinière; 12½ in. high; incised decoration by Hannah B. Barlow, borders by Frank A. Butler; c. 1885.

XIV. (*opposite bottom*) *Left to right*: (1) Salt-glaze Doulton Ware jug; c. 9½ in. high; Hannah B. Barlow; 1875. (2) Salt-glaze Doulton Ware vase; c. 10½ in. high; Florence E. Barlow and Lucy A. Barlow; 1883. (3) Salt-glaze jug; 8¼ in. high; Hannah B. Barlow; c. 1893.

XV. Salt-glaze Doulton Ware ewer; 12½ in. high to top of handle; Hannah B. Barlow; c. 1895.

XVI. Salt-glaze Doulton Ware by Frank A. Butler illustrating changes in his styles. *Left to right*: (1) Tobacco jar; 5½ in. high; 1873. (2) Jug; 12 in. high; c. 1872. (3) Vase; 10 in. high; 1905. (4) and (5) Pair of vases in Art Nouveau style on Chiné background; 14½ in. high; c. 1895.

XVII.   Salt-glaze Doulton Ware vase; 14 in. high;
Frank A. Butler; 1906.

XVIII.   Salt-glaze Doulton Ware vase; 12 in. high;
Frank A. Butler; c. 1898.

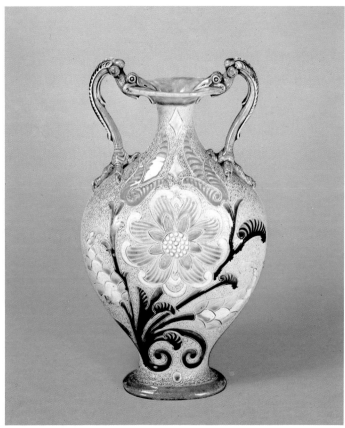

XIX. Salt-glaze Doulton Ware vase; $6\frac{3}{4}$ in. high; Eliza Simmance; 1883.

XX. Salt-glaze Doulton Ware jardinière; 10 in. high; Eliza Simmance; 1884.

XXI. (*opposite*)   Salt-glaze Doulton Ware vase; $13\frac{1}{2}$ in. high; monogram of Eliza Simmance and initials of Rosina Brown; c. 1890.

XXII.   Doulton Silicon Stoneware vase;
10 in. high; Eliza Simmance; 1884.

XXIII.   Salt–glaze Doulton Ware vase; $11\frac{1}{4}$ in.
high; signed in full 'Edith D. Lupton, Lambeth
School of Art'; 1878.

XXIV. Doulton Carrara Stoneware
vases. *Left to right*: (1) 7¼ in. high;
Edith D. Lupton; c. 1889.
(2) 7½in. high; Eliza Simmance; c. 1889.

XXV. Doulton Carrara Stoneware vase;
6¾ in. high; Mark V. Marshall; c. 1890.

XXVII.   Doulton Carrara Stoneware vase; 10 in. high; painting of children by Ada Dennis, scroll work by Mary Denley; c. 1887–90. (Vase also has initials of Josephine Durtnall, assistant.)

XXVI. (*opposite*)   Doulton Carrara Stoneware vase; 12 in. high; Kate Rogers; c. 1892.

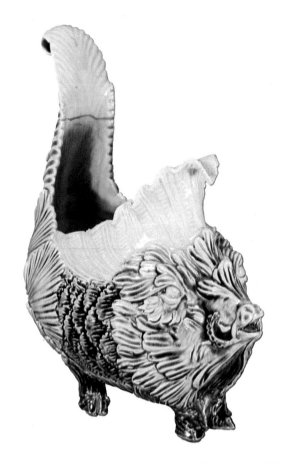

XXVIII.   Salt-glaze Doulton Ware vase (inspired by Borogrove in *Alice through the Looking Glass*); 8 in. high; Mark V. Marshall; c. 1892. (Other vases from same mould show different colouring and other slight variations.)

XXIX.   Salt-glaze Doulton Ware study of lizard on rock; 5 in. high; Mark V. Marshall; c. 1901.

XXX.   Salt-glaze Doulton Ware vase;
10½ in. high; Mark V. Marshall; c. 1904.

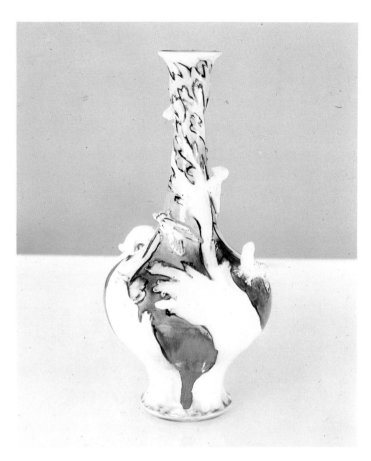

XXXI.   Salt-glaze Doulton Ware vase, slightly
lustred; 10½ in. high; George H. Tabor; 1883.

XXXIII. Salt-glaze Doulton Ware water filter with lid and tap; 14 in. high; c. 1885.

XXXIV. Salt-glaze Doulton Ware vase; 11 in. high; monograms of Louisa J. Davis and Mary A. Thomson; 1878.

XXXII. (*opposite*) Salt-glaze Doulton Ware vase; 9½ in. high; monogram of Mary A. Thomson and initials of Jessie Bowditch, assistant; 1880.

XXXV. Salt-glaze Doulton Ware vase; 5¾ in. high; Bertha Evans; 1886.

XXXVI. Salt-glaze Doulton Ware vase; 12 in. high; Emily Stormer; c. 1891.

XXXVII. Brown salt-glaze Doulton Ware jug commemorating the jockey, Fred Archer (see page 75); 6¾ in. high; 1887.

XXXVIII. Salt-glaze Doulton Ware three-handled silver-rimmed loving cup designed by John Broad with applied white relief figures of cricketers (believed to represent Dr. W. G. Grace, K. S. Ranjitsinhji and George Griffen); 6½ in. high; registered at the Patent Office in December 1880.

XXXIX.   Salt-glaze Doulton Ware 'Isobath'; 6¾ in. high; c. 1889. (See page 167.)

XL. (*opposite*)   Salt-glaze Doulton Ware jug with long spout; 8¾ in. high; Rosina Brown; c. 1892.

XLI. Salt-glaze Doulton Ware trinket box with lid; 8½ in. long; Francis C. Pope; c. 1902.

XLII. Light-brown salt-glaze Doulton figure of
Queen Victoria (inscribed at back: 'Queen
Victoria 1819–1901'); 11¾ in. high; designed by
John Broad for reproduction; 1902.

XLIII. Light-brown salt-glaze Doulton figure of
Boer War soldier on darker brown and green base;
12½ in. high; designed by John Broad for
reproduction; c. 1901.

XLIV.   Salt-glaze Doulton Ware commemorative items. *Left to right*: (1) Coronation of Edward VII and Queen Alexandra; with relief-moulded portraits of the King and Queen, the future George V and future Edward VIII as a child; 7 in. high; 1902. (2) Trafalgar Centenary; with relief-moulded portrait of Nelson and inscription 'England expects every man will do his duty'; $10\frac{1}{2}$ in. high; 1905. (3) Chicago Exhibition; relief-moulded portraits of Christopher Columbus and George Washington by John Broad; $7\frac{1}{4}$ in. high; 1892–93.

XLV.   Salt-glaze Doulton Ware 'Virago' inkwell; $3\frac{1}{2}$ in. high; designed for reproduction by Leslie Harradine; c. 1905–08. (See page 79.)

XLVI. (*opposite*)   Salt-glaze Doulton Ware 'Toby on Barrel' or 'Double-XX' jug; 8 in. high; designed by Harry Simeon for reproduction; 1929.

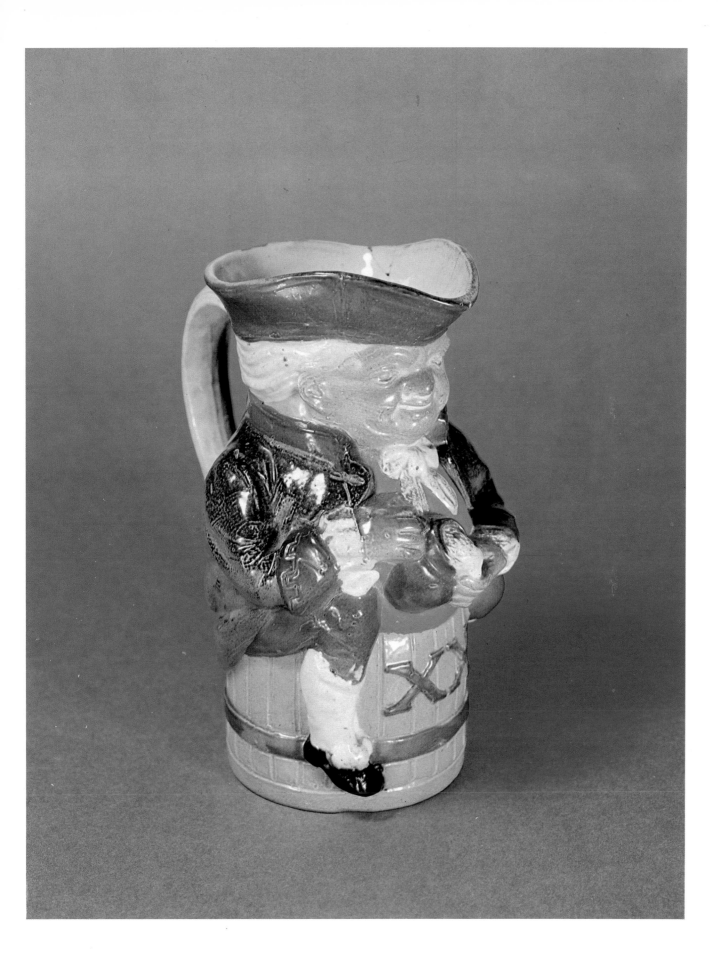

XLVII.   Brown salt-glaze Doulton Ware vase; 7 in. high; Vera Huggins; c. 1930.

XLVIII. (*opposite top*)   Salt-glaze Doulton Ware pots; tallest item (lamp-base) 14½ in. high; Agnete Hoy; 1952–56. (Also with Helen Walter's symbol.)

XLIX. (*opposite bottom*)   Cream-glazed Doulton Ware pots with coloured decorations under an applied 'Bristol' glaze; diameter of largest bowl 8½ in.; Agnete Hoy; 1953–54. (Also with Helen Walter's symbol.)

L.   Salt-glaze Doulton Ware cat; 10 in. high to tip of tail; Agnete Hoy; 1955. (About 12 were made from the mould, all varying in colouring.)

LI.   Doulton Lambeth Faïence tea-pot; 6½ in. high. (This is an early example of Lambeth Faïence made possibly in 1872.)

LII. Doulton Lambeth Faïence vase; $10\frac{1}{4}$ in. high; 1875.

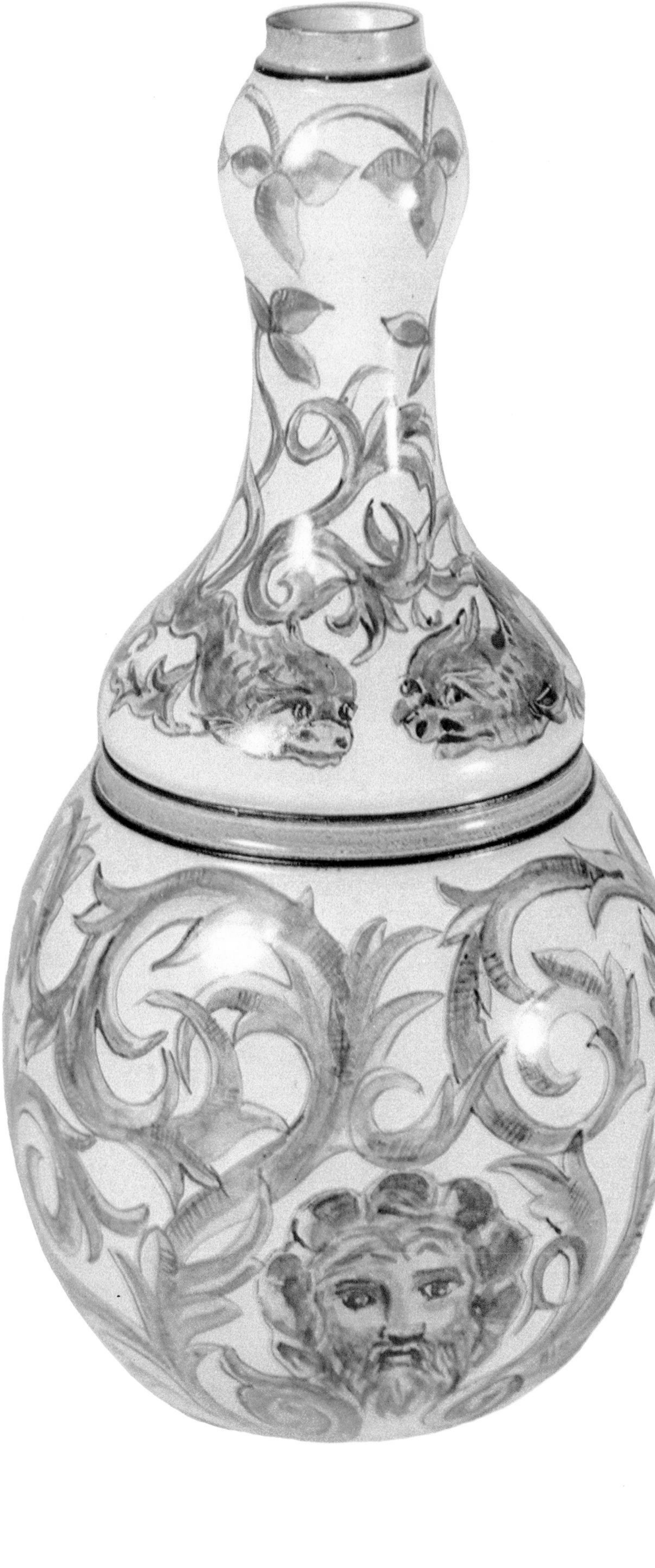

LIII. Doulton Lambeth Faïence wall-plaque entitled 'Old Bridge, North Wales'; 21 in. high; Esther Lewis; 1877.

LIV. Doulton Lambeth Faïence vase; 12 in. high; with monogram of Minna L. Crawley and initials of Nellie Garbett, assistant; 1879.

LV. Doulton Lambeth Faïence vase marked 'CYPRUS' and decorated in style of early Cypriot pottery (see page 160); 10¾ in. high; 1879.

LVIII.   Doulton Lambeth Faïence vase; 12 in. high; Minna L. Crawley; 1877.

LVI. (*opposite top*)   Doulton Lambeth Faïence. *Left to right*: (1) Vase; 13 in. high; Minna L. Crawley; 1877.
(2) Jug; 12½ in. high; A. Euphemia Thatcher; c. 1882. (3) Vase; 13½ in. high; Kate Rogers, c. 1892.

LVII. (*opposite bottom*)   Doulton Lambeth Faïence. *Left to right*: (1) and (5) Vases; 6 in. high; Helen A. Arding;
1879. (2) and (4) Vases; 8½ in. high; Alberta L. Green; c. 1882. (3) Vase; 7 in. high; Mary M. Arding; 1883.

LIX.   Doulton Lambeth Faïence vases; 9½ in. high; Mary Butterton; c. 1885.

LX.   Doulton Lambeth Faïence vase; 10 in. high; monograms of Mary Denley and assistant Josephine Durtnall; 'Doulton Lambeth' written in on base; c. 1885.

LXI. (*opposite*) Massive Doulton Lambeth Faïence vase; 41 in. high; monograms of Florence Lewis and assistant Josephine Durtnall but apparently no Doulton trade-mark; c. 1889.

LXII.   Doulton Lambeth Faïence vase; $9\frac{3}{4}$ in. high; painted scenes by Hannah B. Barlow, additional decoration by Katherine B. Smallfield; c. 1887.

LXIII. Doulton Lambeth Faïence jug; 10 in. high; painted decoration and Chiné (Doulton & Slater's Patent) background; c. 1895.

LXIV. Doulton Lambeth Faïence vases. *Left to right*: (1) 9½ in. high; Helen A. Arding; c. 1880. (2) 16½ in. high; Mary Butterton; c. 1883. (3) 12 in. high; unidentified artist; c.1909.

LXV. Doulton Lambeth Faïence vase; 14½ in. high; seascapes by Esther Lewis; additional decoration by Ada Dennis and Mary Denley; c. 1890.

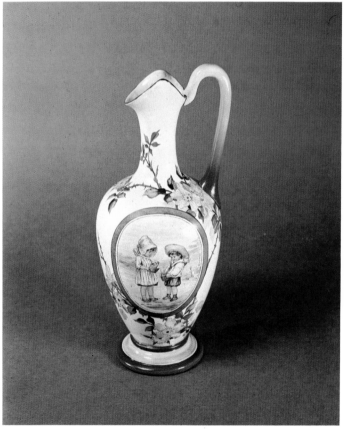

LXVI. Doulton Lambeth Faïence jug; 9½ in. high; monogram of Ada Dennis and initials of Josephine Durtnall and Gertrude Smith; c. 1894.

LXVII. Doulton Impasto Ware vase; 10 in. high; Kate Rogers; 1883.

LXVIII. Doulton Marqueterie Ware vases. *Left*: 10¼ in. high; Ada Dennis and Josephine Durtnall; c. 1892. *Right*: 6 in. high; c. 1889.

LXXI. Two of a series of Doulton Lambeth Faïence tile panels designed and painted by J. H. McLennan for the Birkbeck Bank (later the Westminster Bank), Chancery Lane, London; 1899.

LXXII. One of a series of Doulton Lambeth Faïence tile panels designed and painted by W. J. Neatby for the Blackpool Winter Gardens; 1896.

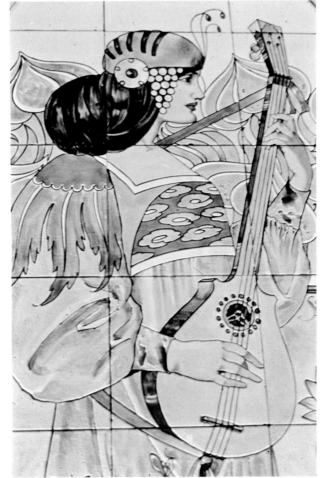

LXIX. (*opposite top*) Doulton Marqueterie Ware tea-pot; $3\frac{1}{4}$ in. high; Ada Dennis; c. 1893.

LXX. (*opposite bottom*) Doulton Marqueterie Ware bowl; 8 in. diameter; c. 1889.

LXXIII. *Left*: Doulton Velluma Ware vase; 8¼ in. high; designed by Margaret E. Thompson for reproduction; c. 1912. *Right*: Doulton Crown Lambeth vase; 13½ in. high; Florence Lewis; c. 1895.

LXXIV. Doulton Crown Lambeth vase; 8½ in. high; c. 1896.

LXXV. (*opposite top*) *Left*: Cream salt-glaze Doulton Ware bust of Charles Dickens; 6½ in. high; designed by Leslie Harradine for reproduction; 1912. *Right*: Doulton hard-paste glost porcelain figure of Doris Keane; 9 in. high; designed by John Broad for reproduction; c. 1919.

LXXVI. (*opposite bottom*) Two Doulton 'Persian Ware' vases; 4¼ in. and 5½ in. high; William Rowe; c. 1925; and salt-glaze Doulton Ware figure of a reaper; 7½ in. high; designed by Leslie Harradine for limited reproduction; c. 1910.

HIGH STREET
LAMBETH

LXXVII.   Doulton Lambeth Faïence painted tile panel, composed of 6 in. × 6 in. square tiles, showing the
High Street approach to the Lambeth Pottery in the 1880s; John Eyre and Esther Lewis.

1. John Doulton: 1793–1873.

2. The Doulton & Watts Lambeth Pottery, c. 1840. (From a painting by Thomas Wakeman.)

3. Brown salt-glaze stoneware Doulton & Watts tobacco jar, with applied relief decorations of topers, trees, etc.; top-dipped darker ochre brown; 9 in. high; c. 1835.

4. Brown salt-glaze stoneware Doulton & Watts jugs with applied relief decorations; top-dipped darker ochre brown; 3½ to 7 in. high; early 19th century.

5. (*opposite top*) Brown salt-glaze stoneware Doulton & Watts spirit flasks; 'Man on Barrel'; 8½ in. high; 'Miss Prettyman'; 6 in. high; Mr. & Mrs. Caudle; 7½ in. high; c. 1840–1850.

6. (*opposite bottom left*) Brown salt-glaze Doulton & Watts spirit flask; top-dipped darker brown; 7¼ in. high; c. 1846. (The other side shows Punch and Dog Toby and is inscribed 'The Triumph of the Pen'.)

7. (*opposite bottom right*) Light-brown salt-glaze Doulton & Watts fish-shaped spirit flasks; 8½ to 11½ in. long; early 19th century.

8. Sir Henry Doulton: 1820–1897. (From a drawing by Frederick Sandys.)

9. Early examples of attempts to produce salt-glaze Doulton Ware, c. 1866. The tankard on the right, 7½ in. high, has an incised classical scene, probably by W. Christian Symons, filled in with cobalt blue – most of which has vanished during the firing. The vase, 6½ in. high, has simple turned and stamped decoration filled in with blue and brown. (See Colour Plate V for another early specimen of Doulton Ware.)

10. (*opposite top*)   Further examples of early salt-glaze Doulton Ware of the kind shown at the Paris Exhibition of 1867; light cream stoneware with turned, incised and applied decoration in cobalt blue; 5¼ and 6¼ in. high.

11. (*opposite bottom*)   Salt-glaze Doulton Ware jugs with carved, incised and applied relief and slip decoration in tones of brown, blue, green and cream. *Left to right:* (1) 10½ in. high; George Tinworth; 1874. (2) 10½ in. high; Arthur B. Barlow; 1873. (3) 9 in. high; George Tinworth; c. 1874.

12. Salt-glaze Doulton Ware jugs by George Tinworth with incised, impressed and applied relief decoration, in tones of blue, brown and green. *Left to right:* (1) 9½ in. high; assistant's monogram of Emma Martin; 1877. (2) 11¼ in. high; 1874. (3) 9¾ in. high; assistant's monogram of Sarah Gathercole; 1876.

13. Massive salt-glaze Doulton Ware vase with incised, carved and modelled decoration, depicting twenty scenes from British history and twenty kings, queens and other rulers (including Oliver Cromwell – described as 'tasting the misery of power'); c. 72 in. high; George Tinworth; 1892 for the Chicago Exhibition of 1893.

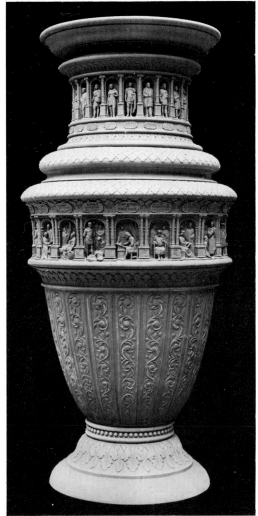

14. Massive salt-glaze Doulton Ware jug with carved, incised and modelled decoration, inscribed with texts and comments relating to the modelled biblical scenes and figures around the middle of the jug; c. 50 in. high; George Tinworth; 1873. (Shown at the Philadelphia Exhibition of 1876.)

15. Terracotta group depicting 'The Presentation of the Child Jesus in the Temple', one of five groups, each comprising three figures, inserted in the panels of a large Doulton Ware pulpit exhibited at Philadelphia in 1876; George Tinworth, 1875.

16. Salt-glaze Doulton Ware 'Nautilus Shell' escorted by cupids on sea-horses; modelled by George Tinworth, with incised seascapes by Hannah B. Barlow; c. 1878. (A similar piece, dated 1878, with a circular opening for a clock-case in place of a seascape, has been recorded.)

17. George Tinworth in his studio at the Lambeth Pottery, in 1887, working on part of his largest and most ambitious terracotta panel, 'Christ before Herod', the overall length of which was 20 feet. The figures are lifesize. The scene illustrated shows two soldiers bringing a sick man to be healed.

18. Terracotta bust of Henry (later Sir Henry) Doulton by George Tinworth; 18 in. high; 1888.

19. 'The Wheelwright's Shop'– a terracotta panel, 8 in. square, depicting an incident in the sculptor's own life (see page 108). George Tinworth; c. 1877. (There are at least three other copies extant, each with slight variations probably made when Tinworth touched them up after they came from the mould.)

20. Two of a set of 'Four Seasons' in salt-glaze Doulton Ware, carved in high relief and glazed in shades of brown and blue; 8½ in. × 4 in.; George Tinworth; 1876.

21. (*opposite top left*) 'The Football Scrimmage', salt-glaze Doulton Ware humoresque; c. 4½ in. high; George Tinworth; c. 1885.

22. (*opposite top right*) Salt-glaze Doulton Ware umbrella stand in the form of a brown kangaroo, holding a dark brown ring and standing on a green base; 38¾ in. high; George Tinworth; c. 1885.

23. (*opposite bottom*) Three salt-glaze Doulton Ware menu-holders; 3¾ in. high; George Tinworth; c. 1884. (Tinworth modelled a set of 40 different 'Mice Musicians' for the 1884 Exhibition of Invention and Music. He produced many variations on the same theme, especially in the 1880s and 1890s – mice groups at the base of spill-vases and incorporated in menu-holders, etc.)

24. Three of a set of brown salt-glaze stoneware 'Boy Musicians'; 4¼ to 5¼ in. high; George Tinworth. (Tinworth modelled at least 55 figures of boys, including two conductors, playing some 37 different instruments, but not all were put into production. The figures were partly moulded and partly modelled and there are many minor variations in facial expressions, hats, positioning of limbs, etc. in the reproductions. Tinworth began work on this set c. 1889 and was still adding to it in 1910. One hundred of these figures were made in 1910–11 with *white* faces; most of these went to Australia.)

25. Salt-glaze Doulton Ware vase; incised, applied relief and *pâte-sur-pâte* decoration; blue, brown and pale straw colouring; 12 in. high; George Tinworth; 1883.

26. (*opposite top*) Two salt-glaze Doulton Ware pots by Arthur B. Barlow, with incised and applied decoration in tones of blue, buff and cream. *Left:* Beaker; 4 in. high; c. 1872. *Right:* Mug; 4¾ in. high; 1873.

27. (*opposite bottom right*) Salt-glaze Doulton Ware jug, white body with deeply incised decoration in tones of deep blue and olive green; 5 in. high; Arthur B. Barlow; 1873.

28. (*opposite bottom left*) Salt-glaze Doulton Ware tea-pot with incised and applied decoration in blue and brown tones; 4½ in. high; Arthur B. Barlow; 1875.

29. Two salt-glaze Doulton Ware jugs by Arthur B. Barlow, with incised, applied and carved decoration. *Left:* 9¾ in. high; 1873. *Right:* 7¼ in. high; c. 1871.

30. (*opposite top*)   Three salt-glaze Doulton Ware pots by Arthur B. Barlow. *Left to right:* (1) Jug, incised dark brown foliage on mottled pink ground with stiff blue leaves on neck; 10 in. high. 1874. (2) Vase with incised blue and pale green foliage on brown ground; 10 in. high; 1874. (3) Jug with incised pink and blue foliage on pale green ground; 10¼ in. high; 1874.

31. (*opposite bottom*)   Three salt-glaze Doulton Ware pots by Arthur B. Barlow. *Left to right:* (1) Ewer with deeply incised foliage and geometric patterns, applied flower-heads in blue and brown tones; 10½ in. high; 1874. (2) Vase with incised brown foliate scrolls and applied white flowers on buff ground, impressed with blue flower heads; 9½ in. high; 1874. (3) Jug with incised green and brown foliage on white ground, impressed with blue flower-heads; 10 in. high; 1875.

32. (*opposite top*)   Three salt-glaze Doulton Ware pots by Arthur B. Barlow. *Left to right:* (1) Jug with incised green and brown scrolling foliage on white ground; 8¾ in. high; 1873. (2) Jug with incised blue foliate scrolls on white ground; 8 in. high; silver mount hall-marked 1872. (3) Ewer with incised leaf motifs in blue, white and green, incised blue scrolls on neck and shoulders, and applied flower heads; 10 in. high; 1875. (Also has the monogram of Mary A. Thomson.)

33. (*opposite bottom left*)   Salt-glaze Doulton Ware jug with incised decoration in brown, blue and buff tones; 9½ in. high; Hannah B. Barlow; 1875.

34. (*opposite bottom right*)   Salt-glaze Doulton Ware vase, the sides modelled in high relief with wolves chasing deer, glazed dark brown on a buff ground; 11¼ in. high; Hannah B. Barlow; c. 1872.

35. Salt-glaze Doulton Ware umbrella stand with dark brown incised decoration on buff ground; 26½ in. high; Hannah B. Barlow; 1874.

36. Salt-glaze Doulton Ware vase with incised frieze of deer pursued by wolves within incised foliate borders, filled with blue and brown slip; 15¾ in. high; Hannah B. Barlow; c. 1872.

37. Three salt-glaze Doulton Ware pots by Hannah B. Barlow. *Left to right:* (1) Jug with incised white decoration against a stippled buff ground; 6½ in. high; c. 1895. (2) Tobacco jar and cover with incised decoration filled in with brown and green slips; buff ground painted with white vermicular pattern; 6½ in. high; c. 1895. (Also bears the monogram of Eliza Simmance.) (3) Jug with incised decoration of lions on buff ground with stippled sky; 8½ in. high; c. 1895.

38. Salt-glaze Doulton Ware vase with incised decoration filled in with brown against buff ground; 12 in. high; Hannah B. Barlow; 1873.

39. Salt-glaze Doulton Ware vases with incised decoration of cattle; applied and tube-tool decoration painted with pigments; 18½ in. high; Hannah B. Barlow; c. 1895.

40. Massive salt-glaze Doulton Ware vase with incised kangaroos; tube-tool and pigment-painted decoration in tones of brown, green, blue and cream; mottled blue-green glaze effects; 28 in. high; Hannah B. Barlow; c. 1900. (This vase also bears the monogram of Florence E. Barlow.)

41. Salt-glaze Doulton Ware vase with incised horses; other incised and applied decoration; mottled blue-green glaze effects; 17 in. high; Hannah B. Barlow; c. 1892. (This vase also bears the monogram of Florence C. Roberts.)

42. Salt-glaze Doulton Ware tea-pot, cream jug and sugar bowl, each piece with incised frieze of rabbits, and green and blue foliate borders; tea-pot 4½ in. high; Hannah B. Barlow, borders by Lucy A. Barlow; 1883.

43. Massive salt-glaze Doulton Ware vase, with incised scenes of lions in two shaped buff panels; impressed blue flower heads, relief scrolls, handles with lion-mask terminals and base modelled with paws; 33 in. high; Hannah B. Barlow and Frank A. Butler; 1886.

44. Terracotta panel with animals modelled in high relief, entitled 'So near and yet so far'; 10 in. by 7 in.; Hannah B. Barlow; 1890. (One of several pieces exhibited at the Royal Academy between 1881–90.)

45. Salt-glaze Doulton Ware vase decorated with birds and foliage in dark olive and white *pâte-sur-pâte;* stone-coloured ground, the surface roughened with regular pattern of small impressed dots; 14½ in. high; Florence E. Barlow; 1883.

46. Three salt-glaze Doulton Ware pots by Florence E. Barlow. *Left to right:* (1) Jug incised with herons on a white ground; 7½ in. high; 1874. (2) Vase incised on buff ground with finches, glazed blue and brown, incised leaf borders; 11 in. high; 1878 (borders by Mary A. Thomson). (3) Jug with incised horses in blue and brown slip on buff ground; base with incised border of green and blue leaves; 6¾ in. high; 1877.

47. Three salt-glaze Doulton Ware pots by Florence E. Barlow. *Left to right:* (1) Vase with incised brown foliate scrolls on buff ground with painted diaper pattern; shoulders similarly decorated with blue foliage, the base with incised blue and green leaves; 10 in. high; 1878. (Also bears the monogram of Mary A. Thomson.) (2) Jug with incised scrolling brown foliage and applied white bead-work and flower-heads on mottled blue ground; 6¾ in. high; 1876. (3) Vase with incised and cut out stylized flowers and foliage in various shades of blue; 10¾ in. high; 1878. (Also bears the monogram of Eliza L. Hubert.)

48. Three salt-glaze Doulton Ware vases with *pâte-sur-pâte* paintings of birds by Florence E. Barlow. *Left to right:* (1) Vase; 17½ in. high; c. 1899. (2) Vase; 10½ in high; 1883. (Also has Lucy A. Barlow's monogram.) (3) Vase; 6 in. high; 1886.

49. Massive salt-glaze Doulton Ware vase with *pâte-sur-pâte* paintings in white and green tones, base with brown and blue incised panels outlined with bead-work; 26½ in. high; Florence E. Barlow; c. 1880.

50. Massive salt-glaze Doulton Ware vase; *pâte-sur-pâte* paintings of birds by Florence E. Barlow; other carved, incised and modelled decoration by Frank A. Butler; c. 32 in. high; 1892 for the Chicago Exhibition of 1893.

51. Salt-glaze Doulton Ware vase with *pâte-sur-pâte* paintings of ducks by Florence E. Barlow; other details not recorded but carving and modelling probably by Frank A. Butler; c. 1901.

52. Massive salt-glaze Doulton Ware vase with incised, impressed and slip-outline decoration filled in with pigment-painting; 28 in. high; Florence E. Barlow; c. 1898.

53. Salt-glaze Doulton Ware plant pot with incised and applied relief decoration; 5 in. high; Frank A. Butler; 1879. (Also has initials of Mary Aitken and Arthur Willcock.)

54. *Left:* Salt-glaze Doulton Ware tankard with incised, stamped and applied relief decoration; 8 in. high; Frank A. Butler; 1882. (Also has initials of Anne Gentle and Arthur Willcock.) *Right:* Salt-glaze Doulton Ware jug with incised decoration; 8 in. high; Frank A. Butler; 1872.

55. Three salt-glaze Doulton Ware pots. *Left to right:* (1) Vase with incised and carved decoration, painted with light and dark brown slips; 7 in. high; Frank A. Butler; 1874. (2) Vase with incised and carved decoration, painted with light blue and light and dark brown slips; 9 in. high; Frank A. Butler; 1876. (3) Vase with carved and stamped decoration, painted with blue, green, brown and white slips; 8 in. high; Florence E. Barlow; 1878.

56. Three salt-glaze Doulton Ware pots by Frank A. Butler. *Left to right:* (1) Jug with incised, applied and impressed decoration in tones of green, blue, pink and brown; 17 in. high; 1874. (2) Jardinière with frieze of applied moulded portraits of Queen Victoria, Victor Emmanuel of Italy, Napoleon III, Empress Eugenie and Kaiser Wilhelm I, each portrait separated by applied reliefs of shamrocks, thistles and roses; 8¼ in. high; 1874. (3) Vase with incised scrolls and leaves and applied flower heads in mottled tones of green, brown and blue; 14¼ in. high; 1876. (Also has the monogram of Eliza L. Hubert.)

57. Three salt-glaze Doulton Ware pots by Frank A. Butler. *Left to right:* (1) Vase with incised green and blue foliage and brown cross-hatched panels; 7¾ in. high; 1884. (Also has initials of Mary Aitken and Fanny Clark.) (2) Bowl decorated with incised leaves and foliate scrolls in brown, blue and green tones, applied flower-heads and bead-work, the rim with four sections of pierced scroll-work; 10¼ in. diameter; 1880. (Also has Mary Aitken's initials.) (3) Jug with carved and incised blue leaf patterns on stippled buff ground, the incised borders with coloured bead work; 13½ in. high; 1881. (Also has Isabella Miller's monogram.)

58. Three salt-glaze Doulton Ware vases by Frank A. Butler. *Left to right:* (1) Vase with incised dark green stylized plants on brown ground in Art Nouveau manner; 17½ in. high; 1909. (2) Vase with incised stylized plants with pale blue stems and green leaves against a grey ground; 13¾ in. high; c. 1895. (3) Vase modelled with projecting stylized flowers, green leaves and brown stems against dark brown and pale green grounds; 14¾ in. high; 1909.

62. Four salt-glaze Doulton Ware pots by Emily J. Edwards. *Left to right:* (1) Jug, hatched buff ground with brown glaze, further decorated with incised blue-glazed leaves; 9½ in. high; c. 1872. (2) Jug with incised green scrolls and blue leaves on scored brown ground; 7¼ in. high; 1873. (3) Dish with incised decoration, green and purple leaves and white bead-work on brown ground; 10½ in. diameter; 1876. (4) Jug, brown ground, with incised leaves and flower sprays filled in with blue slip; 8½ in. high; c. 1872.

59. (*opposite top left*) Salt-glaze Doulton Ware vase decorated in Art Nouveau style with dark blue flowers and seed pods on a pale blue ground with grey borders; 13 in. high; Frank A. Butler; c. 1900. (Also has initials of Rosina Brown.)

60. (*opposite top centre*) Salt-glaze Doulton Ware jug with incised and coloured decoration in blue, green and brown tones; 7½ in. high; Emily J. Edwards; 1871.

61. (*opposite top right*) Salt-glaze Doulton Ware jug with incised and coloured decoration in tones of brown; 7¾ in. high; Emily J. Edwards; 1871.

63. Three salt-glaze Doulton Ware pots by Eliza Simmance. *Left to right:* (1) Vase painted with green foliate scrolls on darker green ground, borders in yellow and brown; 8¼ in. high; 1884. (Also has Emma Martin's initials.) (2) Bowl painted with alternate floral panels in pale green and blue on dark green ground, borders in yellow and brown; 7 in. high; 1883. (Also has Emma Martin's initials.) (3) Vase painted with pale green and blue leaf sprays with raised seed-pods on darker green ground with yellow borders; 9¼ in. high; 1883. (Also has Rosina Brown's initials.)

64. Three salt-glaze Doulton Ware vases by Eliza Simmance. *Left to right:* (1) Vase with incised pale blue flowers and brown foliage edged in white on royal blue ground; 14 in. high; c. 1895. (Also has Rosina Brown's initials.) (2) Vase with incised blue and white flowers and green foliage on dark green ground; 14 in. high; c. 1895. (Also has Rosina Brown's initials.) (3) Vase with incised blue flowers against a buff panel of white scrolls and green borders on a mottled brown ground; 14 in. high; c. 1895.

65. Three salt-glaze Doulton Ware vases by Eliza Simmance. *Left to right:* Large ribbed vase painted with blue leaves and pale blue flowers with green stalks against mottled sepia ground; 15 in. high; 1906. (2) Vase painted with pink pomegranates against green ground; 19¼ in. high; 1910. (3) Vase painted with long-tailed birds on flowering branches between large yellow leaves against pale mottled blue ground; 15¾ in. high; 1916.

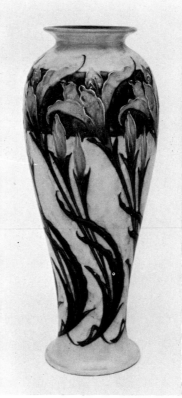
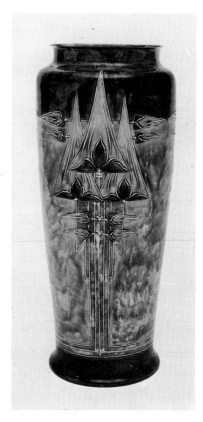

66. (*opposite top left*)   Salt-glaze Doulton Ware vase with incised and tube-tool outlines filled in with greens, pinks and mauves; 11 in. high; Eliza Simmance; c. 1900. (Also has initials of Bessie Newbury.)

67. (*opposite top centre*)   Salt-glaze Doulton Ware vase with incised, tube tool and painted decoration of magnolia blossom and leaves in tints of deep cream, mauve and olive green; 14 in. high; Eliza Simmance; 1907. (Also has initials of Jane Hurst.)

68. (*opposite top right*)   Salt-glaze Doulton Ware vase with tube-tool decoration of stylized flowers and leaves in brown, green and blue tints; 17 in. high; Eliza Simmance; 1904.

69. (*opposite bottom*)   Three Doulton Silicon Stoneware vases by Eliza Simmance. *Left to right:* (1) Vase with incised and painted green and white flowers and leaves against cream ground, the blue neck with impressed gilt flowers; 7¾ in. high; c. 1890. (2) Vase, brown ground painted with white blossom and dark brown leaves, gilt rim; 4 in. high; 1884. (3) Vase, brown ground with three shaped panels with incised and painted white flowers between blue borders, the neck painted with flowers; 8 in. high; 1884.

70. Salt-glaze Doulton Ware vase with three panels painted *pâte-sur-pâte* with flowers on stippled buff ground, borders pierced and carved with pale blue flowers, base and neck incised with leaves; 14 in. high; Edith D. Lupton; 1882. (Also has Mary A. Thomson's monogram.)

71. Doulton Silicon Stoneware vase with carved and painted decoration in blue, black, white and gold; 11 in. high; Edith D. Lupton; 1888.

72. Doulton Silicon Stoneware vase, background washes of white and dark brown slips, *pâte-sur-pâte* and perforated decoration of stylized flowers in blue; 16 in. high; painting by Edith D. Lupton, carving probably by Arthur Beere; 1882.

73. Three salt-glaze Doulton Ware pots. *Left to right:* (1) and (2) Altar vases with incised impressed and applied relief decoration; 13¾ and 6 in. high; E. D. Lupton; 1881 and c. 1892. (3) Vase, possibly replacement of one of a pair originally designed and decorated by Edith D. Lupton, with incised cornucopia of green foliage and brown berries on pale green ground; 12½ in. high; c. 1902.

74. Three salt-glaze Doulton Ware vases by Edith D. Lupton. *Left to right:* (1) Vase, stippled buff ground with incised fruiting vine within blue and brown scroll borders; 10 in. high; 1886. (Also has Emily Welch's initials.) (2) Vase with incised green leaves, painted blossom and berries on buff ground with white vermicular pattern; 6¾ in. high; 1886. (Also has Emily Welch's initials.) (3) Vase with incised mottled foliage and seed pods, carved blue flowers on buff ground with white vermicular pattern; 14 in. high; 1886.

75. *Left:* Doulton Silicon Stoneware vase with chocolate panels painted with blue flowers alternating with light brown panels with incised white scrolls and gilt vermicular pattern; 9½ in. high; Edith D. Lupton; 1884. *Right:* Doulton Silicon Stoneware covered vase, brown unglazed body with impressed flower heads below turquoise and brown panels enriched with gilding; 8¾ in. high; Frances E. Lee; 1885.

76. Three Doulton Silicon Stoneware pots. *Left to right:* (1) Vase, brown
ground painted with chocolate foliage, stippled frieze glazed blue, with pale
blue scrolls; 10½ in. high; Martha M. Rogers; 1883. (2) Vase, light grey
ground with incised and painted brown plants with small blue flowers and
gilt foliage; 7¼ in. high; Eliza Simmance; 1884. (3) Vase, light-brown body
with stippled panels, incised blue and white scrolls within dark brown
borders; 9½ in. high; Martha M. Rogers; 1883.

77. Salt-glaze Doulton Ware vase with incised, impressed and applied
decoration; blue, brown, green and fawn tones; 11 in. high;
Louisa E. Edwards; 1879.

78. Salt-glaze Doulton Ware bowl with incised, impressed and applied decoration, blue, brown and green tones; 3½ in. high; Louisa E. Edwards; 1880.

79. Salt-glaze Doulton Ware vase with carved decoration, tones of blue and olive green; 11 in. high; Louisa E. Edwards; c. 1885–90. (Also has Emma Martin's initials.)

80. Three salt-glaze Doulton Ware pots by Louisa E. Edwards. *Left to right:* (1) **Vase,** pale blue ground with finely incised foliage, with overall incised blue leaves and flowers; 10 in. high; 1881. (Also has Rosina Brown's initials.) (2) Vase with incised blue flowers and foliage on pale blue ground; 11 in. high; 1879. (Also has Eliza L. Hubert's initials.) (3) Jug with incised green and yellow plants with blue flowers on white background; 7¼ in. high; 1878.

81. Salt-glaze Doulton Ware vase, deep blue and light brown tones, with incised decoration and lively modelling of fox stalking hens superimposed on the thrown vase and base; 18½ in. high; unsigned but almost certainly by Cund (see page 96); 1882.

82. Salt-glaze Doulton Ware vase, blue with two modelled monkeys clinging to the sides and two modelled gorillas on base coloured naturalistically; 18 in. high; also attributed to Cund; 1881.

83. Salt-glaze Doulton Ware vase in tones of brown with *pâte-sur-pâte* painting in deep cream of stylized flowers and foliage; 11 in. high; Florence C. Roberts; 1883. (Also has Rosina Brown's initials.)

84. Salt-glaze Doulton Ware tazza, in tones of brown, green and cream; *pâte-sur-pâte* painted flowers by Eliza Simmance, modelled decoration by C. Vigor; 11 in. high; c. 1880.

85. Four salt-glaze Doulton Ware pots by Florence C. Roberts. *Left to right:* (1) Vase, buff ground stippled and modelled in relief with blue flowers and mottled green foliage; 12 in. high; 1885. (Also has Rosina Brown's initials.) (2) Mug, combed buff ground with impressed flowers, further decorated with applied brown flower spray; 5¼ in. high; 1884.
(3) Mug, with incised panels of blue foliage and applied bead-work divided by incised lovat leaves; 5 in. high; 1879.
(4) Vase, buff ground modelled in relief with green, blue and brown stylized flowers and leaves, neck painted with pink and white blossom; 10¼ in. high; 1884. (Also has Rosina Brown's initials.)

86. Three salt-glaze Doulton Ware vases by George Hugo Tabor. *Left to Right:* (1) Vase, buff stippled ground with incised brown masks, urns and foliate scrolls, the pale blue neck deeply scored with spiral grooves; 10¾ in. high; 1881. (2) Vase with carved blue oak-branches and acorns on a hatched ground, the blue neck with yellow bands; 9¼ in. high; 1883. (Also has monogram of Harriett E. Hibbut.) (3) Vase, the green ground with overall incised blue masks, scrolls and flowers; 9½ in. high; 1884. (Also has monogram of Harriett E. Hibbut.)

87. *Left:* Salt-glaze Doulton Ware vase; 10¼ in. high; carved and modelled by John Broad; 1880. *Right:* another vase 10½ in. high; carved and modelled by Harry Barnard; 1881. (Further details not recorded.)

88. Three salt-glaze Doulton Ware vases by William Parker. *Left to right:* Vase with incised continuous blue branch bearing yellow fruits against pale blue ground; 9½ in. high; 1884. (Also has monogram of Harriett E. Hibbut.) (2) Vase with incised flowers on pale buff ground, the shaped borders incised and coloured yellow; 7½ in. high; 1883. (Also has monogram of Harriett E. Hibbut.) (3) Vase with incised foliate scrolls in shades of blue on white ground divided by bead-work; 11¾ in. high; 1879.

89. *Left:* Salt-glaze Doulton Ware vase with carved and modelled decoration, white, light blue, light green and tones of brown; 14 in. high; William Parker; c. 1890. *Right:* Doulton Lambeth Faïence vase with pale and dark blue and pink painted decoration; 11½ in. high; Minna L. Crawley; 1879.

90. Four salt-glaze Doulton Ware vases. *Left to right:* (1) Vase with carved panels of blue foliage surrounded by painted white flowers, the dark blue ground with incised green leaves; 8½ in. high; Eliza S. Banks; 1882. (Also has initials of Annie Gentle.) (2) Vase, white ground with painted cream lattice-work and incised flowering foliage in green and white *pâte-sur-pâte;* 8 in. high; Margaret Aitken; 1881. (Also has initials of Florence Hunt.) (3) Vase, incised and carved brown and blue leaves on hatched ground, with applied shell motifs; 7½ in. high; Margaret Aitken; 1882. (Also has initials of Georgina White.) (4) Vase, the buff ground with incised scale pattern and four panels, two with ears of corn and two with blue flowers; 7 in. high; Elizabeth Atkins; 1883.

91. Three salt-glaze Doulton Ware vases by Frances E. Lee. *Left to right:* (1) Vase, royal blue ground with four stippled buff panels painted with dolphins and flowering foliage in white and green; 9¾ in. high; 1883. (2) Vase, buff ground with finely incised foliage, painted overall in *pâte-sur-pâte* with blossom; 9 in. high; 1882. (3) Vase, buff ground with painted white foliage, incised green leaves and blue flowers; 10¾ in. high; 1884.

92. (*opposite top left*)   Two salt-glaze Doulton Ware vases by Elizabeth M. Small. *Left:* Vase with mottled blue ground with incised bright blue flowering foliage, the edges piped and gilt; 12½ in. high. 1884. *Right:* Vase with incised blue and brown berried foliage on mottled pale blue ground; 10¼ in. high; 1884.

93. (*opposite top right*)   Two salt-glaze Doulton Ware vases by Edith Rogers. *Left to right:* (1) White ground with thick dark olive-green glaze with incised foliage, over-painted in *pâte-sur-pâte* with white foliate scrolls; 10¼ in. high; 1882. (2) Overall incised white and buff scrolls, with three plaques inscribed Scott, Burns and Keats; 11½ in. high; 1882. A similar vase has the names Byron, Milton and Cowper. (Also has Rosina Brown's initials.)

94. (*opposite bottom left*)   Salt-glaze Doulton Ware vase, pale olive-green ground deeply incised, blue flowers, brown leaves; 10½ in. high; Louisa J. Davis; 1882.

95. (*opposite bottom right*)   *Left:* Salt-glaze Doulton Ware vase, buff ground with painted white Y motifs, incised long lovat leaves, brown foliage and blue flowers; 9¾ in. high; Louisa J. Davis; 1877. *Right:* Salt-glaze Doulton Ware vase, white ground with incised spiral band of foliage with blue flowers; 11¾ in. high; Louisa J. Davis; 1877.

96. Salt-glaze Doulton Ware vase with *Chiné* (Doulton & Slater Patent) background with impressed, incised and painted decoration in white, yellow, brown and green tones; 10 in. high; c. 1896.

97. Four examples of salt-glaze Doulton Ware pots with *Chiné* (Doulton & Slater Patent) background, with incised, applied, painted and gilded decoration; bowl 4 in. high, vases 10 to 10¾ in. high; late 19th or early 20th century.

98. Brown salt-glaze Doulton stoneware 'Sea-horse'; 30 in. high;
Mark V. Marshall; c. 1906.

99. Brown salt-glaze stoneware vase with mottled 'orange-skin'
surface; incised, carved and modelled decoration; 9 in. high;
Mark V. Marshall; 1875.

100. Massive salt-glaze Doulton Ware vase, deep blue ground
with applied, carved and modelled decoration in tones of blue
and green against deep blue ground; 36 in. high;
Mark V. Marshall; 1882.

101. Three salt-glaze Doulton Ware pots by Mark V. Marshall. *Left to right:* (1) *Art Nouveau* jug with incised blue and white panels, base of handle modelled with a hare's head; 10¾ in. high; 1909. (2) Vase, shading from white through purple to blue at base, with buff-coloured fantastic creature modelled in relief; 10½ in. high; 1904. (3) Vase with lime-green glaze, incised and modelled in relief with fruiting foliage in brown and white; 10½ in. high; 1904.

102. *Left:* Salt-glaze Doulton Ware flattened disc-shaped bowl, painted with purple foliage in shaped sepia panels, the underside with shaded blue glaze; 4 in. high, 14½ in. diameter; Mark V. Marshall; c. 1890. *Right:* Salt-glaze Doulton Ware vase painted with blue foliate designs against white ground; one side modelled with portrait, the other with a bird amongst flowers; 15 in. high; Mark V. Marshall; c. 1895.

103. Four salt-glazed Doulton Ware vases by Mark V. Marshall, pigment painted on white slip ground in tones of blue, green, brown and pink in colour schemes devised by Walter Gandy; tallest vase 16 in. high; 1906.

104. Brown salt-glaze stoneware vase and lid, designed, carved and modelled by W. G. Hastings; awarded First Prize in Society of Arts competition in 1889; 16½ in. to top of lid.

105. Salt-glaze Doulton Ware figurine, matt white stoneware painted in tones of blue; 7 in. high; Mark V. Marshall; c. 1910.

106. Salt-glaze Doulton Ware vase in tones of blue and brown; designed and modelled by W. G. Hastings; 34½ in. high; c. 1888.

107. (*opposite top*)   Group of four salt-glaze Doulton Ware pots by Mark V. Marshall. Details not recorded.

108. (*opposite bottom left*)   Doulton Silicon Stoneware water filter, buff, grey and light blue, with impressed, applied relief and incised decoration, figures and flower-heads in white relief; 14½ in. high; c. 1885.

109. (*opposite bottom right*)   Doulton Silicon Stoneware water filter, light buff with incised, carved and applied decoration in tones of brown and blue; c. 14½ in. high; c. 1885.

112. (*above*) Salt-glazed Doulton Ware motto jug
with applied relief decoration, inscribed
'BREAD AT PLEASURE, DRINK BY
MEASURE, WHEN YOU DOUBT, ABSTAIN';
6 in. high; designed by John Broad for
reproduction; c. 1896.

110. (*opposite top left*) 'The Lambeth Potter'; unglazed buff terracotta study; 27 in. high; John Broad; 1883. (A few smaller versions 7 in. high were also made for reproduction c. 1903.)

111. (*opposite top right*) Salt-glaze Doulton Ware motto jug with applied relief decoration; inscribed 'FILL WHAT YOU WILL AND DRINK WHAT YOU FILL'; 7¾ in. high; designed by John Broad for reproduction; c. 1896.

113. (*opposite bottom right*) Doulton Silicon Stoneware vase, matt green ground, birds and flowers in glazed relief in white, blue, green and brown; 16 in. high; John Broad; c. 1882.

114. Unglazed dark grey Doulton terracotta bust of William Pitt; 13¾ in. high; John Broad; 1906. (See page 95.)

115. Salt-glaze Doulton Ware clockcase, glazed in shades of blue and brown with carved and incised details and applied bead-work, supporting cherubs moulded and glazed, the back with overall incised yellow and blue foliage on lovat ground; 15½ in. high; monograms of John Broad and Mary A. Thomson; 1879.

116. Brown salt-glaze Doulton stoneware medallion of William Pitt; 7½ in. high; modelled for reproduction by John Broad; 1906.

117. 'Girl and Lizard' or 'The Bather' – off-
white salt-glaze Doulton stoneware figure;
12¾ in. high; John Broad; c. 1914. (A
similar figure was reproduced c. 1923 in
white, purple, brown and green colour
scheme devised by Vera Huggins.)

118. Doulton hard-paste porcelain figure;
7¼ in. high; modelled by John Broad for
reproduction; c. 1919–21.

119. Three Doulton hard-paste porcelain
figures; the tallest 8 in. high; modelled by
John Broad for reproduction; c. 1919–21.

120. Three 'sporting jugs' designed by John Broad for reproduction; applied vignettes of golfers and cyclists; coloured Art Nouveau borders; 7¾, 5 and 7¼ in. high; c. 1900.

121. Three salt-glaze Doulton Ware pots by Francis C. Pope. *Left to right:* (1) Buff stoneware vase modelled in relief with mermaid riding on a fish, covered with copper applied by electrolysis; 11¾ in. high; c. 1905. (2) Vase with incised mottled blue, pink, and green leaves with purple stems against a pale ground; 15¼ in. high; 1904. (3) Slip-cast vase of hexagonal section with mottled green glaze; moulded with pale blue winged beasts in relief; 11 in. high; c. 1910.

122. Three brown salt-glazed Doulton stoneware pots with incised, applied and moulded decoration and 'leopard-skin' surface; 6 in. to 11¾ in. high; designed by Francis C. Pope for reproduction; c. 1910–12.

123. Three salt-glaze Doulton Ware pots by Francis C. Pope. *Left to right:* (1) Vase modelled in relief with white bird among white foliage and blue flowers on pale green ground; 9¾ in. high; c. 1905. (2) Vase painted with green flowers growing from black stems with purple leaves on a pale sepia ground; 10 in. high; c. 1905. (3) Slip-cast vase for reproduction; moulded on each side with a blue bird in a tree, the borders olive-green; 8¾ in. high; c. 1920.

124. Five salt-glaze Doulton Ware vases designed for reproduction by Francis C. Pope, with incised and painted decoration in wide range of slips and pigments in colour schemes devised by Walter Gandy; the tallest vase 18 in. high; c. 1900.

125. Three salt-glaze Doulton Ware vases designed for reproduction. *Left to right:* (1) Slip-cast vase with green leaves and black and white checkered design on yellow panels; 8¾ in. high; c. 1910. (2) Vase with incised and pigment-coloured decoration; 10¼ in. high; Francis C. Pope; c. 1912. (2) Vase with decoration in purple, sepia and pale blue pigments and slips; 8 in. high; Mark V. Marshall; c. 1912.

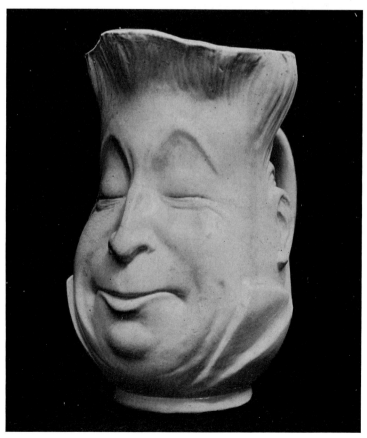

126. Brown salt-glaze Doulton stoneware figure of
French Legion soldier on black pedestal; 9½ in. high;
designed for reproduction by Leslie Harradine;
c. 1905. (Three other models of similar soldiers
have been noted.)

127. Brown salt-glaze Doulton stoneware spirit
flask depicting Dr. Johnson; 6 in. high; designed
for reproduction by Leslie Harradine, c. 1909.
(Some of these flasks are marked with the name of
the 'Ye Olde Cheshire Cheese' in addition to the
Doulton trade-mark.)

128. Cream salt-glaze Doulton stoneware figure
jug depicting Mr. Pecksniff; 7½ in. high; designed
for reproduction by Leslie Harradine: 1912.

129. Salt-glaze Doulton Ware slip-cast cockatoos; 6 in. high; designed for reproduction by Leslie Harradine; c. 1911–12.

130. Three brown salt-glaze Doulton stoneware spirit flasks depicting, left to right, Lord Balfour, Lord Haldane and Austen Chamberlain; c. $7\frac{1}{4}$ in. high; designed for reproduction by Leslie Harradine; c. 1908–11.

131. Three light-brown salt-glaze Doulton stoneware figures designed for reproduction by Leslie Harradine for the Dickens Centenary 1912; c. 9½ in. high; depicting the Fat Boy, Mr. Pecksniff and Uriah Heep. (Other figures depict Sam Weller, Sairey Gamp, Mr. Pickwick, Mr. Squeers and Mr. Micawber. Some of these figures are also found in white-glazed and dark brown stoneware and on square bases; Harradine apparently modelled two different sets.)

132. Two white glazed Doulton stoneware figures, with blue checker decoration, entitled 'Dutch Woman' and 'The Toiler', 7¾ and 8½ in. high; designed by Leslie Harradine for reproduction; c. 1907.

133. Brown salt-glaze Doulton stoneware figure of Sidney **Carton**. (Dickens' *Tale of Two Cities*): 10½ in. high; designed for reproduction by Leslie Harradine; c. 1912.

134. White salt-glaze Doulton stoneware figure, 'Motherhood'; 5 in. high; designed for reproduction by Leslie Harradine; c. 1912–13.

135. Salt-glaze Doulton Ware vase with mottled green neck and base, and paintings of birds amid stylized foliage and flowers; 15½ in. high; Harry Simeon; c. 1922.

136. Two salt-glaze Doulton Ware jugs with ivory glaze background and pigment decoration; 8 in. and 6½ in. high; Harry Simeon; c. 1911.

137. Salt-glaze Doulton Ware vase, with semi-matt amber running glaze on dark brown base. 9¾ in. high; J. H. Mott; 1920.

138. Salt-glaze Doulton Ware jar with deep blue and pearl decoration; 6 in. high; Harry Simeon; 1927.

139. Three salt-glaze Doulton Ware vases designed for reproduction. *Left to right:* (1) Ribbed vase moulded with cellular pattern and glazed olive-green; 6½ in. high; c. 1921. (2) Vase cast into square section, decorated with laburnum on rich blue ground; 8¾ in. high; Leslie Harradine; c. 1912. (3) Vase with moulded yellow flowers growing from blue, purple and green panels in Art Nouveau manner; 9¾ in. high; Leslie Harradine; c. 1909.

140. Three salt-glaze Doulton Ware pots decorated with coloured slips, designed c. 1922 for reproduction. *Left to right:* (1) Slip-cast vase; 7 in. high; Harry Simeon. (2) Slip-cast two-handled vase; 5½ in. high; William Rowe. (3) Vase; 6 in. high; Margaret E. Thompson.

141. Salt-glaze Doulton Ware bowl, raised appliqué brown outline, green and yellow decoration outside, inside mottled blue; 7 in. diameter; Harry Simeon; 1929.

142. Salt-glaze Doulton Ware plaque c. 17½ in. diameter by Harry Simeon and vase by William Rowe, c. 1921–22. (Details not recorded.)

143. Four salt-glaze Doulton Ware vases by Harry Simeon c. 1920–22. *Left to right:* (1) White lilies and green leaves edged in white piping against pale blue ground; 13 in. high. (2) Polychrome colours with a cockerel and blue pheasant among flowering branches outlined with blue piping against a cream ground; 9¾ in. high. (3) Painted with ears of corn in brown, green and purple against a mottled blue ground; 9 in. high. (4) Painted with a parrot among green tropical foliage on a pale green panel above a mottled blue ground; 10½ in. high.

144. Three salt-glaze Doulton Ware vases designed for reproduction by Margaret E. Thompson; 6½ to 8½ in. high; c. 1910/11. (Other details not recorded.)

145. Six salt-glaze Doulton Ware bibelots for use as ash-trays; ring trays, etc.; 3¼ to 4¼ in. high; designed in the 1920s by Vera Huggins, Harry Simeon and other artists for reproduction.

146. Five salt-glaze Doulton Ware pots, with various types of glaze, slip, incised and carved decoration; 1930s; Vera Huggins. (Heights and other details not recorded.)

147. Another group of five salt-glaze Doulton Ware pots, with various styles of decoration; height of largest pot 13 in.; Vera Huggins; 1930s. (Other details not recorded.)

148. Salt-glaze Doulton Ware cylindrical vase with incised and slip-painted decoration; 11½ in. high; Vera Huggins; c. 1930.

149. Salt-glaze Doulton Ware loving cup in light and
dark brown and cream tones, with carved, incised and
modelled decoration; 7 in. high to top of lid; signed in
full by Agnete Hoy; 1953 to commemorate the
Coronation of Queen Elizabeth II. (Limited edition of
100; a smaller version 4¾ in. high was produced in a
limited edition of 25.)

150. Three salt-glaze Doulton Ware pots by Vera
Huggins. *Left to right:* (1) Vase with incised green
flowering foliage on a mottled blue ground; 12¾ in.
high; c. 1925. (2) Bowl painted with pink and blue
flowers against a brown ground, the rim and centres of
the flowers pierced; 5 in. high; 1926. (3) Vase glazed
in green, blue and brown with incised and raised
borders; 11¼ in. high. c. 1925.

151. Group of four salt-glaze Doulton Ware pots by Agnete Hoy, with incised, impressed and painted decoration in several shades of buff, brown and blue, the two small shapes derived from a lotus flower and the fruit of a poppy; the lamp bases 16 in. high; 1954. (Also have the symbol of Helen Walters.)

152. Two views of a salt-glaze Doulton Ware Coronation tankard in light and dark brown and cream, with incised and applied relief decoration; 4 in. high; designed for reproduction by Agnete Hoy; 1953. (Also has the symbol of Helen Walters.)

153. Doulton Lambeth Faïence dish with painted underglaze decoration; 14 in. long; Mary Butterton; 1875. (Bought at Philadelphia Exhibition of 1876 by the Victoria & Albert Museum.)

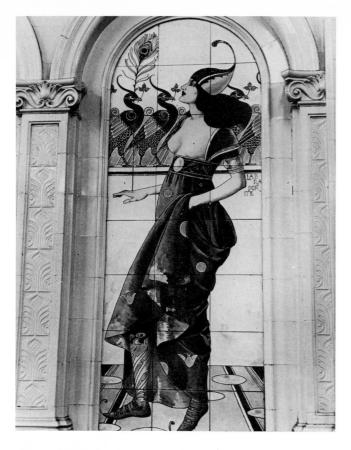

154. One of a series of 28 Doulton Lambeth Faïence
tile panels designed and painted by W. J. Neatby for
the Blackpool Winter Gardens; tiles 6 in. by 6 in.; 1896.
(See also Plate LXXII.)

155. Doulton Lambeth Faïence plaque with painted
portrait of Handel; J. H. McLennan; 1880. (See page 131.)

156. Doulton Vitreous Fresco panel after Botticelli,
12 in. by 9 in.; painted with matt colours and gold by
William Rowe; c. 1907.

157. (*opposite top left*) Doulton Lambeth Faïence 'Orpheus' vase on Greek amphora shape; light and dark green, yellow, brown and turquoise underglaze colours, dark green handles and base; 13½ in. high; John Eyre; c. 1888.

158. (*opposite top centre*) Doulton Lambeth Faïence vase painted in under-glaze colours; 16½ in. high; Mary Capes; 1879.

159. (*opposite top right*) Doulton Crown Lambeth vase and lid, with perforated, modelled and incised decoration, painted in underglaze colours; 24 in. high; Mark V. Marshall 1892 for Chicago Exhibition of 1893.

160. (*opposite bottom*) Group of three Doulton Lambeth Faïence vases painted in underglaze colours and gilded. *Left* by Esther Lewis and Mary Denley; *centre* by John Eyre; *right* by Mary Denley; c. 1890. (Further details not recorded.)

161. Doulton Crown Lambeth vase and lid; 'Ariadne Lamenting', painted in underglaze colours by John Eyre; c. 1890. (Further details not recorded.)

162. Doulton Crown Lambeth vase and lid, 'The Mermaid', painted in underglaze colours by John Eyre; c. 1890. (Further details not recorded.)

163. Doulton Marqueterie Ware tea-pot, gilded; 5 in. high; c. 1887–91.

164. Doulton Marqueterie Ware cup, saucer and bowl, gilded; cup 2¾ in. high, bowl 5 in. diameter; c. 1887–91. (See also Plates LXVIII to LXX.)

165. Salt-glaze Doulton Ware vase with modelled relief decoration, amber coloured glaze; 24 in. high; Richard Garbe, R.A.; 1931.

166. Salt-glaze Doulton Ware sea-lion, bronze glaze; 26 in. high; from model by Richard Garbe, R.A.; 1931–32.

167. Salt-glaze Doulton Ware roundel (one of a series) made in six sections, coloured with blue, white and fawn slips; Gilbert Bayes; c. 1933.

Appendix I

ARTISTS AND ASSISTANTS
AND THEIR MONOGRAMS, SYMBOLS
AND OTHER MARKS

THE lists which follow comprise over 450 artists and assistants with their monograms, symbols and other identifying marks. They include the principal designers and artists concerning whom records have survived, also most of the assistants who worked in the Lambeth Studios for more than a short period.

Almost all the principal artists were also original designers, not just executants of others' ideas. For convenience of reference, stoneware artists and assistants are listed separately from those who specialized in Lambeth Faïence, Crown Lambeth, Marqueterie and the other wares. (Some artists, such as the Barlow sisters, who are known primarily for their stoneware worked occasionally on other media, but these are exceptions.)

Where *dates* are printed in *italics*, this indicates that it is known (either from dated pots or from some surviving record) that the artist or assistant in question was at the Lambeth Pottery during the years mentioned. He or she may, however, have been there *before the first date* and *after the second*. Any help that readers in possession of dated pieces may be able to give to extend these dates will be welcomed.

The Doulton Lambeth Wares fall into two distinct groups:

(A) Pieces designed and mainly or entirely executed by the artist whose monogram or signature appears. Of these, except for pairs of vases and moulded pieces such as figures and animal studies, only one was normally made.

Where two or, in rarer instances, three or more artists collaborated in special (and usually rather elaborate) pieces, the monograms of each of them will be found. On many pots the marks appear also of the assistants who carried out, under the principal artist's supervision, subsidiary aspects of the decoration such as applying beading or bosses, rouletting, stippling and filling in broad uniform areas of background colouring.

An incised or hand-painted number is found near some artists' monograms. It was formerly thought that the number 306, for example, indicated the 306th piece executed by the artist in question since joining the Lambeth Studios. A detailed study and record of many pieces by the same artist shows that this assumption was incorrect, for the sequence of numbers does not tally with the sequence of dates. Nor do the numbers appear to refer to shapes, and so their significance remains a mystery.

Certain figures, animal studies and other hand-moulded or slip-cast items designed by Tinworth, Broad, Marshall, Pope, Harradine, Simeon and a few other artists were reproduced from plaster moulds taken from the artists' original models. Some of Tinworth's smaller terracotta and stoneware plaques (intended for general sale and not specially commissioned or made for exhibition purposes) were also reproduced from moulds. These items were usually assembled, finished and signed by the artist concerned and sometimes (in the case of Tinworth's comical mice, frog and similar groups, for example) there are noticeable variations in detail between different examples of the same subject.

(B) Wares, designed by a principal artist but reproduced in varying quantities by assistants. (See page 55.) Such wares generally bear an impressed or printed number preceded by the letter X. Of these anything from a gross to some 2,000 or 3,000 were made, according to their popularity. The average run seems to have been in the region of 1,500 over a few years, after which the design was usually withdrawn. The only 'repetitive' or 'series' wares of which really vast quantities were made were the relief-figured 'hunting' or 'Toby' wares (see pages 8 and 10).

Impressed or printed factory order numbers, usually larger than the X-numbers, are found on some wares, also letters such as C, WC, FC, denoting various types of clay. The letters HW on teapots indicated that they had been made from a heat-resisting body.

*   *   *

Some pots bear dates. The dates of others can usually be deduced within a few years by combining information derived from trade marks, artists' and assistants' marks, year codes, registration marks and other indications described on pages 89–150.

STONEWARE ARTISTS

(The figures in brackets after the dates refer to illustrations of the artist's work shown in this book. Colour illustrations are indicated by Roman numerals.)

AITKEN, Margaret: *1875–1883* (90)

ATKINS, Elizabeth: *1876–1899* (90)

BANKS, Eliza S.: *1874–1884* (90)
Sparkes said of her in 1880: '(She) has taken up the painting on stoneware by the *pâte-sur-pâte* method, and has invented and executed some excellent designs on a larger and more picturesquely ornamental scale than anyone else. Her work is recognizable by a certain freedom of brush work which perhaps occasionally verges on the natural side of the line that is conventionally held to divide nature from ornament.'
She also used incised and carved decoration very effectively.

BARKER, Clara S.: *1877–1884*

BARLOW, Arthur B.: 1871–1878 (IX, 11, 26–32)

BARLOW, Florence E.: 1873–1909 (XIV, 40, 45–52, 55)

BARLOW, Hannah B.: 1871–1913 (X–XV, LXII, 16, 33–44)

BARLOW, Lucy A.: *1882–1885* (XIV, 42, 48)

NOTE ON THE BARLOWS

After George Tinworth, the artists whose names are most indelibly associated with the rise to fame of the Doulton Wares are Hannah, Florence and Arthur Barlow.

These three, and their sister, Lucy, who also worked in the Lambeth Studios for a few years, were members of a large family of brothers and sisters who grew up in the mid-nineteenth century in idyllic, unspoiled country surroundings, first at Little Hadham in Hertfordshire and later at Hatfield Broad Oak in Essex.

They delighted in an unusual number and variety of pets – among them several different

Hannah and Florence Barlow's Studio, 1887

breeds of cats, dogs and rabbits, a lamb, a tame jackdaw and 'a remarkably sociable pet partridge'. On the 250-acre farm owned by their father, a bank manager at Bishop's Stortford, were horses, ponies, sheep, cows and goats, also a miscellaneous collection of pigeons, doves, pea-fowl and other poultry. During the hunting season fox hounds and stag hounds were frequently out in the neighbourhood.

The young Barlows enjoyed rambling through the woods, fields and country lanes in quest of wild flowers, berries, foliage, birds' nests, fossils and other natural objects. They were encouraged by their father to study natural history and became intimately acquainted with the habits of many animals and birds, and with the metamorphoses of plant life through the different seasons. All this was to bear fruit later in their ceramic art – vividly and realistically in much of the work of Hannah and Florence, more formally in that of Arthur.

In 1859, when he was just thirteen, *Arthur Bolton Barlow* suffered a serious injury to his right hip which gave rise to many complications, confining him to his bed for the next seven years and causing him great pain and inconvenience for the remainder of his life. He had to lie continuously for a long time on his left side, only able to raise himself by resting upon the left elbow. Nevertheless, helped and encouraged by his parents and the family doctor, he eventually managed to take up simple wood-carving. An almost incredible amount of labour and patience was needed in the early stages but his efforts began to show promise and he was greatly inspired by advice and praise from W. G. Rogers, a well-known wood-carver of the period, and from John Ruskin, to whom Rogers showed some of his work. (It is interesting to recall that, some years later, Ruskin encouraged another Doulton artist, George Tinworth, in his early career.)

By 1866, Arthur had improved sufficiently to be able to move around on crutches but his right leg remained permanently useless. He was, however, now able to develop more easily his distinctly individual style of carving groups of fruit, flowers and foliage.

Hannah entered the Lambeth School of Art as a student in 1868 and the following year Arthur joined her there. He remained under the guidance of the director, John Sparkes, for seven years.

Towards the end of 1870 he did several weeks' free-lance modelling for Henry Doulton, as did Hannah, and early the next year they both joined the staff of the Lambeth Pottery, continuing their studies at the Art School in the evenings.

Arthur also studied sculpture at the Royal Academy as an evening student, showing great promise in this field, but unfortunately his health would not stand up to the effort involved. He was, however, able to concentrate on ceramic design and decoration, working – despite his handicap – with extraordinary rapidity and developing a variety of carving, incising and modelling techniques in a highly original way.

John Sparkes spoke warmly of Arthur Barlow's originality. He described his designs as 'a flowing, tumbling wealth of vegetable forms (that) wreaths around the jug, now and then fixed by a boss or pinned down by a point of modelled form', and went on to say: 'his education in the Art School as a modeller was of vast assistance to him, and gave him many methods of dealing with the plastic forms that came under his hands. The occasional use of a gouge or carver's chisel, or other carving tool, gives frequent evidence of his resources. He has carried the system of bossing, or stamping with points, dots and discs to its fullest development. His good taste and perfect mechanical ingenuity have carried his art into fields of decoration of unexpected beauty'.

Arthur Barlow showed his versatility in a wide range of decorations, some fairly simple and restrained, others positively exuberant. He had an exceptional flair for harmonizing decoration with the many different shapes of pots which he designed. His use of the few colours available during his lifetime was particularly subtle.

He died in 1879 at the early age of 34. During the last two years of his life he worked at home, creating numerous new designs in modelling wax and on paper. Although he himself was not able to execute and sign these in clay, some were finished as unique pieces or pairs by assistants and others served as the inspiration for many of the designs which in the 1880s and 1890s were reproduced in some quantity. His influence on several other early Doulton artists is easily discernible.

*   *   *

Hannah B. Barlow, the first woman artist to be employed by Henry Doulton once said that the germ of her life-long vocation as a ceramic designer and artist was 'the coming of a travelling man with a potter's wheel to the village where I lived as a child'. She was only seven at the time and the fascinating sight of the pots 'growing' under the thrower's hand made an indelible impression on the child's mind.

It was a daughter of Rogers, the wood-carver, who introduced Hannah to John Sparkes and the Lambeth School of Art in 1868. There she practised painting, modelling and general design, including the beginnings of the incised or *sgraffito* method of decorating pots which was to become her *forte*. It is thought she was influenced in this direction by the French artist Cazin. (See page 92.) After a short period at Minton's decorating studio in Kensington Gore, she did some free-lance work for Doulton in 1870 and early the next year began to work for him full-time.

Hannah Barlow rapidly developed her special talent, somewhat akin to that of some Japanese artists, which enabled her to draw on paper, or incise in damp clay, almost instantaneous likenesses of animals in a great variety of stances and movements, with the fewest possible lines. These animals were depicted in different settings – pasture, woodland, mountain, forest, tropical desert, jungle, etc.

At her house in the country she had 'a small private zoo', comprising over a hundred creatures of one kind or another. An article in the *Lady* in March 1887 mentions that at that time she had, among other animals, a Scotch deerhound, a black mountain sheep called 'Lady Gwen Morris', a pet goose, a fox terrier, a Russian cat ('much admired by the Prince of Wales when he visited her studio') and 'the latest addition, a little fox, just brought from South Wales, which was at first very savage but is now both tame and gentle, and follows Miss Barlow about as quietly as a well-trained dog'.

She visited regularly the London and other public and private zoological gardens to study various animals and although she made innumerable pen and pencil sketches from life, she was never known to use these for copying on to the clay. She would sometimes observe the animals' movements for hours on end and then reproduce them from memory. As the author, C. Lewis Hind, put it: 'She knows the anatomy and ways of animals by *cumulative experience* and scratches the forms on to the clay . . . a method demanding a precision of touch rare even among artists of distinction.' 'Her art,' wrote Tom Taylor of *Punch*, 'is a living art, derived from close and sympathetic study of life, and having life in it, and so working freely, joyously and profusely as all life works – not in a dead, dull and formed fashion, as mechanical dexterity works.'

It is an interesting side-light on the attitudes of the period in which she lived that Hannah – despite her country upbringing, her experience of numerous pets, and her wonderful powers of observation – seems to have managed to avoid depicting in her otherwise vividly life-like studies of animals any sign of what she would have perhaps called their 'private parts'.

It has often been said that in her *later years* at Lambeth, Hannah, because of the constant handling of damp clay, lost the use of her right hand. In fact this happened (as recorded in a report in the Berlin *National-Zeitung*, 3rd September, 1876) when she had only been at the Lambeth Pottery for three or four years. Her hand was put in splints for several months and remained partly paralysed for the rest of her life. For many wearisome weeks she practised assiduously, making strokes with her left hand, until she gained as complete a mastery over her tools with that as she had formerly had with the right hand. In her determination to overcome her handicap she was greatly encouraged by the example of her brother, Arthur.

Hannah painted occasionally in *pâte-sur-pâte* or combined this with incised outlines. She sometimes modelled animals in high relief on the sides of bowls and vases but examples of these are rare as are those of her plaques with low relief and painted decoration, and her painted tiles and tile panels. Specimens of her painting on Lambeth Faïence and of incised sketches on stoneware of harvesters, children and other humankind are also uncommon.

Between 1881 and 1890, ten studies, mainly of animals, modelled in high relief in terracotta, were exhibited by Hannah at the Royal Academy. She won numerous gold medals and other awards for her work at many national and international exhibitions.

* * *

Florence E. Barlow joined Arthur and Hannah in the Lambeth Pottery in 1873. Some of her early work in foliate scroll and similar types of decoration shows something of Arthur's influence. She also used the so-called *sgraffito* technique fairly extensively for a few years but then branched out in other directions, most notably *pâte-sur-pâte* painting, which after 1878 is the most characteristic feature of almost all her work in stoneware.

It has been said that, in their early incised work, both Florence and Hannah were influenced by Jean-Charles Cazin, a French landscape artist and stoneware potter who succeeded Alphonse Legros as a teacher at the Lambeth School of Art in the early 1870s. Cazin's signature appears on some stoneware made at the Fulham Pottery and a monogram which might conceivably be his has been noted on some early Doulton Ware.

Hannah and Florence depicted both animals and birds on some of their pots up to about 1877–78. It is said that they then came to an agreement that in future Hannah would concentrate on animals and Florence on birds, and with a few rare exceptions they seem to have kept to such a pact for the remainder of their days at Lambeth. It was probably a wise decision, and may have been suggested by Sparkes, for the rare examples of Hannah's birds that one comes across seldom approach the standard attained by her sister.

Florence was particularly successful in producing a sense of light and shade in her *pâte-sur-pâte* paintings of birds in their natural surroundings. Examples of her work are found also on Lambeth Faïence, Crown Lambeth, Marqueterie, Silicon and Carrara Wares. The great bulk of her designs were, however, on salt-glaze stoneware.

Like Hannah, Florence won many awards at the Great Exhibitions.

*   *   *

Lucy A. Barlow, another sister, worked at Lambeth for a few years, probably from 1882 to 1885, judging from dated pieces that have been noted. (She is not mentioned in articles about the Barlows which appeared in 1886 and after.) Little is known about her but it is apparent from the specimens of her work which have survived that, compared with the other three Barlow artists, hers was a minor talent, confined largely to executing borders and surrounds for designs by Hannah and Florence.

One sometimes comes across pots with the monograms of two, or, more rarely, all three sisters. These naturally arouse great interest among collectors of Barlow wares.

Although their basic styles did not change greatly after the 1880s (the main concessions to new trends being in shapes, borders and surrounds), Hannah and Florence both maintained a high standard of execution, all the more notable when one considers their prodigious output. Even in their last few years at Lambeth, the speed and spontaneity with which they decorated pot after pot, without ever repeating themselves, was a constant source of amazement to visitors to their shared studio.

BARNARD, Harry: 1879–1894 (87)

Barnard, while still a youth, came to the Lambeth Pottery, on Sparkes' recommendation, from the South Kensington School of Art, where he had been a student for nearly three years. He continued his art studies for a further three years, in the evenings, at the City Guilds School in Kennington Road. Henry Doulton offered him the choice of assisting Tinworth, Pearce, or Marshall and he chose the latter because he thought it would offer more variety.

He became a versatile designer and decorator in most of the techniques practised at Lambeth in the stoneware medium but it is perhaps in his relief modelling of harpies, gryphons, sphinxes, dragons and other fabulous creatures on vases and bowls that he excelled. Some of these he also modelled as separate pieces. In this field he was no doubt influenced by his mentor, Marshall, but none the less his work is in no sense imitative.

He collaborated not only with Marshall but also with Hannah and Florence Barlow, Eliza Simmance, Esther Lewis, Arthur Pearce and other artists in producing unique pieces for large international exhibitions. A number of Doulton Ware lamp bases were designed by him and among other activities he modelled relief portrait medallions of Disraeli, Gladstone, John Bright and General Gordon for commemorative wares.

After leaving the Lambeth Studios, Barnard became curator of the Wedgwood Museum at Etruria. He was the author of a book entitled *Chats on Wedgwood* published about 1924.

BARON, W.: *1876–1883*

BEARNE, George W.: *1881–1890*

BEERE, Arthur: *1877–1881* (72)
Stoneware and terracotta modeller. His work included figures of the four seasons and others entitled 'Waiting' and 'Valour'. He also modelled figures, medallions and other embellishments in terracotta for architectural use.

BISHOP, Ernest R.: *1881–1884*
Listed in 1882 as an Assistant Artist.

BROAD, John: 1873–1919 (XXXVIII, XLII–XLIV, LXXV, 87, 110–120)
Modeller, sculptor, designer and decorator. He designed many large figures and figure-groups, also fountains, items of garden statuary, busts and portrait medallions in both stoneware and terracotta.

Broad was a versatile and prolific artist, equally at home with large or small works. His merits failed to receive the full recognition they deserved during his lifetime, mainly because he was overshadowed by George Tinworth's fame. Although by the turn of the century Tinworth had done his best work, he continued to be lionised until his death in 1913 as the 'grand old man' of the Lambeth Studios.

Among Broad's many works were: a moulded octagonal vase with relief head of Alexander in the centre of one panel, c. 1880; blue stoneware vases with decoration of green modelled dragons, c. 1880; a large terracotta group for Brisbane, 1880; silicon stoneware vases decorated with birds and flowers in high relief, 1882; a statue of General Gordon for a memorial at Gravesend, 1893;

a statue of Queen Victoria, 8 ft. high, erected on the Albert Embankment, 1899; figures and portrait medallions for the Birkbeck Bank, 1899; a large fountain for Colombo, 1901; a Queen Victoria memorial for Newbury, Berks., 1903; a fountain as a Queen Victoria memorial for Malacca, 1904; figures of 'Youth', 'Age' and 'The Four Seasons' for Ingram House, Stockwell, 1906; Birch Memorial, Ipoh, Perak with four life-size figures symbolizing 'Fortitude', 'Loyalty', 'Justice' and 'Patience', 1909.

Broad designed numerous applied reliefs for commemorative wares, sporting items, motto jugs and the like. Among his smaller figures were 'The Bather' and 'Atalanta' in porcelain and stoneware; 'Madame Pompadour', 'The Minuet' and 'Romance' (Doris Keane) in porcelain; 'Our Lady', 'Pomona' and 'The Potter' (two sizes 7-ins. and 27-ins. high) in terracotta; Queen Victoria on her Throne in stoneware and King Edward VII standing against a column in terracotta and stoneware and faïence figures of Nelson standing against a bollard.

Among his smaller works his striking studies of Boer War soldiers and his bust of William Pitt (produced in a limited edition of, it is believed, only six copies for the centenary of Pitt's death in 1906) are particularly admired.

The above represent but a small fraction of Broad's remarkable output but may suffice to give some idea of his versatility.

See also under FRITH on page 164.

BUDDEN, Alice E.: *1881–1891*
Listed in 1882 as a senior assistant artist; promoted in 1884.

BUTLER, Frank A.: 1872–1911 (X, XIII, XVI–XVIII, 43, 50, 51, 53–59)
Butler, during nearly forty years at the Lambeth Studios, designed and decorated many thousands of vases, jugs, bowls and other pots, large and small, and his work has a great appeal for numerous collectors because of its scope and the way in which it reflects the changing styles of the Doulton Wares from the 1870s up to and beyond the *Art Nouveau* manner at the turn of the century.

One thing at least in which Queen Victoria and Gladstone were fully at one was in their admiration for Butler's work. John Sparkes said of him in 1880: 'Another artist who has made his mark on the ware by the originality of his forms is Frank A. Butler. He is quite deaf and almost dumb, one of many thus heavily afflicted who have passed through the School. He began his artistic life as a designer of stained glass but his invention was not needed nor, I dare say, discovered in the practice of an art which is almost traditional. I introduced him to the new work and in a few months he brought out many new thoughts from the silent seclusion of his mind. A bold originality of treatment and the gift of invention are characteristic of his work. He has struck out many new paths. A certain massing together of floral forms and an ingenious treatment of discs, dots and interlacing lines indicate his hand. He not only produces designs for himself to execute but keeps three or four assistants busy by designing forms and patterns for them to carry out. His best work, perhaps, is that where the ground is carved, leaving the pattern in relief, and he is *facile princeps* in the treatment of the wet clay vessel by squeezing it into shapes other than circular.'

See also pages 29, 35 and 63.

CALLAHAN, James E.: 1883–1936
A talented etcher of landscape and figure subjects and formal ornament for borders, etc.

 CLEMENTS, Frances: *1885–1895*

Joan Cowper COWPER, Joan: 1936–1939
See page 68.

CUE, Charles G.:
Listed in 1895 as a modeller and designer.

CUND, W.? or A.? c. 1878–c. 1881 (81, 82)
A modeller about whom and his work unfortunately little information has been discovered. He was at Lambeth when Harry Barnard came there in 1879, and for one or two years afterwards he worked in the same studio as Marshall and Vigor. He is not listed in 1882 and presumably had left by then. Barnard describes him as 'a modeller of all sorts of animals, real and imaginary; the latter he used to make very dexterously and rapidly in a perfect freehand manner, twirling and creeping round good shapes of simple outline. These were greatly admired and called for in the old days by Howells and James; he must have made scores of them, all different'.

Sparkes said of him in 1880: 'He has an absolute gift for perceiving the devilries in the Japanese and Chinese dragons. These beasts form his favourite subject and he manages to introduce a spirit of fiendish energy into their expressions, their lean reptile proportions and their destructive claws that is to my mind entirely remarkable.'

DAVIS, Louisa J.: *1873–1894* (XXXIV, 94, 95)
A stoneware designer and decorator who specialized in designs based on conventionalized flowers and leaves. Some of her work shows Persian and Indian influence. Sparkes described her treatment of certain plants – notably reeds, sedges and grasses – as having 'a masculine vigour and power of drawing that remind one of old Gerard's woodcuts'.

DAVISON, W.: Late 19th and early 20th century (?)
Doulton designer and decorator mentioned by Mr. J. H. Mott who recorded his monogram.

DUNN, W. Edward: c. 1882–c. 1895

DUNN, Edward: Late 19th and early 20th century (?)
It was formerly assumed that this was W. Edward Dunn, but Mott, who must have known them, listed them as two distinct individuals and gave different monograms for each. Unfortunately nothing more has been found about either of them.

DURTNALL, L. Imogen: *1880–1901*
In her first few years at Lambeth as a Senior Assistant Artist she used the code letters dd.

EDWARDS, Emily J.: 1871–1876 (60–62)
One of the first women designers and decorators at the Lambeth Studios. She specialized in carved and incised foliate patterns.

'Her work,' said Sparkes, 'is ornament made up of an ingenious mixture of classical or conventional forms with natural growths. There is usually great flatness of treatment in her work, with which elaborately diapered backgrounds in no wise interfere. The colour clings to the small stamped patterns on these backgrounds and flows into the deeper depressions, to the manifest enrichment of the piece. She often gave indication of close study of antique methods of decoration.'

Miss Edwards died at an early age and specimens of her work are much rarer than those of many other Doulton Ware designers and artists.

EDWARDS, Louisa E.: c. 1873–c. 1890 (XI, 77–80)
She specialized in incised (often very finely incised) foliage and flowers and scroll-work. Some of her designs suggest Persian and

Turkish influence. She sometimes combined *pâte-sur-pâte* painting with incised and carved decoration.

EGGLETON, Edward E.: 1927–1956 (intermittently)
Served as a draughtsman and lettering artist in the Architectural Terracotta Department at Lambeth from 1927 to 1935 and then went into the Art Department as a general designer with a special responsibility for lettering and tile-painting in which he excelled. His work was interrupted by war service, and later by transfer to another Doulton works, but he returned to supervise from 1950 to 1956 what was left of the Lambeth Art Department after the Second World War.

He worked mainly on designs for mural plaques and panels, indicator tablets, hand-painted tiles and advertising pottery for shipping companies, brewers and other concerns.

ELLIS, Herbert: c. 1877–1928
A versatile modeller of stoneware and particularly of terracotta figures, architectural features, garden ornaments, fountains etc. He collaborated with John Broad on some large groups of statuary. He occasionally signed his work in full.

FISHER, Elizabeth: 1873–c. 1888
Her designs, mainly incised foliate scrolls, formalized leaves and flower-heads, were at first rather over-elaborate with much bead-work and bosses and were much influenced by Tinworth. She later branched out into more original and generally simpler patterns.

GANDY, Walter: 1880–1932 (103, 124)
Gandy was head of the architectural office and catalogue section from about 1890 but also assisted the Lambeth Art Studios greatly with his wide knowledge of historical art and ornament – a subject which he made a life-study. From the turn of the century he collaborated with designers in arranging colour schemes for tile panels, plaques and large faïence vases. He himself designed and decorated a number of pots, and others which he designed were carved and incised by his wife, Ada Dennis (see page 128).

A gifted musician and water-colour painter, he exhibited at the Royal Academy and won a Gold Medal at the St. Louis Exhibition of 1904. Signed pieces by Gandy are quite rare.

HARDING, J. B.: early twentieth century
A modeller whose main work was assisting John Broad on large

figures and figure groups. He also modelled some smaller figure studies for reproduction in stoneware.

LH HARRADINE, A. Leslie: 1902–1915 (XLV, LXXV, LXXVI, 126–134, 139)

A gifted designer and modeller who is admired especially for his figure creations for limited reproduction in brown and white salt-glaze stoneware and coloured Doulton Ware. Among these are studies of North African Spahis; a series of figures of Dickens' characters (Sam Weller, Sairey Gamp, Pickwick, Micawber and Squeers), a bust of Charles Dickens, a figure-jug depicting Mr. Pecksniff, and a mug with relief figures of Sam Weller, Old Weller, Pickwick and Arthur Jingle – produced for the centenary of Dickens' birth in 1912; figures of 'A Dutch Woman', 'Mother and Child', 'A Reaper', 'A Coalman', 'A Sower', 'A Peasant', 'A Peasant Girl' and 'Mermaids'; studies of dogs, cockatoos and other animals and birds; terracotta busts of King George V and Queen Mary; a set of spirit flasks somewhat in the style of the 1832 'Reform flasks' (see page 11) depicting Lloyd George, Asquith, Haldane, Balfour, Chamberlain, Theodore Roosevelt and Dr. Johnson.

After serving in the First World War, Harradine retired to the Channel Islands to work as a freelance designer and modeller; during the next 45 years he modelled many figurines for Doulton's Burslem Pottery for reproduction in bone china, some of which have remained popular favourites to this day.

W HASTINGS, W.: c. 1885–c. 1891 (104, 106)

A designer who specialized in large and small modelled vases in classical and Renaissance styles. In 1889 he gained a Society of Arts First Prize for one of his vases.

AH HOY, Agnete: 1952–1956 (XLVIII–L, 149, 151, 152)

See page 68.

ELH HUBERT, Eliza L.: 1876–1883 (47, 56, 80)

Apart from decorating her own original designs this artist assisted Tinworth with his fable groups and some other models, including clock-cases. Her monogram is also found with that of Butler on some pieces.

V·H *YH* HUGGINS, Vera: 1923–1950 (XLVII, 117, 145–148, 150)

See page 66.

99

HUSKINSON, John: c. 1878–c.1883
Listed in 1882 as a Doulton Ware artist. Apparently not at the Lambeth Studios for very long and examples of his work are rare.

JARRETT, Ernest: *1885–1889*
All that is known about this artist is that he designed and decorated a Doulton Ware vase for which he won First Prize in a Society of Arts Competition in 1889.

JOHNSON, Doris: 1922–1956 (intermittently)
An assistant artist up to 1950, she later designed and executed a number of original vases, bowls and other pots. She painted many of the 'Maxwell Tiles' (see page 67) and also some of the armorial tile panels for the entrance hall of Doulton House (erected on the Albert Embankment, London, S.E.1 in 1938–39).

KEMP, Percy E.: *1881–1890*
Black and white artist and etcher who produced many outline designs for finishing by colouring artists. He left to work for the Press.

LEE, Francis E.: *1877–1894* (75, 91)
Designer and decorator of Doulton Ware and Silicon Ware, specializing in finely incised and carved conventionalized foliage and flowers, combined at times with *pâte-sur-pâte* painting.

LUPTON, Edith D.: c. 1876–c. 1890 (XXIII, XXIV, 70–75)
Her early incised stylized foliate designs were influenced by Arthur Barlow but she later branched out in other directions including delicate *pâte-sur-pâte* painting of flowers and fruits and perforated and carved decoration. She collaborated with Hannah and Florence Barlow, Broad, Beere and Marshall in the production of certain pots.
    She is believed to have retired about 1890 but may have continued to do free-lance work up to her death in 1896.

LYONS, Annie: c. 1890–1939
Doulton Ware, Lambeth Faïence and tile decorator, specializing in painting and enamelling. She worked with Doris Johnson on the 'Maxwell Tiles' (see page 67).

MACKAY, W. W.: Early 1900s?
Recorded by J. H. Mott as a Doulton Ware designer.

M·Y·M MARSHALL, Mark V.: c. 1879–1912 (XXV, XXVIII–XXX, 98–103, 105, 107, 125, 159).

Before coming to Doulton's Lambeth Studios towards the end of the 1870s, Marshall had been a stone-carver working on Victorian Gothic Revival churches. He had also spent some time assisting the Martin Brothers. It was perhaps from them that he derived his taste for the impish and grotesque; this, however, was a fairly general peculiarity of the period and although Marshall's name, in the minds of some collectors, is particularly associated with lizards, dragons and mythical creatures trailing round vases and resting on rocks, this is but one aspect of the creative output of a gifted modeller, designer and decorator who was one of the most versatile and imaginative artists ever to work at Lambeth. Harry Simeon, who knew him in his later years, said of him: 'I could never understand how easily he worked out an idea – much as a bird sings.'

J. F. Blacker, who also knew him personally, wrote in his *A.B.C. of English Salt-Glaze Stoneware:* 'He had the most extraordinary ability in carving the wet clay – great architectural details such as grotesque eagles supporting shields; tall vases, some four feet high, with a marvellous wealth of finely designed ornament; jugs with decoration equally ornate in high relief and open-work – these reveal a few of his activities. Then we can turn to some of his statuettes in glazed stoneware, sweetly graceful . . . Much do I value a vase, nine inches high, which came from his hand. It is of perfect pear-shape-inverted form, with a salamander in relief and open-work clinging round the neck and body on a background of low relief foliage, like giant seaweed, exquisitely finished, a marvel of colouring, a proof of the capacity of salt-glaze for colour schemes without a jarring tone – greys and blues, purples and greens with the animal spotted with the nearest approach to peach blossom possible.'

At the Chicago Exhibition of 1893 a salt-glaze ewer, over 6 ft. high, designed and vigorously modelled by Marshall was said to be the largest decorated pot ever to be made up to that time in stoneware. He was equally at home in modelling whimsical paper-weights and salt-cellars, simply decorated vases and bowls, and a highly original set of large 'gargoyles', caricaturing an editor, a printer's devil, a type-setter and other personnel for the façade of a large newspaper office in Canada. He kept in touch with changing trends such as the *Art Nouveau* movement and some consider that he produced his best work under its influence.

Apart from his signed unique pieces he designed a number of others for reproduction from moulds.

MM   MITCHELL, Mary: c. 1876–1887

This designer and decorator is probably best known for her incised representations of human figures, especially children. These vary considerably in talent. She produced also, many pots with incised, carved and relief decoration of foliage and flowers, both stylized and naturalistic.

JHM   MOTT, Joseph H.: 1880–1950 (137)

Art Director at the Lambeth Pottery from 1897 to 1935: consultant until 1950. See page 63 for further details.

NIGHTINGALE, H. Bone: *1873*

According to Sir Edmund Gosse, Nightingale was one of the Lambeth School of Art students who came to the Lambeth Pottery in 1873; no further record has been found.

WP   PARKER, William: c. 1879–c. 1892 (88, 89)

General and architectural modeller, designer and decorator.

P   **AP**   PEARCE, Arthur E.: 1873–1930

Although one does not come across many signed pots by this designer and artist, he played an inestimably important part in the development of the Doulton Lambeth decorated ceramics.

The son of an architect, he first studied architectural design at South Kensington and then general design at Julien's studio in Paris. He began in London as an illustrator and teacher of drawing. He could use pencil or brush equally well with either hand. He contributed etchings to *The Portfolio* and other art magazines and exhibited at the Royal Academy.

He came to the Lambeth Studios in his early twenties and remained there for 57 years. For some years he continued to study at the Lambeth School of Art.

'He was,' wrote Harry Barnard, 'swift and prolific in his ideas.' He had a vast knowledge of historical styles and ornament, was a gifted etcher, water-colour painter and illuminator, and was constantly consulted by, and collaborating with, other Lambeth Artists. He played a big part in the development of Lambeth Faïence and hand-painted tiles and tile panels, and co-operated with many well-known architects in the design of architectural features in terracotta. Nearly all the Doulton Pavilions at the big International Exhibitions were designed by him.

FP   POMEROY, F.: 1880s

Modeller and designer.

P *F·C·P* POPE, Francis C.: 1880–1925 (XLI, 121–125)
Doulton Ware and terracotta designer and modeller. He also
worked as a free-lance designer for Starkie, Gardner & Co., well-
known wrought-iron makers.

A versatile artist, Pope designed some very pleasing pots in the
early 1900s decorated by the brush-line method. Among his many
other productions were copper- and silver-plated vases, moulded
in relief with fishes, mermaids and other mythological beings,
sea-weeds, etc.; 'leopard-skin' wares – some in simple gourd-like
shapes; garden ornaments; architectural features such as medallions,
portrait busts and *putti* riding on dolphins.

Apart from the signed pieces which he personally designed and
decorated, Pope created many designs for reproduction, especially
by the slip-casting process.

R PRITCHARD, R.: Early 1900s?
Recorded by J. H. Mott as Doulton Ware artist. Further details
not known.

RIX, Wilton P.: 1868–1897
The first Art Director at the Lambeth Pottery. See pages 26 and 158
for further details.

FCR ROBERTS, Florence C.: 1879–1930 (41, 83, 85)
As well as the usual incised and carved techniques practised by
many of the Doulton Ware artists, she was fond of relief modelling
of flowers and foliage. She collaborated with several of the leading
artists, especially Hannah Barlow.

EER ROGERS, Edith: *1881–1888* (93)
Designer and decorator of Doulton Ware, Silicon Ware, Carrara
Ware and Impasto. The daughter of the well-known wood carver,
Alfred Rogers, she was a versatile artist; pots decorated by her
with very finely incised and carved designs and delicate *pâte-sur-pâte*
painting show considerable originality.

MMR ROGERS, Martha M.: *1879–1885* (76)
This designer and decorator was apparently not at the Lambeth
Studios for many years. Her monogram is found on Silicon Ware
and Doulton Ware, usually with incised and *pâte-sur-pâte* decoration.

WR ROWE, William: 1882–1939 (LXXVI, 140, 142, 156)
Designer and decorator, trained at the Lambeth and Westminster

Schools of Art. He was a talented etcher and water-colour painter and exhibited at Royal Academy and other exhibitions. Signed pots by him are fairly rare; he specialized in tile-painting and was responsible, among many other commissions, for the design and most of the execution of the largest set of hand-painted tile panels ever produced at the Lambeth Pottery. (See page 67.) The revival of the 'Persian Ware' in the 1920s was largely due to him and Simeon.

Rowe created a great many designs of vases, scent bottles, bibelots and other pots for reproduction in the 1920s and 1930s. He continued to work occasionally at Lambeth until 1945. With his wide knowledge of historical design and ornament he was frequently consulted by other artists, especially after Pearce's retirement.

EAS SAYERS, Elizabeth A.: *1877–1883*
Listed in 1882 as Doulton Ware artist; apparently not at the Lambeth Studios for many years.

HS SIMEON, Harry: 1896–1936 (XLVI, 135, 136, 138, 140–143, 145)
Simeon worked as a youth with his father who was a monumental mason near Huddersfield. He studied modelling and sculpture at the Huddersfield School of Art where he won a scholarship to the Royal College of Art at South Kensington. He studied there between 1894 and 1896 before coming to the Lambeth Pottery.

Simeon was an extremely modest but gifted designer, decorator and modeller. He was an admirer of Mark V. Marshall's dexterity and ingenuity but regretted his tendency (though it was, he said, 'a tendency of the time') to overcrowd some of his work with excessive ornament.

Among Simeon's wide range of productions were some attractive large hand-painted wall-plaques; many pieces of 'Persian Ware' and leopard-skin stoneware; an original series of 'Toby' jugs, match-strikers, ink-pots and other bibelots; and a range of terracotta garden ornaments. He created many designs for reproduction.

ES S SIMMANCE, Eliza: 1873–1928 (XIX–XXII, XXIV, 37, 63–69, 76, 84)
Although rather over-shadowed in the nineteenth century by the famous Barlow sisters (with whom she often collaborated by designing surrounds for their incised decorations) Miss Simmance later became more and more recognized as an original and versatile designer and decorator, especially of the Doulton Wares and Silicon Wares. Her work during more than half a century, because

of its variety and volume, has great attractions for the present-day collector.

John Sparkes said of her in 1880: 'First among those who have thrown their whole energy into their work is Miss Eliza Simmance. Her work is not only designing with the stylus but especially she excels in painting the *pâte-sur-pâte* patterns. These are examples of her work which are so eminently graceful and well-drawn as to emulate the same qualities in the work of the Italian ornamentists. She, too, has so many ideas to spare – more than she can work out by herself – that she keeps a staff of rising artists occupied in carrying out her instructions.'

She practised most of the decorating techniques in vogue at the Lambeth Pottery and often combined two or three of these on the same pot – incising through coloured slips, carving, perforating, applied relief-figuring, bold modelling, etc. Her finely incised and *pâte-sur-pâte* decoration is particularly attractive.

Like her colleague, Frank Butler, she was very much alive to changing trends in the art world and some of her designs in *Art Nouveau* manner are outstandingly attractive. In her later years she liked to be called Elise rather than Eliza.

She won many high awards at international exhibitions.

JMS SMALL, Elizabeth M.: *1881–1884* (92)
Listed in 1882 as Doulton Ware artist.

EES STORMER, Emily E.: *1877–1895* (XXXVI)
Miss Stormer's monogram was formerly attributed in error to Eliza Simmance. Her style was much influenced by Arthur Barlow and by Frank Butler's early work; it apparently did not change very much during her years at the Lambeth Studios. Her technique and execution were good but some of her pots are over-burdened with decoration.

GTH TABOR, George Hugo: *1881–1889* (XXXI, 86)
Hardly anything has been recorded about this artist and his work. A lustred vase by him, with decoration of fishes and seaweed, made in 1883, is in the Doulton Museum.

TG TINWORTH, George: 1866–1913 (VI–VIII, 11–25)
Sculptor, modeller, designer and decorator of Doulton Ware and terracotta.

John Forbes-Robertson boldly predicted in 1876: 'The name which is destined to make Doulton pottery famous for all time is that of George Tinworth. . . . He is a sort of Rembrandt in clay and unquestionably the most original modeller that England has yet produced.' In his own time, Tinworth – although a few critics dismissed him as merely 'a painter in clay' (referring to Michelangelo's dictum that the more nearly relief sculpture approaches painting the worse it is) – was widely lauded as an original genius. Opinions about his merits and demerits have varied greatly from the time he first began to exhibit at the Royal Academy up to the present day but there is no question of his originality, his uniqueness, and there is no doubt that Forbes-Robertson was largely correct in his prophecy. It *was* Tinworth who first made the name Doulton world-famous, as Sir Henry Doulton himself was always the first to acknowledge, and the two names Tinworth and Doulton have ever since the 1870s been indelibly associated in the minds of collectors and students of late nineteenth-century English ceramics.

*   *   *

The following notes, extracted from a monograph on Tinworth now in preparation, may help to give collectors some idea of this unusual artist and his upbringing.

George Tinworth was born on Guy Fawkes Night, 5th November, 1843, at 6 Milk Street, near Camberwell Gate, Walworth. He spent the first forty years of his life in Walworth, Lambeth and Stockwell, seedy districts of south-east London which had already degenerated sadly from what they had been in the eighteenth century, with their market gardens, orchards and meadows, their Georgian country-houses and their picturesque cottages. By Tinworth's time much of the area had become bleak, dreary and squalid, the result of speculative building and polluting industrialization, with little of beauty or culture to inspire a potential artist.

Tinworth's parents were ordinary people of ordinary hard-working stock. His great-grandfather on his father's side had been a landscape gardener, his grandfather a carpenter, and his father had begun work as a slater's boy, later on becoming a greengrocer with a small delivery van drawn by three or four dogs. Tinworth's mother, Jane Daniel, worked for several years behind the counter of a pastrycook's shop in the Kennington Road, where she was known locally, because of her demureness and piety, as 'the young Quakeress'. She became a member of George Clayton's then celebrated Dissenters' Chapel in York Street, Walworth; Tinworth's paternal grandparents were members of the congregation and it was here that Jane met Joshua Tinworth, the artist's father. (It is interesting to recall that John Doulton also worshipped in this chapel and Henry Doulton was baptized in it.)

During George's early childhood his father, he recalled, had been regarded as 'the most industrious man in the neighbourhood'. But unfortunately the greengrocery venture failed and Joshua, with a brother, started a small wheelwright's business in a back lane in Walworth. This too fell on evil days and by the time George was about eight the family became for a time practically destitute and on at least one occasion, because they could not pay the rent, the landlord put the broker's man in and they had to flit. To make matters worse, Joshua Tinworth became a slave to drink and at times, it was said, was 'an object of terror to his family'. It is clear, none the less, from George's autobiography (unfortunately never completed and very jumbled in places) that he had a deep feeling for his father and a true compassion for his weaknesses. 'My father,' he wrote, 'was a grand man when he was sober.'

The boy grew up in an environment of weary struggling to make ends meet and, at times, of abject poverty. Throughout these trials, his mother's unfailing solace was in her religion; for her the Bible, the chapel, constant prayer, 'the personal walk with God' were the things that enabled her to keep going and to bring up her son in 'the Way of the Lord' who, it consoled her to remember, had said: 'Blessed are the poor.' George was the fourth son born to her but the first one to survive infancy. She vowed that if the child to be born in 1843 were spared to her she would dedicate him to the Lord. Tinworth wrote in his old age: 'Well, I *did* live and she tried to keep her vow but in time I got out of her control and went my own way. But no razor has ever come upon my head, so part of her vow has been kept!' He could indeed have pointed out that his whole life and creative activity had been a continual dedication to the ideals which his mother had instilled into him.

George, it appears, had little regular schooling and none at all beyond the age of twelve. He was, it could be said, brought up on the Bible. His mother told him Bible stories when he was a baby, then as he grew older she read the Scriptures to him again and again. When he had learned to read himself, the Bible became his daily text-book; all other literature was regarded as dross. In an interview he gave to a journalist in July 1897, he said: 'At one time I read practically nothing but the Bible. I steeped myself so in the Scriptures that if anybody asked me whether such and such a passage was in the Bible and, if so, where it was to be found, I could answer him without any difficulty.'

Terracotta medallion, by George Tinworth

In such an environment, it is hardly surprising that Tinworth's evolution as an artist followed an unusual course. 'It was,' he once said, 'at a fair on Camberwell Green I got my first idea of art, when I saw some "Tableaux Vivants".' (These were representations of famous pictures and historical scenes by living persons suitably dressed and in fixed attitudes.) At the time he was about six. His mother bought him slates on which to draw and, later on, paper and paints. When he was eleven or twelve he got to know a shoemaker's apprentice, much older than himself, who used to buy engravings of church windows which he then coloured and re-sold. He showed George how to do this, thereby becoming his first art teacher.

At the age of fourteen, George worked from 7 a.m. to 9 p.m. at a hot presser's in Watling Street, earning four shillings a week which he handed over to his mother. He had to leave home each morning soon after six to walk to work, taking with him some slices of bread and a penny pocket-money. By this time he had begun to carve some butter-stamps out of wood and to model some figures in red clay which he saw some men digging out of a sewer-trench. It was probably a year or so later when the following incident took place: 'I carved a little figure of Samuel out of a piece of mahogany and my mother showed it to a master plasterer who said I ought to go to an art school.'

By this time, after having been sacked from another job in a firework factory, George had begun to work for his father in the wheelwright's shop. Joshua looked on his son's carving as a waste of time. He could quote Scripture for his own ends when he wished and used to say to George: 'Thou shalt not make any graven image!' 'I did my wood-carving,' he recounted, 'at the shop now and then when I could get a chance when my father was out. I would put a boy to look out and let me know when he was coming. When I had the signal I would take the carving out of the vice and throw it to the other end of the yard . . . But sometimes I would show my father what I had done. I remember showing him a serpent I had carved in wood. "Ah, my boy," he said, "you may thank *me* for that wood, and you have enough wood in your head to make another one".'

There are some copies of a terracotta panel by Tinworth, showing the scene in the wheel-wright's shop related above. The original of this almost tragi-comic piece of realism was modelled by the artist about 1877. The copies do not exactly resemble one another and Tinworth must have made some alterations when touching them up after they came from the plaster mould.

Tinworth was by no means the altogether unworldly, narrow-minded puritan he is sometimes made out to be. The following incidents in his early life help us to glimpse that other side of his make-up that comes out so vividly in his humoresques and in some of his quaint, facetious inscrip-tions on panels and figure groups of a highly religious nature. 'As a boy,' he wrote, 'I was always fond of dancing, conjuring and fencing, so I used to go to fairs whenever they came our way.' He loved the annual May Day revels, peeped behind the scenes at circuses, saw the famous Benzoni perform at Ashley's, and got the sack from a firework factory in Peckham for slapping some treacle on another boy's face. He liked boxing and wrestling but drew the line at fighting, even if provoked, on a Sunday! One night he was wrestling with some boys when he fell and broke his arm. He was taken by a stranger to a doctor to have it set. 'But he could see I was a poor boy. He would not set it but said I must go to the hospital. . . . I had to walk home and my father took me to Guy's.' He was left for a long time without treatment, inflammation set in, and he was in great danger of losing his arm. He had to stay in hospital for about 33 weeks.

'I did a bit of conjuring in the street one day,' recalled Tinworth, 'and the schoolmaster was passing and gave me something, though I never longed for money; it was only a bit of fun on my part. But I got into a fix one night when I got my right leg round the back of my neck! I was glad to get it back again and I never tried that trick again!'

*　　　*　　　*

Several differing accounts have been given by Gosse and other writers of how Tinworth came to enter the Lambeth School of Art. He seems to have heard of it for the first time in 1861 and went to look for it in the building where Canon Gregory had founded it seven years before this. The school, however, had meantime prospered and expanded and moved to a new building in Miller's Lane, Upper Kennington Lane. There he eventually located it. Here is what happened then, as told in his own words: 'I saw an old lady going into the school and she invited me in.

When I got inside and saw the statues and the water-colour portraits I felt in a new world! I told this woman that if I had the stone I could carve the statues before us. (I did not know the grandeur of the antique then as I do now.) I asked her if I could come and be taught. . . . I thought I would come and see Mr. Sparkes, the headmaster, so I went the next night and a boy lifted me up to look through the window. Percy Ball was modelling from one of the statues, with hardly anyone there. It was modelling night and I said if there were no more people in the room the next night I would go in. The next night I had another lift up to look in. It was full of people as it was painting night. I had brought a bust of Handel that I had carved in Portland stone. . . . I went round to the side door and Mr. Sparkes was coming out and I showed it to him. . . . I asked him if I could come and be taught modelling. He said: "Come in and see what we are doing." He introduced me to Mr. Bale, the modelling master, saying: "Here's a new student for you, Mr. Bale".'

Tinworth wondered how on earth he was going to get four shillings to pay the entrance fee but his mother pinched and scraped to find it for him. They did not tell Joshua for a long time afterwards but had to in the end for one day he insisted on knowing: 'How is it, George, I give you money but you never have any?' The money nearly all went on buying materials and paying entrance fees for examinations.

Tinworth's first exhibited piece at the school's annual show was a pigeon carved in wood. After a time he won a prize – the first of several at the school – for a carved panel of 'The Saviour being mocked by the Soldiers'. He could not afford to pay for a model at the school so his younger brother, Tom, had to sit for him at home; this meant carting the panel to and fro.

On 22nd December 1864, after three years studying under Sparkes and other teachers at the Lambeth School of Art, Tinworth was admitted to the Schools of the Royal Academy, then near Charing Cross, on the strength of a figure of Hercules copied from the antique. A year later he won Second Silver Medal in the Antique Class and in 1867 First Silver Medal for a Study from Life. He competed for a Gold (Sparkes kindly gave him £10 towards the fee and the cost of models) but was not successful and tried later to be philosophical about it: 'I hardly know what to think about this medal business. It is not worth anything to an artist. You cannot wear the medals if you gain them. If you were a boot-maker you might show them in your window!'

Tinworth was forced to tell his father about getting into the Royal Academy Schools for he had to do his probationership in the morning from 10 to 1. 'So I asked him one morning if he could spare me and he said I might go. When I got home my mother was crying with pleasure, which made me feel like doing the same.'

In 1866, when Tinworth was nearly 23, he exhibited at the Royal Academy for the first time with a small plaster group entitled 'Peace and Wrath in Low Life', an entirely original conception based clearly on his own observations, perhaps even his own experience, in Walworth – two little boys fighting and two little girls trying to separate them, with a dog in the foreground wondering whether or not to join in the fray. It is to be regretted that he did not produce more contemporary studies in this realistic vein.

* * *

The story of how Tinworth came to work for Henry Doulton at the Lambeth Pottery has been told briefly on page 19. After the success of the Doulton Ware at the exhibitions of 1867, 1871 and 1873 in Paris, London and Vienna respectively (a success in which Tinworth had played a major role) his career at Lambeth became a story of one triumph after another.

In 1874 he exhibited at the Royal Academy three large terracotta panels 'Gethsemane', 'The Foot of the Cross' and 'The Descent from the Cross'. The following year eight small terracotta panels, also inspired by biblical themes, were shown at the Academy and evoked a glowing tribute from Ruskin: 'Full of fire and zealous faculty breaking its way through all conventionalism to such truth as it can conceive.'

Further exhibition successes followed and commissions for a reredos for York Minster Cathedral and a series of 28 semi-circular lunettes for the Guards' Chapel in Birdcage Walk – the first two of many important commissions which, it has been said, were enough to keep several ordinary sculptors busy for decades, without taking into account the thousands of vases and hundreds of humoresques which also poured forth from his studio.

A list of some of Tinworth's works in terracotta and stoneware up to 1883 is given in a catalogue of his exhibition at the Conduit Street Galleries, Regent Street, in that year. An interesting introduction by Edmund Gosse gives an account of the artist's life and career up to that time.

In 1894, Tinworth told Harry Barnard, after consulting a note-book, that he calculated he had done at least 500 panels in terracotta 'of important size' and he could not tell how many smaller ones. He continued to produce panels, memorials, figures, figure groups and medallions up to the time of his sudden death in 1913 when on his way to work. By the turn of the century, it is generally agreed, his best work had been done although there were still brilliant flashes of the old genius.

As for his vases and other pots in salt-glaze stoneware, Sparkes said that by April 1874 he had done 'quite a thousand, all different'. In 1880 Sparkes told the Society of Arts that Tinworth had by then designed and decorated 'many thousands of vases'. Harry Barnard, who knew him intimately for many years, said in 1931: '(He) was an indefatigable artist and very rapid. He would, for recreation, as it were, suddenly conceive the idea of decorating some vases. He would forthwith go to the thrower and get him to make some shapes to his instructions, then keep him *all day long* making others like them. As quickly as they were made they would be carried up to his studio in the soft state and he would quickly decorate them with a wonderful spiral-spring sort of scroll-work which was exactly suitable to receive the stoneware coloured glazes and formed a selling-line of which the showroom could never get enough. *I have known him decorate 70 such vases in a day!*'

In his comical groups of animals in human situations, Tinworth also found relief from his more serious and larger works. 'It is a change,' he said, 'to go from one subject to another. . . . I cannot finish off a piece satisfactorily with a tired mind.'

Walter Fairhall knew Tinworth in his later years and has given some interesting recollections of him. 'In 1902,' he wrote, 'Tinworth had a studio on the top floor of the building at the corner of High Street, Lambeth, and Black Prince Road. (This has a terracotta panel by him over the corner entrance, depicting Henry Doulton, Hannah Barlow and Tinworth himself, among other figures.) By this date his best work was behind him but he continued to pour out panels, groups, vases and also the humoresques in which his impish humour found an outlet. He was working then on the panels illustrated in a little booklet entitled *From Sunset to Sunset*. These panels were reproduced from moulds by his assistant, William Hollowell (see page 166), but the demand was disappointing. Most of his other panels, except some fairly small ones, were unique. Some of the smaller panels 8½ ins. square or even smaller were conceived as rough sketches for large works.

'The large panels had to be cut into convenient sections while still soft, with the joints as far as possible coinciding with the lines of drapery, etc. They were reassembled after firing on a reinforced cement base – a method for which there was plenty of precedent from Lucca della Robbia onwards. In the case of life-size or over life-size groups, great skill was necessary to ensure that the jointing would come where least noticeable and at the same time to build up an internal cellular structure to take the weight and maintain structural strength.

'By 1902 commissions for Tinworth's terracotta sculptural work had practically ceased but he was given an absolutely free hand to carry on regardless of expense.

'Although personally genial, Tinworth had little or no contact with most of his fellow artists at Lambeth. This was not from lack of goodwill but from the peculiar circumstances of his life and upbringing. He lacked contact with the wider world; his ideals though noble were narrow; he had no small talk, no general conversation, yet he was pleased when visitors to his studio showed an intelligent interest in his work.'

*   *   *

See also pages 18, 20, 22 and 58.

M̄T THOMSON, Mary Ann: *1875–1890* (XI, XXXII, XXXIV, 32, 46, 47, 70, 115)
Some of this artist's vases with scaly dragons modelled in high relief remind one of somewhat similar pieces by Mark V. Marshall or Harry Barnard but, as already pointed out, a taste for the grotesque and reptilian was a fairly general characteristic of the late 1800s. She collaborated with several other artists of her period, especially Arthur Barlow, Butler, Barnard and Gandy.

F̄ TOMKINS, Louisa E.: *1882*
Listed in 1882 as a Doulton Ware artist.

C.V. VIGOR, C.: *1878–1881* (84)
Vigor was a modeller at the Lambeth Pottery when Barnard came in 1879. Barnard admired his 'very charming low relief work'. He exhibited several times at the Royal Academy. Examples of his work for Doulton are very rare; vases have been noted with relief panels depicting scenes from Greek mythology, also tiles with figuring in low relief.

He had apparently left Lambeth by 1882. He later became well-known as a society portrait painter on the Continent and on his return to England also had many commissions from the aristocracy here.

WHITING, Onslow E.: *1889*
Doulton Ware designer and decorator mentioned in 1889 catalogue of Art-workmanship Exhibition. No other record.

WILSON, Edgar W.: *1880–1893*
Wilson etched plates of ships, landscapes, castles, views of Cambridge and Scottish scenery for reproduction on stoneware. He later became an art critic for the *Pall Mall Gazette*.

YOUATT, Bessie J.: *1873–1888*
Listed in 1882 as Doulton Ware artist. She also designed and decorated some Marqueterie Ware.

DOULTON WARE ASSISTANTS

The letters S.A. stand for senior assistant, J.A. for junior assistant and L.N.E.T. for late 19th and/or early 20th century.

It may be assumed that some of the assistants listed as juniors in 1882, and a few of those listed as seniors, were later promoted but details are not generally available.

Some Doulton Ware assistants helped also with Lambeth Faïence and other decorated wares.

Many assistants used code letters. A lower-case letter usually gives the clue to the first letter of the assistant's surname, e.g. b: Budden; br: Boucher; bbb: Baker. Sometimes the same letter is repeated inverted (see Palmer) or on its side (see Hibberd). Occasionally the first letters of both Christian name and surname are used, e.g. mr: M. Ruckstuhl.

Where dates are given in *italics*, this means no more than that it is known from dated pots or from some surviving record that the assistant was at the Lambeth Studios during the period indicated. She may well have been there longer. Any information readers may be able to give to extend these dates will be appreciated.

AARON, Adelaide: Listed in 1882 as J.A.

ABBOT, Christine: S.A., L.N.E.T.

ADAMS, Elizabeth J.: Listed in 1882 as J.A.

aa   ADAMS, Ella H.: Listed in 1882 as J.A.

AITKEN, Mary: Listed in 1882 as S.A. *1875–1894* (53, 57)

ALLEN, Emily: Listed in 1882 as J.A. *1882–1889*

ASKEW, A. (Miss): S.A., L.N.E.T.

AXFORD, Lizzie: Listed in 1882 as S.A.

AYLING, Louisa: Listed in 1882 as S.A. *1877–1895*

BAKER, Clara: Listed in 1882 as J.A. *1879–1882*

BAKER, Emily: Listed in 1882 as J.A.

BALL, Edith H.: Listed in 1882 as S.A.

BANFIELD, E. (Miss): S.A., L.N.E.T.

BARANYAI, H. (Miss): A Hungarian lady who worked as an assistant in the Lambeth Studios c. 1919–1920.

BARKER, Alice M. E.: Listed in 1882 as S.A. *1882–1895* (She produced some original designs.)

BARNES, V. (Miss): S.A., L.N.E.T.

BARRETT, Mary A.: Listed in 1882 as J.A. *1882–1889*

BEARD, Ethel: S.A. *1890–1930*

BIRNIE, Augusta M.: Listed in 1882 as J.A. *1882–1887*

BIRT, Florence M.: Listed in 1882 as J.A.

BISHOP, Ernest R.: Listed in 1882 as Assistant Artist. *1881–1884*

BISSMIRE, Eborah: Listed in 1882 as J.A.

BLAKE, H. (Miss): S.A., L.N.E.T.

BOUCHER, O. (Miss): S.A., L.N.E.T.

M B   BOWDEN, Maud: S.A., L.N.E.T.

▪b▪   BOWDITCH, Florence: Listed in 1882 as J.A.

.B.   BOWDITCH, Jessie: Listed in 1882 as S.A. *1878–1883* (XXXII)

bb▪   BOWEN, Eliza: Listed in 1882 as S.A.

LℱB   BOWEN, L. F. (Miss): S.A., L.N.E.T. (There is some doubt as to whether or not this is the same assistant as Eliza Bowen.)

W.B   BOWSTEAD, Winnie: S.A. 1896–1947
She assisted several of the later artists. One of the most important assignments she worked on (in 1838–39) was the painting of the Gilbert Bayes frieze 'Pottery through the Ages' over the entrance to Doulton House, Albert Embankment, London, S.E.1.

J·B   BOYCE, Jessie: S.A., L.N.E.T.

D.B   BRIANT, Daisy: S.A., L.N.E.T.

R.B.   BROWN, Rosina: Listed in 1882 as S.A. *1879–1901*
Her initials appear on many pots by Butler, E. Simmance and other artists and on later pieces by themselves. Presumably she was promoted (XI, XXI, XL, 59, 63, 64, 80, 83, 85, 93)

AℰB. **b**   BUDDEN, Alice E.: Listed in 1882 as S.A. *1881–1891*
She exhibited original work in 1889 and had been promoted in 1884.

obo   BUDDEN, Mary: Listed in 1882 as J.A.

ALB. *B*   BURLTON, Alice L.: Listed in 1882 as S.A. *1881–1887*

b+   *G.D.B*   BURR, Georgina: Listed in 1882 as S.A. *1882–1885*

ⓑ   BURRELL, Eleanor: Listed in 1882 as S.A. *1877–1883*

o b   BURROWS, Emma A.: Listed in 1882 as S.A. *1881–1889*

bb *M.B* BUTTER, Mary: Listed in 1882 as J.A. *1882–1885*

A.C. CASTLE, Annie M.: Listed in 1882 as J.A.

c CASTLE, Kate J.: Listed in 1882 as S.A.

m.c. ₍c₎ᶜ₍c₎ CAUTY, M. (Miss): S.A., L.N.E.T.

Ɔ ℓ̰ CHANDLER, Emily M.: Listed in 1882 as S.A. *1881–1884*

■c■ CHURCHER, Clara: Listed in 1882 as J.A.

E.C. CLARK, Emily: Listed in 1882 as J.A.

FC CLARK, Fanny: Listed in 1882 as S.A. *1876–1895* (57)

CO COCKS (Miss): S.A., L.N.E.T.

E.C. COLEMAN, Edith M.: Listed in 1882 as S.A.

R C COLLINS, Rose: S.A. Short period in 1920s.

c■■ CONGDON (Miss): S.A., L.N.E.T.

ccO COOKE, Alice: Listed in 1882 as J.A. *1882–1895*

cOO CROSBY, Emily: Listed in 1882 as S.A.

cc CUPIT, Annie: Listed in 1882 as S.A.

C c■ *L.C.* CURTIS, Lilian: Listed in 1882 as S.A. *1881–1897*

dO DAINTREE, Lizzie M.: Listed in 1882 as S.A. *1881–1890*

d■ DALE, Olive: S.A. c. 1915–1921

KD.   DAVIS, Kate M.: Listed in 1882 as S.A.

MD **d+**   DAVIS, Mary A.: Listed in 1882 as S.A. *1881–1884*

ⓓ   DAYTON, Elizabeth: Listed in 1882 as J.A.

(DENNIS, Ada: see page 128)

dd▪   ⟁   DENNIS, Florence: Listed in 1882 as J.A. Later became a faïence S.A. *1881–1891*

ꝺꝺꝺ   DOUTHWAITE (Miss): S.A., L.N.E.T.

dd   DURTNALL, L. Imogen: Listed in 1882 as S.A.; promoted later. (See page 97.)

▪ɛ▪   EARL, Alice K.: S.A. *1886–1897*

e▪▪   EARL, Florence: Listed in 1882 as S.A.

e▪   *A.E.*   ECKENSTEIN, Alice: Listed in 1882 as S.A.

ee○   ECKENSTEIN, Lottie: Listed in 1882 as S.A.

Sɛ   ELLIS, Sarah: Listed in 1882 as J.A.

Ɛ̵   **e**   EVANS, Bertha: Listed in 1882 as S.A. Later did original work. *1881–1887* (XXXV)

ee   EVERETT, Kate: Listed in 1882 as S.A. *1881–1892*

f▪   FELTON (Miss): S.A., L.N.E.T.

SF   ⓕ   FISHER, Sarah: Listed in 1882 as S.A. *1879–1883*

f○   *Ɛ.A.F.*   FORSEY, Emily A.: Listed in 1882 as S.A. *1882–1889* *ff*   FORSTER, Minnie: S.A. *1895–1915*

ff   FOSTER, Constance F.: S.A., L.N.E.T.

f   FRANCIS, L. (Miss): Listed in 1882 as J.A.

fr   FREAKES, May: S.A. *1911–1956*

ff   FRENCH, Lizzie: Listed in 1882 as S.A. *1879–1882*

Æ̸F   FRENCH, A. E. (Miss): S.A., L.N.E.T.

f■■   FRICKER, M. (Miss): S.A. *1900–1940*

g.**8**   GADSDON, Elizabeth A.: Listed in 1882 as J.A. *1876–1882*

J.G. **go**■   GANDY, Jessie: Listed in 1882 as J.A. She later became a faïence painter. *1881–1889*

EG   **g**   GARBETT, Nellie: Listed in 1882 as S.A. *1879–1882*
(LIV)

NG **gg**■   GATHERCOLE, Ellen: Listed in 1882 as S.A. *1880–1883*

Ⓖ   GATHERCOLE, Sarah P.: Listed in 1882 as S.A. *1873–1883*
(12)

AG.   GENTLE, Annie: Listed in 1882 as S.A. *1879–1883*
(54, 90)

G   **go**   GIBLIN, Kate R.: Listed in 1882 as S.A. Later married John Broad.

■**g**■   GILLMAN, Elizabeth M.: Listed in 1882 as J.A.

g g   GOODE, Mary A.: Listed in 1882 as S.A.

gg○   GOODERHAM, Laura: Listed in 1882 as J.A. *1881–1896*

■g GOODING, M. (Miss): S.A., L.N.E.T.

GOODMAN, Emily: Mentioned by Rix as colouring artist in 1873.

G GREEN, Edith: Listed in 1882 as J.A.

g■ GREEN, Laura: Listed in 1882 as S.A.

OgO GREIG, Lydia: Listed in 1882 as J.A.

g ■■ GRIGGS, A. (Miss): S.A., L.N.E.T.

.G. *ℋG* GROOM, Alice E.: Listed in 1882 as S.A. *1881–1911*

gOO GUEST, Jessie: Listed in 1882 as J.A.

h HARMAN, B. (Miss): S.A., L.N.E.T.

hOO HARRINGTON, Edith: Listed in 1882 as J.A. *1881–1888*

RH. HARRIS, Rosina: Listed in 1882 as S.A. *1879–1883*

hn HARRISON, Nellie: S.A., L.N.E.T.

h k HAWKINS, Ethel: S.A. *1897–1915*

hh■ *E.M.H.* HAWKSBY, Emily M.: Listed in 1882 as S.A.

hh̄ HAYNES, Emily: Listed in 1882 as J.A.

Aℋ HAYS, A. (Miss): S.A., L.N.E.T.

hd HAYWARD, E. Violet: S.A. c. 1897–1942

■h■ HAZELDINE, Rosetta: Listed in 1882 as J.A. *1881–1883* hOh   HEATH, O. (Miss): S.A., L.N.E.T.

h⊐   HELLIS, Alice G.: Listed in 1882 as J.A.

H   h▪   A.M.H   HERAPATH, Alice M.: Listed in 1882 as S.A.

hh   HERAPATH, Edith: Listed in 1882 as J.A.

hhh   HEWITT, F. (Miss): S.A., L.N.E.T.

⊂⊐   HIBBERD, E. (Miss): S.A., L.N.E.T.

HEH   HIBBUT, Harriett E.: Listed in 1882 as S.A. *1876–1884* (86, 88)

(h)   HINCHLIFF, Jessie: S.A., L.N.E.T.

M,H   HOLBROOK, Marion: S.A., L.N.E.T.

hhO   E.H.   HOLLIS, Eliza J.: Listed in 1882 as S.A.

JH   HONEY, Joan: S.A. 1930s. (She designed some pieces for reproduction.)

H̄   hO   HORNE, Agnes S.: Listed in 1882 as S.A. *1877–1894*

hO▪   HORTON, Annie: Listed in 1882 as J.A.

K,H   h▪▪   HUGHES, Kate: S.A., L.N.E.T.

J.H.   HUNT, Florence L.: Listed in 1882 as S.A. *1881–1884* (90)

JH   HURST, Jane S.: Listed in 1882 as S.A. *1881–1914* (67)

⊢J   JONES, Florrie: S.A., L.N.E.T.

J̇ JOYCE, Gladys: S.A. 1913–1956

J JOYCE, Ivy: S.A. 1911–1930. Ivy and her sister, Gladys, were responsible for decorating many of the later 'series' wares and also assisted several of the leading artists on important assignments.

ƐK K KEMP, Edith L.: Listed in 1882 as S.A.

k KNIGHT, Harriette E. E.: Listed in 1882 as J.A.

ll
O LACY, Alice: Listed in 1882 as S.A. *1881–1895* (She also worked in faïence.)

CL LAMB, Charlotte: Listed in 1882 as S.A. *1879–1883*

LATHAM, Jenny: S.A., L.N.E.T. (Engaged primarily on enamel and gilt decoration on Chiné Ware.)

ll LAYZELL, Marion: S.A. c. 1917–1930

L ll LEE, Harriette E.: Listed in 1882 as S.A.

+++1 LEGGE, Nellie: S.A., L.N.E.T.

ll: LILLEY, Ada C.: Listed in 1882 as J.A. *1881–1887*

1: LILLEY, Mary M. S.: Listed in 1882 as J.A. (She later became S.A. for faïence.) *1881–1889*

l LONDON, Ada: Listed in 1882 as S.A.

EA L LONDON, Emily A.: Listed in 1882 as S.A. *1881–1883*

1:: LONGHURST, Alice: Listed in 1882 as J.A.

1d LORD, Jessie: S.A. 1930s.

m▬m   MARLYN, Matilda: Listed in 1882 as J.A.

ⴴⴴ   MARRIOTT, Emma: Listed in 1882 as J.A.

m   MARSHALL, Susan: S.A., L.N.E.T.

m m   MARTIN, Eliza: Listed in 1882 as S.A. *1878–1883*

EM.   MARTIN, Emma: Listed in 1882 as S.A. *1875–1884*
(12, 63, 79)

m▪m   MARTIN, M. (Miss): S.A., L.N.E.T.

mmm   MARTYN, Matilda: Listed in 1882 as J.A.

mO   MATTERSON, Louisa: Listed in 1882 as S.A.

m▪   MAYCOCK, Ada: Listed in 1882 as J.A. *1881–1889*

m   MAYES, Emily: Listed in 1882 as J.A.

EM.   MAYNE, Emily W.: Listed in 1882 as S.A. *1881–1884*

mt   MEDLICOTT (Miss): S.A., L.N.E.T.

mi   MIDDLEMISS (Miss): S.A., L.N.E.T.

▪▪m   MILBORROW, Alice: Listed in 1882 as J.A.

M   MILLER, Isabella: Listed in 1882 as S.A. *1881–1884*
(She may have done some original work.) (57)

ⓜ   MILNE, Annie: Listed in 1882 as J.A.

mOO   MORGAN, Ada: Listed in 1882 as J.A.

ⓝ   NAISH, H. (Miss): S.A., L.N.E.T.

n   NEAL, Annie: Listed in 1882 as J.A.

BN   NEWBERY, Bessie: Listed in 1882 as J.A. for faïence but probably promoted soon afterwards as S.A. to Doulton Ware artists. Her initials are found mostly on stoneware pieces by Tinworth, Butler and other artists. She may have done some original work. By 1911 she had become a supervisor. (66)

N   NEWNHAM, Josephine E.: Listed in 1882 as S.A. *1881–1919*

mn   NEWSON, Mary: S.A., L.N.E.T.

∎n∎   NOBLE, E. (Miss): S.A., L.N.E.T.

   ORCHIN, A. (Mr.): S.A. *1881–1885*

P   L P   PADBURY, Lizzie: Listed in 1882 as S.A.

Op   PALMER, Ellen: Listed in 1882 as J.A. *1881–1895*

EP   PARTINGTON, Emily J: Listed in 1882 as S.A. *1880–1912*

LP   PARTINGTON, Lily: S.A., L.N.E.T.

P∎   PARTRIDGE, Annie: Listed in 1882 as J.A. S.A. in 1890. *1882–1913*

P∎P   PEARSON, Georgina: Listed in 1882 as J.A.

PP   PENNETT, Helena M.: Listed in 1882 as J.A. *1881–1883*

∎P∎   PHEBY, E. (Miss): S.A., L.N.E.T.

Pᒎ   PICKERSGILL, E. (Miss): S.A., L.N.E.T.

rrO   RABBIT, Jane: Listed in 1882 as S.A. *1881–1884*

E.R.   RANDALL, Emily: Listed in 1882 as J.A.

rg   RAWLINGS, L. (Miss): S.A., L.N.E.T.

R   𝒯ᵂ𝑅   READER, Frank W.: Listed in 1882 as S.A. *1881–1885*

𝓕𝑅   r▪   REDFORD, Constance E.: Listed in 1882 as S.A.

r▪   RICKARDS, S. (Miss): S.A., L.N.E.T.

𝒜𝑅   RITCHIN, Alice M.: Listed in 1882 as S.A. *1881–1911*

(r)   ROBJENT, Alice: Listed in 1882 as S.A.

r   ROSEVEAR, Letitia: Listed in 1882 as S.A.

mr   RUCKSTUHL, M. (Miss): S.A., L.N.E.T.

ER   RO   RUMBOL, Ellen: Listed in 1882 as S.A. *1882–1914*

rOO   RUMBOL, Jane: Listed in 1882 as J.A.

▪r▪   RUSSELL, Alice: Listed in 1882 as J.A.

rɹ   RUSSELL, Kate E.: Listed in 1882 as J.A.

R   ↄc   LR   RUSSELL, Louisa: Listed in 1882 as J.A. *1882–1893*

rO   RYMER, Clara: Listed in 1882 as J.A.

𝒜𝒮.   sO   SAYERS, A. (Miss): Listed in 1882 as S.A. *1882–1915*

sOO   SAYERS, Fanny: Listed in 1882 as J.A. *1882–1892*

ssO   SCOTT, Rosalie: Listed in 1882 as J.A.

sr   SHEARS, G. (Miss): S.A., L.N.E.T.

ss▪   SHUTE, A. (Miss): S.A., L.N.E.T.

ЄS.   SHUTE, Emma: Listed in 1882 as S.A. *1880–1886*

ss▪   SHELTON, Annie: Listed in 1882 as J.A.

OsO   SKIDMORE, Alice M. M.: Listed in 1882 as J.A.

A.S.   SMITH, Alice G.: Listed in 1882 as J.A. *1882–1889*

S.   **ss**   E.B.S   SMITH, Ellen B.: Listed in 1882 as S.A. *1879–1882*

GS   SMITH, Georgie: S.A., L.N.E.T.

Ⓢ   SPONG, E. (Miss): S.A., L.N.E.T.

SMS   s▪   STAREY, Mary: Listed in 1882 as S.A.

s   STOCK, Eliza: Listed in 1882 as J.A.

s▪s   STRATFORD, Emilie M.: Listed in 1882 as J.A.

st   STRATTON, E. (Miss): S.A., L.N.E.T.

tl   TALBOT, Winifred: S.A., L.N.E.T.

tO   TEGETMEIER, Florence: Listed in 1882 as J.A.

tt   THOMAS, Elsie S.: Listed in 1882 as J.A.

tx   THOMPSON, Marie E.: Listed in 1882 as J.A.

MGT   THOMPSON, Minnie G.: Listed in 1882 as S.A. *1882–1883*

W   THORNEMAN, Walter: Listed in 1882 as S.A.

AT   TOSEN, Ada: S.A., L.N.E.T.

ttt   TOSEN, Eleanor: S.A. *1885–1920*
(She produced some original designs.)

t■■   TOWNSEND, Ellen C.: Listed in 1882 as J.A.

tOO   TRANTER, Ethel: Listed in 1882 as J.A. *1881–1891*

U: UNWIN, M. (Miss): S.A., L.N.E.T.

v   VARNEY, Bessie M.: Listed in 1882 as S.A.

w: WAKELY, E. (Miss): S.A., L.N.E.T.

LW w   WAKELY, Louisa: Listed in 1882 as S.A. *1882–1892*

✕   WALTERS, Helen: Senior assistant to Agnete Hoy (q.v.) from 1953–1956. Later taught from 1956–1963 at Hornsey College of Art and since 1964 at Goldsmiths College. Has produced and exhibited much original work. (XLVIII, XLIX, 151, 152)

MW   WEBB, Minnie: S.A., L.N.E.T.

wO   WEEKES, Jenny F.: Listed in 1882 as J.A.

EW   WELCH, Emily M. R.: Listed in 1882 as S.A. *1879–1888*
(74)

G.W.   WHITE, Georgina: Listed in 1882 as J.A.
(90)

W   WILLCOCK, Arthur: Listed in 1882 as S.A. Left to become textile and wallpaper designer. *1879–1882*
(53, 54)

wOO   WOOD, Ada M.: Listed in 1882 as J.A.

ww   WOOD, Emily: Listed in 1882 as J.A.

A W. WORTHEY, Ada L.: Listed in 1882 as J.A. *1882–1886*

Y YOUNG, L. (Miss): S.A., L.N.E.T.

Z ZURCHER, A. (Miss): S.A., L.N.E.T.

FAÏENCE DEPARTMENT ARTISTS

See notes re abbreviations, dates, etc. on page 87.

Many Faïence Department artists and assistants were associated with the production not only of Lambeth Faïence but also of Crown Lambeth, Carrara, Impasto, Marqueterie and other wares in which hand-painting formed an important or major element of the decoration (including on-glaze enamel painting on stoneware).

MsA ADAMS, Matilda S.: *1882–1886*

Æ ALLEN, Fannie J.: *1882–1883*

A ARDING, Helen A.: *1879–1883* (LVII, LXIV)

M.M.A ARDING, Mary M.: *1880–1883* (LVII)

ARMSTRONG, Margaret M.: *1880–1889*
Some of her designs were adapted from works by H. S. Marks, R.A., a former student of the Lambeth School of Art. She appears to have specialized in figure-painting.

(Her mark was formerly wrongly attributed to Mary M. Arding.)

ÆB BAIGENT, Agnes E. M.: *1901–1910*
Naturalistic floral ornament and designs in *Art Nouveau* style are characteristics of this artist's work.

AB BUTTERTON, Mary: *1874–1893* (LIX, LXIV, 153)
Examples of her painting are found on Carrara and Marqueterie Wares as well as on Lambeth Faïence. Sparkes said of her in 1880:

'(She) has done very much in original design, mainly treatments of natural forms, often circumscribed by geometrical limits that are suitable to the form of the vase to be decorated. A firm decision of drawing is observable in her work.'

CAPES, Mary: *1876–1885* (158)
Her delicate designs were often influenced by Japanese art. She had, however, an inventive all-round talent and seemed equally at home in natural or stylized forms, geometrical or conventional ornament. Among other things, she developed a painting technique with enamel colours on stoneware that had been glazed by dipping and fired in a salt-glaze kiln.

CHALLIS, Margaret M.: *1878–1884*

COLLINS, F. M. (Mrs. Vale): *1878–1880*
A pioneer in the field of Impasto painting, the successful launching of which owed a great deal to her talents. Unfortunately she died two years after joining the Lambeth Studios and signed pieces by her are very rare indeed.

CRAWLEY, Minna L.: *1878–1885* (LIV, LVI, LVIII, 89)
Much of her work shows the influence of Persian and Rhodian pottery designs. She was particularly talented in depicting the thread-like stems and small leaves and flowers of twining plants, and in her use of subtle blue and green tones of colour.

CRUICKSHANK, James R.: c. 1881–c. 1889
This artist specialized in painting historical scenes on tile-panels and figures, especially heads, on plaques. Harry Barnard recalled that for one of his panels 'Bewick and his Apprentice', Willie Rowe, then a boy, posed as the apprentice.

Cruickshank co-operated also in painting a number of mural panels designed by Eyre.

DENLEY, Mary: *1884–1894* (XXVII, LX, LXV, 160)
Designer and painter, particularly of Lambeth Faïence and Carrara Ware. One of her large vases, painted with Italian-style scroll-work was shown at the Chicago Exhibition of 1893. She specialized in classical shapes and Renaissance ornament.

DENNIS, Ada (Mrs. W. Gandy): *1881–1894* (XXVII, LXV, LXVI, LXVIII, LXIX)
Designer and painter of Lambeth Faïence, Carrara and Marqueterie Wares, she excelled in the depicting of woodland and rustic scenes and children. She also did on-glaze enamel painting on stoneware and decorated pots designed by her husband, Walter Gandy.
(She was listed in 1882 as a Stoneware S.A.)

DURTNALL, Josephine A.: *1882–1895* (XXVII, LX, LXI, LXVI, LXVIII)
Listed in 1882 as J.A. but was exhibiting original work in 1889.

ELLIOTT, Fanny: *1882–1889*
Faïence and Carrara Ware artist. She also painted in on-glaze enamel colours on stoneware.

EYRE, John: c. 1883–1897 (157, 160, 161, 162, LXXVII)
One of the most versatile and outstanding of the Lambeth Faïence designers and painters. His work ranged from flower studies and landscapes to classical and romantic portraits; from delicate and fanciful evocations of fairies, goblins and mermaids in misty ethereal settings to historical scenes full of vigorous action and authentic detail.

Lambeth Faïence Vase, by John Eyre

He had an extensive knowledge of classical and modern art and considerable ability as a figure painter. His monogram is found on a great variety of large and small vases, plaques and mural tile panels. Some of his Impasto panels at the Paris Exhibition of 1889 were over 16 ft. high by 7 ft. 6 ins. wide.

Before coming to Lambeth, Eyre had been with Minton and Copeland.

 GILLMAN, Emily J.: c. 1898–1913

 GREEN, Alberta L.: *1878–1887* (LVII)

 HALL, Alice: *1878–1882*
Mentioned by Sparkes in 1880 as having done some excellent treatments of natural flowers and foliage. (She was then Miss Alice Shelley.)

E.H. HAMILTON, Elizabeth: Listed in 1882 as a Faïence Department artist.

HL HAUGHTON, Lizzie: *1881–1883*
A Lambeth Faïence and Impasto artist about whom little is known.

RK KEEN, Rosa: *1882–1890*

UL LARCHER, Ulrique: Listed in 1882 as Faïence Department artist.

EL LEWIS, Esther: *1877–1897* (LIII, LXV, LXXVII, 160)
One of the most accomplished exponents of painting on Faïence, Impasto and Carrara Ware, she specialized in woodland scenes, mountain landscapes and seascapes. Her portrayal of sunlight and moonlight effects on water is particularly good.

Also very effective was her use of thick slip painting on Impasto Ware to give almost a modelled effect.

Sparkes spoke in 1880 of her 'broad, breezy representations of nature in quiet grey and warm tones'.

FL LEWIS, Florence E.: *1874–1897* (LXI, LXXIII)
Florence Lewis studied at the Lambeth School of Art. John Sparkes introduced her to Henry Doulton about 1874.

'She has,' said Sparkes, 'a remarkable power of design and a skill in painting that is seldom surpassed. Her designs are of flowers, foliage and birds and whether she is working out a large design or a small tile her energy and power are equally shown'.

By the time she left the Lambeth Studios as a full-time artist in 1897 (having come into a legacy), she covered a much more extensive field than that mentioned by Sparkes, not only in pottery but also in her oil and water-colour painting. She exhibited frequently at the Royal Academy, the Royal Institute and the principal London galleries. After 1897 she travelled extensively on the Continent but continued to do free-lance work for Doulton, several examples of which were shown at the Paris Exhibition of 1900.

Apart from her own work as a designer and painter, especially of Lambeth Faïence, Crown Lambeth and Marqueterie, she played an important part in the development of these wares by directing for several years a group of some seventy young women as trainee painters.

She occasionally did some *pâte-sur-pâte* painting on stoneware. She also did occasional designing and painting on china for Doulton of Burslem. A dessert and tea service which she had painted with primroses was bought by Queen Victoria in 1887. A book written by her on *China Painting* was published by Cassell & Co. in 1883.

She continued to paint oils and water-colours up to her death in 1917. At an exhibition of her work in 1916 Queen Mary bought one of her pictures.

LEWIS, Isabel: c. 1876–1897
Isabel was Florence's sister and also worked in the Lambeth Studios as a designer and painter of faïence and other wares.

What Sparkes tactfully said of her work in 1880 remained more or less true during the succeeding years until she and Isabel both retired in 1897. 'Her work', he said, 'gives great evidence of taste although her original design suffers a little by the close comparison with her sister's'.

She designed and decorated many pots for exhibitions and her painting of exotic flowers was particularly admired.

LINNELL, Frances M.: c. 1879–c. 1885
Specialized in flower painting in a broad style on Impasto Wares. She was mainly responsible for the development of this ware after the death of Miss Collins.

McLENNAN, John H.: c. 1879–1910 (LXXI, 155)
Designer and painter of faïence vases, plaques, wall tiles, mural panels, etc., characterized by vigorous drawing and harmonious colourings. He is believed to have been only seventeen when he

came to the Lambeth Studios, continuing his art studies at the Lambeth and other Schools of Art. A year later, at an exhibition at the Alexandra Palace, he won a silver medal for what was described as an 'exquisitely-rendered portrait of Handel' painted on a plaque (see illustration No. 155). He also painted about this time portraits on pottery plaques of Gladstone and several members of his Cabinet.

McLennan was represented at many international exhibitions. He designed and painted tile panels for the King of Siam and the Czar of Russia, also panels for the Birkbeck Bank and the Children's Hospital, Great Ormond Street, London. Some very large tile panels by him in Vitreous Fresco, depicting incidents from Mallory's history of King Arthur were shown at the Paris Exhibition of 1900.

A.M. MARSHALL, Alice: c. 1897–1914
A daughter of Mark V. Marshall, the famous stoneware designer and decorator, she specialized in floral decoration on Lambeth Faïence and Crown Lambeth Wares.

WJN NEATBY, William J.: 1890–1907 (LXXII, 154)
Before coming to the Lambeth Pottery's Architectural Terracotta Department in 1890, Neatby had been apprenticed to an architect and had later spent ten years at Burmantoft's Pottery in Leeds. Although he apparently had no art school training he developed a considerable talent for ceramic design and painting in a flexible and original vein, especially of faïence mural tile panels, richly coloured, in *Art Nouveau* style.

Unfortunately much of his work has been destroyed during the redevelopment of valuable sites in London and other cities (such as Frascati's famous restaurant where he did some magnificent work for the Freemason's Banqueting Hall). Excellent examples are, however, still to be seen in Harrods' Food Halls in Knightsbridge, where there are some colourful murals depicting hunting and pastoral scenes.

Neatby also designed and executed some striking polychrome painted tiles and slabs for the external facing of the Everard Printing Works in Broad Street, Bristol; a set of 28 panels with paintings of women in Pre-Raphaelite costumes for the Winter Gardens in Blackpool; a set of medallions illustrating the history of costume for the Theatre Royal, Birmingham; panels for the John Lines showroom in Tottenham Court Road, London; and mural panels for the King's Café, Birmingham.

In a review of his activities in *The Studio*, in 1903, Aymer Vallance wrote: '(It is) the strength of Mr. Neatby's work that he is no mere theorist but at once a designer, vivid in imagination, and a handcraftsman who has thoroughly mastered the ways and means of his material.'

Further details and illustrations of Neatby's work will be found in *Victorian Ceramic Tiles* by Julian Barnard (Studio Vista, London, 1972).

 NUNN, W. J. W.: *1886–1890*

(PEARCE, Arthur E.: see page 102)

 RHEAD, George Wooliscroft: Faïence designer and painter listed in 1882.

Doulton Ware Vase (left), by Florence E. Barlow; Lambeth Faïence Vase (right), by Emma Roberts

 ROBERTS, Emma: *1882–1912*
Some of her work reflects the influence of Italian maiolica. In her later years at Lambeth she supervised a group of assistants decorating Natural Foliage and other wares.

 ROGERS, Isabel: Late 19th century.

 ROGERS, Kate: *1880–1893* (XXVI, LVI, LXVII)
Faïence and Impasto painter, specializing in floral decoration with a strong, firm touch.

 RUDDOCK, E. (Miss): Late 19th century.

(SHELLEY, Alice: see HALL)

 KBS SMALLFIELD, Katherine B.: c. 1881–1912 (LXII)
Listed in 1882 as a senior assistant in the Faïence Department, she was later promoted and specialized in figure subjects.

132

CAS SPARKES, Catherine A.: 1870s.
A talented all-round artist, the wife of John Sparkes, she did free-lance work for Doulton in the 1870s and perhaps later, and assisted her husband particularly in his efforts to develop faïence at the Lambeth Pottery.

A tile panel designed and painted by her, comprising 252 tiles, 6 in. by 6 in., depicting the Pilgrim Fathers saying farewell to friends in England, was greatly admired at the Philadelphia Exhibition in 1876.

F.S. STABLE, Fanny: *1879–1883*
According to Sparkes in 1880, Miss Stable had 'taken as her model the treatment of large surfaces by the Japanese, and by the study of these great teachers succeeded in producing paintings of excellent interpretations of nature'.

Examples of her work have been noted which also show Persian and Rhodian influence and French rococo style of floral decoration.

STURGEON, Katherine: *1875–1883*
She specialized in figure painting on tiles and plaques.

THATCHER, A. Euphemia: *1879–1889* (LVI)

THOMPSON, Margaret E.: c. 1889–c. 1926 (LXXIII, 140, 144)
She continued in a completely different vein the work of painting on mural tile panels begun by John Eyre, specializing in scenes inspired by legends, nursery rhymes and children's stories. These were mostly designed as mural decorations for hospital wards and had the great advantage, for such applications, of being easily cleaned.

Some good examples of her work are still to be seen in St. Thomas's Hospital, London.

Miss Thompson also designed some attractive Doulton Ware vases and bowls in *Art Nouveau* style in the early 20th century.

VARGAS, C. (Miss): L.N.E.T.

VARGAS, R. (Miss): L.N.E.T.

Watt WATT, Linnie: *1875–1890*
Faïence artist specializing in rustic scenes and figure painting. She exhibited paintings at the Royal Academy and examples of her

work were shown at the Philadelphia Exhibition of 1876. (The *New York Times* on 20th August of that year referred to her as 'the daughter of a potter'.)

Sparkes spoke very highly of her, saying: '(She) has a most distinguished gift for conveying the impression of a picturesque scene with rustic figures, in excellent colour and with artistic breadth of effect, quite admirable in its truth. Her works will speak for themselves to every artist who sees them.'

 WRAY, C. M.: L.N.E.T.

*　　*　　*

FAÏENCE DEPARTMENT ASSISTANTS

See notes re abbreviations, code letters, dates, etc. on page 112.

The arrows, curves and other symbols used by many principal assistants who worked at the Lambeth Studios between about 1890 and 1914 generally give little or no clue to the names of these assistants. The following tables should help to locate most of them.

ARROWS OR SIMILAR

E. Archer	E. Nash
N. Brake	A. Spurrell
L. Hayward	K. Whitton
A. Lacy	

STRAIGHT LINES

G. Barker	L. Parker
F. Dennis	L. Rogers
M. Edermaniger	A. Rohss
E. Harrison	N. Taylor
L. Marriott	F. Tomlyn
M. Neal	

CURVES OR WHORLS

M. Gray   A. Marshall

E. Henderson   F. Norrish

K. Heywood   E. Smith

E. Jessett   N. Straker

F. Lewis   R. Wilson

ONE CURVE AND ONE STROKE

A. Bentley (with dot)   E. Forsyth

J. Chandler   A. Mills

E. Clark   A. Tranter (no dot)

A. Duncan

ONE CURVE AND TWO STROKES

N. Atkins   A. Lyons

D. Broad   G. Nye

C. Bunn   F. Sawyer

D. Cordero   H. Toland

A. Daniels   A. Turner

M. Dunton   K. Walker

E. Graver   M. Welsby

ONE CURVE AND THREE STROKES

E. Brooke   E. Norris

B. Macnae   F. Perrin

L. Mear

TWO CURVES AND ONE STROKE OR DOT

N. Beeden	M. Pryce
G. Benson	G. Sharpe
F. Blackstaffe	F. Shipman
D. Frampton	H. Wilkinson
E. Henderson	C. Wood
M. Lilley	

TWO CURVES AND TWO STROKES

D. Crofts	F. Russell
M. Driver	M. Thornton
J. Lasham	A. Tosen
F. Maskell	A. Wilson

TWO CURVES AND THREE STROKES

A. Potterton

*   *   *

The Faïence Department assistants were often involved in decorating wares other than Lambeth Faïence in which painting was an important part of the overall design, e.g. Carrara, Marqueterie, Impasto, Chiné and Chiné-Gilt, Vitreous Fresco and Persian Wares.

In the case of Faïence Department Assistants the abbreviation L.N.E.T. (late 19th and/or early 20th century) signify dates approximately somewhere between 1890 and 1914. Unfortunately it is not so far possible to be more precise.

ARCHER, E. (Miss): L.N.E.T.

ATKINS, N. (Miss): L.N.E.T.

BARKER, G. (Miss): L.N.E.T.

BECK, Acidalia E. C.: Listed in 1882 as J.A.

BEEDEN, N. (Miss): L.N.E.T.

BENSON, G. (Miss): L.N.E.T.

BENTLEY, A. (Miss): L.N.E.T.

BLACKSTAFFE, F. (Miss): L.N.E.T.

BRAKE, N. (Miss): L.N.E.T.

BROND, D. (Miss): L.N.E.T.

BROOKE, F. (Miss): L.N.E.T.

BUNN, C. (Miss): L.N.E.T.

CAFFIN, Alice: Listed in 1882 as J.A.

CAMPBELL, Alice: Listed in 1882 as J.A.

CAPES, Bertha M.: Listed in 1882 as S.A.

CHANDLER, J. (Miss): L.N.E.T.

CLARK, L. (Miss): L.N.E.T.

CLARKE, E. (Miss): L.N.E.T.

CORDERO, D. (Miss): L.N.E.T.

CROFTS, D. (Miss): L.N.E.T.

CROSBY, Ellen: Listed in 1882 as S.A.

DANIELS, A. (Miss): L.N.E.T.

(DENNIS, Florence: see page 116)

A.D. DRAKE, Amelia A.: Listed in 1882 as S.A. *1881–1892* (Original work by 1890s.)

 DRIVER, M. (Miss): L.N.E.T.

 DUNCAN, A. (Miss): L.N.E.T.

 DUNTON, M. (Miss): L.N.E.T.

D DURTNALL, Beatrice M.: Listed in 1882 as S.A. *1881–1890*

J.D DURTNALL, Josephine A.: Listed in 1882 as J.A. *1882–1895*

FＪ EDERMANIGER, M. (Miss): L.N.E.T.

E EMERTON, C. (Miss): L.N.E.T.

ÆF FIMISTER, Ada E.: Listed in 1882 as S.A.

Ⴘ FORSYTH, E. (Miss): L.N.E.T.

M.F. FOX, M. (Miss): L.N.E.T.

⊤ FRAMPTON, D. (Miss): L.N.E.T.

F FRANCIS, Catherine: L.N.E.T.

(GANDY, Jessie: see page 117)

ℒℊ GOLDSACK, L. (Miss): L.N.E.T.

ℋ GRAVER, E. (Miss): L.N.E.T.

ㅅ GRAY, M. (Miss): L.N.E.T.

H   HARRISON, Emma C.: Listed in 1882 as S.A. *1881–1889*

   HAYWARD, L. (Miss): L.N.E.T.

(·)   HENDERSON, E. (Miss): L.N.E.T.

   HEYWOOD, K. (Miss): L.N.E.T.

H.x.   HULFORD, Annie M.: Listed in 1882 as S.A.

   JESSETT, E. (Miss): L.N.E.T.

   KELSEY, Edith: L.N.E.T.

(LACY, Alice: see page 120)

   LASHAM, J. (Miss): L.N.E.T.

LATHAM, Jenny: L.N.E.T. (She also did enamel and gilt work on Chiné Wares.)

(LILLEY, Mary M. S.: see page 120)

(LYONS, Annie: see page 100)

   MACNAE, B. (Miss): L.N.E.T.

÷   MARRIOTT, L. (Miss): L.N.E.T.

   MASKELL, F. (Miss): L.N.E.T.

MASON, Ellen: L.N.E.T.

   MEAR, L. (Miss): L.N.E.T.

   MILLS, A. (Miss): L.N.E.T.

EM MUNDAY, Iza M.: Listed in 1882 as S.A.

NAISH, E. (Miss): L.N.E.T.

NEAL, Minnie (Miss): L.N.E.T.

(NEWBERY, Bessie: see page 122)

N NOTTINGHAM, Lilla: Listed in 1882 as S.A.

NORRIS, E. (Miss): L.N.E.T.

NORRISH, F. (Miss): L.N.E.T.

NYE, Gertrude: L.N.E.T.

P PAINTER, D. (Miss): L.N.E.T.

PARKER, L. (Miss): L.N.E.T.

P. PEARSON, S. (Miss): L.N.E.T.

PERRIN, F. (Miss): L.N.E.T.

POTTERTON, A. (Miss): L.N.E.T.

PRYCE, M. (Miss): L.N.E.T.

R ROBINSON, Emily L.: Listed in 1882 as S.A.

ROGERS, L. (Miss): L.N.E.T.

ROHSS, A. (Miss): L.N.E.T.

RUFF, Agnes M.: Listed in 1882 as S.A.

RUSSELL, F. (Miss): L.N.E.T.

S.S   SANDERSON, Susanna M.: Listed in 1882 as S.A.

A.S.   SANDES, Agnes D.: Listed in 1882 as J.A.

SAWYER, F. (Miss): L.N.E.T.

SHARPE, G. (Miss): L.N.E.T.

E.S   SHELLEY, Elizabeth: Listed in 1882 as S.A. (Exhibited original Carrara vase in 1889.)

SHETTLEWORTH, Lizzie: Listed in 1882 as S.A.

SHIPMAN, F. (Miss): L.N.E.T.

M.S.   SLATTER, Mary: Listed in 1882 as S.A.

MBS   SMALLFIELD, Mildred B.: Listed in 1882 as S.A.

SMITH, E. (Miss): L.N.E.T.

F.S.   SMITH, Frances: Listed in 1882 as J.A.

SMITH, Gertrude: Listed in 1882 as S.A. *1882–1895* (Exhibited original work in 1889.) (LXVI)

SPURRELL, A. (Miss): L.N.E.T.

STRAKER, N. (Miss): L.N.E.T.

TAYLOR, N. (Miss): L.N.E.T.

THORNTON, M. (Miss): L.N.E.T.

TOLAND, H. (Miss): L.N.E.T.

TOMLYN, F. (Miss): L.N.E.T.

TOSEN, A. (Miss): L.N.E.T.

TRANTER, A. (Miss): L.N.E.T.

TURNER, A. (Miss): L.N.E.T.

VINER, Emily M.: Listed in 1882 as S.A. *1881–1887*

WALKER, K. (Miss): L.N.E.T.

WATERS, L. (Miss): L.N.E.T.

WELSBY, M. (Miss): L.N.E.T.

WHITTON, K. (Miss): L.N.E.T.

WILKINSON, H. (Miss): L.N.E.T.

WILSON, A. (Miss): L.N.E.T.

WILSON, Louie: Listed in 1882 as S.A.

WILSON, R. (Miss): L.N.E.T.

WOOD, Christina: Listed in 1882 as J.A.

WOODINGTON, Edith H.: Listed in 1882 as S.A. *1882–1889*

WOODS, Rosetta S.: Listed in 1882 as J.A.

Appendix II

TRADE-MARKS, BACK STAMPS AND OTHER AIDS TO DATING

1	DOULTON & WATTS	Impressed, moulded or incised marks on stoneware and terracotta products, c. 1827–1858.
2	DOULTON & WATTS LAMBETH POTTERY LONDON	*Notes:* (i) No marks have been traced for the Vauxhall Walk period 1815–1826. (ii) No. 15 High Street, Lambeth, was renumbered 28 in 1838. (iii) John Watts retired in 1853 and the name of the firm became Doulton & Co. The name Doulton & Watts may, however, have been continued in trade-marks for some time.
3	*Lambeth Pottery.* DOULTON & WATTS 15 HIGH STREET, LAMBETH.	

4	DOULTON LAMBETH	Impressed or printed marks on plain brown- and cream-glazed stoneware c. 1858–c. 1910. Also found impressed on some of the earliest Doulton Ware with simple incised decoration 1866–1869. After 1891 the word 'England' was added.

5	DOULTON LAMBETH ENGLAND	There are several minor variations of this impressed or printed mark, used on plain brown- and cream-glazed stoneware c. 1891–1956. It is also found very occasionally on Doulton Ware and Lambeth Faïence.

6	HENRY DOULTON H. DOULTON H. DOULTON & CO.	George Tinworth, who always regarded Henry Doulton as his personal patron used these names, roughly incised, on many of his panels and plaques. (The old firm known as Henry Doulton & Co. had in fact made drainpipes and had ceased to exist long before Tinworth came to Lambeth.)

| 7 | | Impressed mark on early Doulton Ware c. 1869–1872. |

| 8 | | Impressed mark on Doulton Ware. The date was added between 1872 and 1877 and occasionally between 1877 and 1887. A circular printed variation of this mark is also found. |

| 9 | | Impressed or printed mark on Lambeth Faïence c. 1873–c. 1914. After 1891 the word 'England' was added. A date was sometimes inserted in the centre of the mark. This mark is found also on Doulton Ware. |

| 10 | | Impressed mark on Doulton Ware c. 1876–1880. A date is usually found impressed nearby. Occasionally found on Lambeth Faïence. |

| 11 | | Impressed or printed mark on Lambeth Faïence c. 1873–c. 1914. After 1891 the word 'England' was added. Sometimes both No. 9 and No. 11 appear on the same pot. |

| 12 | | Impressed or printed mark on Doulton Ware c. 1880 to 1902. After 1891 the word 'England' was added. The year of production also occurs occasionally. This mark is sometimes found on Lambeth Faïence along with No. 11. |

| 13 | DOULTON LAMBETH ENGLAND | Impressed or printed mark on ashtrays and other small items of Doulton Ware. Occasionally found also on larger pots; c. 1891–1956. |

14      Impressed or printed mark on Impasto Ware 1879–c. 1914. After 1891 the word 'England' was added.

15   Impressed or printed mark on Crown Lambeth Ware 1891–c. 1903.
(Mark No. 12 with the word 'Crown' above it is also found, especially before 1894.)

16   **DOULTON & SLATERS PATENT**   Several variants of this mark, used in conjunction with Doulton Ware or Lambeth Faïence marks are found on Chiné and Chiné-Gilt Wares 1885–1939.

17      Impressed or printed marks on Marqueterie Ware 1887–c. 1906. After 1891 the word 'England' was added.

18   Impressed or printed mark on Carrara Ware 1891–1924. Between 1887 and 1891 Mark No. 12 is found on Carrara Ware.

19   Impressed or printed mark on Silicon Stoneware c. 1880–1932 The word 'England' was added after 1891.
Mark No. 12 is also found on some early Silicon Ware.

| 20 | KERAMET DOULTON LAMBETH ENGLAND | This mark, in conjunction with No. 12 or No. 21, is found on some pots made in the early 1900s, with a metallic coating obtained by the electro-deposition of silver and copper. |

| 21 | | This new mark, available for use on all the decorated Doulton Lambeth and Burslem Wares, was introduced in 1902 after the Company had been given the right, the previous year, to use the description 'Royal Doulton' for its products. (Some of the marks for specific wares were continued in use with or without No. 21.) The lower portion (without the lion and crown) was used on smaller pots from 1902 to 1956. |

| 22 | | Impressed or printed mark on Doulton Ware 1922–1956. |

| 23 | ROYAL DOULTON LAMBETH ENGLAND | Impressed or printed mark on slip-cast Doulton Ware such as figures and non-circular pots c. 1912–1956. |

| 24 | MADE IN ☩ ENGLAND | Printed mark on hard-paste porcelain figures c. 1918–1933. |

| 25 | | This monogram is also found on some hard-paste porcelain c. 1918–1933. It is made up of a combined M and T, denoting not the designer but J. H. Mott, art director, and W. Thomason, chief chemist, who developed the new porcelain body. |

26

Impressed or printed mark on 'Persian Ware' c. 1920–1936.

27

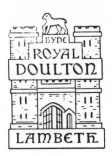

This mark is found on a range of pigment-decorated pots introduced in the mid-1920s. It has also been found on some large wall-plaques. It appears to have been discontinued by 1939.

Further Aids to Dating

As already explained on page 88, a number preceded by an X indicates that the design was reproduced in quantity.

The approximate date of *introduction* of such patterns may be estimated from the following table. It must be borne in mind that some patterns, if they proved popular, were continued for several years after their first introduction. The trade-mark will also help to determine the approximate date of manufacture.

X. 1–1500: 1883–1886	X. 7601–8240: 1912–1920
X. 1501–4000: 1887–1893	X. 8241–8450: 1921–1923
X. 4001–5200: 1894–1896	X. 8451–8700: 1924–1927
X. 5201–5940: 1897–1902	X. 8701–8800: 1928–1929
X. 5941–6600: 1903–1905	X. 8801–8900: 1930–1933
X. 6601–7600: 1906–1911	X. 8901–9000: 1934–1945

It will be noted that after Sir Henry Doulton's death in 1897 the average number of new introductions a year dwindled considerably.

Between 1902 and 1925 impressed lower-case date-letters are found on some pots. These letters run in consecutive order from c in 1902 to z in 1925. They usually but not always appear inside a shield.

On slip-cast wares the month and year of manufacture were sometimes indicated by impressed figures, e.g. 10.21 for October 1921.

REGISTRATION MARKS AND NUMBERS

(The author is indebted to Mr. Geoffrey A. Godden for the following details.)

On designs registered at the Patent Office between 1842 and 1883 a diamond-shaped mark will usually be found in addition to the normal trade-mark. Two different patterns of diamonds were used but so far as the Doulton Lambeth Wares are concerned one need only consider the following:

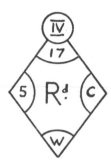

The most important item here is the letter on the *right-hand side* of the diamond (C in the above illustration) which indicates the year of registration (1870).

The following is the key to these letters:

A: 1871	I: 1872	S: 1875
C: 1870	J: 1880	U: 1874
D: 1878 (part)	K: 1883	V: 1876
E: 1881	L: 1882	W: 1878 (part)
F: 1873	P: 1877	X: 1868
H: 1869		Y: 1879

The letter at the *bottom* of the diamond indicates the month of registration as follows: A: December; B: October; C or O: January; D: September; E: May; G: February; H: April; I: July; K: November; M: June; R: August; W: March.

From 1884 onwards Registration Numbers were used instead of the diamond-shaped mark. The following table shows the first number issued each year up to 1909. The numbers from 1903 to 1909 are approximate. A slight overlap may occur between the end of one year and the beginning of another.

1884: 1	1893: 205240	1901: 368154
1885: 19754	1894: 224720	1902: 385500
1886: 40480	1895: 246975	1903: 402500
1887: 64520	1896: 268392	1904: 420000
1888: 90483	1897: 291241	1905: 447000
1889: 116648	1898: 311658	1906: 471000
1890: 141273	1899: 331707	1907: 494000
1891: 163767	1900: 351202	1908: 519500
1892: 185713		1909: 550000

Appendix III

A DOULTON WARE GLOSSARY

(Note: Not included in this Glossary are (i) the
artists and designers listed separately in Appendix
I, and (ii) commemorative wares already
described in Chapter V.)

AESOP'S FABLES   In 1882 George Tinworth modelled a series of miniature reliefs in Doulton Ware illustrating the following subjects taken from Aesop's fables: (1) The Frog who would be as big as an Ox; (2) The Wolf and the Crane; (3) The Cats and the Cheese; (4) and (5) The Fox and the Stork; (6) The Frog and the Mouse; (7) The Drunken Husband; (8) The Crow and the Pitcher; (9) The Eagle and the Fox; (10) The Man and the Lion; (11) The Ass in the Lion's Skin; (12) The Two Travellers and the Oyster; (13) The Cat and the Sparrow; (14) The Vain Jackdaw; (15) The Porcupine and the Snakes; (16) and (17) The Fox and the Ape; (18) The Cat and the Sparrows (another version); (19) The Nurse and the Wolf (an elaborate work which also depicted incidents from The Two Rabbits, The Fox and the Grapes, and The Kite and the Pigeons); (20) The Quack Doctor.

Tinworth later modelled variations on some of these themes, both as panels and as free-standing figures, and also developed amusing studies of mice and frogs going to the Derby, playing leap-frog, cycling, boating and so forth, based entirely on his own fertile imagination.

Some of these works were reproduced from moulds in varying quantities over the years. Those which bear Tinworth's monogram were given their finishing touches by him and no two pieces are exactly alike. It is thought-provoking to find that 'The Frog Cyclist', for examples of which collectors will now gladly pay many pounds, was sold to the trade in the 1890s for half-a-crown!

Clockcases and vases depicting incidents from Aesop's fables were also designed by Tinworth.

ALTAR VASES, CANDLESTICKS, ETC.   A series of Doulton Ware vases in three sizes, also candlesticks, flower stands and font ewers, was introduced about 1876. The seven basic designs, named 'York', 'Oxford', 'Ely', 'Dorchester', 'St. Albans', 'Lambeth', and 'Salisbury', were ornamented with different religious and ecclesiastical symbols based on designs by the Rev. Dr. Lee, F.S.A., the then Vicar of All Saints, Lambeth. The shapes and the remainder of the decoration were, it is believed, designed mainly by Edith Lupton and Eliza Simmance. Reproductions were made until about 1904 when a new range with less elaborate tube-tool decoration was introduced.

Edith Lupton, Eliza Simmance, Tinworth, Butler and possibly other artists designed and decorated special vases for a number of cathedrals and churches.

ANIMAL AND BIRD SUBJECTS   There is great scope for collecting Doulton Wares featuring animals and birds. They include Tinworth's comical studies of mice and frogs and his

153

reliefs and groups based on Aesop's fables; rare terracotta reliefs by Hannah Barlow; sea-horses, birds, lizards, salamanders and other creations by Mark Marshall; sea-lions and ducks by Richard Garbe, R.A., cats by John Broad and Agnete Hoy; owls by Vera Huggins and cockatoos by Leslie Harradine. There are also kangaroos, cormorants, monkeys, squirrels, koala bears, pelicans, ibex, rabbits, pigeons, cockerels, dolphins designed by various artists for reproduction from moulds.

Ashtrays, match-box holders, ring stands and other bibelots featuring animals, birds and fishes will also be found. Well worth looking out for are the colourful studies of birds on wall plaques painted by Simeon.

Apart from the many figures there is, of course, an amazing variety of incised and painted studies of animals and birds on pots designed and decorated by Hannah and Florence Barlow.

ARCHER, FRED   See page 75.

ARCHITECTURAL WARES   In addition to the standard stoneware, faïence and terracotta blocks, slabs, balusters, columns and tiles supplied for building purposes, a great deal of special work was undertaken, in collaboration with architects, in the form of figures, figure groups, medallion portraits, hand-painted tile panels, gargoyles, grotesque rain-water heads and other decorative features designed by Broad, Neatby, Pearce and other Lambeth artists.

When buildings of the Victorian and Edwardian eras are being demolished to make way for redevelopment schemes, it is sometimes possible to acquire hand-painted plaques and tiles; fireplace surrounds (those with 'Persian-style' tiles are particularly attractive); cherubs, dolphins and other figures; medallion heads; eagle terminals; etc. For those with suitable gardens to display them in, large figures in terracotta may occasionally be acquired.

Unfortunately most of this kind of work is destroyed or damaged beyond repair during demolitions – those involved in the redevelopment of the site being unwilling to bear the extra cost which would be involved in taking special steps for its preservation.

It is not generally realized what a big part was played by the architectural section of the Lambeth Art Pottery in the construction of many well-known buildings. The following list of a few of these may be of interest: The Savoy, Russell and Imperial Hotels in London; University College Hospital; the Royal Observatory at Greenwich; Harrods Stores, Knightsbridge; the former Birkbeck Bank in Chancery Lane; theatres at Chelsea, Peckham, Hastings, Middlesbrough; the Refuge Assurance Buildings, Manchester; the Roman Catholic Cathedral, Westminster; the Royal Waterloo Hospital; Hyde Park Gate Mansions; Pagani's Restaurant; the Kursaal, Ostend; extensions to the Victoria and Albert Museum, South Kensington; Lloyds Bank, Temple Bar (a particularly fascinating example of the use of Doulton ceramics); Everard's Printing Offices, Bristol.

See also pages 13 and 51–53.

ARMORIAL TILES, PLAQUES, ETC.   Tiles, tile panels, plaques and tablets were made at various times to special order, depicting in hand-painted colours, and sometimes in relief, the armorial bearings, crests and symbols of individuals, schools, colleges, businesses, regiments, towns, etc.

Crested tobacco jars, mugs, tankards and other items were also designed to order, for clubs, societies and other organizations.

ART UNION OF LONDON Between about 1885 and 1902 the Lambeth Studios supplied many signed artists' pieces for this Union, the members of which took part in annual draws for works of art, ranging from paintings exhibited at the Royal Academy to small ceramic figures and vases. Such pieces, in addition to the Doulton trademark and the artist's monogram, were indented or printed with the words 'Art Union of London'.

ASHTRAYS AND ASHBOWLS Many hundreds of different designs, some in more or less conventional shapes, some incorporating figures of children, elves, animals, birds, fish, etc., were reproduced from moulds.

In addition to those made for the pottery trade, many others were supplied for advertising purposes to brewers, distillers, taverns, hotels, restaurants and other enterprises seeking a durable and artistic publicity medium. These were impressed or otherwise marked with the names and/or symbols of the customer concerned.

ASKEW, WILLIAM One of the most accomplished throwers at the Lambeth Pottery in the 80s and 90s. He shaped many of the pots designed by Tinworth, the Barlows, Butler and other leading artists, besides creating many shapes himself. He won many prizes in competitions organized by the Society of Arts and the Worshipful Company of Turners, and several times demonstrated his talents before Queen Victoria and other important visitors to the Lambeth Studios and the great exhibitions.

'ASSYRIAN' AND 'EGYPTIAN' WARES From about 1889 to 1914, jugs, tobacco jars, tea- and coffee-pots, bowls, mugs, tankards and other items were made in brown salt-glaze stoneware with cream or off-white relief decorations of Assyrian and Egyptian figures. The tops and bottoms were dipped in dark brown ochre glaze and the lips of the jugs and coffee-pots were usually in the form of a sphinx. Another variety, less often found, has gold figures on a black background.

Similar motifs are seen also on Silicon Ware pots. This ware was revived in 1923 for a short period in connection with the discovery of Tutankhamun's tomb; the range included butter dishes, tobacco jars with both ordinary and patent clamp lids, low and tall candlesticks, cruet sets, bulb bowls, fern and flower pots, tea-pots, cream jugs and sugar bowls.

ATKINS, ROBERT A highly skilled turner who was responsible for finishing off many of the early Doulton Ware pots on the lathe to give them a smooth surface for decorating. He was succeeded as chief turner by George Martin.

BABB, S. NICHOLSON Extramural modeller, friend of William Rowe, who designed a salt-glaze stoneware figure of a 'Lute Player', of which only a few reproductions were made c. 1912. No other Doulton items by this modeller have so far been traced.

See illustration on page 30.

'BABY INKWELLS' See page 79.

'BACCHANALIAN' JUG This was the name given by Henry Doulton to a brown salt-glaze jug, first produced in the 1840s, with relief mouldings depicting a drunken Silenus and satyrs. Examples are becoming rather difficult to find.

'BACCHUS' JUG   Another similarly inspired jug but with off-white applied relief decoration of dancing children and vines. Designed by John Broad, it was introduced in the 1880s and was still shown in a 1910 catalogue.

Some of these 'Bacchus' jugs have the motto 'Good is not Good enough: The Best is not too Good'. Others are found with only half the motto or no inscription at all.

BALL CLAY   See page 158.

BARRELS, SPIRIT   Salt-glaze brown stoneware containers, generally in barrel shape were made over a long period from the early days of the Doulton & Watts Pottery in the 1820s up to the time of the First World War. They were produced in several sizes. Some large specimens are to be seen in the Royal Pavilion at Brighton; these are said to have been supplied by John Doulton to George IV.

The barrels usually have light, medium or dark brown simulated hoops and applied hop and vine decoration, and often, the Royal Arms, but some are quite plain. Some are marked in front with the name of the spirit to be contained and the name of the licensee to whom they were supplied.

Very rare are the spirit barrels in coloured Doulton Ware. These were made infrequently to special order. A few were made as recently as 1955, designed by Agnete Hoy; these are just as rare now as nineteenth century specimens.

BARTLETT, ALFRED J.   A thrower at the Lambeth Pottery, mentioned in an Art-Craftsmanship Exhibition catalogue of 1889.

BAYES, GILBERT   See page 67.

BENNETT, JOHN   See page 43.

BLACK LEATHER WARE   See page 46.

'BODY'   The name given by potters to the finally prepared mixture of clays and other ingredients from which a particular ceramic ware is made; e.g. 'stoneware body', 'porcelain body', 'earthenware body'.

BREADPANS   Large quantities of inexpensive brown- and cream-glazed stoneware breadpans were made at the Lambeth Pottery from the 1870s – up to as recently as 1940. Decoration, if any, consisted of a stencilled design in black.

These breadpans, covered with a perforated stoneware or metal lid, were supplied mainly through ironmongers and hardware stores.

Breadpans in coloured Doulton Ware are extremely rare and were probably made only to special order.

BROWNING SETTLEMENT   A salt-glaze Doulton Ware memorial fountain, presented by Henry Lewis Doulton in memory of his father, Sir Henry Doulton, was unveiled in June 1898 in the Browning Garden behind the Robert Browning Settlement in York Street, Walworth. (Sir Henry was baptized in 1820 in the York Street Nonconformist Chapel associated with the missionary hero, Captain Wilson.)

BRYON, A. Mentioned by Walter Gandy as one of the earliest decorators of the Doulton Ware. Possibly a Lambeth School of Art student who did some free-lance work for Henry Doulton.

CANDLESTICKS These were made in the early days of the Lambeth Pottery in plain brown salt-glaze or cream-coloured stoneware, and from c. 1870 onwards in coloured Doulton Ware.

Made usually in pairs, some were designed and decorated by Tinworth, Butler, Pope, Marshall and other well-known artists. Good specimens of the artist-signed candlesticks are becoming rare but examples of those made for reproduction (some in very attractive shapes and all-blue, all-green and all-brown colourings) can be found without too much difficulty.

Among the latest made were some designed by Simeon in the late 1920s as part of his 'Toby Ware' series. (See page 65.)

CAPEY, RECO See page 67.

CARAFES See DECANTERS, page 160.

CARRARA WARE See page 50.

CAUDLE FLASKS See page 13.

CAZIN, JEAN-CHARLES See page 92.

CHESHIRE CHEESE, YE OLDE Relief-decorated 'Toby' or 'hunting' jugs and mugs, flagons, punch bowls, condiment sets and other brown salt-glaze stoneware productions were supplied for many years, in fair quantities, to this famous old London tavern both for use and for sale to American and other tourists.

Those made from c. 1886 up to c. 1910 had the name of the proprietor (B. A. Moore) and often a view of the tavern. Those made from c. 1910 to 1930 had just the name of the tavern and the date – 1667 – when it was established (not, as some have imagined, the date of manufacture!).

Some Dr. Johnson figure flasks, designed by Harradine, were also supplied to the Cheshire Cheese between about 1910 and 1915. These had its name printed on the bottom.

CHINÉ WARES See page 48.

CHOISY, H. B. This name is found on some Lambeth faïence plaques and dishes. A monogram which could be H.B.C. has also been noted on some Doulton Ware of c. 1878.

CHURCH, ARTHUR (SIR) See page 23.

CINERARY URNS Terracotta cinerary urns, designed in collaboration with Sir Henry Thompson (author of *Modern Cremation*, Kegan Paul, 1889), were made at the Lambeth Pottery in the 1890s. New ranges of relief-figured Doulton Ware urns were introduced in 1903 and again in 1925.

These are hardly likely to come into the hands of collectors in the near future but they may be of interest to archaeologists in a later epoch!

CLAYS AND OTHER MATERIALS In a lecture given in February 1885 to the staff of the Lambeth Art Department, Mr. Wilton Rix, the then art director, described the principal clays and other raw materials used at the Lambeth Pottery. Though, in later years, various refinements were introduced in methods of preparation, there were no great changes in the basic materials used.

For ordinary small brown jugs and pots the ball clays from Dorset and Devon needed only to be ground and mixed with sand and water to prepare them for use. For large pots a proportion of 'grog' or 'rough stuff' (i.e. ground-up fragments of already fired pottery) was added to the mix to 'open' the ware and make it more stable in the kiln during firing.

The shade of brown was said to be dependent partly on the amount of iron compounds in the clay and partly on the position of the ware in the kiln and the extent of its exposure to the salt fumes. The dark brown seen on the tops and bottoms of many pots was obtained by dipping them in an ochre glaze before firing.

Throughout the whole period of stoneware production at Lambeth, several artists used this ordinary body from time to time. Although it did not lend itself to decoration with coloured pigments, it could be carved and modelled effectively, or ornamented with incised designs through a lighter-coloured slip, or with applied figuring in a lighter clay or slip. Arthur Barlow, Butler, Marshall, Pope, Broad, Simeon and others produced some attractive pots in this ordinary body. It was used also for relief-figured 'hunting' jugs and similar wares.

For most of the Doulton Wares special bodies, much lighter in hue, varying from buffs and creams to near-white, were evolved. Between 1867 and 1875 an attractive warm cream-coloured body was much used which made an excellent background for the quiet colour schemes, based on the simple browns, blues and occasional greens to which the artists' palette was then more or less confined.

For the lighter-coloured bodies, other ingredients were added to the basic ball clay, in varying proportions according to the particular hue and texture required. These might include ground calcined flint made from large pebbles from the Sussex coast, white-firing Cornish china clay (similar to the Chinese kaolin), Cornish stone (a kind of felspathic rock similar to the Chinese petuntse), felspar from Scandinavia, silica sand, and various types of 'grog'. For some finer bodies ground porcelain might be added in small quantities.

The clay and other prepared materials were mixed with water into a semi-liquid slip, passed through fine-meshed sieves, and then pumped into wooden presses (later replaced by metal ones) where the bulk of the water was forced out again through canvas cloth, leaving behind soft sheets of clay. These were then put through a kind of mincing machine called a 'pug' from which the clay emerged in a continuous block or cylinder, ready to be cut into suitable sections and taken to the throwers. (For wares intended to be made by the slip-casting method – see page 177 – the slip was conveyed at first in buckets, later through pipes, to the casting benches.)

According to Rix, the addition of ground calcined flint made the body more capable of taking a high salt-glaze during the firing; for this reason it was not suitable for Silicon Ware. If too much flint was added to the stoneware body, however, this developed a tendency to crack and would not respond well to incised or carved decoration. Felspar and Cornish stone were used to render bodies and any applied glazes more fusible. China clay was used sparingly for whitening a stoneware body; too high a proportion prevented the salt glaze from 'taking'.

When a really white-burning clay or slip was required, the mix had to be passed in liquid form over magnets to extract iron impurities. Used as a slip, and stained with colours derived from copper, manganese, iron, cobalt and other metallic compounds, this produced very pure colour tones.

On some Doulton Wares letters such as W, WC, FC and C will be found; these indicate different types of body. The letters HW indicate a special body for teapots and jugs which would withstand very hot water. In itself it was nearly white but apparently had the peculiarity of turning bright orange if used as a slip on a darker body.

The bodies used for the lighter-coloured stonewares were also used for Lambeth Faïence which had its *first* firing at the same high temperature as stoneware (c. 1,250–1,280° Centigrade).

The evolution of the various types of body, especially the self-coloured ones and the Marqueterie, involved a great deal of patient research by Rix who was also largely responsible for the development of pigments, glazes and slips suitable for use with them. Many of the coloured glazes, derived from metallic oxides, would be more accurately described as thin coloured slips. They were very different from the usual earthenware glazes and contained clay to add body and sometimes tin oxide to give opacity. They were usually applied by brush. Two or more of these 'glaze-slips' were often dabbed over each other on the same part of the design, giving that marbled or cornelian effect which is so characteristic of a good deal of Doulton Ware after 1890.

CLOCKCASES From about 1877 onwards clockcases, mostly in salt-glaze Doulton Ware but some in Silicon Stoneware, terracotta and Lambeth Faïence, were made for the wholesale clock trade in Clerkenwell, Birmingham and other centres. 'Clock garnitures', comprising a clock and two matching vases, were also made.

On many of the clockcases the decoration is entirely or mostly moulded and these were presumably reproduced in some quantity. Among the artists who designed and decorated some unique cases were Hannah Barlow, Matilda Adams, Eliza Simmance, Josephine Durtnall, Mary Thomson, Tinworth, Broad, Marshall and Harradine.

CLOISONNÉ This name was originally given to enamel decoration involving a network of raised metal enclosures or *cloisons* into which the enamel is poured, allowing the different colours to be kept quite separate. As applied to Doulton Ware it was sometimes used to describe decoration within raised outlines applied from a tube-tool in a rather similar way to icing a cake. (See page 39.)

COGGINS, J. A Lambeth Pottery thrower of the 1880s and 1890s. He threw some exceptionally large vases for Tinworth, Marshall, Hannah Barlow and other artists. Apart from his work for the Art Department he made some enormous 'Ali Baba' jars and other vessels for the chemical industry.

COMMEMORATIVE WARES See Chapter V.
For commemorative wall plaques see MURAL TABLETS, page 172.

CONDIMENT SETS A great variety of condiment sets (salt, mustard and pepper pots) was made over a long period of years from the 1870s until the 1930s. Some of these, particularly those with relief-figuring of topers, windmills, etc., were made in large quantities but there are also to be found unique artist-signed sets by Hannah Barlow, Emily Edwards, Tinworth, Marshall, Simeon and other artists.

COPPER WARES   See page 46.

CORONATION WARES   See Chapter V.

CRESY, EDWARD   See pages 17 and 19.

CRICKET SUBJECTS   See under SPORTING SUBJECTS, page 177.

CROWN LAMBETH WARE   See page 51.

CYCLING SUBJECTS   See under SPORTING SUBJECTS, page 177.

'CYPRUS'   This name is found on some Lambeth Faïence vases and bowls dated 1879. Only a few have been noted so far and probably not a great number was made. They have stylized lotus and hatched and lozenge designs. It has been pointed out by Mr. Michael Collins, who has one of these vases in his collection, that the designs were influenced by early Cypriot pottery, a fair amount of which was excavated in the 1870s.

It is interesting to note that it was in 1878, after the Congress of Berlin, that Cyprus was ceded to Britain as part of the Balkan settlement after the Serbo-Turkish War.

DECANTERS   Salt-glaze Doulton Ware decanters and carafes of 27 fluid ounces capacity were made between about 1875 and 1914 in both circular and square shapes. They were often supplied in sets of two to five, with or without oak, mahogany or wicker containers.

The standard design had grooved sides in light brown and blue, with single or double acanthus decoration on the neck, and with pewter tops to the corks. The decanters were often marked 'R' for rum, 'B' for brandy, 'G' for gin, 'W' or 'SW' for Scotch whisky, and 'IW' for Irish whiskey.

Other designs were produced from time to time for special customers. These were designed, decorated and signed by the artists concerned. Even the standard designs are becoming difficult to find nowadays.

See also FLAGONS.

DICKENS SUBJECTS   See under HARRADINE, page 99.

DOMESTIC AND UTILITARIAN WARES   Apart from the coloured salt-glaze Doulton Wares and other decorated Doulton ceramics, some collectors are interested in other products in plain brown or cream-coloured stoneware which were made for everyday use in quantities sometimes running into hundreds of thousands. These include ginger beer, blacking, ink and other bottles, extract pots, jam jars, mustard jars, butter pots, pickling and preserving jars, snuff jars, footwarmers, carriage warmers and boot dryers. (See also page 10.)

Such articles are very difficult to date as the designs were often unaltered over several decades and the marks are not helpful except that those incorporating the word 'England' indicate a date after 1891 and those with 'Limited' in the name of the firm must have been made after 1899.

DOULTON, JOHN   See pages 5, 7–11, 13 and 15.

DOULTON, HENRY (SIR)   See pages 11–15, 17–33, 40, 43 and 54–60.

DOULTON, HENRY LEWIS   See pages 60–63.

DOULTON & SLATER PATENT (CHINÉ WARE)   See page 48.

DOULTON & WATTS   See pages 10–15.

DRINKING FOUNTAINS   From about 1870 until well into the twentieth century, terracotta, Doulton Ware and faïence drinking fountains were made at the Lambeth Pottery in a great variety of sizes and designs. Many of these were standard but some were individually designed for special commissions by Tinworth, Broad, Pearce and others.

DWIGHT, JOHN   See page 7.

'EGYPTIAN' WARES   See under 'ASSYRIAN' on page 155.

ELECTROPLATING   For a short period around the turn of the century a number of pots designed by Pope and Marshall (and possibly other artists) with relief-moulded decoration (generally of mermaids, dolphins, fish and dragons) were given a plated finish of silver, deposited on a resist over a layer of copper.

ELLIS, THOMAS   Ellis was the talented thrower who was first entrusted with shaping the new Doulton Wares which demanded a lighter and more delicate style of manipulation than necessary for ordinary industrial wares. He was highly praised by John Sparkes in a lecture given to the Society of Arts in 1874; he won many awards in competitions and designed some of the shapes decorated by the Barlows and other artists. Some of his pieces are preserved for posterity in the foundations of the so-called 'Cleopatra's Needle' on the Victoria Embankment, London.
  One of Ellis's sons, SAMUEL, also became a thrower at the Lambeth Pottery where he was apprenticed c. 1870.

ENAMEL DECORATION   This is a method of decoration used extensively on china and porcelain but less often on earthenware and stoneware.
  Enamels are vitreous ceramic pigments compounded with other materials so that they will fuse, when applied over-glaze, at a much lower temperature (usually from about 700°–800° Centigrade) than under-glaze colours. Derived from metallic oxides, such as copper, cobalt, iron, antimony, manganese, they lend themselves to a much wider colour palette than is possible with high-fired under-glaze decoration.
  Enamel decoration was introduced – very sparingly at first – at the Lambeth Pottery, about 1880, to accent certain details in faïence colour schemes. It was later used extensively, with or without gilding, on the Chiné Ware. Its use involved three or more firings.
  Enamel decoration on the ordinary Doulton Wares and on Carrara Ware is comparatively rare.

ENCAUSTIC TILES An 1894 catalogue shows over 70 different designs of Doulton 'encaustic ornamental tile pavements'. These were specimens of the immense number of different combinations which could be built up from a wide range of tiles and bands.

Encaustic comes from a Greek word meaning 'burnt in'. The term was first applied to medieval inlaid tiles made by monks. The art was revived by Herbert Minton in 1830 and then developed on an industrial scale. These tiles have an inlaid pattern in coloured clay fused into the body during firing.

ENGOBE A thin coating of liquid clay (slip) applied to pottery of a contrasting colour.

ENGRAVING AND ETCHING See PRINTING, page 174.

EXHIBITIONS
Great (Crystal Palace) 1851: page 13.
London 1862: page 16.
Paris 1867: page 20.
London 1871: page 20.
London 1872: page 24.
Vienna 1873: page 24.
Philadelphia 1876: pages 28 and 42.
Paris 1878: pages 31 and 42.
Chicago 1893: page 58.

FAÏENCE, LAMBETH See page 40.

FIGURES Many small figurines and animal models as well as large figures and figure groups were made at Lambeth between c. 1870 and 1956, the last of all being some delightful studies of cats by Agnete Hoy.

They were made either as individual pieces or in limited editions seldom exceeding a few hundred. The smaller figures were in plain brown or cream salt-glaze stoneware, coloured Doulton Ware and Lambeth Faïence or occasionally in terracotta and, after about 1918, a few were produced in hard-paste white porcelain. The larger figures were mostly in terracotta although stoneware was also used where the overall dimensions permitted.

Among the artists who modelled figures were Leslie Harradine, Arthur Beere, John Broad, M. V. Marshall, George Tinworth, Herbert Ellis and Charles Vigor. Figures were occasionally modelled also by extramural artists, e.g. Gilbert Bayes, Allen Howes and H. Nicholson Babb.

FILTERS Circular filter cases with lids and taps were made from the 1830s in plain brown and cream-coloured stoneware, with little decoration other than the Royal Arms. From the 1870s until 1914 other designs were made in both Doulton Ware and Silicon Ware and some of them are extremely attractive. Some were quite small for table use; others of larger dimensions for use in kitchens and sculleries. To develop new ideas for filter cases was one of the first tasks set George Tinworth and he produced some remarkable designs in a very Gothic vein. One wonders what has become of them.

The fact that the firm could supply *decorated* filter cases gave them an advantage over competitors.

FIREPLACE SURROUNDS From the late 1870s until the 1930s the manufacture of fireplace surrounds in Doulton Ware and terracotta, and up to 1914 in Lambeth Faïence, formed an important section of the Lambeth Pottery's activities. Up to about 1910 'Persian Ware' surrounds were also made.

The Doulton Ware and terracotta surrounds were formed from tiles, slabs and hollow blocks. The Lambeth Faïence and 'Persian Ware' surrounds were generally in tile form.

The majority of these surrounds were made up from standard units but Doulton also received commissions from time to time for exclusive hand-painted tile surrounds. The painting of these was done by Lambeth Faïence artists and assistants.

FIRING   See KILNS, page 167.

FLAGONS, SPIRIT   In addition to decanters and flagons made for sale to the general public, either as single items or in sets (see DECANTERS, page 160), large quantities of commercial flagons were made for publicity purposes, especially between c. 1880 and 1935, for Scotch and Irish distillers – chiefly but not entirely for the export trade. These have become very popular indeed with certain collectors, especially, it would seem from correspondence, in Australia, Canada and the United States.

Some of these flagons, particularly in the nineteenth century, were decorated in colours and/or with relief figuring but the majority were of plain brown stoneware with printed or embossed trade-marks and lettering, with the tops glazed a darker brown or blue. Some very attractive examples are found with an overall deep mottled blue colouring. Between c. 1883 and 1895 a special range was produced decorated with etchings of Scottish landscapes and castles, and views of Cambridge, by Edgar Wilson, Arthur Pearce and Willie Rowe. Eliza Simmance designed a flagon for Melrose Highland Whisky about 1875 and she and other Lambeth artists were responsible, in collaboration with the distillers, for almost all the designs.

A series was introduced around 1906 with what was called 'hog coin' decoration (see page 166). One of the last orders for flagons received by the Lambeth Pottery was in 1955 for several thousand in the shape of a bell for the well-known distillers, Bells Limited. After the Lambeth factory closed, Doulton of Burslem continued to make similar flagons. The Burslem Pottery has also supplied flagons to a large number of firms.

The names of some twenty different distillers have been noted for whom the Lambeth Pottery made flagons, and there may well have been more. Some, moreover, ordered flagons in different shapes, decorations and sizes at various times. There is, therefore, considerable scope for collectors in this particular field.

FLASKS, FIGURE   See pages 10, 11, 13 and 64.
See also Chapter V on COMMEMORATIVE WARES.

FLOWER AND FERN POTS   A great variety of small and large fern and flower pots, some with pedestals, was made from the mid-nineteenth century until about 1915. Many of these were in brown salt-glaze stoneware and Silicon Ware but others, often profusely decorated, were made in coloured Doulton Ware, especially between 1890 and 1914. After 1920 some very attractive flower pots, with restrained decoration, designed by Rowe and Pope, were reproduced in small quantities.

FOOT-WARMERS, ETC. Foot-warmers and hot-water bottles, in several different shapes and sizes, were made over a very long period from the early Doulton & Watts days. Manufacture declined in the 1920s, with the coming of lighter alternatives, but was revived between 1939 and 1950 when aluminium and rubber were in short supply.

It is clear from correspondence that many people of the older generation still treasure and use their 'Reliable', 'Improved', 'Thermette' and other types of warmers. It is very difficult to date these and other utilitarian wares, and marks, unlike those on the decorated Doulton Wares do not help much – except that those incorporating the word 'England' indicate a date after 1891, those with 'Limited' in the name are after 1899, and those with 'Royal Doulton' are after 1901.

In the nineteenth century such things as stoneware boot-warmers, carriage-warmers and breast-warmers are also mentioned in surviving records.

FOUNTAINS In addition to the large, often monumental, fountains designed by Tinworth, Broad and Pearce for international and other exhibitions – of which the Glasgow Fountain (see below) is one of the few surviving examples – a great variety of smaller garden fountains was made in terracotta and Doulton Ware from the 1870s onwards. The last examples, in terracotta only, were produced in the early 1930s.

See also DRINKING FOUNTAINS (page 161).

FRITH, W. S. Frith designed and modelled a large terracotta figure of Queen Victoria and the 'Canada' group for a Doulton fountain exhibited at the Glasgow Exhibition of 1887. He also designed the 'South Africa', 'India' and 'Australia' groups for the same fountain but these were modelled by Ellis, Broad and Pomeroy respectively. The overall design of the fountain was by Arthur Pearce.

The fountain was presented by Sir Henry Doulton, after the Exhibition, to the City of Glasgow and was re-erected on Glasgow Green.

Frith studied at the Lambeth School of Art and the Royal Academy Schools. He returned to Lambeth to teach and succeeded Aimé-Jules Dalou there in 1880, becoming one of the outstanding teachers of sculpture during the late nineteenth century.

FULHAM POTTERY See page 7.

GARBE, RICHARD See pages 66 and 154.

GARDEN WARES Terracotta garden seats, vases, fountains, sundials, figures, window boxes, animal ornaments, etc. were made over a long period from c. 1829 to 1915 and again from 1927 to 1936. Among the designers were Tinworth, Pope, Marshall, Pearce, Broad and Simeon. Some garden ornaments were also made in Doulton Ware and plain brown salt-glaze stoneware.

So-called garden 'majolica' ware was introduced about 1875 and discontinued about 1910. Jardinières, garden tables, fountains and other items were made in this ware from rough clay of great strength, coated with fine cream-coloured slip on which, after firing, royal blue, yellow, grey, wine and other coloured pigments were painted; these, after a further firing showed up with great clarity. The wares were often ornamented with garlands, wreaths and scrolls in rococo style. Broad and Pope were the principal designers of garden 'majolica'.

GAS BURNERS   See page 168.

GILDING   On individually designed stoneware and faïence pots, and on Marqueterie Wares, best gold was used for any gilded decoration required. This was applied as an amalgam of mercury and gold, the mercury being driven off during firing. The resulting dull surface then required burnishing with an agate tool. This gilding was very durable and handsome in appearance.

On the repetition wares so-called 'liquid' or 'bright' gold was used. This was a solution of gold resinates and a flux; it required no burnishing but had neither the appearance nor the durability of best gold when used as decoration.

'GILT CIRCLE' WARE   Tobacco-jars, plant- and fern-pots, and occasionally jugs and vases, in Doulton Ware and Silicon Ware, were sometimes decorated with a more or less continuous background of whorls in low relief applied to the soft clay before the first firing. Enamel colours were then added to the top and bottom rims and the whole of the background gilded before refiring. On some pieces applied relief decoration was also applied over the whorled surface.

This type of decoration was used intermittently between about 1880 and 1914 and was revived for a period in the 1920s. It is often singularly attractive.

GLAZES   See under CLAYS AND OTHER MATERIALS, pages 158–159.

GLASGOW FOUNTAIN   See under FRITH, page 164.

GOLFING SUBJECTS   See under SPORTING SUBJECTS, page 177.

GOSSE, EDMUND (SIR)   See pages ix, 14, 108 and 110.

GRAY, KRUGER   See page 66.

GREGORY, ROBERT (CANNON)   See page 16.

GRÈS-DE-FLANDRES   See pages 16, 17 and 24–25.

'GROG'   See under CLAYS AND OTHER MATERIALS, pages 158–159.

'HANDYMAN'   See page 77.

'HERCULANEUM'   The name given to a shape (based on a Roman pot found at Herculaneum) made at Lambeth c. 1880–1895 in blue, fawn and brown colour schemes with raised ornament applied by hand moulds.

Several other shapes during this period were inspired by Greek and Roman prototypes. Sir Henry Doulton built up a small but choice collection of Greek pottery in the Lambeth Art Department Museum. Most of this was later presented by his grandson, Eric Hooper, to the British Museum and the Hanley Museum.

'HOG COIN' DECORATION This strange name was given to a type of decoration, used mainly on flagons, jugs, teapots, mugs and tankards. It is characterized by brown, white and bronze medallions or coins, varying in number usually from four to fourteen, according to the size of the article to which they were applied. Made mainly between c. 1905 and 1914.

HOLLOWELL, WILLIAM G. Although not a creative artist, Hollowell was a remarkably versatile 'workman-craftsman' who could turn his hand to clay-preparation, mould-making, carpentry, etc. For many years he was invaluable to George Tinworth in a great variety of ways. Among other things he was an expert photographer who photographed Tinworth's works on 24″ by 15″ plates from which prints were made by the Platinotype Company; these were sold to small chapels and meeting-places which could not afford original Tinworth works or reproductions in terracotta. Hollowell also prepared sets of slides about Tinworth for use in lantern lectures. (See also page 110.)

HOWES, ALLAN See page 66.

'HUNTING JUGS' See pages 8, 10, 56, 64 and 88.
    As well as the jugs with applied reliefs of topers and hunting scenes, jugs with *moulded* reliefs of boar, stag and fox hunting were made from about 1840, possibly earlier, and were still being made in the 1880s. They were of ordinary brown stoneware, top-dipped in a darker ochre glaze before salt-glazing. They are found in at least three different sizes. Those with the *Doulton & Watts* mark are quite rare nowadays and those with *Doulton Lambeth* are also becoming difficult to find.

ILLINGWORTH, NELSON Illingworth designed and modelled a Doulton Ware lamp for the Paris Exhibition of 1889. Apart from this there is no record of his having worked for Doulton. The lamp was decorated by Mary Thomson.

'IMPASTO' WARE See page 44.

INDICATOR TABLETS In 1924, at the suggestion of Mr. J. A. Parker, A.M.I.C.E., a keen mountaineer and member of the Cairngorm Club, Doulton made an indicator tablet to be placed on the summit of Lochnagar, showing distances and directions to neighbouring peaks and other places of interest. This was regarded as a trial piece to see if it would stand up to the severe weather conditions to be encountered.
    A year later, Mr. Parker reported that, in spite of an extremely hard winter, the cream-coloured stoneware tablet, with underglaze lettering and map in black, was in perfect condition. This was the beginning of a series of such commissions for Scottish, New Zealand, Canadian and other peaks.
    These tablets are of course only of indirect interest to collectors. Requests for information about them are, however, received from time to time. The maps and lettering were the work mainly of Edward Eggleton.

INKBOTTLES AND INKWELLS Large quantities of inkbottles and inkwells were made over a long period, beginning as early as 1815 and extending into the 1930s. The largest customer was the famous Stephens firm; many were supplied also to the Admiralty, War Office, Board of Education and other Government Departments, as well as to universities, colleges, schools and other institutions. They were made in many different shapes and sizes in plain brown and cream and sometimes blue-coloured stoneware. Some have the customer's name stamped or printed on them.

The total number made probably ran into millions over the years yet some collectors will pay pounds for unusual early marked specimens which were originally sold for a few pence. Certainly a glistening collection of varied designs can make an attractive and interesting display.

Great numbers of inkbottles and inkwells are found in old rubbish dumps; the Thames Estuary and other marshes, river beds and canals are other sources of 'finds'. It says much for the strength of the stoneware body that so many have survived in perfect or near-perfect condition.

Besides the plain inkwells supplied to schools, etc. a number of attractive and rather more expensive designs were made in decorated Doulton Ware. These are less frequently to be found. A 'Toby' inkwell designed by Simeon in 1924 was apparently the last to be produced.

See also pages 7, 9 and 79.

INKSTANDS Among a variety of inkstands made in Doulton Ware, mainly between the 1870s and 1914, the one called the 'ISOBATH' calls for particular mention.

This unusual object (see illustration XXXIX) was introduced in 1888 for the well-known De La Rue Company. Inside the Doulton Ware surround a half-sphere of vulcanite was suspended on an axis swivelling from two recesses cut in the sides of the large ink reservoir. The pen was dipped into the little spout on the outside of the 'Isobath' and, as the ink was taken up, the half-sphere moved slightly, allowing the ink that had been used to be replaced.

Some of these inkstands have been noted with Eliza Simmance's monogram. It is not known how many were made but they are seldom seen nowadays and are regarded as very unusual collectors' items.

ISLINGTON CHAPEL See page 75.

JONES, MARTHA See pages 8–10.

JONES, WATTS & DOULTON See pages 8–10.

KILNS AND OVENS Except where on-glaze enamelled, gilded or lustred decorations were involved, all salt-glaze Doulton Ware was fired once only, at a temperature reaching 1,250° C. to 1,280° C., in the same large kilns used by the general factory for firing chemical and industrial stoneware. The Doulton Ware was placed on slabs in the centre of the kiln where there was least risk of it being damaged from grit and scorch; the top, bottom and sides of the kiln were then filled to capacity with industrial wares.

Certain other decorated wares, such as Lambeth Faïence, Carrara and Impasto wares, and most of the Silicon, were given their *first* firing in saggers (oval or round fireproof containers) in large 'Bristol' kilns at the same high temperature as for the salt-glaze wares. (These were the kilns used for firing industrial wares which had an applied instead of a salt-glaze.)

For enamelling, gilding and similar finishing processes smaller muffle kilns or ovens were used in which, as the name suggests, the ware was protected by an inner wall from direct contact with flames or smoke. These muffles, of which there were several different types, were fired at varying temperatures according to the decorating process involved and in all cases very much lower than that required for salt-glazing.

From about 1830 the firing processes at the Lambeth Pottery were carried out under the supervision of a member of the Speer family, the last head burner of that name at Lambeth retiring in 1955.

'LACE' WARE   This name was occasionally applied to the Chiné Ware. See page 48.

LAMBETH FAÏENCE   See page 40.

LAMPS   Doulton Ware lamp bases were first made about 1872 for the lamp trade and manufacture continued well into the twentieth century. Apart from more conventional shapes, some were in the form of owls and other birds. Lambeth Faïence bases were made to a lesser extent. Figures in terracotta were also supplied to hold electric light fittings; some of these were designed by Broad about 1909.

Standard designs were reproduced in fair quantities; individual lamp bases were also designed and decorated by several artists, including Hannah and Florence Barlow, Edith Lupton, Eliza Simmance, Mary Butterton, Kate Davis, Francis Lee, Edith Rogers, Tinworth, Broad, Marshall and Barnard. The scope for collecting is thus quite extensive.

In 1881, Harry Barnard recorded in his diary that he had been designing Doulton Ware lamp bases and also gas burners for firms in Sheffield and Birmingham. One of the firms was named J. Hinks and Son. Barnard's lamp bases are particularly attractive and original, being often partly modelled, partly incised, with additional *pâte-sur-pâte* decoration of fishes, animals, birds and fabulous monsters.

Lamp bases – including some large ones for showroom use – were designed by Vera Huggins between 1925 and 1939; others by Agnete Hoy in the 1950s. Being made in very small quantities they are even more difficult to find than the earlier ones.

'LEATHER' WARE   See page 46.

'LEOPARD SKIN' WARE   See page 64.

LOVING CUPS   Doulton Ware loving cups of various designs and sizes, with from two to four handles, were made to order with special inscriptions over a long period from about 1877 to 1950. Such cups were also often presented to Lambeth employees on marriage or retirement; these were usually signed by their colleagues in the damp clay before firing.

Loving cups were produced at times to commemorate historical events and personages; details of these will be found in Chapter V. Others were made in standard designs, some with mottos. (See under MOTTO JUGS, page 171.)

LUSTRED STONEWARE AND FAÏENCE   Lustre decoration – on-glaze painting with thin coats of compounds derived from metals, especially copper and silver, which produced in certain lights a metallic sheen – was little practised at the Lambeth Pottery. Some examples were shown at the Paris Exhibition of 1900 and Mott produced others from time to time into the early 1930s.

MAJOLICA   See page 48.

'MAORI' WARE In 1907 (probably to mark New Zealand's attaining dominion status) a series of unusual Doulton Ware pieces – vases, bowls, jugs, teapots, candlesticks and decanters – was produced. The colouring was cobalt blue with Maori-inspired designs in brown and the words 'Kia Ora', meaning 'good luck'.

Apparently the series was not repeated and specimens are now fairly rare, even in New Zealand to which the bulk of the few thousand pieces produced was exported.

MARKS, H. STACY A well-known student of the Lambeth School of Art who later became an R.A. He knew many of the Doulton artists and designed a number of tiles and tile panels at Henry Doulton's request, among them some depicting farming scenes and others symbolizing the five senses. The latter were exhibited at the Howell & James Galleries in Regent Street, London, in 1875.

Some of his figure designs were adapted for Lambeth Faïence tiles and plaques by Margaret Armstrong.

'MARQUETERIE' WARE See page 49.

MARSHALL, ALEX J. See page 66.

MARTIN BROTHERS Three of the famous Martin Brothers had associations with the Lambeth Pottery; see page 27.

MARTIN, GEORGE Martin was responsible in the 1880s and 1890s for turning (finishing to a smooth surface on the lathe) many of the pots then decorated by Tinworth, the Barlows and other artists. He won awards in competitions held by the Society of Arts and the Worshipful Company of Turners.

MATCH AND MATCH-BOX HOLDERS Various designs in ordinary stoneware and in Doulton Ware were made from about 1835 to 1930, including several incorporating models of animals, fishes, birds, Toby Philpot and other figures.

One of the most interesting of these holders from a historical viewpoint was designed in the late 1830s by a young man called Crampton who afterwards became a famous engineer. About this time 'lucifer' matches (the first phosphorous matches) had begun to supersede the earlier tinder-boxes and the 'friction lights' which were smeared with chlorate of potash and sulphate of mercury and struck by placing the head in a folded piece of sandpaper and then jerking it away. At first the lucifers were highly inflammable and likely to go on fire in strong sunlight or in a warm room, or if the box containing them were dropped. Crampton had the idea of making a stoneware box with a separate compartment for each match. He called to see Henry Doulton and after watching the factory methods of working with clay designed a die-pressing machine which Doulton described later as being 'as perfect a machine as I have ever had to do with. Having put some lumps of clay on a projecting shelf and set the machine in motion, the boxes were rapidly delivered, finished and perfect'.

Thousands of these stoneware boxes were made but they were expensive and did not sell well, especially after the lucifers were improved. The remaining stock was carted off in 1850 or there-abouts to be used as hard core for new roads in Brixton and Tulse Hill.

MAXWELL TILES   See page 67.

MEDALLIONS   Reference has already been made on page 19 to the terracotta medallions designed by Tinworth soon after he came to the Lambeth Pottery and which were still being reproduced from moulds in the early 1900s. These varied in diameter from 2 ft. 2 in. to 3 ft. 9 in. Tinworth also designed a smaller medallion, about 1 ft. 4 in. diam. depicting Isis.

Medallions made to order in terracotta and Doulton Ware to ornament the façades of hotels, banks and other buildings were designed by Tinworth, Broad, Ellis and Pearce.

MENU AND PLACE CARD HOLDERS   In addition to several types of plain blue, brown and cream stoneware menu holders supplied to hotels, restaurants and taverns, and often bearing the name of the establishment concerned, Doulton Ware holders (some designed by Tinworth, Marshall and Barnard) were made for sale to the general public. Such things were used quite regularly by hostesses in the nineteenth and early twentieth centuries, not just for large banquets but for even small dinner parties. Menu cards designed by Kate Greenaway, Beatrix Potter, Walter Crane, Harry Furniss and other popular artists could be bought from stationers to go in the stands. Smaller Doulton Ware stands to take place cards were also made.

Most sought after of all are the holders designed by Tinworth, such as those incorporating little figures of mice playing musical instruments. Another amusing example is the one entitled 'Apple Stall' showing a little mouse stealing an apple while the stall-holder mouse is asleep. Other designs in the same vein by Tinworth are known, entitled 'Conjurers', 'Organ Grinder', 'Italian Music', 'Trumpet', 'Bass and Fiddle', 'Wheelwright', 'Barber', 'Gardener', 'Harp and Violoncello', 'Potter', 'Harp and Cornet', 'Bass Viol', 'Artist' or 'Painter', and 'Electricity'. Nearly all of these were in Doulton Ware but the 'Gardener' is found also in Silicon Gilt.

Most of these menu holders were designed by Tinworth in the mid- or late-1880s and early-1890s but several were repeated in slightly varying versions well into the next century. Though reproduced from moulds, they were finished by hand by Tinworth and (as in the case of similar groups made without any slot to hold menus) no two treatments of the same subject are ever exactly the same.

MERRY MUSICIANS, THE   This is the name given to a well-known set of brown salt-glazed figures of boy musicians modelled by George Tinworth. Photographs exist of fifty-six different figures, including two conductors but not all of these were put into production. It is believed that Tinworth began modelling the first of these figures about 1895 and he was still at work on others when Doulton's Australian agent visited his studio in 1910. Some 37 different subjects were eventually produced. The number of reproductions of each particular subject varied according to its popularity but in no case, it is thought, were more than one hundred made.

About a year after Tinworth's death a small final group of musicians was made from the original moulds which were then destroyed.

All these musician figures are now very scarce; rarest of all are those with cream instead of brown faces of which a small quantity was made for the agent mentioned above.

The figures were partly moulded and partly modelled and no two were ever alike, there being noticeable variations in expression, posture and headgear.

See illustration 24.

METALLIZED VASES   See ELECTROPLATING, page 161.

MIALL, MISS One of the early Lambeth Faïence painters, possibly a free-lance, some of whose work was exhibited at Philadelphia in 1876.

MICE MUSICIANS, THE A quaint series of 40 Doulton Ware figures of mice playing musical instruments was modelled by Tinworth for the 1884 Exhibition of Invention and Music. The subjects included some of those later adapted as MENU CARD HOLDERS (q.v.).

Two further complete sets were made in 1888 and thereafter individual subjects were reproduced from time to time in small quantities.

The same remarks made about variations in THE MERRY MUSICIANS apply also to these whimsical mice figures.

MILES, A. AND H. G. A. These two signatures have been noted on tiles depicting scenes from 'A Midsummer Night's Dream', dated 1878.

MINIATURES Miniature vases, jugs, bottles, bowls and the like were often made in Doulton Ware, as well as in plain brown stoneware, between about 1875 and 1939. They were especially popular in the latter part of the last century.

Nearly all of these miniatures were thrown on the wheel and even the smallest jugs (some under one-inch in height) are perfectly proportioned. Some of the throwers at Lambeth would demonstrate to visitors the shaping first of all of a very large vase and then that of a tiny jug with walls so thin and an opening so small that it seemed almost incredible that the potter could control the shape.

Many of these miniatures are attractively decorated with incised, carved, beaded and *pâte-sur-pâte* designs by Hannah Barlow, Edith Lupton, Eliza Simmance, Alberta Green and other artists; others bear only assistants' initials. The majority range between 2½ to 5 inches in height.

MOLD A Miss Mold helped Florence Lewis with a china-painting class at the Lambeth School of Art. She originated a style of underglaze painted relief decoration on terracotta.

MORTLOCK & CO., JOHN This famous Victorian firm of china and glass dealers was established in Regent Street in the early nineteenth century and later moved to Oxford Street. Doulton's connection with them dated from about 1880 and several exclusive designs of Doulton Ware were produced for them; these bore their name as well as the current Doulton trade-mark.

MOTTO JUGS At least forty different designs of brown salt-glaze, Doulton Ware and Chiné jugs, inscribed with mottos, quotations and verses were produced between about 1880 and 1914. A further series of twelve with printed or tube-tool decoration was made between 1924 and 1939. Tinworth, Butler, Broad, Simeon and Rowe were responsible for some of the designs.

A special design inscribed with the American National Anthem was produced for the American market.

Among the mottos found on these once very popular jugs are the following:

> 'There's many a slip 'twixt the cup and the lip'
> 'Fill what you will and drink what you fill'
> 'Merry meet, merry part'

'Use me well and keep me clean'
'Bitter must be the cup that a smile will not sweeten'
'Take fortune as you find her'
'Remember me when this you see'
'The more the merrier'
'Say when'
'Heaven helps those who help themselves.'

Typical of the verses are:

'Remember me
When this you see
Though many miles
We distant be.'

'This is the tree that never grew;
This is the bird that never flew;
This is the bell that never rang;
This is the fish that never swam.'

'He who buys land buys stones
He who buys flesh buys bones
He that buys eggs buys shells
He that buys good ale buys nothing else.'

There is an interesting variant of this in which by mistake the word 'bones' was repeated (instead of 'shells') in the third line.

MOUNTAIN INDICATORS   See INDICATOR TABLETS, page 166.

MURAL TABLETS AND PLAQUES   Although they are available for 'collection' only in a visual sense, these inscribed stoneware mural tablets and plaques, commemorating famous people and historical houses and sites have a great fascination, especially for visitors to London.

The earliest were produced in the late 1880s for the Society of Arts. Subsequently, hundreds of others were made for the London County Council, the City of London Corporation, and various official bodies and private societies and groups in Britain and overseas, celebrating personages as diverse as Bob Fitzsimmons, Bligh of the Bounty, Oscar Wilde, Charles Lamb and Robert Louis Stevenson (on whose plaque at Hyères is the quotation: 'I was only happy once; that was at Hyères').

These plaques were made in several designs and colour schemes but by far the best known are those in blue and white sponsored by the London County Council. They look very attractive, especially against the dark background of London brickwork.

The production of commemorative plaques led to an extensive business in designing tablets for use as house-marks by brewing firms and these are to be seen on the walls of many British hotels and pubs.

The manufacture of these plaques and tablets was discontinued at Lambeth in 1956.

'NATURAL FOLIAGE' WARE   See page 47.

In 1926 a new form of natural foliage decoration was introduced and used for a few years. Casts were made in plaster from leaves and berries; these moulds were then used to produce thin clay reliefs which were thumbed on to the pot.

NIGHTINGALE, H. BONE   According to Sir Edmund Gosse, this was one of the students from the Lambeth School of Art who came to the Lambeth Pottery in 1873. He probably stayed only a short time.

NIXON, SAMUEL   See page 13.

PAPERWEIGHTS   Tinworth, Marshall and Simeon, and possibly other artists, designed some attractive Doulton Ware paperweights. Tinworth's 'Mouse and Bun' proved especially popular over a long period from about 1884; a new edition was brought out in 1913, the year of his death. Among Marshall's paperweights are some inspired by Lewis Carroll's Cheshire Cat and Mock Turtle. Simeon designed a Toby paperweight about 1924.

Compared with glass, pottery does not seem to have been widely used for paperweights. The Doulton examples were not made in large quantities and are rarely seen today.

PÂTE-SUR-PÂTE DECORATION   See page 31. Other exponents of this method of decoration included Frances Lee, Edith Rogers, Edith Lupton, Harry Barnard, Louisa Edwards, Margaret Aitken, and (occasionally) Hannah Barlow.

PAULIN, GEORGE   See page 67.

PEACOCK, HARRY   Peacock was one of the leading throwers at the Lambeth Pottery in the 1900s. He demonstrated his art at several exhibitions and during the first run of 'Chu Chin Chow' he appeared nightly as the potter in the bazaar scene.

'PEPSALIA'   This name, probably that of a soft drink, is found on stoneware bottles made between c. 1890 and 1900. From the earliest days of Doulton & Watts and well into the twentieth century vast quantities of stoneware bottles and 'cans' for holding beer, ginger beer, cider and other beverages were supplied.

'PERSIAN' WARE   See pages 47 and 65.

PHILLIPS   Phillips were well-known china dealers to whom Doulton supplied special designs of stoneware beakers, jugs, cigar lighters and other items, mainly between c. 1887 and c. 1910. Among the items noted, bearing Phillips' name as well as the Doulton mark, are some 'black jacks' (imitation leather jugs) inscribed with a crown, the letters CR and the date 1646 – the year Charles I surrendered to the Scots. A rather similar 'jack' was, however, made for Watson & Co. of Salisbury (see under SARUM, page 175).

'PIGGY BANK'   A few stoneware money boxes were made as samples for the trade in the early 1900s. Apparently there was not much enthusiasm for them and the idea was not proceeded with. These money boxes are thus among the rarest examples of Doulton Ware.

PITTAR, BARRY   A water-colour painter and etcher who produced designs for the Lambeth Studios, c. 1895–1901.

PLAQUES   See under MURAL TABLETS, page 172.

POLYCHROME STONEWARE   This name was given to a type of stoneware used mainly in mural work from 1897 to 1939, the last example made being the frieze over the entrance to Doulton House, the former headquarters of the Royal Doulton Potteries on the Albert Embankment, London, S.E.1. This imposing panel, symbolizing 'Pottery through the Ages' was designed by Gilbert Bayes.

The stoneware body was coated with a white slip on which, when dry, the colours were painted. In the firing (at 1,250° C.) the slip and the colours partially fused – the result, in its purity of colour and fatness of glaze, being somewhat similar to Della Robbia work but far more resistant to extremes of temperature and atmospheric corrosion.

PRINTING   Printing was used as a decorating process from about 1877, either in landscape and figure subjects for hand-colouring or as an outline for repetitive pattern ornament.

The plates were engraved from Doulton artists' drawings by outside engravers or were hard or soft ground etchings by the artists who specialized in this work – mainly Edgar W. Wilson, Barry Pittar, Arthur Pearce, William Rowe and James Callahan. Pulls from the inked plate were taken on twiffler paper, transferred to the ware when this was white hard, and then washed off with soap and water. The resulting print was either hand coloured or left as a black print on the ware. Plain black printing was extensively used on utilitarian wares such as footwarmers, breadpans, ginger-beer bottles and filter cases.

PUNCH AND DOG TOBY FLASK   See page 13.

PUZZLE JUGS   Made in ordinary brown salt-glaze stoneware in small quantities between c. 1880 and 1914. Examples in coloured Doulton Ware are very rare.

These jugs were based on seventeenth- and eighteenth-century examples with three to six spouts around the rim and, generally, a humorous verse alluding to the difficulty of drinking the contents without spilling. The secret was to cover all but one of the spouts, and the little hole under the handle, with the fingers; by sucking at the remaining open spout the liquid could be drunk safely.

REFORM BOTTLES AND FLASKS   See page 11.

REGISTRATION MARKS AND NUMBERS   See page 150.

RELIEF FIGURING   Raised ornament (such as used on the 'Toby' or 'hunting' jugs) made from small face-moulds and fixed by adhesion to the surface of the pot with a little slip.

REPOUSSÉ WARE   This name was sometimes given to the early 'Natural Foliage' Ware. (See page 47.)

RING TRAYS AND STANDS These were made intermittently in Doulton Ware from about the 1880s to the 1920s. Some of the most attractive incorporate birds, rabbits, mice, undines and other figures.

'ROUGH STUFF' See under CLAYS AND OTHER MATERIALS, page 158.

RUGBY See under SPORTING SUBJECTS, page 177.

RUSKIN, JOHN See pages 19, 90 and 110.

SARUM (SALISBURY) Many different articles in both brown salt-glaze stoneware and Doulton Ware were made in fairly large quantities between c. 1888 and 1939 for the Salisbury firm, Watson & Co. of 'Ye House of John A'Port', for sale to tourists. (A'Port was a wealthy merchant of Sarum – the old name for Salisbury – who is said to have been Member of Parliament and six times Mayor, and who about 1425 built part of the premises occupied by Watson & Co.)

Apart from such things as flower- and fern-pots, candlesticks, matchstands, inkpots, tobacco jars, ashtrays, shaving mugs and cruet sets, three rather unusual items call for special mention:

(i) 'The Old Sarum Kettle': a reproduction, reduced in size, of a red slip-coated earthenware egg-shaped vessel in Salisbury Museum. It has a loop handle at the top, a spout on one side, and a funnel-like filler on the other. The original vessel had in fact no ancient link at all with Salisbury; the museum authorities believe it to be an olive oil pitcher from North Africa, presented to the museum in the 1890s.

The reproductions have an emblem in relief about half-way down below the handle. There are two different forms of emblem, both chosen at different times by Watson & Co. to add local colour:

> A. Mark of merchant John Halle, wool merchant and Mayor of Salisbury in the late 15th century. It incorporates a staple, probably as symbol of the wool trade and a cross, circle and triangle as symbols of Christianity, eternity and the Trinity. 'Kettles' with this emblem were made, it is believed, between c. 1888 and c. 1925.
>
> B. Mark of John A'Port, consisting of his initials J. A. P. combined with cross, circle and triangle. This emblem was used on wares made between c. 1925 and 1939.

(ii) 'The Old Sarum Leather Gill': a reproduction based on an old leather jug in the Salisbury Museum. (Generally a gill is regarded as a quarter of a pint but this jug would hold twice that.) The date on the original is 1646 but on the reproduction it appears as 1658 and emblems A or B have been added. Some of the 'gills' have patent pewter lids.

(iii) 'The Old Sarum Leather Jack': a reproduction, $1\frac{1}{2}$-pints capacity, of an original said to have been in the Salisbury Museum but which the authorities cannot now trace. The original is said by Watson & Co. to have been 'made locally for King Charles I when he visited Salisbury in 1646 and used by him at the Banquet'. The stoneware reproductions have a crown, the initials C.R. and the date 1646 in relief. Made from c. 1905 to 1939. (See also PHILLIPS, page 173, for details of another version.)

SCENT BOTTLES Some 40 different shapes and decorations have been noted, mostly designed by Rowe, Simeon and Pope between c. 1900 and 1914, and in the 1920s.

SCULPTORS Among the sculptors whose work has been reproduced in Doulton salt-glaze stoneware are the following: Adrian Allinson, Josephine Vasconcellos Banner, Gilbert Bayes, David Evans, Richard Garbe, R.A., George Kruger Groy, A.R.C.A., Allan Howes, Harry Parr, George Paulin and James Woodford, R.A.

SERIES WARE See pages 55, 88 and 149.

SGRAFFITO, SGRAFFIATO A term derived from an Italian word meaning 'scratched'. As applied to the early Lambeth Doulton Wares it usually denotes a design drawn with a stylus or needle-tool on the plastic clay. The effect was often strengthened by printing a blue or other coloured stain over the whole area of the incised design; when dry the stain was brushed off, leaving enough in the incised lines to sharpen the effect.

The term is more usually applied to decoration formed by scratching through a covering engobe or slip to expose a differently coloured body beneath. This method of decoration was also practised at Lambeth but not nearly so often as that first described.

SGRAFFITO WARE This description was at first applied to the decorated salt-glaze Doulton stoneware made in the 1870s but was soon generally superseded by the term 'Doulton Ware'.

SHAKESPEARE SERIES In 1914, probably in connection with the 350th anniversary of Shakespeare's birth, the Lambeth Pottery introduced Doulton Ware jugs in three sizes, fern-pots in two sizes, a teapot, a tobacco jar and possibly other items, illustrated with scenes from 'Hamlet', 'Much Ado about Nothing', 'The Merchant of Venice', 'A Midsummer Night's Dream', 'As You Like It' and 'The Merry Wives of Windsor'.

SILICON WARE See pages 45–46.

SLAB MOSAIC DOULTON WARE This was a special development of Doulton Ware decoration for architectural use. A mosaic design was outlined on a clay slab with deeply incised lines. The pieces of clay formed by these lines were taken out one by one and dipped in a glaze of the particular colour required. They were then replaced in their original positions and mastic was run into the incised outlines. The result, after firing in a salt-glaze kiln at 1,250° C., was a fine lustrous mosaic, the mastic outlines becoming as hard as steel. Slab Mosaic was introduced in 1902 and probably discontinued in 1914.

SLATER, JOHN Art director at the Doulton Pottery in Nile Street, Burslem, Staffs. from 1877 to 1914. He was the co-patentee with Doulton & Co. of Chiné Ware (see page 48).

SLIP   Clay in a semi-liquid state of more or less cream-like consistency used for making, lining and decorating pottery.

SLIP-CASTING   This is a method of making pottery by pouring slip into plaster moulds formed in easily removable sections as negatives from the designer's original model. The plaster absorbs water from the slip and an outline shell of clay begins to adhere to the walls of the mould. When this shell is sufficiently thick, the surplus slip is poured away and the mould sections removed, leaving a replica of the original model which is then trimmed and finished by hand.

'SLIPWARE, OLD ENGLISH'   About 1919 the Lambeth Pottery produced a series of bowls, cups, vases and two- and three-handled tygs, the designs of which were remotely inspired by seventeenth-century Staffordshire earthenwares decorated with slip designs trailed on from a quill or tube, in much the same way as icing a cake. Some of the vessels bore proverbs such as 'A Bird in the Hand is worth Two in the Bush'.

SPARKES, JOHN   See pages 16–20, 23, 26, 31–32 and 34–38.

SPEER FAMILY   See page 38.

SPIRIT BARRELS, DECANTERS, FLAGONS   See under BARRELS, DECANTERS, FLAGONS.

SPORTING SUBJECTS   Doulton Wares featuring sporting subjects offer an interesting and quite wide field which appeals to many collectors. Various activities – cricket, golf, boating, shooting, Rugby and Association football, cycling, running, jumping, putting the shot, etc. – were depicted, usually in the form of applied relief vignettes, on jugs of different sizes, mugs, beakers, two- and three-handled loving cups, biscuit barrels, and tobacco jars.

The range was widened by interchanging the relief-figuring so that on jugs of the same shape, for instance, one finds different combinations of subjects. Other pots again were devoted to various aspects of the same sport. On one of the earliest sporting jugs produced in 1880 or 1881, the famous cricketer, Dr. W. G. Grace, is shown in eight different stances; beakers made at the same time show three different impressions of him in action. Other cricketing items show a bowler, a batsman and a wicket-keeper, said to represent K. S. Ranjitsinhji, W. G. Grace and George Griffen.

The majority of the vignettes were designed by John Broad and Harry Barnard. Production of some of the items continued intermittently until about 1914.

(See illustration 120.)

STAG-HUNTS   Relief-figured salt-glaze stoneware jugs and mugs in the so-called 'Toby' or 'hunting' jug style, but with stags instead of the more usual foxes, were produced in the 1840s. They are now fairly rare.

STAMP, J.   This name has been noted on some Lambeth Faïence tiles dated 1884.

STAMP-DAMPERS Three designs of these in brown salt-glaze stoneware and coloured Doulton Ware were produced at Lambeth in 1912, including one with the head of David Lloyd George. They were apparently made only for two or three years and are quite rare.

STATUES In addition to statues and statuary groups made by Tinworth, Broad and other artists for special commissions, a number of standard designs in unglazed terracotta were illustrated in late nineteenth and early twentieth century Doulton catalogues.

They include a statue 7 ft. 6 in. high on a 1 ft. 8 in. high base, holding an electric light standard in the form of a torch. Among other figures are those entitled 'Morning', 'Evening', 'The Bather', 'Pomona', 'Flora', 'Spring', 'Summer', 'Autumn', 'Winter', 'Faith', 'Victory', 'Loyalty' and 'Fortitude'. There was also a lion 6 ft. by 2 ft. 6 in. by 3 ft. 6 in. high.

'SWASTIKA' WARE A range of teapots, tobacco jars, mugs, ashtrays, matchstands, loving cups, fern-pots and other items decorated with swastikas and horse-shoes and inscribed 'Good Luck' was produced in relief-figured Doulton Ware and also in Chiné-Gilt Ware for a few years from about 1907.

SYMONS, W. CHRISTIAN See page 20.

TAM O'SHANTER See page 13.

TERRACOTTA See pages 13, 19, 51, 58, 108 and 110.

THROWING The great majority of Doulton Ware vases and other pots were formed by a 'thrower' on the potter's wheel – an art which dates back at least to ancient Egyptian and Near Eastern times. Lambeth Faïence, Carrara Ware and other decorated pots were nearly all similarly formed.

The term throwing is not as is sometimes said, derived from the fact that the potter throws a lump of clay on to the wheel. It comes from an Old English word meaning 'to twist' or 'to turn'. A thrown pot is one spun on the wheel and if it is not subsequently smoothed on a lathe one may often see the horizontal 'ribbing' of the surface. It is always fascinating to watch a lump of clay spring to life, as it were, almost by magic, in the hands of a good thrower, as by skilful manipulation he gradually creates the shape he requires. An excellent description of the process was given by Longfellow in his poem *Keramos*.

TILES AND TILE PANELS See pages 42, 47, 50, 53 and 67.

'TOBY' WARE See pages 8, 10, 56, 64 and 88. Up to about 1875 only jugs and mugs were made in the traditional relief-figured Lambeth and Fulham style. About that date production was extended to include tea- and coffee-pots, condiment sets and other articles of household use. The figuring on these was usually in a white clay but light brown or buff figuring was continued for jugs and mugs up to 1889. The tops were usually dipped in a darker ochre brown glaze but a blue glaze was occasionally used.

Miniature jugs, some less than ¼-in. high were made from time to time, especially between about 1880 and 1914.

Large three-handled relief-figured tygs with the handles in the form of hounds are among the rarer types of this ware.

See page 65 for details of a new 'Toby' series produced between 1924 and 1939 in the style of the eighteenth century standing or seated Tobies.

TUBE-TOOL   A tube from which liquid clay (slip) was extruded to form raised outlines in much the same way as the icing on a cake. (See page 39.)

TURNING   After they had been shaped on the wheel, vases and other pots were often smoothed and finished to exact dimensions by turning on a lathe.

VAUXHALL WALK POTTERY   See pages 8–11.

VELLUMA WARE   See page 51.

VIEW INDICATORS   See page 166.

'VIRAGO' INKWELL   See page 79.

VITREOUS FRESCO   See page 45.

WATTS, JOHN   See pages 8–11 and 15.

WILLOW PATTERN   'Willow Pattern' pseudo-Chinese designs in blue and white relief-figuring on a buff ground are found occasionally on tankards, jugs, tobacco jars, sugar-basins and other items produced in the early part of this century.

WOODFORD, JAMES   See page 67.